Shooter's Bible GUIDE TO SPORTING SHOTGUNS

Shooter's Bible GUIDE TO SPORTING SHOTGUNS

A Comprehensive Guide to Shotguns, Ammunition, Chokes, Accessories, and Where to Shoot

ALEX BRANT

SKYHORSE PUBLISHING

Skyhorse Publishing books may be purchased in bulk at special discounts for sales promotion, corporate gifts, fund-raising, or educational purposes. Special editions can also be created to specifications. For details, contact the Special Sales Department, Skyhorse Publishing, 307 West 36th Street, 11th Floor, New York, NY 10018 or info@skyhorsepublishing.com.

Skyhorse® and Skyhorse Publishing® are registered trademarks of Skyhorse Publishing, Inc.®, a Delaware corporation.

Visit our website at www.skyhorsepublishing.com.

10 9 8 7 6 5 4 3 2 1

Library of Congress Cataloging-in-Publication Data is available on file.

Cover design by Kai Texel

Print ISBN: 978-1-5107-0465-7
Ebook ISBN: 978-1-5107-0467-1

Printed in China

Dedication

To Peter L. Horn II: Hunter, conservationist, explorer, author, and great friend

This book is dedicated to my good and great friend Peter L. Horn II, with whom I've shot birds from New York to Georgia, from Ireland at my shoot, to the great shoots he runs in Hungary; and with whom I've shared African adventures in the wilds of The Sudan and Ethiopia decades before cell phone or satellite communication was available in the bush.

It is also dedicated to Bubba, the fourth generation of our Humewood line of Labradors and who was most regrettably "the last of the Mohicans," passing away in the fall of 2016, and also to Wellington, my brilliant spaniel, who like Bubba acted as a model and tester of products in this book and who hopefully will outlive me, as I don't think I can handle putting down another friend.

CONTENTS

Acknowledgments

I need to thank all of the PR and marketing individuals for all the different companies who provided samples for field testing, photographs, and in-depth information, as well as the manufacturers and companies themselves.

First and foremost at Beretta, Dr. Franco Beretta, Dr. Pietro Beretta, Peter Horn, Ed Anderson, Kim Eveland, Robert Booz, and Ian Harrison. And for help with photos for the book, Travis Haglin and Alberto de Carli.

Then (in no particular order):

Tom Rosenbauer at Orvis; Al Kondak at Perazzi; George Kollitides, the former president of Remington, and Jessica Kallam, head of PR at that company; JJ Reich and Tim Brandt from ATK/Federal/Vista; Kelly Sorensen, formerly with Hevi-shot and Ralph Nauman, president of the company ENVIRON-Metal, Inc., Makers of HEVI-Shot; Nathan Robinson and Jason Gilbertson from the Olin Corporation for the help with Winchester ammunition; Roger Bills and Steven Matt from Yamaha and G3 boats; Scott Newby from Yamaha all-terrain vehicles; Melissa Nichols with Streamlight; Josh Lantz—Traditions Media, PR for Avian—X, Tenzing and Plano; Jon Reddout from Negrini; Mac McKeever from L.L. Bean; Anthony Matarese; Aaron McCaleb, Source Outdoor Group and PR for Trulock chokes; Outdoor Writers Association of America; Professional Outdoor Media Association; Lori Yunker at Burris; Carlotta Fiocchi, Jackie Stenton, Carlo Fiocchi, Travis Franklin, Elizabeth Segura and Buel Collins at Fiocchi; Pat Mundy and Dave Domin at Leupold; Sarah Waszkiewicz, Randolph Rangers; Guy Bignell at Griffin and Howe; Niles and Kim Wheeler at Safari Outfitters; Heather Miller from Costa; Heather Pleskach at Otis technology; JD Rentz and Mars Freudenberg at Americase; Howard Gray of RedOxx; Kim Emery for Irish Setter Boots and Orion Coolers; Rachel Rogers and Stephanie Young, Buck Knives; Heather Bennett/ Heather Pleskach at Otis; Gretchen Goodson at SportDog; Roy Hill at Brownells; Ted Gartner from Garmin; Jackie Abreu and Pauline O'Keeffe of Thermacell; Dave Larsen of Gamehide and Elimitick; Fort Knox's Doug Tarter; and Joseph Hall and John Ward President of War Eagle boats. Jake Pike at Casa de Campo; Peggy Long from Orvis Sandanona; NSSA/ NSCA Nicki Broekhove-Martin, Sherry Kerr; ATA Ashley Johnson; HELICE Michael B. Higgins; JAMES JULIA/ Lisa Oakes for great photographic support on Golden age of American shotguns; Jon Brown from Boyt Harness and Mud River; Jim Eyster of Heritage Gunsmiths; Ross Roberts and Alex Brouwrer of Truck Vault; Addy McDaniel and Matt Soberg of *Covey Rise* magazine; Don Currie; and Nancy Whitehead (htt://www.nancywhitehead.com/)

Game Shooting Venues

Doug and Jackie Coe of Pine Hill Plantation; Brays—Paul Burton; J. Reid Bryant, wingshooting services manager, The Orvis Company, Inc.; Dan Michels, Crystal Creek Lodge; Chad Hoover, Hoover Outfitting; Jennifer Miller, Greystone Castle Sporting Club; Trent Leichleiter, Pheasant Bonanza; Kyle Waggoner, 3 Corners Outfitting; Matt And Jess Libby, Libby Camps; Michael Browning, Grouse Haven Wingshooting; Matt Anderson, Brush Creek Ranch; Michael Bollweg, Tumbleweed Lodge; Mark Nissen, Classic Bird Hunts; Caroline St-Pierre, The Ledges; Linea Brant at Highland Hills Ranch; Brittany Heyn at Cheyenne Ridge Outfitters; George Goldsmith and Richard Seaman at Goldsmith Sporting estates (the information and photographs on Scottish sport). To Stephen Matt, a special thanks for his photos accompanying Yamaha G3 boats and to Charles Sainsbury-Plaice (cspgreetings.manifesthq.com agripix@mac.com) and Glyn Slatterly (glyn@glynsatterley.com; www.glynsatterley.com 011 44 1875 853103) for permission to use the photographs they took of me and my dogs in Britain.

A special thanks to Philip Steinkraus for writing the excellent chapter on FITASC for the book. And to Tom Roster for his excellent chapter on nontoxic shot shells.

My editors over the years, including Diana Rupp at *Sports Afield* magazine; Ralph Stuart and Vic Venters at *Shooting Sportsman* magazine; Elizabeth Hutchison and Dave Mezz at *Garden and Gun* magazine. In the U.K.: Mike Barnes, first at *The Shooting Gazette*, and then at *Fieldsports*; and Will Hetherington after he became editor-in-chief of *The Shooting Gazette*. And also a special thanks to Will for permission to use the photographs that accompanied my articles in *The Shooting Gazette*. Most important, Jay Cassell, from thirty-five years ago at *Sports Afield* to current work on this book at Skyhorse Publishing, and Lindsey

Breuer-Barnes at Skyhorse, who suffered through my computer illiteracy.

And to a few of my great shooting friends: J. Pepe Fanjul, for being my great friend and the force behind shooting at Casa de Campo; Charles Conger, a brilliant shot who was America's best shoot manager before moving on to Remington; Jake Claghorn for being my unofficial co-chair for shooting at our club and who does the heavy lifting; Pierre Villere, Majid Jafar, Hans Depre, FM Claessens for shooting with me in many countries and always exhibiting great sportsmanship; and Clint Smullyan, a dear longtime friend with whom I have shot from New York to Britain; to Gary Herman the original chief shooting instructor for the USSCA and who is my go-to friend if I am having trouble with a target presentation. Robert J. Castelli, a shooting friend for 40 years who took some photos of me, and who served as a model for many instructional pictures.

Apologies in advance if I have forgotten anyone. At my age, easily done.

▲ The author with Fab 4. Left to right: Dusty, Maggie, Sam, and Darky. Sam is the son of the two black labs. Photo courtesy of Renata E. Coleman.

Prologue

I had hoped to personally field test every major item included. That just was not possible. It was neither feasible from an economic point of view (I would've needed a staff of helpers, sort of like Consumer Reports) nor with the time constraints given to me. Luckily, having been a shotgunner since the age of 12, I have been fortunate to have over time functionally field-tested hundreds of shotguns and loads and boots and glasses and vests and jackets and brush pants and waders.

So while this has been labor intensive for me I hope that you will find, dear reader, much useful material between the covers.

▲ When a pheasant is flapping its wings, it is gaining speed but is rarely at top speed. Courtesy *Shooting Gazette*.

Foreword

The Development of Sporting Guns in North America versus European Sporting Guns

In order to appreciate the evolution of the shotgun, it is important to understand differences in the types of guns in common use in Great Britain, Continental Europe, and the American Colonies in our formative years. Until the early 1700s, most of the guns in North America were imported from Europe. Typically these were smooth bore flintlocks from England and France. However, as eighteenth-century American gunsmiths began to flourish, the type of guns preferred diverged.

British Sporting Guns

Throughout much of its history hunting in England was an activity of the upper class, as legally only land owners could hunt (stalk or shoot in their nomenclature) and the vast majority of the land was in large estates owned by the wealthy, often nobility. To reduce poaching, the right of individuals to possess firearms was greatly restricted. Thus, ownership of a shotgun or rifle was not even a choice for the average Brit. Moreover, deer hunting was further restricted to landed gentry and generally carried out on horseback with hounds.

The affluent British sportsmen of the eighteenth and nineteenth centuries were primarily interested in hunting various types of birds. Most of their arms were designed for wing shooting. Rifles were considered an oddity. In the book titled *British Field Sports*, author William Henry Scott (1818) described rifle shooting as a "nice and curious branch of gunnery."

Photos of early fowling guns, courtesy of J. Julia. Top left is flintlock; other two are of high-grade percussion firearms.

Colonel Peter Hawker, one of the most prolific authors among British sportsmen of the early nineteenth century, kept detailed diaries. In his book, *Instructions to Young Sportsman*, Hawker provides details regarding the design of the firearm to be used by the British sportsman. Today we would call it a shotgun; however, he employed the terms "fowling piece" or "gun" interchangeably.

The book *British Field Sports*, published in 1818, described the firearms as falling into four categories–and all of them shotguns: the Fowling Piece, the Double-Barrel, the Long Shore, or the Duck Gun. By the early 1800s, American gunsmiths were more interested in rifles and handguns.

▲ English gent firing black powder at partridge. Setters and pointers are hunting them much as they do now.

While driven shooting has reached its pinnacle of perfection in Britain, it actually began in France. Indeed, wing shooting itself became a sport in France long before England, as they adapted their flintlock designed "fowling pieces" for the task. (The French invented the flintlock in the early 1600s). Exactly when bird shooting on the wing began in Britain is tricky to establish, especially the aspect of driving birds over standing sportsmen. In the early days of the sport, known as "shooting flying" from the French 'tir au vol', the guns walked along with the beaters as they marched through the woods with birds primarily flying away like American hunters pushing roosters out of South Dakota cornfields; shooting the birds as

we would over pointers or flushing breeds. "Shooting flying" in Britain most probably coincided with the Restoration, with Charles II's returning courtiers carrying the lightweight French flintlocks. Richard Blome, writing in his *Gentleman's Recreation, 1688,* "it is now the mode to shoot flying."

▲ Lord Ripon was clearly the most famous game shot of his day, and possibly the best game shot of all time in Britain.

The French term for driven shooting as we know it today is battue. The first reference that I can find of anyone shooting driven birds in the British Isles was Sir John McGill in County Down in the 1670s. But this may be apocryphal. (It is believed that pheasant were brought to Britain by the Romans during their occupation, not for sport but as a quality food source—the way we would raise chickens or those large white "Long Island" ducks). By the second half of the nineteenth century, driven pheasant shooting replaced walked up or rough shooting as the sport of choice for the gentry. Queen Victoria's husband Albert—Prince Consort, not King, like Prince Philip—did much to popularize it. His son, Edward Albert, later King Edward VII took it to a whole new level especially at his Sandringham estate. It was the great Edwardian shooting house party around which much of the British social season revolved. The timing for this King could not have been better as breech loading blackpowder shotguns were coming into production in the 1860s, allowing much more rapid reloading though generally a trio of guns was required by these gentlemen. It was at this point where driven shooting, with birds being pushed over the guns, really took off—no pun intended. These days of the lavish house parties, great shots and big bags, part of the Edwardian era, undoubtedly bankrupted many who wanted to keep up with the Joneses—or more accurately, keep up with the King.

And while the history of the shotgun in Britain may not mean much to you, lo these many centuries later, it profoundly influenced early American gun makers like Fox, Baker, and Lefever, and these designs were the foundation for the modern side-by-side guns which we love.

▲ The development of the modern shotgun coupled with large swaths of public land and friendly farmers allowed American sportsmen to hunt wild upland gamebirds to an extent never known in Britain.

▲ Many society figures went broke trying to keep up with the Prince of Wales.

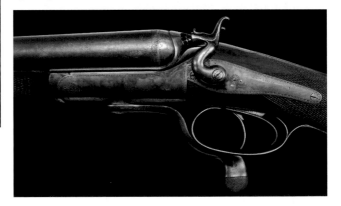

CHAPTER 1
Basics

Fifty years ago, the world was a much simpler place. Esteemed writers like Warren Page and Jack O'Connor would often write an article on creating an appropriate battery of firearms to cover most of our sport. Invariably, it would boil down to a .22 LR, as everyone needs that to practice inexpensively and without much recoil or noise; a 12-gauge shotgun along the lines of their favorite endeavors; and suggesting a .270 or .30–06 if one lived in the West, or perhaps a lever-action in .30–30 or .358 for hunting in the brush and woods from Maine to Minnesota.

Eastern rifle hunters were advised to get a 2.5X or, at most, a 4X scope, most likely with a post reticle. (I still have my original Lyman All-American 2.5X with its post reticle as a memento of that era, although it is no longer mounted on any gun that I own.) The western hunter would be well advised with either a 4X or 6X scope, most commonly had with a very simple crosshair. If memory serves, magazine articles of the time argued the advantages of a crosshair versus a dot. (Remember this was before the days of variable powers, duplex or BDC scope reticles, and decades before illuminated reticles.) Some high-powered .22-caliber centerfire would be suggested for those who shot woodchucks or prairie dogs, and something more powerful for those lucky enough to have access to elk or moose or grizzly. (If one shot all the above, that would total six firearms.)

There was an old saying among the writers of that

▲ A covey rise in the traditional tall Pines of Brays Island offers one of the splendors of classic southern sport. Photo courtesy of Brays Island.

generation: "Beware the man who has only one shotgun," meaning such a man could probably shoot that one firearm well, as he shot it often and at everything. It is almost impossible today to be a one-shotgun man, unless one concentrates solely on one sport, be it skeet or trap or waterfowl. Non-lead shotshell loads required by the federal government for waterfowling made sure of that, as did improved recreational shooting opportunities and hunting applications for the shotgun, everything from sporting clays and Helice to turkeys and predators. If one were fortunate enough to compete in skeet, trap, sporting clays, and their respective sub-gauge events, hunt South Dakota for ringnecks, Wisconsin for grouse, Cape May for woodcock, quail in the plantation belt, geese on the Canadian prairies, ducks in the flooded timber of Arkansas, etc., one would need a lot of different shotguns to do it all right. It would also mean you have enough money to buy them all, and probably even that you are retired, if you have enough time to do it all. Congratulations—and do you need any new friends?

Still, some of us yearn for efficiency and multi-tasking (and not everyone, of course, has a bank account with which to address every shotgun whim). So, in this section I will show you ways your shotguns can perform multiple tasks. For example, your waterfowl gun can be quite effective for predator hunting if you add optics and lights. While skeet shooters historically prefer a shorter barrel than sporting clays competitors, with multiple screw-in chokes in just one shotgun, a person could get by at both games. Alternately, one could, I suppose, have a set of 26-inch or 28-inch barrels with skeet chokes for that game, and 30- or 32-inch barrels choked differently for sporting clays. (Shorter barrels are more suitable for women, youngsters, older, weaker, or shorter individuals.) Barrel length should be in proportion to the shooter.

Then it comes down to autoloader versus over/under. Pumps are rarely a contender for serious clay bird competition these days; in the old days, Winchester's famous pump model 12 with a Cutts compensator was common on the skeet grounds, but very few top competitors, if any, would go that route today. Shooting the 12-gauge in competition means a lot of recoil over the years, so more tournaments have been won at American skeet with the semiautomatic

Remington 1100 than any other firearm. Most sporting clays guys prefer over/unders. But some individuals shoot over/unders better than they shoot autoloaders and vice versa, and that is just a fact of life. No one shoots competitive trap any longer with a side-by-side, though some of the traditional British and Golden Age American manufacturers made side-by-side live pigeon and trap guns, both hammer and hammerless. There was a point at which British pigeon guns were relatively inexpensive on the secondhand market, especially from some of the less-famous makers, because they were heavy and stocked too high. Today, for many in England who prefer shooting extremely tall driven pheasant with side-by-sides, new homes have been found for these wonderful guns, and their prices have increased dramatically.

Making the Case for One Shotgun

▲ There are special joys to birdshooting in the West including amazing vistas. On a hunt like this for chukar partridge, fitness is required. Photo courtesy Highland Hills ranch.

A hypothetical upland hunter who pursues ringnecks or sage grouse or Hungarian partridges out West would probably be well suited with a side-by-side or over/under—individual preference, nothing more, nothing less—choked Modified and Full. Some hunters prefer autoloaders or pumps, both for the cost advantage and additional third shot. For such hunting, I prefer the 12-gauge for work of this kind, but certainly 20-gauge with a 3-inch is awfully close. (Remember, every time one goes down a gauge, the effective pattern for any given choke narrows a bit until one gets to .410-bore, wherein it narrows tremendously and one must go to

▲ An upland bird hunter in the West would probably be well-suited with a side-by-side or over/under, choked Modified and Full.

Full choke to have sufficient density to kill clays in the 20-yard range on the skeet field.)

If this fellow also pursues ruffed grouse or occasionally heads south from Oklahoma through Texas to the classic tall pines of the American South in pursuit of Gentlemen Bob and wants to stick to one shotgun, then the 20-gauge becomes the better choice. By switching shotshells to something faster with smaller pellets, and with a felt or fiber wad, the same gun used for those pheasants and chukars should produce Improved Cylinder and Modified patterns from those Modified and Full barrels, respectively. Testing and analysis on the patterning board is the only way to see how your gun actually performs, of course. As Ken Eyster once told me, "Each barrel is a law unto itself."

Let's change the hypothetical of our western upland hunter once more. Instead of heading south for quail, he enjoys the occasional day of waterfowling but does not pursue it so much to warrant the investment in a

◀ A good waiting position when expecting a flush as barrels can go swiftly to the bird.

▲ Upland bird hunting in the West. Photo courtesy of Classic Bird Hunts.

3½-inch 12-gauge behemoth. He prefers double-barreled guns to autoloaders. If our hypothetical upland hunter in the paragraphs above is also an avid sporting clays shot and can afford only one gun (and assuming when he competes he wants to win in his division rather than just have fun), he would be better served with an over/under than with a side-by-side.

Again, the 12-gauge has the edge over the 20-gauge 3-inch, but it depends on the waterfowling. If those few days are spent shooting geese, I would say the 12-gauge is a lock. If it's early season teal or wood duck or mallards coming in nicely to decoys, then the 20-gauge is fine.

In the case where waterfowling is part of our hunter's mixed bag of tricks, it is a real question as to which non-lead load to use. If he's using his grand-dad's Fox or Parker or Model 21, bismuth or Hevi-Shot Classic Doubles has to be the load of choice, especially for chokes tighter than Modified. If he's using a modern double (and please do check with your gun's manufacturer if you are this hypothetical individual), the barrels may be perfectly fine with steel shot or tungsten.

The Great Choke Debate

I suppose I might be a dinosaur. The more I shoot and the older I get, the more I like fixed chokes. I have seen barrels ruptured because of interchangeable choke tubes. This is most common when the choke tube has not been screwed in tight enough. This is particularly common for fellows who shoot extended choke tubes and tighten them in by hand, rather than using a proper choke tube wrench. Chris Batha, if memory serves, once wrote in a magazine about choke tubes not properly cleaned and the pressure of the gas getting under the tubes and creating the same effect. As I did live in Ireland and in Scotland for years, shooting on wet days was common. As the guns need deep cleaning after those soggy days afield, the interchangeable choke was just one more thing to worry about. Also, at some point one of my flush chokes was over-tightened, or perhaps not sufficiently greased/oiled, and I needed to take the gun to the gunsmith to have it removed. The choke needed to be thrown away at that point. Finally, do remember that a thin-walled tube that falls on the floor and is dented even in the slightest must be discarded, or, again, the chance of rupturing a barrel is just too high.

Barrels of Barrel Choices

To get the best accuracy possible with a slug gun, either auto-loader or pump, one needs to tune the trigger, perhaps drill and tap the gun for scope mount bases, use a rifled barrel, and, if the gun is being used only as a slug gun, should probably have the barrel "pinned." If you want to skip the pinning, then one can certainly get a camo waterfowl gun with the appropriate slug barrel added to it or, perhaps the appropriate slug gun with a waterfowl barrel as an add-on. Hastings makes among the best aftermarket slug gun rifled barrels.

The competitor who shoots sub-gauge skeet, sporting clays or Fitasc events would probably best be served with a set of carrier barrels for a 12-gauge gun with 20, 28, and .410 tube inserts for the other gauges. The other alternative for shooting sub-gauges will be found in three- or four-barrel sets (three-barrel sets based on a 20-gauge frame, four-barrel sets if based on a 12-gauge frame). Most likely, if you are at that stage of your competitive career, you probably already have quite a good idea about what you want and what suits your style and technique best.

Whether you prefer an over/under, side-by-side, auto-loader, or pump is a very personal decision. (I'm ignoring the very specialized single barrel trap guns for this general discourse; similarly, I am also ignoring bolt-action shotguns for slugs and the odd lever-action used in some Cowboy Action matches.) When we get to sporting clays, I will discuss my favorite over/unders and my favorite auto-loaders, as these are the two platforms of choice for the competitive shot. When we get to game guns, side-by-sides and pumps will once again play a role.

Guns for the Upland Hunter

In my shotgun selection overview, I primarily spoke about over/unders and side-by-sides. This probably illustrates more about my opinions (read prejudices) than it does about the sport. My first shotgun was a Browning Auto 5, over fifty years ago, my second a Remington 1100 claimed on Green Stamps (I trust some of you reading this are old enough to remember what those were), so my first shots at clay targets and pheasants and ducks were all done with these two wonderful guns.

▲ When hunting in a group, blaze orange becomes important. For this type of shooting many hunters prefer the extra shots an autoloader provides. Photo courtesy Cheyenne Ridge.

The Argument for Two Barrels

My firearm of choice for over 90 percent of waterfowling today would be an autoloader. And if I was shooting 3½-inch 12- or 10-gauge shells, no other firearm would even be considered. For upland game, though, I prefer double-barreled guns. There are two reasons for this. The primary one is safety. If I'm hunting with a friend and I break open my gun or he breaks open his, we are aware of this safe mode of carry via a quick visual inspection of the other. This certainly is not possible with autoloaders, if you're standing to the left of your friend (given the right-hand orientation of the receiver opening on most autoloaders) or vice-versa. Same thing with pump guns, although I suppose with sufficient visual acuity you might be able to see the fore-end pulled all the way back. For crossing barbed wire or streams, this safety aspect of a plainly visible open and inert shotgun is a bonus (to be completely safe, of course, empty the shotgun of cartridges first).

The other reason I prefer double-barreled guns, and here the edge probably goes to side-by-sides, is that they are lighter and shorter and, therefore, quicker. This is a real advantage if one is hunting thick cover. With the same length of barrel, double-barrels are a few inches shorter than their semiauto and pump brethren, as the auto action is typically 5–8 inches in length but trigger placement mitigates some of this disparity and this translates to a quicker gun when

▲ Dressed in an Orvis jacket and Beretta hat, both with orange highlights, I should be quite visible to other hunters. This side-by-side is a pleasure in the uplands, from Garbi, one of Spain's better makers.

pursuing woodcock or ruffed grouse. Also, if you're hunting wild birds, you're probably covering miles. Over miles, ounces feel like pounds. And day after day those pounds add up—or perhaps I'm just feeling my age.

Upland Gauges

If you are 12-gauge guy, and I must admit I love the 12-gauge gun, go for it. All the same, it's only real advantage in upland shooting is seen on longer shots and bigger birds. The ringneck pheasant demonstrates this need well. If you are shooting behind flushing dogs, with the birds more likely to get up at distance, the bigger gauge enables you to go up in shot size without significantly diminishing the pattern density. Penetration is a concern with such a bird as well.

▲ A 20- or 28-gauge will serve you well when hunting bobwhite quail.

Remember, on a going-away bird—and pheasants always seem to travel away from the folks with the guns—you need to push through all the feathers, fat, and even the entrails before you reach the hearts and lungs for a quick kill.

The hunter of woodcock or grouse or quail, especially Gentleman Bob, is probably better served with a 20- or 28-gauge. (The 16-gauge is a great compromise, but has two distinct disadvantages: It is hard to find shells for it at most retail stores, and, when it is available, choices within the gauge are woefully limited. Some call it survival of the fittest, I call it a shame.) There is almost no difference in performance between a 20-gauge $^{7}/_{8}$-ounce load and a 28-gauge $^{3}/_{4}$-ounce shell. All other things being equal, they kill as well. The 28 is a bit lighter, and at some point guns can, indeed, become too light and too quick. Really strong guys need to soften their mount to deal with superlight guns. But this is something only you can determine for yourself.

If you do shoot small, quick birds most of the time, but occasionally hunt ringnecks behind flushing dogs (where your shots at least on most days should be farther than if you were shooting over pointing breeds), then the 20-gauge 3-inch is the hands-down winner. Being able to shoot $1^{1}/_{4}$-ounce loads that pattern well puts the 20 in a class of its own amongst sub-gauges for this type of shooting.

The .410 has to be considered a gun for experts. To have patterns dense enough, you must use Full choke. Even then, at modest ranges, say 20 to 25 yards, the pattern won't be much bigger than a good-sized dinner plate. That said, in the right hands and at relatively close range, the .410-bore is a great gun for any bird the size of a quail or partridge or smaller. If you use a .410 and kill efficiently and humanely with it, you probably know enough about the gun and the game so that this section can be skimmed over.

For any of the small birds hunted over pointing breeds, open chokes are most efficient: Cylinder, Skeet, and Improved Cylinder are all fine. If you are shooting a single-barrel gun, take your pick, and if you are shooting a double barrel, pick two out of three. If you are shooting larger birds or at long distance, Modified or Improved Cylinder for your first barrel, good to about 35 yards, and Full for your second shot at a bird now presumably farther away, should work quite well.

Double triggers certainly have a place on upland guns. Without a doubt, they are the quickest way to select the barrel you want to shoot first. Single triggers, either selective or nonselective, are fine too. Personally, for this type of shooting, and if this is your only type of shooting, there is hardly any advantage to a selective trigger. The one advantage to them I do find is that if I'm shooting in a situation, for example doves, where I've shot one bird and want to load another cartridge quickly, it is easier to load it into the top barrel of an over/under, so I will select the top barrel before the day begins and leave it there until it concludes. With a side-by-side, it makes no difference. The dissimilarity in opening in size of/angle of opening, for anyone who cares, is called the "gape."

If shooting an over/under for hunting, I must admit I prefer a solid top rib to a ventilated, as I feel the heat dispersion aspect of the latter is overrated and, on a wet day, it is just another area that needs drying and cleaning to prevent rust.

On a side-by-side, flat, filed, or concave ribs are all equally good. The choice comes down to personal preference. I must admit I do not like the look of a raised, ventilated rib on the side-by-side, and certainly it means a different gun fit than a rib more or less on the same plane as the barrels. But that's just me. If you have a Model 21 that was offered with a high ventilated rib and you like it, I make no judgment. (My wife keeps telling me that I'm self-righteous. However, her use of "righteous" is a malapropism, implying, rather, that I prefer to be right than wrong and I see little to favor wrongness—although I must admit that these sentences are a bit self-righteous, if not downright egotistical. Might she have a point?)

If you are shooting double triggers, a straight grip is the obvious choice, although a very shallow Prince of Wales or semi-pistol grip as found on an old Belgian Browning works almost as well. If not straight, though, the grip must be very shallow. I prefer rounded fore-ends on over/unders and preferably a semi-beavertail along the lines of Italian manufacturers on side-by-sides, but this, too, is a personal decision.

Length of barrels—I thought you'd never ask! Shorter barrels are definitely falling out of favor, especially amongst target shooters. For the grouse woods, however, shorter is definitely more maneuverable. This is even more important if you are shooting an autoloader or pump-action. There is no ballistic disadvantage to 26 inches, but it's about as short as you should go, especially if you want the gun to hold value on the resale market. Barrels at 28 inches are probably as long as I would go with the double-barrel gun to carry as I'm pushing my way through the alders. If shooting quail or dove or pheasant, the choice is personal and there is no one correct answer. Certainly you can go longer. But if I were shooting numerous species from woodcock to pheasant, one probably couldn't go wrong with the compromise of 28 inches.

There is also another factor to be considered choosing barrel length. It is the size and strength of the shooter. The taller and stronger the shot, the more appropriate longer barrels become. Similarly, a smaller or weaker individual is better suited to shorter barrels. A 5'4" woman is more likely to shoot well with 26- to 28-inch barrels than she would with 32 inch. However, strength also is a factor. If the 5'4" woman is a power lifter, she may well prefer 30-inch barrels. All of these factors interact. And all are based on the presumption that the shotgun stock correctly fits the shooter.

The Mount is the Shot

▲ This good gun mount on an incoming target is shown on this and the next photo. I would like to see the feet closer together.

▲ Shooting incoming targets: Notice how the weight is on the rear foot and the front leg is bent, allowing a good transfer of weight backwards while staying on the line of the bird.

Ed Anderson is the gunsmith of the Beretta Gallery in New York City and a Master-class sporting clays shot. He once told me something that really opened my eyes about shooting. I knew it on an unconscious level, but I had never heard it verbalized before: "The mount is the shot," he said, simply. Truer words have never been spoken. The mount starts with good footwork, but as you see the target, whether it's game or a clay pigeon, you steadily move the barrels toward it, focus on the bird, then blend the speed of the barrels and the bird until you've established the proper sight picture.

The Stance

Footwork is one of the keys to shooting well. You need to be erect, balanced with your weight slightly

▲ My great and good friend Bob Castelli purposely showing incorrect form and a bad gun mount. His body is all scrunched up, weight is too far forward and bending forward from the waist. . . . This is not Bob's style but a staged photograph.

forward, and relaxed. Ideally, your heels should be no farther apart than your shoulders, and depending on your conformation, they can actually be as close together as six to nine inches. The front knee should be slightly bent, with the weight somewhat over the front foot; fifty-five to 60 percent of the weight should be on the front foot. The toe of the leading foot should be pointed at the spot where you plan to connect with the bird.

During your mount, the gun will be coming across your body at about a 45-degree angle before making contact with the pocket formed just inside the shoulder as you raise your arms and the gun. The heel of the buttplate should settle about the top of your shoulder. Your gun should reach your face and shoulder simultaneously or at least close to it. The plane of your face should be perpendicular to the rib. Don't cant your face or tilt it more than minimally forward. Your neck should be slightly forward but not enough to cause any strain, and your eyes should remain as level as possible.

Perfect Pocket

Just inside the shoulder there is a pocket that is easy to feel. Raise your right arm, keeping it bent at the elbow and parallel to the ground. Now move it forward slightly. Use your left hand to explore the pocket; this is where you want to place the buttplate. Depending on your physique, the top of the butt may be level with the top of this pocket or a bit below.

The gun needs to be locked into this pocket. Your left arm (or right for Southpaws) should be held at a naturally comfortable angle. Holding your leading arm directly below the gun as you might do when you're shooting a rifle, doesn't work for shotgunning. But keeping it parallel to the ground would quickly tire your arm and cause you to start missing the targets. (From Kay Ohye's book *You and The Target*, some trap shooters

▲ This image illustrates a common mistake, especially among beginners. Weight is too far rear and the head is too far back and erect on the stock. The Winchester model 42 is lovely though.

▲ In this staged shot, the gun is placed too low in relation to the shoulder, and the face is too far forward.

keep their arm above parallel to use "bone to bone" to lock the stock in place.) A 30- to 45-degree angle below horizontal is about right for the majority of shooters.

Never lower your face to the gun. This often happens to shooters who make the common mistake of mounting the shotgun above the bicep or on the point of the shoulder. Ouch! Do this a few times, and I guarantee you will never do it again. Some shooters will find the exact spot more easily by standing square to the gun. In shooting situations, however, it's generally best to have the gun going across your body that 45-degree angle I spoke of. You must learn to find this pocket with unconscious effort—in time and with practice, it will become muscle memory.

Every shooter is different. After you've spent enough time shooting, you will eventually develop your own natural style and technique both in mounting and in target acquisition. Always try to keep it based on sound fundamentals. That is the key to hitting birds.

▲ This is like the previous photo but even more extreme in wrongness.

The Twist

One of the keys to target shooting, indeed to all shotgun shooting, is twisting from the waist, with the actual movement being generated from the feet and lower legs and moving upward. Too many shooters incorrectly sway or shift weight from one foot to the other, which causes them to come off the correct line—"rainbowing" it's called. You must learn to twist, or to pivot, from the waist. This keeps the shoulders level and barrel on the line, but you must also work from your legs to accomplish this correctly and consistently. In fact, the best shooters work their move from the legs, getting their knees involved.

The easiest way to get a feel for this movement is to take a broom handle or something similar and place it behind your neck, holding it near the ends. Then stand in front of a mirror with your feet directly below your shoulders and twist to the left and the right. This is the way to move your shotgun to a target. So, now pick up your shotgun, double-checking that it is empty, of course, and practice moving to the left and the right by twisting from the waist in the same manner.

In this mounting process, your head must remain still and your eyes level. (To keep your eyes almost level, the gun fit must be perfect.) In an ideal mounting process, the tips of the barrels will barely seem to move.

Heads Up

When you are being fitted for a gun, the gun-fitter will try to get your eye directly over the center of the rib, with your face as perpendicular as possible. Turning your face or cocking your head to force your master eye into the correct position creates an imperfect perception of the target, because depth perception is

then inaccurate. Never lower your head down toward the gun. Instead, the gun should always come up to your cheek with a lift of your shoulder. With practice, muscle memory will automatically place the gun in the same spot on your face every time—and when this happens, your shooting will improve remarkably.

▲ Head is nicely upright in relation to the stock and the eyes are pretty close to level in relation to the barrels.

▲ Face is too far forward and angled too far down.

The F Words

When I'm not shooting well, I tend to talk to myself, trying to work out my problems through self-coaching. I normally can tell how I've missed a target—above, behind, below, or in front—but the question is, why? Usually, I can trace my poor shooting to either sloppy footwork or a bad mount, which means my master (dominant) eye is in an incorrect relation to the barrel/s; i.e., while I'm focusing on the bird, the barrels appear as a blur and their relative position just doesn't seem to be right.

I have broken down self-correction into a four F-word mantra: footwork, flow, face, and finish.

▲ Weight is too far back, as is the face.

Footwork—Consistent footwork is absolutely critical to shooting well. Poor footwork equates to running out of a swing and coming off the line to the target. This will cause you to shoot low. By putting slightly more weight on the front foot and pivoting on the rear toe, the right-handed shooter can stay on the proper line for birds going to the left. Stepping into the shot, in the direction where the bird is going, will also do wonders. When a flushed bird flies behind you, turn around and plant both feet so that you're balanced for the shot. If you are not alone, make sure to point the barrels skyward as you move into this position.

▲ While there are a multitude of staged errors, the main one I want you to focus on is breaking at the waist.

Flow—By this I mostly mean don't poke at the bird or "rifle" the shot, which can be tempting to do on shallow angles. While you may get lucky and hit something from time to time, these no-movement shots generally don't work. Some shotgun movement is always necessary.

Another part of flow is to not box the mount. In other words, do not pick up the target too early and then chase it for a long way with a mounted gun. Instead, move the gun to the target and blend the tip of the barrels to the bird as part of the mounting process. As the gun reaches your face, most of the work will already be done and the shot can be quickly and correctly taken.

Face—Hitting the same spot on your face with the stock each time, with a consistent amount of pressure, is also important to a proper mount. Pressure that's too light might cause your master eye to be off-center. This, in turn, would cause you to shoot toward the left (if you are a right-handed shooter)

▲ This staged sequence is designed in an exaggerated form to demonstrate what not to do. In this, the gun comes off the face as the shot progresses, with the bird moving to the shoot. This is a very common fault. Righties stay on the gun better on a target moving to the left.

Finish—Finish, or follow-through, is the fourth element in shooting well. It doesn't have to be exaggerated, but it must occur. The barrel needs to keep moving steadily until the shot has completely exited the muzzle. Do not slow your swing or start to dismount too soon.

Six Inches and The Mental Game

We all have strengths and weaknesses in our lives and in our sports. We all have upper limits of talent, i.e. visual acuity, speed of reflexes. We also have upper limits, largely due to genetics and early stimuli, for our intelligence; no matter how perfect one's environment, only one person in a few billion, give or take, will turn out to be an Einstein. Similarly, myself included, most of us do not have the shooting talent of a George Digweed (arguably the greatest competitive shot of all time); Anthony Matarese, who has won U.S. national titles and a world championship; or the late Smoker Smith who was the top shot of his day. Still, good coaching, a well-fitted gun, and the intelligent use of choke and load will help maximize anyone's individual performance.

There is another aspect to successful shooting that should never be overlooked: confidence. There was a time when I toyed with taking sporting clays very seriously. At my club in Westchester County, New York, in practice I put in a number of 97 and 98 performances, and at competition I set the club record with a 94. Admittedly, it was not the toughest course in the world, but it was still tough enough, and the next closest scores were an 87 and 88 put in by a couple of All-Americans.

I once shot in a sporting clay competition in which I was nowhere close to winning because of an appalling performance on springing teal, my bugaboo. I did, however, post the only straight on the high tower, and the field that day included Smoker Smith, shooting at his peak, Andy Duffy, who went on to win U.S. National and European titles, and Jon Kruger, the U.S. Champion at the time.

For whatever reasons, I often became very self-conscious under the pressure of competition, whereas guys like Smoker flourished in the crunch and loved a gallery. I wilted. Had I been clever, I would have gone to a sports psychologist, and perhaps, and *only* perhaps, as Marlon Brandon said in *On The Waterfront,* "I could have been a contender!" Instead, I quit shooting competitively except at the club level.

Confidence applies to game shooting as well. With a lack of confidence, one tends to become too tentative and too cautious. Triggers don't get pulled or are pulled too late. Birds get wounded instead of killed, or they fail to fall altogether.

On a day of extreme driven shooting, I find if I kill the first couple of good birds well, I can be quite lethal. If I miss the first few, I can have a really bad drive or even an entire day (I do, admittedly, like going for the toughest, tallest, most visually deceptive birds). If I find I can't shoot to my own standard—after all, I am competing against myself not anyone else—I do my best to self-coach and talk myself through the slump. I mumble about moving my feet or locking my face on the stock. Usually I can talk myself into shooting well, though not every time. If the self-coaching fails, I kill a couple birds that I would normally let fly by. "Easy" birds. It puts the image of a well-shot bird into my brain on some subconscious level, lets muscle memory take over, and I can then try and stretch myself again.

Often, especially at trap competitions, if one gun misses a clay, so will the next shooter. The concept of missing creeps unconsciously into the second shooter's psyche. As it turns out, the most important six inches in shooting is not lead or barrel length—it's the six inches between one's ears.

Ethical Limits of Range

A shooting pal of mine, John Milius, who inspired numerous Hollywood household names (Steven Spielberg, Tom Selleck, etc.), to buy fine guns wrote or directed a number of well-known movies. Some films are magnificent, *The Wind and the Lion,* and *Apocalypse Now*; some hugely popular hits such as *Conan the Barbarian.* John is probably best known for the lines from his *Dirty Harry* movies, one of which, uttered by Clint Eastwood, is that, "A man has to know his limitations."

That is the core of divergent points of view. The simple truth is that very few shooters are competent even at the relatively comfortable 30-yard mark. Most people don't judge range accurately (though it can be learned with practice and a rangefinder). Back in the days when I co-owned a successful commercial pheasant and duck shoot in Ireland, I was frequently amazed how often people considered by their peers to be great shots were merely adequate at only a very limited range, generally twenty-five or thirty yards. When watching them shoot, they were lethal on these birds, but would hit a bird five yards higher up in the middle or backend, and with another five yards added on miss completely. These shooters missed the point both figuratively and literally: the sight picture changes with distance.

It is here that the problem with the schools of "instinctive" or "natural" shooting you'll so often see in advertising or in shooting magazines articles exists. There is no "instinct" to shooting. That's a complete myth. Shooting is a hand-eye sport. Humans have learned hand-eye coordination that enables us to perform any number of tasks: drive a car, catch a ball, or place a fly once one has learned how to cast properly in front of a trout. Some acquire this skill set better than others. When it comes to shooting, you are functionally throwing shot where the bird *will* be, not unlike a quarterback throwing a football to his receiver running downfield. But natural hand eye coordination should never be confused with instinct, which is far better illustrated with a Labrador's desire to retrieve or a setter's to point.

To be a competent shot, one must have *technique,* which normally comes only through good training, coaching, and proper practice. And when one is talking about extreme shotgun shooting at fifty yards or greater, one is in a rarefied atmosphere. The great shotgunners, those such as George Digweed, Dan Carlisle, Anthony Matarese, Diane Sorantino, and Kim Rhode, can make such shots routinely but do not think for a minute that they do not work at their proficiency. When I was shooting a lot, I found extreme shooting very natural—because I practiced it. Today, having blown out my shoulder for the third time, I have had to cut back on the number of days I shoot in order to put off having surgery. I rarely shoot clays anymore in an effort to protect that shoulder. But shooting less

▲ Two world champions—Anthony Matarese and Diane Sorantino—and a wannabe—yours truly.

than I used to, I am not always at the top of my game. On days when I am on song, I know it, and I will crumple an extreme bird as easily as a medium one. Knowing my limitations, as Milius would say, I will have shot to my capabilities on that particular day or drive.

Shooting at extreme range is not beyond the scope of the competent shot, but the proper tools need to accompany the effort. One needs large shot, large loads, and tight chokes. One needs to actually pattern their gun to know at what point the pattern of the chosen load goes to hell. Tom Roster, undoubtedly one of the world's great authorities on shotgun ballistics, worked up loads for his guns that provided well over 90-percent patterns at forty yards and retained Full-choke forty-yard pattern configurations at sixty-plus yards. While it is unfortunate that Roster did not pattern his guns beyond the sixty-yard range, it would have been interesting to determine how far adequate patterns were achievable with buffered loads and tight chokes. An educated guess would put that in the seventy-five- to eighty-yard range, though very few people are capable of making sure kills at that distance. (Photos of these patterns were reproduced with Tom Roster's kind permission in my book *The Complete Guide to Wing Shooting.* Terrible title, interesting book, for those with a technical bent).

Let me put this another way: A skeet target is normally shot at about 20 yards. It is 21 yards to the center stake of the skeet field. To my mind, someone who is not shooting good scores on skeet at this modest distance

▲ First barrel patterned at 20 yards. Full choke very tight. This not meant to be for killing birds at this close distance, as there is too much meat damage. Very hot core . . . off-center to the left and way too high.

has no justification to be trying for 40-yard pheasants or ducks. My guess is that great shots probably cripple and lose, on a percentage basis, fewer birds at 50 yards than the average shot does at 30. One should neither extol nor criticize another man's view of sport, as long as that sport is done honestly and within one's abilities. To contemplate shooting at distance on live game, even if you are a good enough shot to make humane kills, it is necessary to pattern your gun at your maximum range. I once patterned a 20-gauge gun of mine and at 50 yards there were sufficient pellets in the pattern to humanely kill a bird whereas at 60 yards there were hardly any pellets in the pattern. Only experimentation and observation will determine your barrel choke load combination at distance.

As another famous Milius line uttered by Dirty Harry: "So you feel lucky, punk, well, do ya?"—should not be in your mind as you are going to a bird. If you can lift

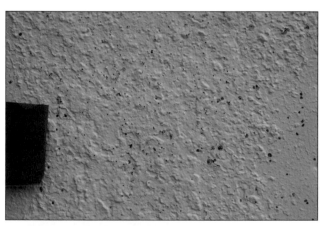

▲ Full choke from my 28-gauge at 30 yards.

▲ Now at 40 yards.

your gun with confidence, assuming that you are going to kill your quarry quickly and humanely, you are shooting within your own scope. If you cannot, especially on more typical birds, I suggest you revisit your technique and equipment and, if necessary, take lessons, change guns, loads, whatever it takes to actually make you proficient and build legitimate confidence.

Shooting Where It Will Be

Wildfowl shooting, upland shooting, and the clay games all have something in common: To be seriously good at any of them, you need to employ different techniques and use different equipment. On a technical sporting clay course, for example, the course designer will often beat you by having a bird that is doing something different than first appears. That, strangely, is also what they all have in common. One must be able to read the target, be it clay or live game.

Live birds often are not actually doing what is first perceived. A pass-shot dove, besides not flying on a straight line, may also be slipping in a side wind—and slipping shots are *very* tricky to read. You have to look at the wings to see if one is slightly higher than the other for curl, and one must be aware of wind direction in relation to the target for slippage. Also, one must read whether its wings are flapping or set. If they are set, the dove is probably gliding downward or dropping to some degree. Personally, I think a pass-shot bird at 40-plus yards with curl and slip is the greatest challenge.

A tall pass-shot bird requires a steady mount, a big sight picture, and the ability to track and read its flight (or line) accurately. This is all aided with longish barrels and a fair amount of overall gun weight; the latter required to minimize recoil with heavy loads (i.e., laws of inertia). For truly tall wildfowl, long barrels, tight chokes (modified or half is max choke for tungsten or steel loads) that have been ideally patterned for a specific load, and large shot are all required. If you can handle the recoil, a minimum 1¼-ounce shot payload on mallard-size game will send enough pellets with sufficient energy to cleanly kill at longer yardages. Geese require heavier loads and larger shot than mallard, and mallard more than teal.

Buffered loads are a plus. Hypervelocity loads do not help much and are not worth their added recoil.

Three's the Minimum

A number of years ago, a couple guys were running a shooting clinic called Optimum Shooting Their names are Gill Ash and Jerry Meyer (their partnership has since split up). The pair was aided by cartridge manufacturers, choke tube makers, clay bird companies and other relative industry support, so they were able to experiment with a fair amount of rigor. If memory serves, they used a trampoline-like mesh to catch clay targets that had not been broken.

Many clays hit with fewer than three pellets were unbroken, with just one or two pellets having penetrated them. In other words, to break off *with consistency* a visible piece of a clay, something needed to score a hit in competition, one needed a minimum of three or four pellets on the clay.

Just like clays, gamebirds need at least three or four pellets of sufficient energy impacting the front half of their body, and ideally in the front third, for a clean, humane kill. (A true sportsman will always use his second barrel to finish off a wounded bird, rather than going to a second bird.)

Different clays also need different pellet sizes for the correct amount of energy to be imparted and make the break. Likewise, the dome of a standard clay target is tougher than the underbelly. A rabbit at distance needs a larger pellet. A mallard or large duck needs heavier shot than a pheasant, a pheasant larger shot than a quail. The gun and load that is best for goose does not work nearly so well on a ruffed grouse.

Slow cartridges should also be avoided, at least in part for their lack of penetration. Long barrels are an advantage in that they aid in momentum, which aids a smooth swing. For heavier loads on big birds, an autoloader such as Beretta's A400 Xtreme or a Remington Versa Max, which handle 2¾-, 3-, and 3½-inch shells, really come into their own. The fact that they are almost impervious to the weather is a huge advantage, especially in salt or brackish water.

Thirty-four-inch barrels have exactly a five-inch advantage over 29-inch barrels. Unlike a rifle, this added barrel length has no ballistic significance. A strong fellow such as George Digweed will undoubtedly prefer something in the 32-inch range. Personally, I am quite happy with 29- to 32-inch barrels, depending on weight and balance, and a woman or small man might in fact find 28 inches preferable.

▲ One of the strongest game shooting teams of all time in Britain. George Digweed and Richard Faulds have around 50 World and Olympic titles between them; Philip Fussell is considered one of the 100 best British shots of all time; my pal Jamie MacLeod and Ian and Liam Botham are all renowned shots. I'm in the back center. This was a day of invited guns by Steve Thomas, who has the Prescombe shoot not too far from London. Photo courtesy of Charles Sainsbury Plaice.

Over/unders have the advantage of a more precise sight picture. The term "single sighting plane" is a misnomer. The issue at hand is actually one of width (compared to the sight picture of a side-by-side and even the receivers of a semiauto or pump), otherwise sighting planes would be on different levels. For both-eyes-open shooters, another advantage of over/unders expresses itself when, with a high hold point on a trap target or a directly overhead incomer, one can often see the bird "suspended" underneath the barrels like a half-tone in photographic lingo which allows a more consistent sight picture to develop. (For those not conversant with photographic nomenclature, it means that the image will not be crisp and distinct, but will still be apparent though fuzzy or blurred.) This is why, for example, a two-eyed shooter has a higher hold point at the trap house–he can see the bird coming out of the house, beneath his barrels.

While one wants to be steady and consistent for tall to

extreme pass shooting, one needs to be slightly aggressive, even reckless, in their approach to shooting grouse or quail. By reckless I do not mean dangerous, but rather shooting out of one's comfort zone, pulling the trigger much earlier and with much less hesitation than one would on a tall bird. A tall goose or mallard or, indeed, dove may only be in range when he is close to vertical, and that takes some studying and timing to get correct. To shoot a covey rise of quail well, on the other hand, one needs to get the first shot off as fast as possible, though not so close as to produce "Georgia snow." That probably means telling your brain (or is your brain telling you?) to pull the trigger when that first quail is somewhere between 15 and 20 yards. By the time neurons are fired, primer ignited, and pellets sent downrange to the target, that should translate into a kill about somewhere between 20 and 25 yards in front. (And that gives you time for a second shot also still in range.)

Again, birds need to be read. Is the bird dropping in relation to the horizontal or is it climbing slightly? If it is dropping, often the case, then one needs to shoot low. I like to think of dangling legs on the target and come down from the body to these imaginary feet, then fire and follow through. To a bird at a slight angle, I would go from those dangling feet towards the wing in the direction of flight to establish my line, fire, and follow through. More lead is obviously required on quartering shots, more again on a crossing shot.

There is a world of difference between the ideal waterfowl gun and an upland gun. Indeed, there are all sorts of different firearm, ammunition, accessory, and technique requirements between each sport. Certainly, I would consider a lightweight 20- or 28-gauge for small ducks like teal when they are decoying well. For spooky ringnecks getting up far in front of a flushing dog, I would want a 12-gauge or a 20-gauge 3-inch with a 1¼-ounce load of No. 4 or 5 coupled with tight chokes to penetrate from behind.

Triggers and Flinches

One of the worst things that can happen to a shooter's confidence is to develop a flinch. Flinch tends to be caused by the pounding that one endures while shooting, though the noise associated with shooting can be a factor, too. Shooting a heavy load hundreds of times is like standing still while someone beats on your shoulder again and again and again. Throw in the barrel flip, which after a long day can cause quite an ache against your cheek or neck, and a flinch might just be in your future.

The best way to deal with a flinch is to not develop one. The good news is that it is more easily prevented than cured. This lies partly in knowing your own physical limitations. For example, some shooters never develop a flinch from a shooting normal 1⅛-ounce trap loads from an over/under, while others might develop one while shooting a light 1-ounce load in an auto-loader.

Flinches come in all shapes and sizes. I've seen all sorts. Sometimes the shooter steps forward. Sometimes one seems to push the gun, other times they'll seem to pull the gun, or drop the barrels. Whatever form it takes, a miss is sure to ensue. Let's look at some basic principles for avoiding flinch.

Light loads recoil less than heavy loads, but it's not as easy as reading "Reduced Recoil" on the box and assuming that will do the trick. There are cartridges from some manufacturers that do seem to be more pleasant to shoot than others, even when they produce the same exterior ballistics.

A heavier gun generates less recoil than a lighter gun with the same load-laws of inertia. Auto-loaders absorb more recoil than fixed-breech guns and spread the recoil over time, though some autoloaders are more pleasant to shoot than others. Gas-operated designs such as found in the Beretta or Remington semiautos seem to do the best job at creating a mild shove.

While trap and wildfowling are primarily 12-gauge sports, 20- and 28-gauges can be used effectively in practice sessions at skeet or sporting clays, for most game shooting situations, and, obviously, in gauge-specific competitions. Many serious skeet competitors use a 12-gauge gas gun, then switch to sub-gauge over/unders. Some competitors use their 20-gauge tubesets in their 12-gauge carrier barrels and their averages are not noticeably affected.

All guns can be made to shoot more pleasantly

via a few different ways. The easiest way is to add a recoil pad that does a good job of absorbing shock. Again, some brands are better than others (Sorbothane-like Kick-Eez leaps to mind). A more labor-intensive and expensive method is to lengthen the forcing cones and back-bore the barrels. This helps create more of a push than a punch (several big manufacturers now offer these as standard features). Barrel porting forces gases upward and reduces muzzle rise, which in turn allows the shooter to get on the next target faster and eases the jolt to the neck over the long term. Adding weight to the buttstock or the barrels (or preferably both), helps keep the balance point where you want it while slightly reducing felt recoil. There are even stocks on the market designed with a hydraulic system that absorbs recoil. ISIS, no relation to the terrorist organization, makes a combination recoil-reducing system and recoil pad that is worth looking into for those who are greatly affected by recoil. They need to be installed properly, not all gunsmiths can do it, and they are expensive—but for many worth the money.

In my old age, I find that a gel pad inserted into my shooting vest does a great job at making a long shooting day more comfortable. I prefer the soft versions of these pads. The drawback, of course, is that if you wear one consistently it will slightly alter your length of pull.

A bad trigger may lead to flinching. The worst triggers have a significant amount of slack and/or a significant amount of creep. Both destroy your timing. Most competitive shooters require a trigger pull of about three to four pounds and completely devoid of creep or slack.

It is easier mentally to accept a heavier trigger pull than it is to deal with creep or slack. When you pull the trigger you disengage the sear, which allows the hammer to fall. Some shooters develop a flinch by lightening their trigger so much that, on some unconscious level, they become afraid of touching it for fear of a premature discharge. (No need to call Dr. Freud, just go to a trigger expert—less expensive, more rewarding.)

If you develop a flinch and can't cure it through the means described above, there is another alternative: the release trigger. Release triggers are not for the beginner, the uncommitted, or the absent minded, because you pull the trigger *first*, call for the bird, and then *release* the trigger to disengage the sear.

The safety implications for such a trigger setup should be obvious. More than one trap house has been shot by someone whose mind wandered while holding down the trigger. Release triggers are pretty much limited to the clay field. Some clubs require guns so equipped to sport a warning sticker on the buttstock. No hunter should ever use one.

Some serious trap shooters develop a flinch on only the first shot of doubles, without the bad reaction tainting other parts of their game. Some of these gents have overcome the problem by using a release/pull-trigger system. In other words, the trigger releases on the first shot and is pulled normally on the second. If you do go to a release trigger, make sure that it is installed by a manufacturer or gunsmith with a solid reputation, warranty, and design. Once installed, do *not* tinker with this trigger at all on your own. If it needs work, return it to whomever installed it.

I suppose this is as good a spot as any to go into "lock time." This is the time between when you pull the trigger and when the firing pin is struck by the falling hammer. Theoretically, the faster the lock time is, the less follow- through you'll need; practically, unless your lock time is abysmal I'm not sure how much this really matters. The truth is that while some guns are much quicker than others in their lock time, as long as your gun isn't too terribly slow it won't matter much. There is one caveat. Let's say, for example, that you shoot an old autoloader with a slow lock time on your normal trap shots and handicap targets, but switch to an over/under with much faster lock times for doubles. This difference between guns may affect your timing. If your favorite auto-loader has a particularly slow lock time, you may be able to purchase a kit from companies like Brownells that will speed it up. Your goal should always be to make as many things as possible consistent in your shooting.

Chapter 2
Breaking Down the Modern Shotshell

"*L*ong live lead!" say I, but that may be short-lived as more states and federal land are requiring non-lead shot.

As I've explained, the ban on lead for waterfowling led to new generations of cartridges and shotguns designed specifically for that task. That was necessary because your dad's or your granddad's shotguns, those old pumps or side-by-sides with fixed full-choke barrels, though a joy to shoot, are unsuitable for use with any shot that's harder than lead. It is here, then, at this time in history that demanded U.S. waterfowlers shoot non-lead shot, that shotshell design and components realized their first big innovations since the invention of the plastic wad and shell hull.

Bismuth was an early answer for the call for "non-toxic" shot (a.k.a. "non-lead" shot). But early bismuth pellets were too light and too brittle. Lucky for us, bismuth is much better today than it was even 10 years ago, so, if you do choose to use Old Betsy and her Full chokes, then bismuth answers your desires. Indeed, with any fine old gun, even those with relatively open chokes, I wouldn't risk using anything as hard steel shot.

It was this ban of lead and especially the introduction of steel and other shot of harder materials such as tungsten, that has witnessed most 12-gauge wildfowl guns increasing their chamber to 3 and 3½ inches, in order to pack as much punch as possible in the payload. But, as Newton's third law states, for every action there is an equal and opposite reaction—and these heavier loads generate considerable recoil.

While many modern autoloaders do a good job of absorbing the blow, 3½-inch loads still kick significantly. To think otherwise would be foolish, so, while this length is offered in pump-actions if 3½ inches is your shotshell of choice, I would definitely do some testing with these super magnum loads before purchasing that action. Don't get me wrong, Winchester's old Model 12s are a thing of beauty, but firing multiple 3½-inch shells through any pump will beat you up. I think that modern autoloaders offer the best bang for the duck buck, combined with as much recoil mitigation as is possible, plus that third shell advantage over a double, makes it the gun of choice for most serious waterfowlers.

For those who go after geese or large sea ducks

▲ Winchester XPERT employs their Diamond Cut Wad designed for high pattern density.

▶ Drylock system is designed to keep powder dry in wet conditions.

like eiders, yes, 3-inch and 3½-inch 12-gauge and, in some cases, even the mighty 10-gauge, should be considered. All have a terminal advantage over anything smaller. That said, if you're happy to shoot 2¾-inch shells, say at decoying mallards or black ducks, then any action you prefer is fine (and in those situations, smaller gauges and over/unders work well with the right loads and chokes).

Get to the Vitals

There was an article just a few years ago in the U.K.'s well-known British magazine, *The Field* (once upon a time *the* magazine), that restated the adage that "pattern fails before penetration." That is hugely incorrect. For example, one could have a great pattern of No. 9 and never do anything more than wound a duck at 30 yards due to lack of penetration.

In that article, and so many others, the important aspects of shotshell construction are either unknown to the writers or ignored. Pellets do not kill through massive tissue damage and energy being absorbed by the animal as is the case with rifle or pistol bullets. One must think of it more like a knife wound, or an arrow with a pointed rather than broadhead tip, where penetration *to the vitals* is critical.

▲ I've used Fiocchi's nickel-plated Golden Pheasant load with great success even in small gauges.

Far too many supposed ballistic experts think of shotguns and their pellet payloads in rifle terms. When I was the Founding Editor of *Combat Handguns*, I worked with some guys in law enforcement on projects showing that rate of twist can affect tissue damage. The hydrostatic shock that works so effectively with rifle or handgun projectiles, though, has a minimal impact when it comes from shotgun pellets. There is relatively little hydrostatic shock from *any* pellet. Some writers, especially in the British sporting magazines, confuse terminal ballistics of a rifle with that of a shotgun. Statically, one needs three or more pellets of an appropriate size to reach a vital organ and kill—*most* of the time. Hard pellets are more likely to penetrate to a vital organ. Soft pellets pattern less well (obviously a disadvantage) and are less likely to penetrate far enough consistently to reach organs.

The Lowdown on Lead
I love the smell of gunpowder in the morning. But unlike my screenwriting friend and shooting pal John Milius's line in *Apocalypse Now*, it does not smell like victory. That said, the smell of a freshly fired shotgun shell spurs autumnal memories. Memories of my childhood hunting pheasant and woodcock behind my English setters: hunts on my own and those taken with friends. Memories of shotguns expectorating lead.

Lead was an issue of concern in America decades before it had any impact in Britain or Europe. That concern was based on a study at Patuxent (by USF&W) on ingested lead and lethality of lead and steel in waterfowl. Strangely, it was neither opposed by the gun manufacturers or the cartridge makers, as both saw it as an opportunity: sportsmen would need new barrels or shotguns to handle steel shot (the first non-lead shot to be introduced), and steel shot was priced much more expensively than lead (though, as a metal, there is little justification for this).

At some point, bismuth came on to the scene as an alternative to steel, which hadn't been well-received in its early years; it is less hard than steel, leaving many hunters furious at the wounded and lost birds that resulted. Bismuth's primary advantage over steel in that it did not damage barrels of old guns or guns with tight chokes. Unfortunately, especially in its early incarnations, bismuth was brittle and simply didn't perform well. Today's bismuth loads with added tin, outperform loads available even a decade ago.

After Bismuth, tungsten-based shot came on the scene. Tungsten is used with additional elements in shot construction, in various matrix forms. Tungsten and iron is an example. Tungsten-based shot made waves when it was introduced. It is significantly harder and heavier than lead, so will outperform it. A number of manufacturers offer tungsten-based shot. First, and perhaps still best on the scene with tungsten shot is the company producing HEVI-Shot, Environ-Metal, Inc. HEVI-Shot has two significant drawbacks and one significant advantage. The good news first: Being heavier and harder than lead, it will kill at greater distances than any other form of shot, as it has more retained energy and provides better penetration. The bad news is that it is unsuitable for really old guns and for any choke greater than Modified in many modern shotgun barrels. The really bad news for HEVI-shot (and bismuth), is that they are far more expensive than lead. Still, if you are hunting waterfowl of any type or are on state lands that have imposed non-lead ammunition restrictions for other game, then you must pay the price.

▲ HeviMetal is a combination of tungsten and steel to make it less expensive than pure tungsten. In the photo you can see the two distinct and different metals. Photo courtesy of Environ-Metal.

When I wrote my book *The Complete Guide to Wing Shooting*, I did various penetration tests. Telephone directories are pretty good for this, especially if they are soaked in water and put in a press. (This was a tip given to me by a CIA operative 40 years ago, who was very much into handgun ballistics and who wrote under a pseudonym for the magazine I edited at the time, *Combat Handguns*.) In these tests of mine, now more than a decade ago, HEVI-Shot penetrated the furthest and lead was quite good. Steel, if one went up in size so that the weight of the steel pellet matched the weight of the lead pellet (approximately) was

surprisingly good, not quite up to lead, but not that far behind. Bismuth, because it was brittle, performed the least well in terms of penetration. But enough said about my experiments. Let's see what ballistics expert Tom Roster has to say about all lead, bismuth, steel, and some of the newer shot types making waves among waterfowlers and upland hunters these days. After that, I'll take you through brands and loads offering the best in shotshell performance.

Making Sense of Today's Non-Lead Loads, by Tom Roster

If I were the average Joe Shotgunner today and not in the business of designing and testing shotshell loads, particularly hunting loads, I'd be at the least confused and more likely absolutely baffled by the amazing array of shotshell ammunition currently sold for hunting. As I primarily deal in waterfowl and upland bird loads, I'll try here to at least demystify these two groups.

Bismuth Loads

The very first effort at an improved pellet type over steel shot that is still with us is bismuth shot. While bismuth offers a density approaching lead, which would up its performance compared to lower density steel, bismuth also has some troubling properties.

Its main negative is its frangibility. If made from pure Bismuth, a high proportion of such pellets bust apart during combustion and while traveling down the shotgun barrel, resulting in numerous pieces, rather than whole pellets, emerging from the muzzle. To overcome this proclivity, Eley, still the world's sole manufacturer of bismuth pellets, had to learn to alloy bismuth with tin in order to control problem. Unfortunately, by the time enough tin is added to bismuth to reduce frangibility to a tolerable level, the resulting density comes in very close to 9.69 g/cc, making this shot intermediate in density between steel shot at 7.86 g/cc and lead shot at 11.3 g/cc.

Translated to current-day use: if you once used No. 4 lead shot for mallards, you will need to use a pellet one size larger in bismuth.

▲ Winchester extended range is available in non-toxic bismuth shot.

The plus side of bismuth shot is that it is relatively soft like lead shot and, thus, creates no problems for shotguns and chokes that cannot safely handle today's modern steel or tungsten-composite pellet types. Choke with Bismuth as you would for lead. Unfortunately for the consumer, bismuth is a rare earth metal, and so the cost of typical bismuth loads today is about three times that of comparable steel loads. For those seeking to give bismuth a whirl, be advised that both Rio and Kent now offer in the U.S. bismuth cartridges in a variety of gauges and shot sizes. Bismuth shot for reloading is also available through Ballistic Products (www.ballisticproducts.com) and Precision Reloading (www.precisionreloading.com).

Upgraded Steel Loads

The customary and traditional shape for steel pellets is the ball. The manufacturing process for steel pellets, unlike that for lead or bismuth shot, makes them exceedingly spherical and uniform in size. Now, recall that because steel pellets are about three times as hard as lead or bismuth shot. This means that steel pellets do not deform during combustion (set-back deformation) or in barrel travel. This results in higher pattern densities and shorter shot strings than either bismuth or unbuffered lead loads can offer. On top of this, steel pellets are relatively inexpensive because iron is such a common element readily available in the U.S. and any other country manufacturing steel shot.

The drawback to steel pellets is that they are less dense than lead pellets. The theorists tell us that because of this single negative property, steel shot must by necessity perform poorly.

Such arguments ignore the results of some fifteen steel-versus-lead shooting tests conducted in the U.S. with voluntary hunters taking thousands of wild ducks, geese, pheasants, and, in 2012, doves under a regimen of scientific field conditions whereby they didn't know whether they were shooting lead or steel. Of the *millions* of rounds fired and the hundreds of thousands of birds bagged, in all cases *the steel pellets of a size equal in weight to the lead pellets tested* performed just as well in bagging as the lead pellets.

Let me make this simple: to achieve the same weight and killing performance of the load you prefer in lead shot, you generally go up two sizes for steel, for example No. 4 lead should be replaced with No. 2 steel, and BBs for geese now require steel T shot.

The only statistically significant difference documented in the above testing was that the hunters missed more frequently with the steel loads than the lead loads. While I have no proof, misses are likely a result of the tighter pattern diameters and shorter shot strings of steel loads. But I do know these test results intimately, as I was personally involved in designing and conducting, then co-authoring the test results in peer-reviewed scientific journals for some eight of the 15 tests run. That said, because lead-comparable steel payloads will be of larger pellets, there will be fewer pellets, a function of the volume restrictions within the cartridge. Yet, this doesn't matter, because as proven over and over in numerous pattern tests, steel pellets pattern so much tighter than lead; a charge of steel No. 2s will place as many pellets in the pattern through the same choke as an equal charge of lead (which, again, will have more pellets in a shot size two sizes smaller, in this case, No. 4).

But be this as it may, the marketers decided to try to give hunters' improved steel pellet shapes and loads. This would also allow charging more for a box of such ammunition. Thus was born Federal's Black Cloud steel loads. These loads featured ribbed, barrel-shaped steel pellets called "Flitestopper" mixed with traditional round steel pellets, all encased in an innovative wad design called "Flitecontrol" that holds the shot in the wad further from the muzzle before separating. The wad was necessary because the barrel-shaped steel pellets, being non-round, simply don't pattern as well as spherical-shaped pellets. But they are cheaper to manufacture than round steel pellets because they require less machining and finishing. So, if steel shot ammunition twice as expensive as traditional steel loads catches your fancy, Federal's Black Cloud loads may be what you're looking for.

Other Steel Loads

Not to be left behind and intended to directly compete with Black Cloud, Winchester put together an extensive line of shotshell loads called Blind Side. These loads contain hex-shaped steel pellets

▲ Winchester Blindside uses six-sided hexagonal shot designed, according to Winchester, to create more transfer of energy and deeper penetration.

reminiscent of the cube-shaped lead pellets manufactured in Italy called *dispersante* and marketed in Europe as spreader loads. Notwithstanding the inescapable aerodynamic fact that a load with cube-shaped pellets simply must open its pattern from any choke very quickly, Winchester manufactures its Blind Side cube-shaped pellets out of steel and markets the loads as suitable for waterfowl. Now, in my testing I can tell you clearly that Winchester's Blind Side loads are terrific for any close-range waterfowling, such as in flooded timber. But they do not and cannot pattern well for anything beyond about 40 yards; to Winchester's credit, it doesn't claim such performance.

Super-Fast Steel Loads

Having run out of the most easily manufactured pellet shape changes that can be made from low-carbon steel wire, U.S. shotshell manufacturers have firmly and universally seized on the idea that if one increases the velocity of steel shot ammunition quite a bit above traditional round-shaped steel pellet loads, it will increase the downrange energy of steel pellets. This has to be a plus, right? Well, it is a small plus out to distances of about 40 yards. But because of the inescapable law of physics regarding balls (i.e., the faster a ball is started, the faster it slows down), higher-velocity steel loads simply shed by about 40 yards most of the velocity and energy they inherited from the increase in launch velocity. Nevertheless, all steel shotshell manufacturers in the U.S. today now offer steel loads in the 1,450 to 1,650+ fps velocity range, which is significantly above the 1,300 to 1,375 velocity range traditional steel loads carry. Indeed, Remington still markets its Hypersonic line that features steel load velocities as high as 1,700 fps.

What the manufacturers forgot to tell shotgunners is the universally known and proven fact that patterning performance degenerates with velocity increase in *all* shotshell loads, regardless of pellet type and shape. Often overlooked is that to achieve the ever-higher speeds of today's high-velocity shotshell loads, such loads are loaded with less shot in order to keep pressures safe. Also overlooked is that very high-velocity shotshell loads come with an inescapable hefty increase in recoil. This is likely the principal reason most waterfowlers today are shooting gas-operated autoloaders.

▲ A most unusual wad configuration.

As a last piece of scientific data for careful consideration, in all of my lethality testing, I have never found any of today's steel loads to kill any better at velocities above 1,450 fps than at velocity ranges of 1,300 to 1,400 fps. If such loads have a plus, for some shooters the added velocity helps them with their ability to connect with the target.

The manufacturers sell both traditional and high velocity steel loads, so the velocity level and price-point choice is yours.

Tungsten-Composite Pellet Loads

Now we come to that group of non-lead loads that are truly a performance improvement over steel, and some of them, an improvement over even lead shot. As the periodic table would have it, tungsten as an element is denser than lead. The most effective of today's tungsten-alloy pellets possess a density of about 12.00 g/cc which is greater than lead pellets at about 11.30 or, if they are hardened with antimony, about 10.90 g/cc. What is more, several of today's tungsten-alloy pellets are about 3½ times harder than lead pellets. Thus, like steel, they

simply do not deform before muzzle emergence. They also pattern extremely well at long range, often exceeding the best buffered lead loads. Like steel shot, guns and chokes must be capable of handling such hard pellets.

The company that brought tungsten composite pellets to the world is Environ-Metal, headquartered in my home state of Oregon. Known as HEVI-Shot pellets, these somewhat bizarrely shaped pellets (until you realize they are basically a ball with an attached boattail) have definitely kicked up a notch long-range shotshell performance.

Just after the turn of the recent century, HEVI-Shot had many competitors, but almost all have died away due to poor sales caused solely by their products' high price-points. The greatest negative of any tungsten-based pellet is that tungsten is an even rarer earth metal than bismuth, with the principal supply located in China. Taking advantage, China charges a whopping price to America for any raw tungsten material imported. This results in 12-density HEVI-Shot pellets, for example, currently selling to reloaders for somewhere around $28 a pound, compared to steel for less than $2 a pound. The same high price-point shows up in factory HEVI-Shot loads, currently selling for something over $4 a shell!

There are softer tungsten-composite pellets available in factory loads only, noticeably Kent's Tungsten Matrix line. These pellets consist of enough tungsten powder mixed with a plastic binder to produce about a 10.50 g/cc pellet at a competitive price-point. Tungsten Matrix pellets are soft like lead and, thus, can be shot in any modern shotgun. But because of their softness, they do not pattern as well as hard steel or HEVI-Shot pellets.

To mitigate the cost of a pure-tungsten pellet load, Environ-Metal now offers several variants of its HEVI-Shot loads, the best-selling and most popular of which is its HEVI-Metal line. HEVI-Metal loads contain a split shot charge consisting of one-half steel pellets and the other half of a smaller HEVI-Shot pellet size that is very close in weight to the larger steel pellet loaded. This increases the total pellet count of the load and, thus, improves lethality over a pure steel load. HEVI-Metal sells for less than half the price of pure HEVI-Shot loads.

◀ Browning TSS stands for tungsten super shot, which is 60 percent denser than lead. A No. 9 pellet has the same energy and weight as a No. 5 lead, which allows for more pellets in the same size load.

Upland Loads

The longstanding list of traditional lead loads for upland bird hunting (pheasants, grouse, quail, woodcock, and chukar), still exist in their original variety of gauges and shot sizes. But due to the marketing success of the mixed-pellet non-lead shot loads, Federal now offers upland bird hunting versions featuring round pellet and barrel-shaped pellet duplex lead loads a la Black Cloud. It's called "Prairie Storm" and has the same Black Cloud Flitecontrol wad. The HEVI-Shot people now also offer mixed-pellet non-lead and lead loads for upland bird hunting, principally pheasants.

In 2015, Winchester brought out its Rooster XR line of pheasant loads containing copper-plated lead shot with an innovative liquid-based buffer. The liquid buffer resin dries hard and then fractures during combustion and barrel travel, resulting in a new way of protecting lead or any other soft shot type from deformation and providing improved long-range performance. (Rooster XR gives quality of patterns that are not much different than traditional dry buffered loads, and they are outstanding.)

There have really been no other innovative upland bird shotshell loads added in recent years, no doubt principally due to the fact that, in the

▶ Winchester's proprietary buffering agent keeps the pellets together for lethal long-range hits.

U.S., more and more of the lands where pheasant hunting takes place are requiring the use of non-lead shot. Lead shot is being legislated out and non-lead shot legislated in more and more every year. This is true also for clay target shooting. Starting in 2018 statewide in California, the required use of shotshell loads and even centerfire rifle and pistol loads for *any* hunting purpose must be non-lead in their composition, no exceptions.

To order Roster's reloading manual on buffered lead and bismuth shotshell loads, HEVI-Shot Reloading Manual, Shotgun Barrel Modification Manual, or his instructional shotgun shooting DVD contact him in Oregon at 541-884-2974, tomroster@charter.net.

◀ Longbeard with special buffering agent. Shot-Lok hardened resin buffering agent and copper-plated shot equals improved density and penetration.

Better Steel

Steel is getting better. Some companies have been experimenting with a steel pellet that has a ring around it—think of the rings of Saturn—that creates a bigger wound channel and more tissue damage (and slightly negating my argument about pellets not creating much of a shock wave, though this must reduce aerodynamics). Also, some steel loads are being designed at true hypervelocity, which translates both into greatly increased recoil and somewhat greater energy and penetration at moderate range, though they quickly lose their competitive advantage as distance increases and velocity sloughs off.

Whereas the use of non-lead shot for waterfowl shooting is annoying, an outright ban for all hunting, as some states like California would like to see and some EU directives are heading towards, would be a disaster. It is absurd to think that the relatively few rifle bullets shot in any specific area would leach into the water systems, and in target range areas, bullet traps could be employed. Bullets taking a deer on a mountainside are unlikely to enter into the food chain or water supply.

We all have our prejudices. For the longest time I hated steel. Part of this had to do with the fact that most of the steel I shot was in the late 1970s and early 1980s and surely its loadings—shot cups, powders, etc.—have improved since then. Or maybe I dismissed it without sufficient experimentation. I have shot it with respectable results in the past few decades in jurisdictions where it is mandated.—A.B.

Modern Shotshells for Things With Wings

Federal

Federal was founded in 1922 by Charles Horn. This company has become an American powerhouse with the widest possible range of products from rimfire to elephant loads and shotshells from self-defense to game birds. Based in Minnesota, it has been used by Olympians and mere mortals. In 1973, almost prescient, it began manufacturing steel shotshells (before the law required non-lead loads for waterfowling), and

among its other innovations, in 2007 it introduced the Flitecontrol wad, which definitively improved its steel shot waterfowl loads. That's just the tip of the Federal shotshell iceberg.

3rd Degree Turkey Load

Turkeys are sometimes shot quite close. Other times they stretch the limits of your skills and your ammunition. These relatively new loads from Federal were designed to deal with both situations simultaneously, sort of along the lines of Forrest Gump's "Life is like a box of chocolates."

In 2015, Federal Premium launched its 3rd Degree in 12-gauge 3-inch and 3½-inch loaded with a whopping 1¾ and 2 ounces, respectively, of shot. In 2016, the new 3-inch, 20-gauge 3rd Degree turkey load gave hunters who prefer this smaller gauge this same unique load in a package for them.

While I always wanted to give someone the third degree (probably saw too many *Dragnet* episodes as a child), I never thought it would be a turkey. It gets its effectiveness from a multi-shot, three-stage payload.

The forward 20 percent of the shot charge is composed of No. 6 Flitestopper pellets which, because of their reduced aerodynamics, rapidly migrate to the fringes of the pattern and thereby cause a widening of the pattern at close range. This will improve the odds of a slightly off-center shot at under 15 yards making a clean kill.

Forty percent of the 3rd Degree payload is in the middle and composed of No. 5 copper-plated lead shot. As this lead shot is truly copper-plated and not merely washed in copper, this shot experiences reduced deformation, which means tighter patterns at distance and enhanced penetration.

The bottom 40 percent of the shot charge uses Federal's No. 7 Heavyweight shot. These tungsten-based pellets carry the energy of lead No. 5s, but, according to Federal, "Because of their small diameter (less friction), spherical shape, and weight, the Heavyweight pellets penetrate deeper than their larger, lead and plated-lead counterparts. Because the hard pellets retain their spherical shape during setback and while traversing the bore/choke, they help maintain a tight pattern core for long-range effectiveness."

◀ Cutaway of the Winchester Long Beard XR that shows why it gets lethal patterns on Toms out to 60 yards. Innovative buffering is the key ingredient.

The 3-inch 20-gauge load has an impressive payload of 1 7/16 ounces. Tight patterns are greatly enhanced by Federal Premium's proprietary Flitecontrol wad.

Federal ammunition utilizing Flitecontrol wads are best used in guns whose chokes/tubes do not have porting or wad-stripping elements. Federal does recommend a Full choke or more. Federal's engineers testing 3rd Degree at 10 yards showed a pattern six inches wide. This is a couple inches wider than most turkey loads fired with the same shotgun. Pellet count at 20 yards in a 10-inch circle averaged 174, and at 40 yards within the 10-inch circle the pellet count was 76. This means good lethal head shots at almost any distance commonly encountered. I shot my last two turkeys with this load and was suitably impressed.

Wing-Shok High Velocity

Many of the better companies are offering properly plated lead shot once again. This is a relatively expensive process and is invariably found only on premium lines. In Federal's case, it is in its Wing-Shok High Velocity loads.

I have been using Wing-Shok in 28-gauge with No. 6 shot and in 20-gauge 3-inch with No. 4 and have found both to be excellent. For taking pheasants from behind, especially over 30 yards, I personally find the ability of the No. 4s to get through feathers, fat, and viscera before reaching the vitals a decided advantage.

Fiocchi

Peter Horn II, VP Emeritus of Beretta USA, is a great friend of mine, and it was because of his suggestion that I field tested just a fraction of Fiocchi's extensive line. Fiocchi was certainly not unknown to me, but I've tended to go to American brands.

Fiocchi is hardly new to the shotshell business, having manufactured cartridges basically from the beginning of breechloading firearms. While not as old as Beretta—nearly 500 years is tough to compete with—nearly a century and a half of manufacturing expertise guarantees this company's place in ammunition history.

Its story is certainly unusual. One-hundred-forty years ago, Giulio Fiocchi was working for a bank, when he was told to go to the town of Lecco to investigate a blackpowder factory that was perilously in debt. Instead of merely liquidating the company, he fell in love with it and organized a loan from the bank so that he could buy it.

His brother Giacomo was an engineer, and the two quickly determined that blackpowder was a thing of the past. Indeed, Fiocchi was an early leader in modern smokeless powder for rifles, pistols, and shotguns. Today, Pietro Fiocchi is the fourth-generation leader of the family business that has over 500 employees and manufactures tens of millions of rounds of military ammunition in addition to their extensive sporting lines. Its American-based subsidiary is Fiocchi USA.

Fiocchi produces ammunition for rifles and pistols in addition to shotguns. Shotshells for the American market, a broad range including those for self-defense and a line of steel shot in 12- and 20-gauge, are loaded domestically in Missouri.

Golden Pheasant

I have been using Fiocchi's Golden Pheasant game loads and am greatly impressed by them. Peter Horn and I shared a stand at our club's recent pheasant tower release. He brought along some 20-gauge cartridges for me to test. Both the 2¾- and 3-inch cartridges performed beautifully. (I was also quite amazed at how clean my bores were after the shoot ended; this last isn't something I normally check that carefully, but

▶ Yellow marks the 20-gauge, so configured to remind shooters not to put in a 12-gauge gun . . . an all too common and catastrophic mistake. Photo courtesy of Fiocchi.

I must admit it was striking.) These loads are well-named. Sometimes one hears of a "golden pellet," that one lucky pellet that strikes the brain or spinal cord to cause instant death at great distance. Maybe that happened on our shoot, but while I can't verify that, I can say that these cartridges brought out the best in Peter and me. The only thing I regret is that Peter brought only a few boxes for the second half of the shoot, so I had to change to two other brands. While not rigorously scientific, I can say with hand to heart that these Fiocchi outperformed my normal loads; birds were often stone dead in the air with the Fiocchi loads. These are not hypervelocity loads, nor do they need to be. What they do have is shot that is nickel-plated, as opposed to nickel- or copper-washed, which keeps the shot rounder and results in more pellets on target and greater penetration into the vitals. Since that day, I've used the Golden Pheasant 12-gauge and 28-gauge loads regularly with similarly impressive results.

High Velocity

▲ Fiocchi's high velocity round proved extremely lethal in my field tests.

Fiocchi's High Velocity shotshells are available in all gauges from 12 to .410 and produce a lot of bang for the buck. With the exception of the .410, which comes in at 1,140 fps, the other loads are what I call high normal velocity 1,200 to 1,330 fps. This is just about ideal,

as the added speed doesn't lead to a ridiculous amount of recoil, yet improves downrange performance. I also like that Fiocchi now offers a High Velocity 28-gauge 3-inch loads designed specifically for Benelli shotguns recently introduced in this gauge. This shell has a 1-ounce payload, while the Golden Pheasant 3-inch 28-gauge's payload is a 1 1/16-ounce.

Target Lines

▲ I've used a lot of Fiocchi target rounds and have found them excellent both at the patterning board and on the sporting clay course.

Fiocchi Exacta Target loads have a loyal following, not surprising considering this is the company's top-of-the-line. As I have shot out my shoulder three times, I have gone to lighter loads from this line that produce less recoil and are gentler on my old joints. The Exacta ⅞-ounce load in my 12-gauge has been great on clay birds. While there are times in competition where I will still go to a heavier load, especially on long targets, I find this ⅞-ounce load has no significant impact on my scores with anything that could be considered a "normal" bird.

What is most impressive about Fiocchi is that it has recently created dedicated lines for trap, skeet, and sporting clays. There are even loads for specific situations encountered in FITASC, for example, the Rapax Crusher load is made to address the sport's longer targets in that the shot cup does not separate from the payload until it has covered approximately 40 yards. This produces consistent hits and breaks at 60 to 70 yards and beyond. Fiocchi also produces a proprietary spreader load that opens up quickly and is very useful for competitors using auto-loaders, in that they can put in this shell for a closer bird and a normal load to be used on the farther target thus maximizing the one choke they are employing. Not to stop there, Fiocchi's 1-ounce Helice load of nickel-plated shot has a velocity of 1,400 fps, something serious competitors will appreciate. Finally, a number of sub-gauge loads and steel target loads round out the company's lineup of competition loads.

Environ-Metal (includes all that follow)

Environ-Metal has been the leader in non-lead shot for decades. The company's HEVI-Shot has been offered by many top companies, including Remington, but for a few years now, Environ-Metal has been manufacturing complete cartridges in addition to shot.

These are the tungsten-based loads against which all other non-lead shotgun ammunition should be judged. Tungsten is both heavier and harder than lead, and that means it hits like a sledgehammer. However, because it is harder than lead, it is not suitable for all shotguns, especially not those older guns with fixed tight chokes. HEVI-Shot (a.k.a. HEVI-Metal) is also now available in combination loads of copper-covered steel.

Classic Doubles

Environ-Metal's Classic Doubles line is available in 12-gauge to .410-bore in a load that's soft enough to use in your grandfather's beloved Parker or Fox. I have used the 28-gauge Classic Doubles in my full fixed-choke model CSMC's A-10. Unfortunately for me, the A-10s do not shoot to a convergent point of impact—POI. This is not a function of the cartridge, but a barrel issue as every single barrel on my four barrel set shoots divergently. The shot, which is U.S. Fish & Wildlife Service (USFWS)-approved non-toxic, is both heavier than steel but soft like lead, and does not harm older barrels. It is also significantly denser and less brittle than bismuth, giving better performance. According to the company's president, Ralph Nauman, "Classic Doubles

is a pressed-powder pellet that contains tungsten and other metals. The materials have been approved by the USFWS as nontoxic since 2004. The pellets are dense, soft, frangible, but lethal on soft targets. After shooting into wood, they look reusable, but shot against steel or rock they turn back to powder. The shotshells are also loaded to relatively low speeds and low pressures. Regular HEVI-Shot pellets are cast products and are not frangible or soft."

HEVI-Shot Pheasant, Goose, and Duck

As the name implies, this load was developed for pheasant hunting. The company says its Heavier than Lead pellets cleanly kill roosters "at distances and in crosswinds where lead can't succeed." While I have used it and it is excellent, I have not shot this load enough to know if that statement is 100 percent accurate. That said, as the shot is heavier than lead shot and hard unlike bismuth, penetration should be greater at further distances. It was specifically designed to increase the knockdown power by, according to the company, "75 percent over traditional steel shot shells." Because it is certified as USFWS non-toxic, it can be used on all lands that require non-lead shot which, as Tom Roster pointed out earlier, may well be the future.

Heavier Than Lead HEVI-Shot Goose is designed for humane, long-range kills on larger birds, geese to tundra swans. Larger shot and bigger loads distinguish it from HEVI-Shot Duck loads, which "smokes fast-flying, small-body birds" according to the company's website. From what I can see, this is true. For mallards and smaller, this will do the trick. I have used this in my 20- and 28-gauge guns and can attest to its staggering terminal properties. Available across all gauges from 10 to .410-bore, if you are hankering to try your 28-gauge on waterfowl, this load should be on your must-try and list.

HEVI-Metal

These shells, a combination of steel pellets layered with HEVI-Shot pellets (two shot sizes smaller to match the ballistics of the steel pellet). The combination puts more pellets on target than steel alone. Available in 10-, 12-, and 20-gauge, there's also a dedicated HEVI-Metal Turkey and HEVI-Metal Pheasant. HEVI-Metal

Fast is a 10-gauge-only load with higher velocity than the 10-gauge load in the original HEVI-Metal line.

Speedball

The Speedball shells from Environ-Metal use a combination of patented MV2 base pellets which have a steel core with thick copper plating. In front of these pellets is a layer of HEVI-Shot. The combo load is designed to bring the performance of HEVI-Shot to more wildfowlers by reducing the price to about half of a full HEVI-Shot load. While two different materials loaded on top of each other may seem gimmicky, I assure you it is not. It patterns well and performs flawlessly. Consider this for your non-lead needs for all but extreme distances.

Hevi-Teal

This is the first all-steel shotshell from Environ-Metal designed specifically for teal and other small-bodied birds. Premium steel pellets keep up with the company's high-quality product line.

Tungsten Super Shot, a.k.a. TSS

A number of shotshell manufacturers, including Federal, now offer TSS turkey loads. Upland and waterfowl hunters can also purchase TSS loads, and a company called Apex will handload them for you in subgauges. More below.

TSS is a tungsten-composite pellet from China. It is offered in both 15 g/cc and 18.1 g/cc densities. TSS pellets are extremely hard and intriguingly are "the roundest, smoothest, most uniform-sized pellets I have ever seen or tested," according to Tom Roster, writing in *Shooting Sportsman* magazine. Remember that whenever using harder than lead pellets, you must have appropriate barrels and maximum choke of modified in most instances. If reloading, wads suitable for material harder than lead must be used.

One of the top shots in England, Dave Carrie, with whom I've shot, told me that he was testing TSS loads in .410 and found that using number 9 shot he was able to get the same penetration as number 6 lead. Because of so many pellets in the pattern when using a number 9, he had sufficient pellets in an 18-inch circle to consistently kill tall pheasant at 60 yards. This was not as rigorous a test as Tom Roster would apply

◄ By combining tungsten-based pellets that are smaller than steel of equivalent weight with steel, one is able to increase the number of pellets in the pattern—read density—for greater lethality. Due to availability and cost, we presume, the company is now currently combining steel with bismuth rather than tungsten for these loads, even though tungsten kills farther than bismuth.

but few men kill as many pheasants at extreme range as Dave (or me). While this needs more investigation, if Dave is correct, this could change the face of long-range, and still humane, shooting for those few individuals who are capable of hitting birds at 60 yards. I do not doubt, however, that in 12 gauge TSS would add 10 to 20 yards of lethality to a comparative lead load.

Two of the industry leaders, HEVI-shot and Federal are offering TSS loads. However, they are extremely expensive; at least 25 percent more expensive than previous tungsten loads, and these were expensive enough.

Apex Ammunition based in Columbus, Missouri, is offering TSS for hunters and will provide sub-gauge loads on request.

Founded by Jason Lonsberry, Jared Lewis, and Nick Charney, they have quickly found a very interesting niche for their TSS company. They are not looking to mass produce their cartridges but rather to have experts handload them to create very high quality cartridges. In addition to tungsten-based loads, they also produce excellent zinc-plated steel cartridges. They are manufacturing cartridges for waterfowl hunters, turkey hunters, predator hunters, and upland sportsman. In some cases the cartridges are a combination of TSS and steel. For more information, contact: info@apexmunition.com and www.apexmunition.com.

CHAPTER 3
Mainstream Shotgun Sport Shooting

Trap

▲ Single-barrel trap gun High Arch Ithaca, $5000-grade Knick Model. Note the engraving and checkering.

In one of my clubs, there's a lovely old print of a gentleman in a park near London standing at his position while a trapper holds a long string, the pulling of which releases a live pigeon from a trap. These fellows trapped local feral pigeons, ergo the term "trapper" so common in our shotgun shooting sports nomenclature, and the tug on the string resulted in the likewise universally accepted "pull" as the order to launch. Indeed, the phrase "no bird," which is now used to mark a clay broken by the trap machine, or less often one launched off course, came from the days when a bird refused to fly upon the opening of its box.

From Pigeons to Blackbirds to Bats—Wait, Bats?

Live-pigeon shooting competitions began in England, probably around 1830, and once it crossed the ocean proved very popular in America. Clubs and competitions were frequent and hotly contested. Britain banned live pigeon shooting in the early part of the twentieth century, out of a goofy sense of political correctness. It is still legal in many U.S. states, and was legal in New York State until just a few years ago when our heroic legislators and anti-gun governor Andrew Cuomo passed legislation forbidding it. That was the same group that came up with the brilliant Safe Act. For anyone who doesn't realize it, I'm using both "heroic" and "brilliant" ironically.

Other early live targets in America included blackbirds and even bats as shown in records from the Sportsman Club of Cincinnati in 1831. Pigeons became the preferred and eventually the standardized target, as they were available everywhere. Pigeons were replaced over time with targets of various types, from glass balls, now considered collectible, to our modern clays. Some of this was out of convenience, as it was often difficult to catch enough pigeons for a competition, but there was also the need for national

MEXICO
GUADALAJARA, OCTOBER 1998

LXII WORLD'S CHAMPIONSHIP BOX FLYERS

$200,000 U.S. cy IN PRIZES

FRIDAY 16 AND SATURDAY 17 President Cup F.I.T.A.S.C. 4 Target - 4 zeroes 26-30 mts	US cy 12,000
SUNDAY 18 America's Grand Prix 1 Target - 1 zero 26-28 mts	US cy 36,000
MONDAY 19 Europe Grand Prix 1 Target - 1 zero 27-29 mts	US cy 36,000
TUESDAY 20 Ending of Europe Grand Prix	
WEDNESDAY 21, THRUSDAY 22 AND FRIDAY 23 LXII Championship of the World 25 Target - 3 zeroes 27 mts	US cy 60,000
SATURDAY 24 Africa Grand Prix 1 Target - 1 zero 26-28 mts	US cy 36,000
SUNDAY 25 Ending of Africa Grand Prix	
17 Consolation Prizes US cy 1,180.00 each	US cy 20,000

Full Entry Fees US cy 1,150.00, F.I.T.A.S.C.
Tax included

6 Shooting stands

CLUB CINEGETICO JALISCIENSE, A.C.
Av. Vallarta # 4446 Vallarta San Jorge C.P. 45120
Guadalajara, Jal. México
Tels. y Fax (3) 122-55-07 y (3) 121-77-81
EMAIL ccj@mail.udg.mx

▲ These shoots bring out some of the top competitors in the world and are as much about money and side betting as glory.

▲ Rare all-option grade 5E Ithaca double-barrel trap gun.

competition standardization—and trap shooting as we know it really came into its own.

Glass ball shooting in the United States was introduced by Charles Portlock in 1866 and competitions were held in 1867 near Boston. The early traps threw the glass balls straight away from the shooter. These early shoots were not considered terribly challenging even in their day.

Captain Adam Henry Bogardus, the renowned world and United States champion shooter, was born in the rural countryside of upstate New York. He is credited with inventing the first useful glass ball trap in 1877, or just about a decade after glass ball competitions began. His trap design threw the balls in a long arc, I presume like a chandelle. Bogardus also patented various glass targets. They had to be tough enough to launch at approximately 60 miles an hour without breaking, but also frangible from pellets striking it.

◀▲ Glass target balls. Photo courtesy Gavin Gardiner Ltd.

Early rules of competition were established. The shooter stood eighteen yards from the traps, and the target had to fly at least sixty feet. Typically, three traps were employed and hidden from view. One trap threw the ball to the left, another straight ahead, and the third propelled the ball to the right. The order of launch upon the call of pull was random.

Hand-blown glass balls were used and were considerably harder to break than modern clay birds. From the website www.traphof.org, we learn with their (ATA) kind permission (paraphrased):

Hagerty Bros. 10 Platt St., New York manufactured the

Bogardus patent glass balls. The Bohemian Glass Works, manufactured Paines Feather-Filled Glass Ball. Whitall, Tatum and Co. were the manufacturer of the Patent Sanded Trap Ball, another popular variation. These were manufactured in many colors and are occasionally used as Christmas ornaments. They were highly visible. The most popular color was amber, with blue second and purple third and even less common was green. A few were nearly black. Plain glass balls cost a penny, embossed balls a bit more. Ira Paines manufactured a ball—"Ira Paine's filled ball "—which was filled with feathers or powder for a more dramatic hit.

◀▲ There must've been quite a lot of interest because a number of companies manufactured glass target balls. They had to be strong enough to be launched without breaking and fragile enough that pellets would break them to score a hit. Photo courtesy Gavin Gardiner Ltd.

The two great competitive glass ball shooters were Bogardus, previously noted, and W. F. Carver, better known as "Doc." Shooting events in those days were challenges promoted almost like a boxing match, and significant prize money as well as glory was on the line. Carver and Bogardus first competed against each other in a live pigeon match in Louisville, in 1883, and Carver won by a single bird.

The second and third matches used clay pigeons instead of live birds, and again Carver triumphed.

George Ligowsky, who invented both the clay pigeon and trap to throw them, both patented in 1880. To promote and popularize his inventions, he approached Carver and Bogardus. He offered $300 to the winner of each match, not an inconsequential amount of money in those days. The two were paid an additional $100 each time a score of 82 or better was shot. The matches were conducted at different venues around the country, and Carver was by far the better shot, winning 94 matches and tying in three, while Bogardus won just three. One-hundred-bird races of Ligowsky's targets were shot in each tournament from the 18-yard line. Ligowsky proved that clay pigeons were a suitable target, but they did not immediately replace the glass balls, instead adding another competition complementing both live boxed bird and glass-ball shooting tournaments.

The main use of target balls after the invention of the clay pigeon was in western shows, most famous of which was Buffalo Bill's Wild West show, and the most famous shot using them being Annie Oakley.

▲ Annie Oakley was much more than just a trick shot, winning many live bird competitions.

Cyril Adams' book *Live Pigeon Trap Shooting* is a fantastic read on the history, and the guns and men who developed the sport. The illustrations are superb. Published by The Sporting Library in Britain, it can be ordered directly from Briley. The author (RIP) also wrote the excellent *Lock Stock and Barrel*. You can also order this book directly from Briley (https://www.briley.com/p-61205-live-pigeon-trap-shooting-book-livepigeon.aspx).

The Game Today
There are really four separate varieties of trap-shooting competitions: 16-yard events, doubles, handicap, and Olympic trap. (The last is found at few facilities and rarely competed in, relatively speaking, in America, so I will not delve into that discipline.) All trap competition in America falls under the jurisdiction of the American Trapshooting Association (ATA), a great American institution.

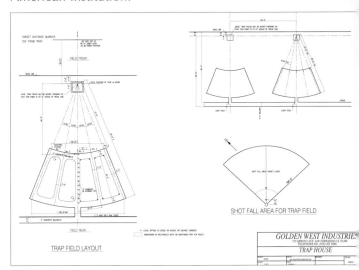

▲ In theory all trap fields are the same. While dimensions and the flight and speed of the bird are regulated, physical settings such as background, altitude, and wind means that each field poses slightly different challenges.

16-Yard Singles
This is the foundation of all trap shooting and it should be mastered to a considerable extent before one considers competing in handicap events or doubles. While the height of the target flight is standardized (assuming a windless day) the targets are thrown at random angles to the left and the right of the trap house center, with an extreme angle of no more than 22.5 degrees. When the trap is adjusted to throw its clays for regulated competition, each target must fly through a three-foot hoop set ten feet above the ground and ten yards distant from the target. That regulated target must also fly a distance between forty-eight and fifty-two yards.

There are five stations from which competitors shoot in turn. The fellow who starts on station No. 1 leads the round. Each shooter fires once and then waits for all the guns to his right to have fired one round before closing his gun and calling for a second target. Assuming a full squad, there is one man at each position, and after the gun on station No. 5 (the furthest to the right on the shooting line) has fired his first five shots, he does a circular permutation to station No. 1, with everyone else moving one station to their right. Thus, a round is comprised of twenty-five shots, five from each station. Most competitions see a minimum of one hundred targets thrown for each competitor. Some of the bigger events are two-hundred-bird competitions.

One of the keys to success in trap is selecting the correct hold point—where the muzzle of the gun is held when the gun is mounted on the shoulder—for each station. A shooter who closes one eye generally has a hold point right at the front edge of the trap house, or slightly above it, whereas someone who shoots with both eyes open will hold higher and see the target first appear beneath the barrel/s.

▲ Winchester's new AA Diamond Grade competition load is copper plated but importantly has a very high antimony component of 8 percent, which should result in better breaks, especially at distance. Double A's have had a loyal following for decades amongst competitive shots in all disciplines.

Handicap

While the targets are the same as in the 16-yard event, the shooter is placed, depending on his competitive record, at one-yard intervals from 17 to 27 yards back from the trap. The further back one goes, the more difficult shooting becomes. To be successful as a handicap competitor, one must take the bird on the rise before it transitions under normal circumstances and never as a dropper. As competitors move further back, the requirements that the gun shoots high becomes more critical. Those who shoot from 27 yards will generally have their guns set up to shoot much higher than when they are shooting doubles or at the 16-yard line.

Doubles

In this event, two clays are launched simultaneously, one to the left and one to the right. The target flight angles stay constant, with only wind affecting them. From station No. 1, the bird going to the right is a straight-away shot, just as from station No. 5 the bird to the left appears as a straight-away. Some shooters prefer to take the going-away bird first, while others prefer the angled shot. Two dead birds are, of course, the goal with each pair, and 25 pairs would constitute a normal round. Registered competitions are usually over a greater number of birds, with most being for 50 pairs.

▲ The new Perazzi High Tech 2020 Competition Gun. Perazzi's did especially well at the 2012 London Olympics.

Becoming a Better Trap Shot

One of the better books on trap shooting is a tiny tome written by Kay Ohye, called *You and the Target*. For many years, Ohye was one of the top trap shooters and coaches in America and I was fortunate enough to take one of his clinics. As he rightly points out, consistency in competition and in practice is the key to success. At the same time, and as I wrote in my first book, *The Complete Guide to Wingshooting*, "Practice makes perfect, but only if you're practicing correctly."

Follow-through is important. Don't think the moment of slapping the trigger is the end of the shot, for it isn't. The gun *must* keep moving until the target breaks. This is especially true when shooting doubles, as it is too easy to go on to the second bird without finishing your first shot, and this will often result in a miss.

Your focus must never be on the tip of your barrel but rather on the target; and it must not waver between the target and the front sight or bead, as that will invariably lead to a gun that does not swing smoothly.

That muzzle-bird, bird-muzzle back and forth results in starts and stops—and misses.

Taking a paraphrased cue from Johnny Cochran: "If the gun don't fit, you just won't hit." Most guns come with a standard dimension for a mythical American. It is worth getting your gun fitted by someone who really knows what they are doing. As a general rule, the shotgun must shoot where you look, but, in the case of trap shooting, you want the gun to shoot a bit high so you don't need to block out the target as you fire.

It's All in the Mount

The gun mount for trap shooting is much the same for skeet and sporting clays, so I suggest all clays shooters read this section.

As described in chapter 1, there is a natural pocket under the collar bone between the chest muscle and the shoulder when the trigger arm is raised. That pocket is where the buttstock should go.

The gun is raised to the face—the face does *not* go down to the gun. Your head should be as perpendicular as possible, but also as far forward on the gun as is comfortable— *without* stretching your neck—so that you are between the drop at comb in the drop at heel. This point along the comb is known as "drop at the face."

Some shooters and some styles feel that the trigger hand (assuming you're righty) does most of the work of raising the gun, whereas others like an active support hand. This is a matter of style.

Once the gun is on the shoulder, the trigger hand will help to mitigate recoil, but do not pull the gun too hard into your shoulder as that will restrict movement. Also, do not keep your support arm elbow too high (i.e., do not make it a "wing" parallel with the ground), nor too low as when supporting a rifle, but, rather, at about a 45-degree angle from the gun. Such a position will minimize fatigue. That said, many *great* trap shooters do shoot with both arms almost parallel to the ground. The great Nora Ross shoots this way. This goes against my sporting clay and game background but never argue with success!

Assuming your gun fits, you need to mount it properly. (Actually, a gun that is fitted for you assumes that you have a good gun mount and that said mount is consistent.) Once your hold point is established, and once the target is acquired in soft focus, you want to move the gun to the target on its flight line, taking a hard focus on the target only near the point of shooting. Concentrating on the target—complete visual and mental focus—is what separates the good from the very good and the very good from the great. If you want to shoot one hundred straight, often necessary to get into shoot offs at top shoots, you cannot let your focus wander.

That said, there is no need to concentrate during the whole round. A certain amount of relaxation when other shooters are shooting is necessary in order to maintain focus when it is your turn. Singleness of purpose must start as you prepare to call for the target, and must increase until the target is broken. It is this methodical, almost ritualistic discipline that will enable you to become your best. The real concentration is for only a short period of time: the time between your mount and the time you break the target. Whether this is a quarter of a second or a couple of seconds depends on you, just know that concentrating when you don't need to will only lead to exhaustion and the inability to focus when it's your shot.

Trap Hold Points

The following presumes a right-handed shooter. If you are left-handed, reverse the directions as in a mirror image:

- Station No. 1—Hold inside the left-handed corner of the trap house about a quarter of the total length of the house's left front edge.
- Station No. 2—Hold inside the left-handed corner of the trap house about halfway between station 1 hold point and center of the total length of the house's front edge.
- Station No. 3—Hold at the center of the house's front edge.
- Station No. 4—Hold inside the right-hand corner of the trap house about a quarter of the total length of the house's right front edge.
- Station No. 5—Hold at the right-hand corner of

the trap house. Indeed some of the top two eyed right-hand trap shots will "cheat" and hold a bit to the right of the house. This makes sense as the severe angle is to the right, and from that position you can see birds going straight away–the most severe angle to the left, from station five.

Shooters who shoot with only one eye open will hold on the front edge of the house or slightly above. Shooters who keep both eyes open take the same positional holds noted for the individual stations, but raise the barrel about twelve to eighteen inches, sometimes higher, though this will vary depending on individual style. In either case, once the target appears, your focus should be so complete that the background almost, or least figuratively, drops away. If you are focusing hard enough on the target, even if it should take an erratic path due to wind, your hand/eye coordination will automatically compensate and a broken target will result.

All the starting hold points are valid but you may need to change them based on your own visual perceptions and reflexes. They are not set in stone.

Point of Impact

Many shotguns do not shoot where you are looking. Even with a gun that is custom fit to you, a defect in barrel alignment within the total gun itself can affect the shot's impact. Before you head to the range and shell out money for practice rounds or entry fees, you should check the point of impact (for both barrels on a double) on patterning targets set at both 30 and 40 yards. This is the yardage span at which most trap targets are broken. Do not presume that both barrels of an over/under (or side-by-side) will shoot to the same point of impact. While they are supposed to do that (the term is "regulated"), I have seen some guns from rather famous makers that shot as much as 18 inches apart—yikes.

Thirty yards is the common breakpoint for 16-yard targets and for the first bird taken when shooting doubles. Forty yards is a pretty good reference point both for handicap targets and for the second bird in doubles. At singles and/or doubles you want a gun that shoots a little bit high—60/40 or 70/30 depending on where you take them and the sight picture you prefer —whereas for handicap shots in the twenty-five- to twenty-seven-yard range, most top competitors want a gun that shoots very high, perhaps as high as 80–90 percent above point of aim. However, in all truth, by time you are shooting at extreme yardage, you know how you want your gun to shoot. By shooting 60 or 70 percent high, the trap shot can see the target as he fires. With the gun that shoots flat, he would have to go through it and blot it out. In any case, as you fire, even when you see the target you must follow through primarily in the lateral but also slightly in the vertical direction of flight. The only lead you will need to see will be to the side on a bird that is not going straight away from you. Obviously, the greater the angle of the target, the greater is the lead that is needed.

Trap Guns and Chokes

Trap is where an over/under with fixed chokes often shines. The lower barrel in Modified or Improved Modified (depending on how quickly you get on target) is the ticket for the first shot at doubles and for singles at the 16-yard line. The top barrel with a tighter choke can handle the second shot and doubles, and often the handicap events, though you may need an adjustable comb you can raise for extended yardages. (Some shooters use different guns for all three events. This is a function of preference and pocketbook.) Combination guns offer a single barrel (a.k.a. Unsingle) for handicap, and an over under set for 16 yards and doubles.

The Mental Game

This (mental toughness) is the key to having great scores and winning. You need to feel confident and you need to think about breaking the target, not worrying about missing or merely hoping that you will break the target and shoot a good score. To be at the top of your mental game, you need to also be at the top of your physical game. You will have worked on the types of targets you will encounter and honed your physical skills and even your visual acuity through numerous practice drills. Weight training can often do wonders for scores. You should consider it.

A History of Skeet

Whereas trap has always been a competition, with its origins in live birds released from boxes (the trap)

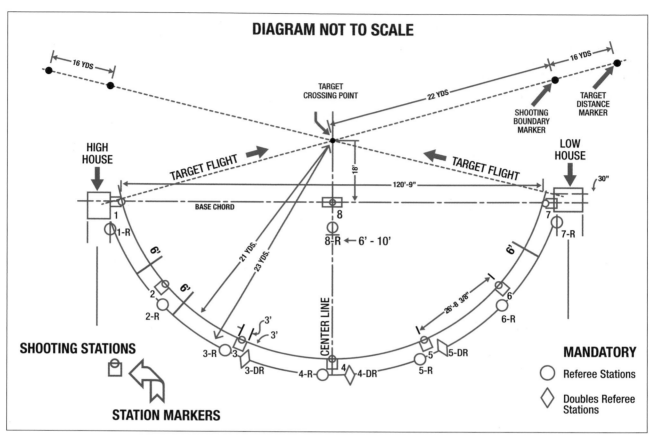

DIAGRAM NOT TO SCALE

16 YDS

TARGET
CROSSING POINT

22 YDS

16 YDS

SHOOTING
BOUNDARY
MARKER

TARGET
DISTANCE
MARKER

HIGH
HOUSE

TARGET FLIGHT

TARGET FLIGHT

LOW
HOUSE

30"

18'

120'-9"

BASE CHORD

1

8

7

1-R

8-R ← 6' - 10'

7-R

6'

21 YDS.

23 YDS.

6'

2

3'

6'

26'-8 3/8"

6'

2-R

3'

6-R

SHOOTING STATIONS

3-R 3

5 5-DR

MANDATORY

3-DR

4-R 4 4-DR

5-R

○ Referee Stations

CENTER LINE

STATION MARKERS

◇ Doubles Referee
Stations

▲ While skeet fields were originally designed to help hunters improve their shooting, they have a loyal competitive following and, in the international version, an Olympic sport. Courtesy NSCA/NSSA.

by a long string, the sport of skeet traces its origins to an upland hunter and dog man named Charles Davis. About one hundred years ago, Davis was working on a method to improve shooting technique under field conditions rather than for a dedicated competition. Originally, the concept entailed a circle with a radius of twenty-five yards. On the circle's perimeter he placed twelve shooting stations. A single trap was positioned at 12 o'clock and set to throw its targets over the six o'clock position. Participants would fire two shots at each of the twelve stations, plus another from the center of the circle, for twenty-five shots total, as that was the number of cartridges per box in those days, just like now. The design was hoped to replicate most of the shots a hunter would see afield. It was either originally called "clock" shooting or "shooting around-the-clock," depending on which writer one believes.

Unfortunately for Davis, but lucky for the rest of us, as his neighborhood grew up there were complaints

▲ Winchester Model 21 Deluxe Skeet.

and he was forced to shoot over his own property without shot falling on his neighbors' lands. The problem was finally resolved, while offering many of the same shots, by installing a second trap, with the shooters now following a very similar shooting format to the one we enjoy today. It was in 1926 that it was renamed "skeet" and became a sport of its own. American skeet has since morphed into an international discipline, which takes place on the same field, but employing a different length of clay flight and target speeds (faster). International skeet also mandates a low gun mount (the gun cannot be brought to shoulder until the bird is seen), and includes the added impediment or variable of a random delay in target launching of up to three seconds after the shooter has called for the target. Another difference is that the sequence to complete the 25 targets in a round of Olympic skeet requires shooters to shoot at doubles, not only on stations No. 1, 2, 6, and 7, as in American skeet, but also on 3, 4, and 5. This includes a reverse double (low house first) on station No. 4. This last double was introduced to the sequence starting in 2005.

The inaugural National Skeet Championship occurred in 1926, and the National Skeet Shooting Association, which still oversees the sport, was formed as a sport grew in popularity.

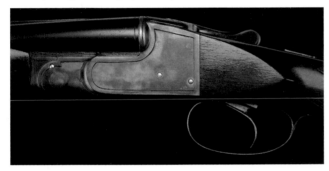

▲ Rare 410 Lefever grade A skeet gun, in excellent condition. Note the single trigger.

For a full list of rules visit www.nssa-nsca.org for NSSA, NSCA, and www.shootata.com for ATA.

Becoming a Better Skeet Shot

The ideal guns for skeet are intrinsically different from trap guns. Certainly, you do not want a gun that shoots excessively high. I prefer seeing the target slightly above my barrel so I will go to about 60/40-point of impact while other shooters prefer a gun that shoots a flat 50/50. Guns that shoot high do not have the same intrinsic benefit as they do in the game of trap. Here it is whichever sight picture the shooter prefers.

The Remington 1100 has probably won more 12-gauge tournaments than any other shotgun. It is a very well-balanced gun for the event and the fact that the gas piston takes a lot of sting out of recoil and spreads it over time means that both flinching and fatigue are less likely to develop. The 26-inch autos were the standard for decades. Now most shooters use 28-inch or longer barrels.

To shoot skeet sub-gauge events, many competitors shoot over/unders, often with carrier barrels and tube inserts so that the gun's overall weight and balance is exactly the same regardless the gauge being shot. Indeed, the advent of sub-gauge tubes by Briley and Kolar are one of the main reasons many shooting small-gauge events have seen significantly better scores.

Like trap, the hold point in skeet is critical. I think this is something that is best developed under the careful eye of a professional coach, though one can also figure it out by trial and error, but generally speaking, you want to have the muzzle of your shotgun held (hold point and at the same level as the flight of the target) out about a quarter of the distance from the house releasing the bird to the center stake (or shot first when shooting doubles). More or less distance from each house as a hold point will depend on your reflexes and style.

It is good to have a routine when you get into each shooting station. I set my feet where I want for the high house, and then realign them for the low. I want a stance that allows me to uncoil so that, when I am shooting, I am completely relaxed, with nothing to interfere with my follow-through. Once my feet are in the right place, I point the gun towards the center stake, raise it to the correct height for the flight line of the target, and then move the muzzle back to my hold point. The correct height could be affected dramatically by a strong wind on the day.

At this stage, I take a soft focus with my eyes halfway between the hold point and the trap house, and then I call for the target.

One of the easiest ways to become proficient at skeet is to work one target at a time until the lead is memorized, indeed, so the action of shooting each particular target from each station becomes muscle memory. When I haven't shot for a while, and assuming I can either shoot with friends who don't care or I'm able to get a skeet field to myself, I will shoot each target until I break five in a row before going on to the next. This discipline leads to consistency. Also, if I have a target that gives me trouble—for whatever reasons, I'm more likely to drop No. 2 high than any other target on the course—I will often shoot a box of cartridges just at that one target. It is important to work on one's strengths, but just as important to mitigate one's weaknesses.

Most top skeet shots use maintained (also called "sustained") lead. The advantage of this is that there is less variation in target acquisition due to speed of reflexes on a given day than one would see with swing-through. Some shooters do use the pull-away method.

The Stations

The following explains the sequence of shots in American (non-Olympic) skeet. There are eight stations or shooting pads total, seven of those arranged around a half-circle circumference behind the line between the high and low house, with the eighth at the center of the line between the two houses.

Station No. 1—High and Low: The high bird on station No. 1 is very straightforward. Starting at the center stake, bring the gun up to about the line of flight and back towards the house the distance that best suits your style. Bring your eyes halfway back to the house from this point to look for the bird and call "Pull." As soon as your muzzle is under the bird and you see a little bit of air, fire and follow through.

▲ Here I am shown shooting a round of skeet at the Greenbrier during the Green Jacket competition circa 20 years ago. Shooting low gun to warm up for sporting clays, I was using a borrowed gun for the first time. The unfamiliar dynamics of the shotgun cost me some targets in the competition. Photo courtesy AAB.

For low bird No. 1, start at the stake and push your gun two-thirds of the way back to the low house. Focus your eyes halfway between from your gun to the house and call for the bird. You should break it close to the center stake. If you're shooting a gun with a Cylinder or Skeet 1 choke, at twenty to twenty-five yards your effective pattern should have a reasonably wide diameter. If you wait for the target to be ten yards from you (past the center stake and seemingly touchable), your pattern is much narrower; you will still be able to break the clay but with a much smaller margin of error. Shoot it the way you prefer, but my advice is to practice shooting this bird at the point where you will break it for doubles.

My friend Eric Steinkraus, a many time All-American Skeet Shot, and Master Class Sporting Clay shot, emailed me in response to a question I had on current thoughts on choking .410s for skeet: *"The best guy ever (Wayne Mayes, who had two hundred 100 straights with the .410) would start out with a pair of .020's and shoot them at eighteen yards indoors off a bench. He would then polish them out until he had a sixteen-inch pattern out of each choke. He said they often didn't mic the same, but they both produced a sixteen-inch pattern at eighteen yards."*

For the pair on station No. 1, you'll take the high bird first, and if you crush it right about at the stake or before, a minimal adjustment in your swing will be all that is necessary to take out the bird from the low house; in other words, the pair can be taken in very quick succession and with very little gun movement between the two shots.

Station No. 2, High and Low: Although I shoot almost all my targets with a maintained lead, I shoot high No. 2 and low No. 6 with an accelerating gun, more pull-away than maintained. In this manner, I never let the bird beat my barrel. Most shooters will see about a two-foot lead on the high bird. When you see the lead that breaks targets for you, memorize it.

Low No. 2 is an easy bird, with the same routine as for No. 1. In other words, start at the stake, go two-thirds of the way back to the house (give or take), look halfway between your hold point and the house, then break the target where you will break it in doubles.

Doubles for station No. 2 should be taken as they are from No. 1, high bird first then low, though you'll experience more transition, more gun movement on this pair then you will when standing in the station No. 1 pad.

Stations No. 3, 4, and 5 High Bird: According to D. Lee Braun, the famous Remington professional and multi-time All-American, the correct lead for the high bird from all these stations is the same—a bit more than three feet will suffice. Nevertheless, he recommends seeing four to four and one-half feet of lead because, if you happen to be one of those who checks your bead and slows the gun, you have built in a margin of error that will enable you to still make the kill. There is much more margin of error to the front, due to the length of the shot string and width of pattern.

YouTube has the classic Braun skeet and trap films and are worth viewing.

Now, this is really important: As soon as the lead looks right, fire and follow through. It *never* gets better, so riding the target and trying to perfect your lead will produce no benefits. This doesn't mean that you can't spend a nanosecond double-checking your sight picture. It just means that if it looks good, *shoot*. Trying to make a shotgun sight picture look exactly perfect, too accurate, makes you hesitant, and hesitation normally leads to focusing on the bead, stopping the gun, and missing behind the bird.

Braun felt that the high bird from station No. 3 the low bird from No. 5 are the two toughest stations on the field for left- and right-handed shooters, respectively. Personally, neither of those has given me the slightest bit of trouble; the high No. 2 and low No. 6 are my bugaboos. If I break station two, there is a 99-percent probability that I will go clear for the round. I improved my shooting on those two stations by shooting them a lot and memorizing the sight picture and timing that work for me.

I'm sorry I never met Lee Braun, as there are many questions I'd have liked to ask him. For one thing, it certainly appears from his book, *Skeet Shooting with D. Lee Braun: A World Champion Shows How Skeet Can Make You a Better Field Shot* (Paperback 1967), by Robert Campbell, that he always shot with a gun not mounted before the call for the bird. I also start this way, as I find a mounted gun gets in my way visually. Still, I doubt there are many top competitive skeet shooters today who don't shoot with a pre-mounted gun. Also, he was an All American both in skeet and trap. There is little to no crossover in top competitors today.

On high house station Nos. 3, 4, and 5, I mount on the center stake at the height the bird flies. I then move the gun two-thirds of the way back to the high house. My feet are lined up so that my front foot is pointing slightly to the right of the center stake. My front knee is bent, and 55 to 60 percent of my weight is on my front leg. When I move the gun back toward the house, I coil myself like a spring, yet I still try to remain relaxed, comfortable, and confident. I dismount the gun at this point and direct my eyes halfway between the hold point and the mouth of the house. Braun talks about looking right into the mouth, but I cannot see the bird there. Perhaps he was one of those individuals who excelled at sports because he had such extraordinary visual acuity. Wherever *you* first see the bird — as a blur or streak—is where you should look for it you should escalate your focus so that the bird is completely locked on and in focus just before and as you fire. The best shots will focus on a part of the target, perhaps the front edge.

I try to break these high house birds within a foot or two of the center stake. Sometimes, in windy conditions or unusual lighting situations, I see the bird late and shoot it late. The important thing is to shoot when the lead looks right, not a moment before, not a moment after.

Stations No. 3, 4, and 5 Low Bird: This is basically the reverse of the high house with a couple of caveats. For the low birds, my front foot is set up with the toe pointing a little bit to the left of the stake. It is important with all targets to start the gun on their line or little bit below. If you start too high, it is easy for the barrel to obscure the target, and then you'll have to compensate by bringing the gun down to the line and likely rush to get in front of it. Your barrel movements should always be performed smoothly to the flight line, not in jagged left or right movements. This is more important with low birds, or least the need for a clear target picture more obvious as the bird launches from below your gun.

As the sight pictures on stations No. 3, 4, and 5 are basically the same, if you can break one of them you can break them all. However, these crossers are often subject to changes in wind, or at least that is the perception of many shooter. It is therefore most important to practice the stations on as many fields as possible to get the feel for them under a variety of conditions. For example, a strong wind from the high to low house will cause the high target to drop quickly. Conversely, the same wind will slow and lift the low target. Staying with the target and a good follow-through are particularly important at these times. Being able to handle adverse conditions by practicing may lead to your shooting well in competition on those days.

Shooting targets from station No. 4 is an outstanding way to practice. It's also helpful for teaching the shooter to call his own shots. For example, if you see that you're breaking the target on its nose, you are shooting well and only the slightest modification needs to be taken to the sight picture in order to totally crush the clay. If, on the other hand, you're breaking the back of the target, you know that you need to increase your lead by at least a foot. Breaks on the top or bottom of the clay can also show you where you're shooting, indeed where on the bird you're specifically focusing.

According to Lee Braun, low No. 5 is the most missed target in skeet shooting for the right-handed shooter. The perception is that the target is getting away from you from this angle, causing you to rush the target. But you actually have plenty of time—the bird is in no way moving any faster than it was from the other shooting stations—so remain focused and relaxed and break the bird.

(I should add that there are many top shooters who coach, give clinics, and have books and DVDs on shooting. I rely on Lee Braun's work as I am of that era. He's also one of the few shots who was top notch both in skeet and trap. Sporting clays and FITASC were unknown in America in those days.)

Good foot position is critical in the middle stations so that you can move your body smoothly. Tension and the concomitant muscle tightening are the kiss of death. You might get away with it for a bird or two, but not if you need to shoot a hundred straight.

Lead as a Function of Angle

Now I'm going to confuse slightly the idea of lead when shooting skeet. The sight picture and lead from station No. 4 will vary slightly with each shooter, depending on how fast one moves their barrels and how they perceive distance. Let us take it as a given, however, that the correct lead is three and one-half feet. The truth is that if the correct lead at twenty-one yards is three and one-half feet for a crosser, it is the actual correct lead for *all* stations, but it is not the *perceived* or *seen* lead.

Let's look at another example. Go to station No. 7 and shoot the low bird going away. Between the time you pull the trigger and the pellets reach the bird, that bird has traveled 3½ feet (with the speed of the pellets and clay remaining, in relative terms, the same). Now step to station No. 6 and shoot the low target. While *visually* the correct sight picture is only, say, two feet here, the target has still traveled the three and one-half feet between the time the trigger is pulled and the pellets smash the bird. Part of this has to do with the side of the shot column intercepting the target. No doubt, when I was in high school or college I knew enough about geometry, trigonometry, and calculus to set up a mathematical model to explain this phenomenon. In my dotage, I do not possess the skills. In the real world of shooting, I'm not even sure that this concern should be addressed, yet, on a theoretical level, I believe it's illuminating.

Station No. 6, High and Low: The high bird taken from station No. 6 is one of the easiest shots on the field. It seems to be coming toward you forever and you can pretty much shoot it where you please. If I'm practicing for sporting clays, I try to take it early, perhaps halfway to the center stake. I will also practice shooting it very late as a dropper, so I can force myself to get under the bird. If I'm shooting in registered target competition, I try to shoot it just before the stake. Some competitive shooters prefer to take the high single a bit after the stake, as this is where they will break it as the second bird in doubles. Indeed, many high-ranked shots take all their double birds at about 18 yards (plus or minus) to be as consistent as possible.

The low bird from No. 6 can be quite tricky. Because it seems to be getting away from you so quickly, there is a tendency to blow past it, realize you've gone too fast too far, stop the gun, and miss behind. A good way to overcome this is to move your hold point a few feet closer to the stake. That way you won't have the feeling of the gun moving overly fast. If you're a swing-through shooter, you just have to touch the bird, fire, and keep going with your follow-through. Otherwise, a foot or so of lead should suffice.

For the pair, you'll take the low bird first, then the high. As it is with the pairs from stations No. 1 and 2, there should be an economy of motion between the two shots. Shoot, slight movement to the next bird, shoot again. No wild swinging to and fro.

Perceived Lead and "Two and One-Half Feet"—An Explanation

Several times in this chapter I've used the phrase "perceived lead." But what is a perceived lead of two and one-half feet or four feet or ten feet?

Perceived lead is the distance you see between the muzzle/bead of your shotgun and the target *at the distance and angle the target is traveling*. Even though your barrel is in one plane and the target in another, it's kind of like looking at two identically sized trees side by side in the distance—"Yup, those look to be about four feet apart." Perhaps it's clear to put it this way: say you are twenty yards back from two trees that are perpendicular to you. As you walk in a semicircle in either direction the perceive distance between the two trees narrow, until they directly in line with each other, at which point there is no perception of separation.

Oddly enough, it's really only when trying to explain it in writing that the question of what defines perceived lead comes up. Almost any coach working with a new shotgunner will ask

their student, whether the clay was broken or missed, "How much lead did you see?" and the student will almost always answer in terms of feet. That's how the brain works, more or less transposing that bead onto the same place as the bird and letting the eyes calculate how much distance is between the two. In that manner, when the student answers after a miss, "I was two feet in front of it," the coach can aid the correction by saying "Increase your lead by doubling it," and then watch their pupil successfully break the clay.

Station No. 7, High and Low: You're on the home stretch now, and should never miss high No. 7 once you're shooting competition seriously. High No. 7 is just like high No. 6 but with a bit less lead. The correct lead will differ depending on where you shoot the target, but I believe killing the bird before it has a chance to drop offers the most consistent results.

For low No. 7 you simply shoot straight at the bird before it has a chance to drop. Do not start so high that you lose the bird under your barrels. Low No. 7 is the easiest shot on the field, but never take any shot for granted. I've done so, and I've missed. Just shoot the damn thing and make sure you do so before it drops and becomes tricky.

Shooting the pair from No. 7 is done just like it is from No. 6: low bird, high bird, economy of motion between the two.

Station No. 8, High and Low: A beginner on the center stage that is station No. 8 feels that these are difficult shots because they take place so quickly. In fact, they are two of the easier targets on the field. The key is to not let the bird beat your barrel and, as always, follow through. In both high and low birds, all you need to do is bring the tip of your barrel to the bird, fire, and finish—*never* swing past the center stake and behind you. Some shooters like to blot the bird out. However, as a both-eyes-open shooter I see the bird the full time it's in flight. If I were a one-eyed shooter or shooting a side-by-side, perhaps it would indeed disappear in the barrels.

My foot position is the same as Lee Braun's, and sometimes I shoot it as he suggests. Other times, I shoot each bird as a sideways shot, maintaining the same foot position. In any case, start your gun along the path that the target will travel. (If you're a new shooter, watch the shooter ahead of you so that you can see what that flight path is.) Look right at the mouth of the trap house, and as you see the target emerge, bring the tip of the barrel to the bird. As soon as you feel that you are accelerating past the bird, fire and follow through. No *perceived* lead is necessary here.

Sporting Clays

Sporting clays came to America with a bang, with a big British American Chamber of Commerce shoot sometime in the 1980s at the Mashomack Preserve Club in upstate New York. There was one team from the House of Lords; another from the House of Commons; a group of old Etonians; a team, I believe, from The Port of Missing Men; I think a team from the old U.S. Sporting

Gary Herman in a good ready position. Note how little his face moves as he brings the gun to it. Courtesy AAB.

Clay Association, now defunct; obviously a team from Mashomack; and then riffraff like me on the outdoor writers squad and a few other squads. Since then, sporting clays has exploded. The National Sporting Clays Association (NSCA) is the main governing body in America, and it does a great job. Considering the fact it also runs the NSSA, that makes sense.

In the early days, sporting clays targets were pretty straightforward, or, perhaps more accurately, less technical in their presentation than they are today. Tournaments tended to consist of 10 stations with 10 birds thrown at each in random combinations of simultaneous pairs, report pairs, and following pairs, the last being less common now. Rabbits, chandelles, teal, and battues, standard, midis et al were thrown; some as low incomers to mimic driven partridge, tall incomers from high towers to mimic driven pheasant,

and dropping birds to mimic decoying waterfowl combined to separate the game of sporting clays from skeet or trap, as did the requirement of an unmounted gun until the bird appeared after "pull" being called. Indeed, in the early days, at many courses it was pejoratively referred to as "skeet in the woods"—but this often was not a fair depiction.

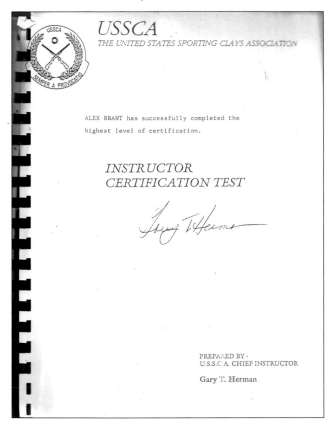

▲ When Gary Herman was the chief instructor for the United States Sporting Clay Association, he actually had me read his written test before anyone else as he felt if I didn't think the question was clear, it might need rephrasing.

Today the rules have changed to allow shooters to pre-mount the guns if they desire, and much longer, more technically deceptive targets—birds dropping when you think they are flat or rising, and just generally more difficult shooting—have taken over as the competitor skills have improved. Dan Carlisle and other great early American sporting clay shooters led the way. Today it is the shooters like Anthony Matarese, shooting his Beretta DT11, who won the World Sporting Clay Championship 2016, who are at the front of the pack. (Matarese is one of the few

coaches from whom I've taken a couple of lessons over the last couple of years. He is a great coach as well as a great shot.)

▲ Anthony Matarese is an amazing shot with eyes like an eagle, and having given so much thought to the game, he is also one of the greatest coaches I've ever met in the sport. Photo courtesy of Anthony Matarese, Jr.

Sporting clays is a mental game, a physical game, a game of hand-eye coordination, and a game of visual acuity. Each aspect has to be honed and refined if you want to make AA or Master Class. If you see sporting clays as a fun day afield with friends, perhaps as practice for actual game shooting, then practice and shooting can be more casual.

▲ Debbie Horn, a former All American Sporting Clay Shot, waits in a good relaxed position. Notice that her gun is pointed in a safe direction while resting her arms; if you're not a safe shot, nothing else matters. Debbie is both a fine shot and a safe one.

If you do take the sport seriously, shooting a practice round doesn't always mean that you are actually *practicing*. You need to get to a good coach, one like Matarese, who will provide you specifics to work on between coaching sessions. Overall trigger time is important, but once that is put in, realize that practice without a goal and self-reflection is merely shooting. Why? Because a problem may not in fact be corrected if you're not practicing properly—you might actually be practicing *missing*. A given practice day for a serious sporting clays competitor may mean working on a single target that's proving difficult, adjusting your footing, hold point, lead, and other factors until you understand how the target should be taken and memorize the sight picture. If you continue to miss a target *without* making modifications, realize that all you're doing is creating the wrong muscle memory (i.e., you are practicing missing).

▲ From the angle, it is obvious that Debbie's first shot is at a rabbit. Notice the Beretta firmly in the pocket, her arms in a comfortable natural position, her weight slightly forward, and her left forefinger on the same line as for barrel.

▲ Debbie is putting a second cartridge in the magazine. Again note that the barrel of her Beretta autoloader is always pointed downrange.

Let's take a closer look at the targets you'll encounter on a typical sporting clays course and more about how the game is played.

Rabbits
Rabbits, the one sporting clays target thrown to roll across the ground (though some courses will throw them airborne since, because they have different aerodynamics than other clays, have such an unusual and challenging flight pattern), must be one of the easier targets to screw up. Because of friction with the ground, they slow in their travel faster than the airborne clay, so they are easy to miss *in front*. This is especially true of rabbits that are on the close side to the shooter. Matarese's solution for me on rabbits was to shoot focusing on the back edge, rather than the front.

A long rabbit target does need lead, but, again, realize

that unless it's right off the arm, it probably needs less lead than you think, simply because it is slowing in its travel more than airborne birds. Now, sometimes a rabbit will be sent airborne as it runs into a hump on a rubber mat, and those jumps tend to be predictable. (Because of random bounces, rabbits are now banned in UK sporting events.) I find I rarely miss a rabbit in the air unless it has jumped just after I finished my shot. But that is the way the cookie, or in this case the rabbit, crumbles—or doesn't crumble. Complicating the successful break of a rabbit target, either on the ground or airborne, is that they are harder and denser than other targets so that they don't break as they hit the ground. It is a very good idea to go to No. 7½ shot for anything other than the closest rabbit. Because of the unpredictable potential jumps of a rabbit, it adds an intrinsic element of unfairness in some competitions. In an ideal world, either a ramp would be added so that all of the rabbits jump at a specific point, or a mat put down and cleaned between squads so that unpredictable jumps are taken out of the equation. Ideal worlds tend not to exist.

Chandelles, a.k.a. Chondels (you will see both spellings used from various sources)
This is not a natural shot for some shooters. I find this one of the easier targets on a course, but chandelles come in different configurations and can prove difficult to many. Thrown as either a standard clay or a rabbit, it comes off the trap's arm and will arc in its flight. Specially designed chandelle traps enhance tilt and

flight path height. Depending on where the shooter is positioned, it can appear on edge before arcing and giving a full flat profile as it drops away, or it can be thrown high in full flat profile to arc away and present the edge. It is a visually deceptive target: Is the bird close, at a medium distance, or far away? Is it a crosser or is it quartering? Is it traveling in a long, shallow arc, or is the distance traveled fairly short but rising before a modest transition period sees it falling rapidly? What is it actually doing it doing after the transition; in other words, is it falling away from me or towards me?

▲ The butt of the gun is well into the natural pocket of my shoulder, arms are where they should be, and soft focus is forward past where I expect to see the bird. In the last bit before firing, take a hard focus on the bird—actually an escalating focus as you get closer to firing. As you take a hard focus on the bird you will be aware of your barrels but only in your peripheral vision.

As with all sporting clays targets, the goal is to break the target where you can kill it most efficiently. Often, Matarese would say to me that point is "where you can see it the best." With the chandelle, that means you can shoot them on the way up, on the way down, or in the transition. Say, for example, the transition is wide but the overall flight path doesn't vary in height much from the beginning of the transition to the end of the transition. In that case, I might wait for the bird close to the transition get in front of it, stay a little bit under it, and shoot it in the transition. For birds on the way down, I tend not to want to let them drop too far, because otherwise they have gained way too much speed as a function of gravity. On any sort of crossing chandelle taken near the transition, the lead is more important than holding above are under in most cases as in most cases the brain will just subconsciously

make that correction for you. If however you find it you are shooting over the bird, as world champion Ben Husthwaite points out it's often good to pretend you're shooting along a tram line below the target. It is important to read your breaks if they are not centered. For example, if you have a small break/chip off the top of a target, you know you need to hold lower. If you're taking pieces off the nose, you should reduce your lead slightly.

Battues

This target is nearly flat and very thin, lacks the aerodynamics of other clay birds. As you might imagine, that makes for unique target presentations.

Never say never, but you rarely want to shoot a battue on its edge. I like to shoot them just as they turn but before they start to drop significantly. There's no dome on this target as there is on the standard clay bird, so when it drops, it *drops*. Again there are many variables and whether you have a pair of battues or single battue, or if it's part of the simo-pair or not will affect where and how to shoot them.

Most shooters are like me and want to take the battue when it presents its full flat face or almost the full face shows. Easy enough to understand, it's a bigger visual, more surface for pellets to hit causing a break; and the bird is slowing then. All the same, with battues, bigger

▲ This series (continued on next page) shows that when dealing with dropping targets, the barrels and the follow-through are very much downward in direction. Gary Herman is a past master at shooting droppers, establishing his lead and matching speed before squeezing the trigger. While slapping the trigger is SOP, on dropping birds squeezing allows you to more easily maintain the correct position of the barrels through the shot. When a simultaneous pair of battues are thrown, while the first bird can often be taken much as a crosser, the second will usually be taken as a dropper.

isn't always better, especially as its speed in full profile can be difficult to gauge. Remember, the optimum place to take a target is where you can best see what it is doing/ read the target. If that's when the battue is presenting only the edge, *shoot it*. You might very well be surprised by how effective the break is and how taking it in a more optimum place on pairs improves your setup for taking your second bird.

Sometimes a battue is thrown like a chandelle or flying rabbit. In this case, it is generally traveling faster than a normal chandelle. When thrown in this manner, it will not turn.

The chandelle tends to be flown in a parabolic arc which, depending on the course designer, can be high or low, crossing or quartering, tilted slightly to its side to make the flight more deceptive. Both standard targets and rabbit targets are used. Indeed, Lincoln traps that great old manual manufacturer offered what they called a flying rabbit. Realize always that rabbits are tougher than standard clays and you might want to go up to size 7½ shot. What gets interesting is the steepness of the parabola. If it's flat at the top and more or less a crossing shot then you can wait with your gun on a suitable line and shoot it almost as a crosser near the top of its flight. On a bird quartering away, you definitely want to shoot it on the way up. You should practice shooting chandelles in various aspects of their flight so that on the day of a competition, you can break it in the best place for shooting a pair. This might mean shooting it on the way down.

▲ Peter Horn shooting Beretta's top-of-the-line autoloader, the Model A400. He uses his index finger parallel to the barrel just as he does on his over under. A good example of relaxed concentration.

As previously stated, a battue comes out on its side, usually too edgy to be shot well and you want to wait for it to turn and start to drop. If you shoot it early as it turns, the dropping aspect becomes less significant. There will be times when it can only be effectively shot as a dropper, often fast dropping bird especially for the second clay if you are shown a pair of simultaneous battues. Battues because of the nature of their design are more affected by wind than any other clay target.

Springing Teal

This is often a very challenging target. Study it. Is it going straight up? On a long teal, the one thing you need to avoid is to shoot it just as it stalls from gravity, as you'll shoot over in the stall and it starts to drop. On close teal, some shooters shoot almost directly *at* the bird at the peak of its flight, or a bit below to account for lock time and the time it takes for the shot to travel to the target. Obviously the longer the shot the more you may need to be below the bird if you are shooting it this way. Sometimes this works, but I find the approach produces inconsistent results. Personally I prefer to shoot them while they are under power, perhaps a quarter of the way from the top. A pull-away or swing-through swing on the way up but before the stall begins can be more effective, though on a really long teal, I will sometimes shoot them on the way down. In those instances, I want to shoot them early in their drop, before they've gained too much speed.

This is a great bird to practice shooting both on the rise and as a dropper—especially since teal can be thrown at angle away from the shooter or toward the

▲ Notice that my head is in a position waiting for the gun to reach my face and my eyes are pretty close to level.

shooter, in addition to the customary presentations. If the bird is not going straight up and down, you may need to start your gun on the side where the bird is moving to or you may want to cant your gun slightly and stay on the edge of the bird in the direction it is flying to be on the correct line as you get over it. In any case, on a teal that is not perfectly vertical you must take the actual line into account for placing your shot. If practicing, consider loading two cartridges and, if you miss it on the way up, try and break it on the way down.

Midis, Minis, and Colors

In addition to the specialty battue and rabbit clays, sporting clays also employ the use of midi clays (90mm in diameter compared to the standard 108/110mm), and minis (60mm). The different sizes, as you might imagine, challenge the read of the target. For instance, a mini thrown along the same path as a standard target will appear farther away, though it isn't, and it may initially fly faster and lose speed more quickly than the standard target.

Finally, sporting clays uses a variety of colored and color-combination targets. In addition to the bright orange, competitors will encounter solid black (hard to read against backgrounds of heavy foliage, making shooting more challenging from a visual standpoint. Personally, I consider this unfair to older shooters especially—black are just fine thrown over the field or with sky as the backdrop); an orange dome with a black rim (I've been told it challenges the reading of the target speed), chartreuse green (very difficult to read when thrown in deep-woods settings), and a bright pink (easier to read against dark backgrounds). Shooting sporting clays should not be designed so that color-blind or older shooters are at a visual rather than an execution of shooting disadvantage. Rabbits come in various colors, though most often in orange or black.

Mounted or Unmounted Gun?

Though it once restricted shooting in registered events to be with an unmounted gun before the call for the bird, NSCA now allows the gun to be pre-mounted on the shoulder. This has proven to be beneficial with presentations that mimic the flight paths of the clays in trap—those with a shallow angle going away or coming in are preferably shot with a pre-mounted gun. Pre-mounting on going-away quartering birds allows getting on going-away birds much more quickly which is a big advantage especially with simultaneous pairs.

A crosser can be shot in either fashion, though I do prefer to shoot crossers with an unmounted gun. Many presentations, especially shallow angles, will benefit from a pre-mounted gun.

From 1 to 5, notice the gun going to the face and the focus always on the target. The head is still. AAB photo.

The Visual Challenge

We all know that visual acuity and shooting go hand in glove. Olympic shots spend a lot of time on various visual acuity exercises. These exercises help shooters of all levels, but it takes a truly committed shooter to practice them on a regular basis.

In just one example, on chandelles, Matarese would have me focus on the rings within the target to make them sharp and in focus in the area where I would shoot the bird (break point). He points out correctly that one does not need a hard focus for the entire shot, just the last critical part when firing the gun. He will also have shooters focus on the front edge rather than the whole bird for some shots, and with practice on close birds for me looking at the dimples on the dome.

Another thing Matarese got me to do was to study the flight of the bird, so as to have a perfect mental picture of the bird's line. In this I would use mental markers, trees, and other landscape fixtures, to determine my hold point for the gun, where to look for the target, and its breakpoint.

In another instance, for shallow-angle birds coming from beneath and to the side of the station, Matarese would set up a hold point where the bird appears under the barrels and the shooter just makes a small movement to break the bird. It worked so well that it almost seems like cheating. It is not. It is intelligent, skilled shooting.

From Smoker Smith I learned, as I mentioned elsewhere, to make the shot as easy as possible. That might mean shooting from the right or left side of the station cage to cut down on the angle of at least one of the targets. Remember, that especially on report pairs, it is important to break the first bird where your gun will be close to your desired hold point for the second target. This makes breaking the *pair* much more consistent.

Footwork cannot be overemphasized, and in sporting clays, it's good to remember that you're not glued in place. You can move within the station between birds, resetting your feet if necessary and if there's time before a second-bird shot. Let me explain.

From 1 to 5, I demonstrate a good ready position. I move back towards the trap, but face is directly above the barrels. Weight slightly forward. Left arm is down between 30 and 45 degrees, which is the most comfortable place for it. As the gun moves into the shoulder and up to the face the movement is smooth and confident. On fast birds coming hard right to left, I often keep all four fingers wrapped under the forend to allow me to pull the barrel a little bit and develop more speed if I need it, more or less subconsciously. I'm shooting my Beretta DT11 Black.

Recall that running out of the ability to swing, which leads to "rainbowing," often leads to missing the target. (In rainbowing, you might actually go up before you start to go down with the tip of your barrel.) You want your feet set so that you are balanced and able to continue your swing to where you will break the bird. Remember too that it is often necessary to move through your legs, bending or unbending knee to keep your shoulders level and your barrel on the line of the target. Now, let's think of a report pair with one bird coming from the left as a crosser and the second bird coming from the right as a shallow but fast quartering target. (I'm always addressing this as though the shooter is right-handed; for lefties please reverse.) I set up with my feet pointed towards the first bird's break zone. Once that shot is complete—and not a moment before—I may move my whole left leg to the left or, if I'm short of time, at least point my toe to the left towards the break zone for the second target. In doing this I don't run out of swing or come off the line on the second bird. I might also take the first bird late if that puts me in a good position to pick up the second target. For example, I'm not taking the bird early and then frantically moving to the right to look for a bird that is rapidly going away from me.

You will find with practice that you have much more time to do this than you think. Obviously, there is usually more time on a report pair, but there is often sufficient time even on a simultaneous pair to move your front foot. If the second bird is a long crosser from the opposite direction of your first target, just moving the toe can mean the difference between a hit and miss.

Chokes for Sporting Clays

When I was shooting sporting clays a lot back in the 1980s to mid-1990s, I was always changing choke tubes and had the luxury of using Eyster 1, 2 and 3s, which sort of translated into perfect Cylinder, a very densely patterning modified, and a perfect Super-Full choke. Each choke was hand-honed for a particular barrel and for a particular load.

The targets on today's courses are longer than they were in the 1980s, so Mod and Improved Mod works fine for me almost all the time. A truly great shot might opt for Improved Modified and Full or Full-Full because they are more concerned about a target getting through a hole in the pattern than in actually missing the bird. About the only time that I will open up my chokes is for an in-my-face rabbit. You have to

view your own shooting abilities honestly and determine what works best for you. If you are shooting an autoloader, for instance, as a general rule, it is best to put in the correct choke for the longer bird, assuming you have confidence that you can break it. If you have a give-me bird with Cylinder and a long bird you feel is beyond your competence, you might want to set up for the close bird so that you know that you come off the stand with at least 50 percent on the scorecard.

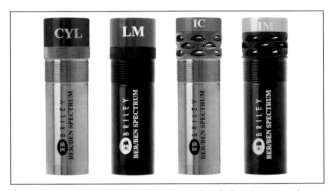

▲ Briley was one of the pioneers of aftermarket choke tubes. Now there are many great aftermarket choke tube makers.

Cartridges and Pellet Size

When I was shooting a lot, and before I developed a slight flinch due to my gun doubling, I generally shot 1 1/8-ounce payloads. Now I rarely shoot anything over an ounce, except on the longest targets, for example a forty-yard rabbit, where I would also use No. 7½, and when feasible and available, I actually prefer high quality loads of ⅞-ounce. (This last even helped me reduce, if not completely eliminate, my flinch.)

In general, almost everything on a sporting clays course can be killed with No. 8 shot. No. 7½ definitely has an edge when retained energy is required, as it is on the resilient rabbit targets and targets at distance. For targets presented at under twenty yards, No. 9 provides both greater pattern density and often a slightly wider pattern, which is why it is the shot size favored by skeet shooters.

I do suggest that you pattern your gun with various loads to see what the gun prefers. Patterning is also important to verify point of impact, especially with double-barrels, i.e., do they shoot to the same point of impact or do they diverge? If you are dead steady, you can check point of impact shooting offhand. If you are not, I would say buffalo sticks as used by African big-game hunters are probably ideal; BOG-PODs and others are the modern versions. You could also shoot off the bench with a rest, as you would with a rifle shooting off a bench.

Methods Creating Forward Allowance

There are three primary methods of creating forward allowance also known as lead. They are maintained a.k.a. sustained lead; pull away and swing through. Each method has its diehard practitioners. Each method has its advantages and its disadvantages. Most shooters would be well served by being able to use at least two or three of these methods.

Maintained lead is definitely the preferred method for skeet shooters. It is also preferred by many shooters for all or most of the shots. To shoot it well the key is matching target speed and the barrel speed and never letting the target beat the barrels.

To shoot pull-away you mount on the front edge of the target travel with it for a certain distance to match the speeds and then, as the name implies, accelerate the gun and pull-away.

Swing through is just that. You come from behind the target and swing through it firing either as you just past the bird or a little bit front depending on the distance and angle of the target. Lead is always a function of speed, distance and angle. All three must be considered.

The problem I always had with swing through was that some days one moves the gun faster than others. It was hard to establish the same consistency as with the other two methods. Recently, I have been watching World Champion Ben Husthwaite's instructional videos on YouTube. He talks about employing swing through a lot. But he does it differently than most. To maintain both a consistent breakpoint and speed, he creates a negative maintained lead. By this he means you start behind the bird and ride with it for a while to establish the same speed as the target and when you are close to the breakpoint you increase your speed, touch the front of the bird or establish a predetermined gap, and fire. Consistency comes from two converging aspects. First, you are in control of your breakpoint rather than just having to fire as you come through the bird regardless of where and when you take it on its flight path. The other is that you are also controlling your own speed—soft or quick moves. For example on a very long bird you might be five feet behind it and then power through. On a slow or close target you might only be one foot behind it and making sure that your hands stay soft as you develop your lead. Through experience, you will know whether you need to start maintaining your negative lead at two, or three feet for example but the beauty is that you are maintaining the same lead and same barrel speed each time you touch the bird.

Ben Husthwaite also shoots many birds using the pull-away method.

Perceptual Differences on Crossing Targets Based on One- or Two-Eyed Shooter's Vision

Don Currie, the chief instructor for the NSCA and one of the top instructors and gunfitters in America, has a column in the organization's magazine answering readers' questions. He was questioned as to why a bird from the left or bird from the right at the same speed, distance, and angle required different leads. (You may recall that in the old days the recommended lead on skeet fields showed 4 and 4½ feet on station four.) This then is the explanation:

"The phenomenon that you are referring to is the comparative difference in "perceived lead" of a left-to-right crosser versus a right-to-left crossing target for a right-handed shooter. For a right-handed shooter, the perceived lead on a left-to-right crossing target will be slightly greater than for a right-to-left crossing target. The actual lead is the same, however. Why the perception of greater lead? Let's start by recognizing that all leads should be subconscious and that measuring is bad, no matter what the reason. Over your shooting life, you will accumulate a subconscious "database" of leads, so this is not something about which you should agonize because we subconsciously adjust for the perceived lead differential. If we were to "measure", however, the perceived lead on a left-to-right will be appear to be greater than that of

(Continued on next page)

a right-to-left crosser because we see binocularly (with two eyes). The perception of incremental lead for a left-to-right crossing target is due to the influence of the left eye on our sight picture. When looking at a left-to-right crosser with two eyes, your left eye sees more lead than the right eye given the angle of offset between the left eye and the rib/muzzle. With a right-to-left flat-trajectory crossing target, your left eye sees the target across the barrel and is often blocked by the barrel so the left-eye bias doesn't occur. It is also important to note that the difference in perceived lead between these two targets will be different for different shooters depending on the degree of dominance of the right eye. If you only had one eye, and shot off the same shoulder as your one eye, then there would be no perceived difference in lead between these two types of targets. For left-handed shooters, this phenomenon is reversed."

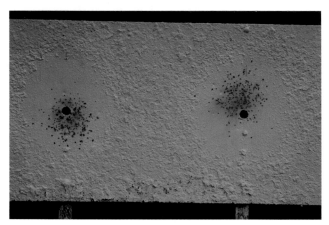

▲ This photo was taken at well under 40 yards—less than 30 if memory serves—to show divergence, as it is easier to see what is really happening in a photograph.

Diverging Barrels

I had a matched pair of over/under sidelock guns made with 20- and 28-gauge barrels.

I have had issues with them from day one — forends were loose on the 28-gauge barrels; some ejection issues; but most disheartening was a greatly diverging point of impact (POI). The manufacturer claimed I did not know what I was doing in terms of testing the guns, and I finally gave up and sent them to Eyster, who is the acknowledged American master on barrels and chokes. Jim Eyster has done a great job filling his father Ken Eyster's very large footsteps.

I shot in a different way than Jim did — as the stocks are very high, he chose to sight down the barrel. I had shot them freehand and off rests. I shot them both at closer and more distant yardage than he did. His SOP is 35 yards. I did it at just over 20 yards and again at something over 40 yards. The former was to allow images that were highly visible when photographed. Even at 20

yards or a bit more, the divergence was great. The more distant the target, the greater the divergence.

Because he shot looking down the rib and I shot as one normally would for guns that were supposed to shoot about 60 percent high, our results look different but in truth the disparity is very similar using both methods.

I will describe his results as he sent them to me: His Notes. "Number 1 gun (comments apply generally to all barrels). When tested barrels are as far off as these in point of impact, it is initially assumed it is from an error in testing and barrels are then tested again differently. All barrels were tested using rests, freehand, and dynamically (moving on water), with similar results. All barrels are off significantly enough that they are uncorrectable in the chokes (except possibly 28gauge number 1) performance issues were not addressed (coverage and efficiency) as they were dependent on having barrels with an acceptable POI."

A synopsis of the errors: most barrels shot left but there was generally a difference between the over barrel and the under barrel and how far left they shot. For example the 20-gauge number 1 gun shot 2 inches to the left with the upper barrel and 7½ inches left with the lower barrel. (Again, remember that all of Eyster's testing was at 35 yards) the under barrel of number two gun shot 10 inches low. The top barrel of the number 28-gauge gun shot 3 inches low and 4½ inches left.

I am still in disputes with the manufacturer. I am hoping that they do the right thing and refund my money . . . but it is uncertain. After approximately eight years of dispute, he has finally accepted Eyster's results though he would not accept mine and is making me new barrels. Whether they are any good or not remains to be seen.

CHAPTER 4
Clay Games and Others (Helice)

FITASC: Don't Fear the Foreign—by Philip C. Steinkraus

If you've ever wondered just who in the world the greatest sporting clays shooter was, realize that the very inquiry itself is kind of a trick question: only English-speaking countries shoot English sporting clays. The rest of the world shoots the international version of the game known to Americans as FITASC.

Let me start by saying that this is just a brief overview of FITASC. If you want all the arcane fine print, I suggest you submerge yourself in the lengthy English translation published in the NSCA rulebook.

FITASC is the French acronym for Fédération International de Tir aux Armes Sportives de Chasse, the sanctioning body of the international form of sporting clays, compak (five-stand), and helice. Because the game was created in France and continues to be headquartered in Paris, most of the technical terms in FITASC remain in that mother tongue.

▲ The author at the ready, holding the FITASC low gun position. *All photos in FITASC section courtesy of Philip Steinkraus.*

Parcours de Chasse (FITASC by another name) is played with a one-ounce cartridge and shot size no larger than 7.5. If a competitor makes the mistake of shooting even a single target with a 1 1/8-ounce payload, he or she is automatically disqualified. It's also a low-gun game with the top of the comb holding at the *ready* position against the body and below a line on the clays vest located at the shooter's breast (25cm below the axis of the shoulder) until the target is called for and appears. If the shooter moves on the call or before the target is visible, the referee can give a warning or even dock the target. Also bear in mind that up to a three-second delay on a pull still qualifies as a good bird!

FITASC may use two different formats, the old-style which remains dominant in the United States, and the new-style, which is the preferred configuration for very large events like the European or world championships. Old-style FITASC employs a layout similar to a large-scale five-stand called a parcour. Each parcour consists of twenty-five targets and FITASC competitions generally range from fifty to two hundred targets. Each old-style parcour has five or more traps, and competitors shoot from three pegs (read stations) of one meter square (usually hula hoops) staked to the ground and strategically located around those traps. Squads are comprised of no more than six and no fewer than three competitors, and at the start of each peg, the lead-off shooter steps into the ring to view targets. A menu board lists the order of individual targets as well as pairs and the standard practice is to regard each single twice. The purpose of this is to become familiar with the flightpath of the bird, to sort out hold points, and to discover any variables or inconsistencies in target or trap performance.

The competitor shoots four two-shot singles (on each parcour there will be one peg with five singles). The lead-off shooter then leaves the ring and the rest of the squad cycles through. At the conclusion of singles, the succeeding competitor in the rotation is designated lead-off shooter for doubles. The majority of pairs are shot on-report, but the rules require at least one true pair per layout. Pairs must consist solely of targets already shot as singles and a shooter may only view pairs if they are simultaneous, and these may be seen twice. Also realize that *full use of the gun* means a shooter cannot only shoot twice at a single target but also double-barrel a sole target on pairs, such as the first clay on a report pair or either bird on a true pair.

After the first peg, subsequent peg placements typically strive to offer a shooter an entirely new perspective thus resulting in what feels like a new course of targets from each succeeding peg.

FITASC parcours can be set anywhere—out in the open or in the woods, on level ground or on a hill, on a skeet or a trap field. FITASC makes liberal use of specialty targets thrown from varying distances. In addition to the standard target (108mm), the most common specialty targets include the 90mm or midi, which flies faster off the trap arm but also slows more quickly than a standard (it appears further away than it really is, creating a false optical illusion); the battue, a flat, wafer-like clay that flies on a rainbow arc and eventually rolls over to show its full face; and the mini (60mm), a rare novelty target that is very wind affected and quite disorienting to shoot. Flying rabbits are also common.

▲ Low gun on a high bird.

The FITASC discipline is supposed to simulate hunting situations with correspondingly reasonable gunning ranges, though this rule of thumb is regularly ignored. Exaggerations abound about the long targets thrown in FITASC but before anyone gets too hysterical, know that probably 90 percent of the presentations will be at a range of thirty to forty-five yards. Sure, the odd clay ranges out to sixty-five yards (especially if the

wind has shifted) and occasionally a one-off is taken at ten feet! Generally though, a good course designer sets a parcour to be enjoyable: a fair challenge which when approached correctly is both achievable and a pleasure to shoot.

A two-hundred-target, old-style FITASC event can comfortably accommodate up to 144 guns, which is usually sufficient. The big championships, however, employ the new-style format where the layouts (known as lines) are spread out and each presentation is just one peg. There can be four pegs consisting of four traps or five pegs consisting of three traps each. While this system is the only practical solution for large events, it plays most like super-sporting and therefore arguably alters the unique character of this discipline.

One of the best things about FITASC is that the referees are very well trained. They know the rules and are the final word on everything regarding their individual parcour—period. While some referees have been known to lord this power over a shooter, the vast majority are fair and are actually a tremendous help. A sound argument can be made that the FITASC ref is the blind justice that guarantees this game is fairer to the average shooter than sporting clays.

In sporting clays referees run the gamut from indifferent college kids and retirees to hero-worshiping clays enthusiasts. The point being that when a particularly aggressive competitor argues a lost target, many refs just don't care and are unwilling to stand their ground in the face of a belligerent onslaught.

Good FITASC refs are immune to this. They don't care who you are or even what the rest of the squad says (though they most often take squad consensus into consideration). A good referee is like a good umpire—often receiving the ire of the shooter but also very much respected, as it is their steadfastness that ensures the very integrity of the game. At the shooter level, there is for all practical purposes no cheating in FITASC. The referees are incorruptible and the only time a competitor ever handles the score card is when they put a signature to their own score. The referee is the sole arbiter of ruling *dead* or *lost* targets but if a shooter feels unjustly aggrieved, they may make a formal protest before a jury panel of shooters and officials. Said jury will then hear the shooter's argument, which must be based solely in the misapplication of rules. (The 2004 World Championship in Signe, France, won by American Gregg Wolf, turned on a protest resulting from a referee's bad call in a shoot-off. Well past sunset, Wolf successfully returned to the parcour and killed the pair to win the championship!)

FITASC parcours are usually temporary, set for an individual tournament and then taken down at its conclusion. This means there is absolutely no home-course

▲ A FITASC peg that creatively integrates topography into the course design.

▲ The shooters perspective from the same peg.

advantage and everyone, total stranger and local hero alike, has exactly the same sporting chance.

The comparison that FITASC is to sporting clays what billiards is to pool is apropos: the two are similar but also strikingly different. My other favorite analogy is that it's like playing a piece of sheet music you've never seen before. Let it also be known that fragile egos perhaps need not apply. There is a lot to remember in FITASC: a wide variety of target presentations and very little repetition. Competitors never have a chance to feel around for a bird or to get *grooved* like they do on multiple pairs in sporting clays. The shooter also has to improvise when shooting pairs. Sure, it helps to watch the others on the squad shoot before you, but the essence of this demanding discipline remains: figure it out correctly the first time and move on.

In FITASC things can turn ugly in an instant and the worst feeling in the world is completely losing one's bearings on a layout. Flailing away inside that ring, suffering the humiliation of one zero after another all the while remaining mindful of the strictly enforced fifteen-second time limit between shots, can overwhelm some shooters. Even accomplished FITASC specialists know that disappointment remains a constant, always at the ready, to deflate a burgeoning self-confidence with a humiliating number on the score board.

The great advantage of sporting clays is that a disaster, no matter how catastrophic, will be over quickly. Everyone shoots the occasional zero on a station and it's easy to shake it off as an anomaly. Shoot a zero on the first peg at FITASC and you're only a third of the way through!

All of this looks overly complicated and nearly next to impossible until you suddenly find yourself able to do it! There is no greater satisfaction than to watch a squad of good shooters struggle with a difficult pair and then to step into the ring, execute correctly, and kill it! And the reward for all this frustration and anguish? A hearty handshake and perhaps a trophy. There has never been prize money in FITASC and the Olympic ideal embraced by the French dictates that the honor of being champion is reward enough.

Don't fear the foreign: we're all terrified of crème brûlée until we actually taste it and realize that it's just delicious cream pudding.

For the record, the greatest clays shooter the world has ever known is "King" George Digweed. The big

Brit has won the World FITASC championship a record twelve times and counting!

Very few nonmember clubs offer FITASC shooting except during competitions open to NSCA members. One of the very few exceptions is Mid-Hudson, located 75 miles north of New York City and only about three miles from the New York State Thruway exit. Instruction is also available and that is probably something one should do if one has never shot FITASC. They are open every day except Tuesday. They also offer sporting clays and five-stand. — P. S.

Mid-Hudson Sporting
411 N Ohioville Rd
New Paltz, NY 12561–3205
contact@midhudsonsporting.com/845-255-7460

Helice

I previously talked about live-pigeon shooting as the basis for trap shooting, and that the common terms of "trap" and "pull" are based on that game. Live-pigeon shooting was legal in New York until just a few years ago when our politically correct, read idiotic, state assembly outlawed it. Pigeons are rats with wings, carrying many dreadful diseases, including *Naegleria fowleri* (though this contamination comes to humans not tactilely but nasally where the amoeba then travels to the brain), known in layman's terms as "brain-eating amoeba." They also carry coccidiosis and other parasites can be transmitted from handling, so care should be taken when touching them, and diligent washing afterwards is a must. Ergo, my rats with wings analogy.

In addition to shooting in the USA, I've been fortunate to have shot live pigeons a number of times at Casa de Campo in the Dominican Republic, as well as in Spain at the famous Club Somontes. To say this game is taken seriously by competitors is a huge understatement. Prize money and side bets are bigger here than any other shooting sport. But with live-pigeon shoots tough

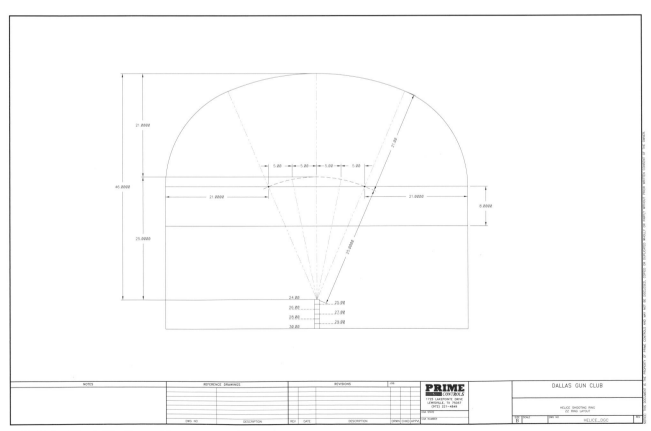

▲ The Helice Ring. Self-loading machines are a recent improvement.

to come by these days—they're rather an underground cult, and if you don't know somebody and haven't been issued a formal invitation, you aren't getting in—I've turned to the target sport of Helice for entertainment.

SOCIEDAD DE TIRO DE MADRID

(S O M O N T E S)

P R O G R A M A

de las tiradas para los meses de

octubre, noviembre y diciembre

de 1985

▲ Club Somontes has always been an important boxed pigeon venue and one of the few in Europe where the sport still flourishes. Helice has its progenitor in boxed pigeon rings. Author's collection.

Helice is also called "electrocibles" and was sometimes known as "ZZ bird," which is the term for the target. On the United States Helice Association website (www.USHelice.com), there is an interview with Chris Potter of the U.K. Helice Association in which he contends that ZZ stands for "zinc zurito." Zurito is the breed of pigeon still used in Spain and specifically bread for the live-pigeon shoots. They have small bodies and are very fast. "Zinc" stands for the first material used to make ZZ birds. ZZ for zinc plus zurito equals ZZ equals olé!

So, Helice is an alternative to using live pigeons. While I don't consider "flyer shooting," the politically correct term for live boxed-bird shooting, inhumane, even friends of animals will have trouble finding something wrong with separating the dome of the ZZ target from its propeller. It is as close as possible to live boxed-bird shooting. Like shooting live pigeons in the competition ring, Helice is a very tough sport, with straights rarely reported; tournament rounds are shot for 30 targets.

Clay Thoughts

If you are practicing, it is fine to practice taking a particular target in different places: for example, waiting longer than normal to practice shooting it as a dropper. However, if you are in competition and you want to have your best scores, you must break the targets in the same place each time. That consistency leads to high scores. If you shoot a clay in a different place each time, the target speed, angle, and distance will change each time and the lead will similarly vary. If you break your first pair in a competition well, shoot all subsequent pairs within a couple of feet of the same breakpoint and use the same hold point.

If you are not connecting, consider changing your hold point or your break point. If the target is slow, consider moving your hand further forward on the fore end, which will naturally slow barrel speed. Correspondingly, for a fast target, you may wish to move your hand closer to you on the fore end as that will increase barrel speed.

The game is very popular in Europe, and this is due at least in part to so many countries having banned boxed-bird shooting. The Hurlingham club on the outskirts of London is where the sport of live-pigeon shooting was codified, but the Brits outlawed it back in the 1920s. Live-pigeon shooters were also big sport in France and Monaco certainly into the 1960s, perhaps later, although I don't think it is practiced at either place anymore. Spain, Portugal, Italy, France, and England are today the core of Helice, but Egypt hosted the 2017 World Championships in Cairo with more than 400 participants.

Like the real thing, Helice targets zig and zag in flight, making them unpredictable. Because they are fast, he who hesitates is lost. Shoot quickly, because even if you do hit it, if the cap sails outside the ring and you'll be scored with a miss (just as a live pigeon dying outside the ring is scored a miss in that sport).

ZZ birds are made from a round, soft-plastic top with plastic wings. The plastic top is called a "witness cap," which is attached to a plastic propeller. The now-defunct American ZZ company used metal wings and propellers, but plastic is used exclusively today. When hit by a sufficient number of pellets yielding sufficient energy, the cap separates from the propeller and, if it falls within the ring, is scored as a hit; the perimeter fence of the ring is twenty-one meters beyond the launchers, and each competitor is allowed two shots per target. As it is with flyer shooting, multiple launchers (five or seven) are placed within the ring, and each machine spins the target at more than 5,000 rpm. Not knowing which trap the target will be launched greatly adds to the difficulty of the sport. To begin the shoot, the shooter calls "Ready" and the trapper replies "Ready." When the shooter calls "Pull" (or indeed any other sound), the target is launched, flying in a fast and erratic fashion.

Helice is not an inexpensive layout to install, nor is it inexpensive to run. Shooting a round of thirty ZZ birds costs about $90, making it much more expensive than skeet or trap. With five-machine layouts, the launchers are positioned between four and one-half and five meters apart on the semicircle arc. Twenty-one meters beyond the traps is a rigid fence twenty-four inches high, and the mesh of the fence must not allow the cap to be able to pass through. This fence marks the outside border of the shooting area into which all scoring targets must fall.

Advances in the machines Helice utilizes have changed the game dramatically, and many machines today are self-loading. All fields employing self-loading machines use the five-box layout (other fields can use seven), which is becoming the standard. With these newer machines, no longer does the shooter need to call "Ready." Instead, the shooter now pushes a button in front of them to arm the system and, upon calling "Pull," the target is released via voice-activation. This arrangement is much less labor-intensive for the ranges, as no one has to run into the field and reset the boxes (a referee to keep score is the only required attendant). It also increases the game's difficulty in that all five boxes are now always live, so the shooter cannot eliminate some of the traps as having already been shot. In the old days, you could narrow your focus with the old hand-loaded machines, as each would eventually empty as the game progressed.

Serious competitors inevitably use over/under shotguns. While the game can trace its origins to Europe, the U.S. team has won Helice World Championship, and its members have seen success a number of times now in various individual categories. The two American hubs of the sport are Texas and California, each having four or more clubs. There are also excellent facilities in Louisiana and Mississippi. A new club in Pennsylvania (see the list below), offers East Coast shooters a place to enjoy the sport, and that club also has an international trap bunker for those so inclined. Many Helice clubs are private, so definitely contact ahead of time and don't just drop by hoping to shoot a round. If you join the U.S. Helice Association, you will be able to shoot various sanctioned, U.S. team-qualifying competitions at the various clubs. To apply for membership in the USHA, download from its website and print, complete, and mail the application form to:

▲ A microphone near the shooter rather than a trapper launches the target.

USHA Membership
7750 N MacArthur Blvd., Suite 120–324
Irving, TX 75063
www.ushelice.com
https://www.ushelice.com/venues

Helice Facilities

ALABAMA

Selwood Farm (New Venue)
706 Selwood Road
Alpine, AL 35014
256-362-3961
email: zach@selwoodfarm.com
www.selwoodfarm.com

CALIFORNIA

Coon Creek Trap & Skeet Club
www.cooncreektrap.com
5393 Waltz Rd, Lincoln, CA 95648
Phone: 916-539-8544

Coyote Valley Sporting Clays
www.coyoteclays.com
1000 San Bruno Ave, Morgan Hill, CA 95037
Phone: 408-778-3600

Martinez Gun Club
www.martinezgunclub.net
900 Waterbird Way, Martinez, CA 94553
Phone: 925-372-9599

Stockton Trap and Skeet Club
www.stocktontrapandskeetclub.com
4343 N Ashley Ln, Stockton, CA 95215
Google Maps: Stockton Trap and Skeet Club
Phone: 209-931-6803
Email: stocktonclays@att.net

GEORGIA

Cherokee Rose
www.crclays.com
895 Baptist Camp Rd.
Griffen, GA 30223
Email: info@crclays.com

ILLINOIS

FLC Shooting Grounds
www.flcoutfitters.com
RR 1 Box 227, County Road 2150, White Hall, IL 62092
Phone: 217-248-9999
Email: FLC@csj.net

IOWA

Westfork Gun Club
1952 240th Street, Sheffield, Iowa 50475
Phone: 641-512-4811
Email: Hejlikj@frontiernet.net

LOUISIANA

GOL Shooting
11919 La Hwy 697
Maurice, La 70555
Tel 337 250 3962
dmouton215@gmail.com

Kiper Farms Cottonland Skeet, Trap, & Helice
www.kiperfarms.com
235 John Rivers Lane, Winnsboro, LA 71295
Phone: 318-366-2194
Email: CottonlandGunGlub@live.com or
kiperfarms@att.net

The Wilderness Gun Club
www.wildernessgunclub.com
7 Teurlings Drive, Lafayette, LA 70501
Phone: 337-804-0818
Email: TheWildernessGunClub@hotmail.com or
edfrancez@yahoo.com

MISSISSIPPI

Prairie Wildlife
www.prairiewildlife.com
3990 Old Vinton Rd.
West Point, MS 39773
Phone: 692–494–5858 or 692 295-2774

PENNSYLVANIA

Keystone Shooting Park
www.keystoneshootingpark.com

610 Game Farm Road, Dalmatia, PA 17017
Phone: 717-903-9009 or 717-362-1966
Email: keystoneshootingpark@gmail.com

SOUTH CAROLINA
Broxton Bridge Plantation
www.broxtonbridge.com
info@broxtonbridge.com
1685 Broxton Bridge Hwy.
Ehrhardt, SC 29081
Phone: 803-824-9651

TEXAS
Abilene Clay Sports
www.abileneclaysports.com
1102 Beltway South, Abilene, TX 79602
Phone: 325-692-9002
Email: contact@abileneclaysports.com; abileneclay
sports@gmail.com

American Shooting Centers
www.amshootcenters.com
16500 Westheimer Parkway, Houston, TX 77082
Phone: 281-556-8199

Austin Gun Club
www.austingunclub.com
reservations@austingun.com
2901 County Rd. 206
Lampasas, TX 76550
Phone: 512-394-4418
Email: reservations@austingunclub.com

Dallas Gun Club
www.dallasgunclub.com
3601 South Stemmons, Lewisville, TX 75067
Phone: 972-462-0043
Email: info@dallasgunclub.com

North Texas Helice
www.iowaparktrap.com
nxthelice@gmail.com

Providence Plantation Sporting Club
10230 FM-521, Rosharon, Texas, 77583
Phone: 713-963-9112
Email: ap@riverway.us

Texas 46 Helice
11300 Hwy 46 W, New Braunfels, TX 78132
Email: jackceast@gmail.com
By Appointment Only. Contact Jack East (owner)
via email for more information or to arrange an
appointment.

Texas Gun Ranch
www.texasgunranch.com
info@texasgunnerand.com
15950 State Hwy. 205
Terrell, TX 75160
Phone: 972-551-0470

CHAPTER 5

On the Wing: Waterfowling and Upland Birds

▲ My fourth-generation Labrador, Bubba. Labradors are the kings of the retrieving breeds both in popularity and field trial success. They make great all-around gundogs, particularly if they are trained to quarter like a spaniel and sit or "hup" to flush. Courtesy Charles Sainsbury Plaice.

Some call it wildfowling, others called waterfowling. I had to "add to dictionary" in my word processor as it didn't believe either was a word. No matter what you call it, I call it great. Few experiences rival being in a blind at dark on an autumnal morning, watching the sunrise and the moon set as one hears the whistling of wings. It is just one of those "great to be alive" moments.

When I started hunting as a boy, duck boats and duck blinds were all pretty much do-it-yourself proposals. If memory serves, Zach Taylor's *Successful Waterfowling* book gave the best directions and plans for both.

Today, one can either be handy or one can find all manner of blinds from suppliers like Cabela's, Bass Pro Shops, and Mack's Prairie Wings, to name a few. As for of duck boats, those suitable for big water to those for shallow water rigs and everything in between are available commercially and usually manufactured to

▲ A great, ready-to-go setup. Courtesy of G3 Boats/Yamaha.

quite high standards. Motors are now designed specifically for getting you through shallow waters and thick mud (mud motors), and some hunters use airboats; this last would have the old-time market gunners spinning in their graves, though perhaps they'd be spinning in envy.

Even duck decoys have changed. Once hand-carved and hand-painted, they have been replaced by decoys made of modern inorganic materials and often come in motorized "action" versions. Many of the old decoys bring small fortunes and are either owned by wealthy collectors or, in some cases, have even made it into museum collections. They are an art form. The newer ones made of plastic will last a very long time if static or until their motors give out.

My early days were of simple provisions. Instead of having a dedicated camo pattern on my waders, I would simply use the same waders I might fish in, and instead of having a matching camo jacket, I would probably just wear my cold weather Eddie Bauer green down coat. It served me well whether I was in the high country of the Rockies or recumbent in the layout boat on the Great South Bay of New York. At some point I did purchase an Orvis waterproof camo poncho that I could wear as the outer layer.

Recently instructional tapes for duck calling were replaced by CDs, and these have now been largely replaced by company links on Google or YouTube. Pretty amazing. As is the quality and breadth of design of the duck calls offered today, be they inexpensive or pricey.

While we certainly do not have the number of birds in our limits that those old market gunners killed from their punt guns to supply the swells at their Park Avenue restaurants, we certainly are spoiled in terms of equipment. (It should be pointed out that wildfowl numbers have generally increased over the decades, and this is primarily due to the amazing conservation work done by Ducks Unlimited and other hunter—conservation groups. While it shouldn't be necessary to point it out, I will nevertheless say that sportsmen weren't responsible for pushing duck numbers down drastically, rather, in the simpler times of the mid- to late nineteenth century, it was unthinking men plying their craft as market gunners in hopes of making money to feed their families that produced the huge, negative declines of U.S. waterfowl populations observed for so many decades.)

I have been very fortunate to have spent more time shooting ducks than almost anyone I know. Yet I am not what I would describe as an expert duck hunter. Let me explain the paradox. From 1996 until 2003, I co-owned and managed the shooting at Humewood Castle in Ireland. We put down roughly 12,000 ducks a year, some of which we hatched and some of which we bought as day-olds and raised to mature flighted birds. We also bought seven-week-old birds to be safe. Although we offered this shooting on a commercial basis, we also saved much of it for ourselves and our friends. It was spectacular shooting sport that received rave reviews in Britain in *The Shooting Times* and *The Shooting Gazette,* and in the United States in the *Bird Hunting Report* and *Shooting Sportsman*. Humewood was considered by most cognoscenti as the preeminent flighted duck shoot in the British Isles.

The birds were put out on the lakes before they could fly. The pen had no top on it, and it was actually designed more to keep predators out than to keep the birds in. An electric wire was placed around each pen to keep fox and mink at bay. (Most years over a hundred foxes were culled.) Young ducks imprint, and because the gamekeeper took care of them from day one, they thought he was Mother. When he whistled they came, often by the thousands. It was an amazing sight to watch the ducks walk from the lake in a line that stretched for four hundred yards to the game crop where he fed them. Still, because they were free to fly, they did as soon as they could. Thanks to this exercise and the lack of confinement, they flew at virtually the same speed as wild mallards.

Often our ducks would fly off for many hours. It was sort of scary to see $200,000 worth of ducks disappear. Fortunately, there were few lakes near our shoot, so they always did come back. The main reason they returned was for the food. (We did lose a thousand ducks once late in the season, when the remnants of a hurricane came by and blew them to Tipperary.)

Most years I shot something in excess of a thousand ducks to my own gun, and I must admit I enjoyed every minute of it. Because of the way they were raised and flushed hundreds of yards from the lakes to which they wanted to return, they tended to present themselves at 35 to 50 yards over the guns. Great sport indeed. This taught me quite a lot about loads and chokes (though we were very fortunate in that Ireland still allows the use of lead shot).

▲ Setting out decoys for ducks. Knowing how to set decoys is critical.

Long Island Waterfowling—Glory Days Living On

In the glory days of American waterfowling, days when market gunners would shoot literally carloads of ducks, there few better area along the Eastern Seaboard for hunting than Long Island. Wealthy New Yorkers formed clubs and bought or leased prime lands so they could hunt in gentlemanly fashion. Serious hunters designed and refined gunning boats, and masterful decoy carvers, probably unaware of the posthumous treasures they were creating, plied their craft.

Nearly 35 years ago, I spent a day hunting with a guide named George Combs who, like his market-hunting great-grandfathers, used gunning boats. In the old days, the men stalked large rafts of birds, killing them with punt guns and shipping the game to the finest restaurants in New York City. George and I towed the layout boats by skiff to the western end of the Great South Bay.

A great advantage to this way of hunting is in its flexibility; it is possible to predict where the birds will be based on weather and tide and then set up there. Leaving the skiff anchored in deep water, we traveled in gunning boats to a small strip of land, where we set in the boats among the sea grass. George quickly set out the Canada goose decoys on one side, black ducks in the middle, and broadbills on the other side. We lay down in the boats,

which were camouflaged by salt grass thatching, and waited.

Buffleheads skimmed across the water well out of range. Brant (no relation to the author) frequently flew in range, but as they were protected birds there, we did not shoot. A black duck came out of the east and was about to land in our decoy spread when we sat up and shot. It quickly veered off, and I didn't connect until the third shot; shooting from a sitting position takes a little getting used to. The Northeast was experiencing an unseasonably warm fall that year, and it made the hunting less productive than usual. We did bag two more black ducks, the only birds that came to our decoys, though we missed a long passing shot at a canvasback.

Though I had one, even in places like Long Island, you don't need to hire a guide to be successful. The bayside of Barrier Beach along the southern shore offers good shooting, particularly for black ducks, though you do need a good four-wheel drive to get your boat trailer in and out, and a good seaworthy duck boat is essential as is the knowledge to pilot it.

According to various wildlife biologists with whom I've spoken, Long Island's sea duck shooting is a largely untapped resource. Access is easy from any north shore harbor into the sound. Peconic Bay also offers good shooting. White-winged scoters and old squaw predominate in the early season. Still, sea duck shooting is not for the amateur. Bob Hand, who was a master decoy carver from Sag Harbor and one of the most dedicated and accomplished gunners on the island, once said to me, "You've got to know the water and your equipment. The sea can look calm when you go out. Then the wind and the tide change and you get a riptide and the boat lands in your face."

Clothing can mean the difference between an enjoyable day in the blind and enduring a frozen hell. In addition to expedition-weight long underwear, I wear insulated waders or boots, depending on the hunting conditions. A warm cap is a necessity, and I often bring a ski mask on really cold

Setting out decoys on a cold morning. Waterfowlers in particular need to wear warm, waterproof clothing.

days. Warm gloves are also a must, as is a waterproof parka. The hunter should be as camouflaged as possible; in snowy weather this entails wearing white instead of traditional camo. In the old days, I wore Hodgeman canvas waders, Duofold long johns, an Eddie Bauer down parka in green, a green baseball cap, and sometimes something from a ski shop to cover my face. Today's waterfowler is spoiled for choice: neoprene waders that come in a multiplicity of camo patterns for the type of cover being hunted keep one both warm and camouflaged. Jackets and parkas come in matching camo, as do gloves caps and even vests for one's retriever pal. Leaky waders, while not a thing of the past, have been largely minimized, and the number of high-tech fabrics and fillers

that block the wind, keep out water, wick out body sweat, and reflect body heat back onto a person are mind-boggling.

The importance of having the correct gear and paying attention to conditions when hunting waterfowl cannot be stressed enough. Indeed, the closest I ever came to dying while plying my sport—and this includes twice being charged by lions and sharing blinds with cobras and other venomous snakes—was duck hunting in Shinnecock Bay with an old-time guide named Frank Downs.

It was the last week of the season, and I arrived to find the saltwater bay completely frozen. The ice had moved Frank's blind a few hundred yards, and everything was encased in ice. It was no longer possible to just get into his boat and cruise out to the blind. Instead, we had to load the boat with decoys and then he pulled and I pushed it across the ice. This alone wouldn't have been too bad, but the ice was not all that thick and every twenty yards or so we would plunge into the water. This was nearly 40 years ago, before thick neoprene waders were available, so by the time we got to the blinds we were extremely cold and wet.

Frank, tough as nails, placed the decoys and every so often went out and re-broke the ice. He needn't have bothered. The only birds we saw all day were geese headed for Southampton at 10,000 feet. Nevertheless, we stayed in the blind for hours before calling it a day.

It was just as bad going back as it was going out, and by that time my energy was depleted by the cold. Every step back was a struggle, and yards from shore I could feel my whole body shutting down—if this wasn't hyperthermia, it was something pretty close. I'm still not sure how I forced myself to shore. My feet were so numb I had to take off my shoes to feel the pedals for the drive back, and it was a struggle to stay awake.

I had brilliant sport at a grand old club called Ottawa on the southern shores of Lake Erie. I shot there with my late good and great friend Tom Roulston, who had been a member for many years. The club itself has been going since the 1860s. It is limited to twenty-five or so members, determined by the number of bedrooms at the club. Each member has his own guide, referred to as a "punter," as in the old days they did actually use punt boats.

Today the club adheres to all fish and game regulations and therefore does not bait. They do, however, encourage ducks to come to their area by constantly improving habitat, including by planting corn and other crops for the birds to feed upon.

In 2003, I shot at Ottawa with Tom about a week after the season opened. We made our way to the far side of the club, where we were going to shoot that afternoon with Tom's punter, Mike Koppleman, who already had a boat loaded with decoys. We traveled the waterways, best described as irrigation canals, and used specially designed rails to move the boat from one canal to another, which kept the portages fairly simple. We were hunting an area where there was no blind, so we merely hid among the reeds and sat on stools. Mike was a master at placing decoys and calling, and it wasn't long before the ducks started to move.

We were in the thick of it virtually every day—mallards, teal, widgeon, and wood ducks all came to our decoys. Tom and Mike like to use oversize decoys and lots of them. Their secret weapons are a couple of oversized decoys set high on stakes with flapping and rotating wings, robo-ducks which were a relatively new addition to the set then.

On days two and three, we shot out of a classic blind built into one of the small embankments along a swamp. It was good to great shooting, and after the high-volume days spent on the dove fields of South America, pheasant shoots in the British Isles, and partridge in Spain, it taught me a wonderful lesson: You don't have to kill a lot of birds to have a spectacular day. This was one of my all-time favorite shoots. The area was pristine, and both of my companions were true sportsmen. In three days of hunting, we shot our limit every day without once shooting each other's birds. Tom noted that in all his years of duck shooting, that had never happened before.

This was my first hunt using Hevi-Shot, loaded commercially by Remington in those days. To say Hevi-shot is great stuff is a huge understatement. It kills better than lead.

The only problem I experienced was that the bolt handle on the autoloader Tom had lent me came off after the second day's shoot. It was lost in the marsh, which wasn't a big deal for us as Tom had brought along a spare gun, but it shows the importance of planning. That lost bolt handle is a fairly common mishap with autoloaders, undoubtedly the most frequent after jamming, which is usually caused by poor gun maintenance. You should always buy a spare bolt handle when you purchase this type of shotgun if you intend to waterfowl, as it costs only a couple of bucks. If you know how to replace it—generally just pushing it in until it clicks—you might save a trip.

INTRODUCTION TO UPLAND SECTION:

If I could only choose one season in which to live, it would be a perpetual autumn. My fondest childhood memories are of time spent afield on a horse, wading a stream, and most especially following pointing dogs in pursuit of pheasant, and when I was really fortunate woodcock and grouse.

When I was quite young, circa 12 years of age, I received my first shotgun, and first shooting lessons.

The shotgun was a Browning Auto-5, and I loved it. But I must admit that some of my enduring bad habits probably have to do with the stock fit on that gun as it had a great deal of drop at the comb. In retrospect,

▲ Photo courtesy of Crystal Creek Lodge and Brian Grossenbacher.

▲ Photo courtesy of Crystal Creek Lodge and Brian Grossenbacher.

I probably would have been better served with a Remington Model 58. In any case, I was a very lucky 12-year-old.

The world was very different then, circa 1960. Often my parents would take me to Grand Central station and put me on train where I was collected in Pawling New York by Joe Cox's wife Helen. I would travel unaccompanied, carrying my shotgun in a long soft case. (Today, in New York City, if a resident, one needs a long arms license with each rifle and shotgun registered—a huge bureaucracy of dubious merit.) I would walk past policeman who were completely uninterested in a 12-year-old with the shotgun. No one thought my intentions were anything other than sporting and that was not frowned upon. Today, with armed reservists patrolling Grand Central in their camouflage, and policemen with bomb sniffing dogs, I would undoubtedly have been tackled, a SWAT team called, my parents arrested on God knows how many charges. . . . But as I say it was a different world.

Joe Cox had one of the few and one of the best shooting preserves near New York City. He was, to put it politely, surprised when a 12-year-old arrived on his doorstep.

His initial response was to send me on the next train back to Manhattan. He then asked me if I could shoot, and I told him I could. So we went out to his trap range where I broke something over 20 of the first 25 targets. (They were easy targets.) So he decided to let me go out with the guide under the strict understanding that if I did anything untoward or even vaguely dangerous the hunt was over and I would never be welcomed again.

▲ A safe way to rest the gun if one is on the right side of the line.

▲ A safe way to walk in on a point, if on the left side of the line.

I have my faults. But I have always been a safe shot. So at the end of the shoot he told me that I was welcome to come back any time—or at least until I screwed up.

Joe was one of those tough guys with a heart of gold. We became quite friendly, and as I got older, I was one of the few people with whom he would actually go out hunting.

If I were there when the woodcock were in, we would spend time hunting them. He had a first rate kennel of dogs. Mostly English pointers as in those days were definitely the dog of choice. He also had a few English setters.

One of his pointers was enough of a pet that it was allowed in the house. I do not remember his lineage but he looked like one of those dogs in the old days from Gunsmoke kennels or Elhew kennels. He was not unfriendly but he was aloof in almost a catlike fashion.

He was a hell of a dog in the field.

When I graduated high school, my grandfather bought me an old Belgian Browning 20-gauge over under to take to college. So I would carry that and Joe would carry his Model 21 12-gauge and we would go hunting.

To this day I can remember the first pheasant I ever shot at his preserve and one or two other birds that were truly memorable. And that was almost 60 years ago.

Gear then: My outfit was simple. A red and black L.L. Bean–style hat, a Viyella shirt, a pair of brush pants, and a pair of leather Russell bird shooter boots which my parents got for me at the great old Abercrombie and Fitch—a store that in no way resembles the company at the same name today.

I recall having some sort of warm vest, something lightweight with the game pouch in the back, and an Abercrombie and Fitch down birdshooting coat which in its day was the bees' knees. Inside it had a flap that could be unzipped and put down and was lined so that one could sit on the ground and have lunch or use in a duckblind without getting one's ass wet.

Now I have so much gear, that I could almost use an extra room.

I have upland outfits for any and all conditions. I have traditional clothes, orange safety clothes, and even clothes from Beretta and Orvis in traditional colors like tan but highlighted in orange for safety.

▲ Buck was the best pointing dog I ever owned, and I owned the Canadian Open Field Trial Champion Cowboys Footsteps. Trained on ruffed grouse, I hunted quail with him from Oklahoma to Florida and woodcock, grouse, and pheasants in various Northeast and mid-Atlantic states. He was prepared to die of old age rather than move on a point unless tapped on the head to relocate.

▲ Photos courtesy of Classic Bird Hunts.

I have heavy coats like the one described above, I have a khaki shell vest from Orvis that must be 30 years old for warm weather hunting, or to slip over warmer clothes; I have dedicated shooting vests again in tan, orange or a combination of the two. I have heavy duty upland bird vest pack from Tenzing that is designed for the hunter who is planning on covering miles, with a built-in backpack, so that one can carry some supplies plus a game bag et cetera et cetera. Easy to carry your electronic collar controls, which today probably includes built-in GPS, some food and water for you and Fido: just let your imagination keep going.

And while we might feel much more comfortable, or quasi-professional with all this paraphernalia, perhaps we made things too complicated.

Brush pants and appropriate boots along with eye and hearing protection go without saying are required for a day afield. But after that it is your choice. While dogs are in some ways better worked with whistles, Delmar Smith believed in using his voice just in case the whistle broke. Instead of GPS tracking devices, one can use a beeper collar, or as they did in the old days a bell, or in areas with a dog can be easily observed even that might not be necessary. I must admit I haven't seen a beeper collar or bell on a pointer in years. An

orange cap for safety makes sense. A dog lead and bowl for watering him, assuming you have a dog, is a good idea. But as long as you have something to carry your cartridges and, hopefully, your birds back, that might be sufficient.

On the other hand, if you going for a long journey through thick woods with which you are not overly familiar then some gear for survival—starting a fire, a compass or GPS to find your way home, should be considered. Garmin make some great ones both as handheld devices and watches.

I have hunted wild quail west to Oklahoma and south to Florida near the southern end of Okeechobee. I have hunted Woodcock from Québec and Maine down to Cape May. I used to be able to find good grouse shooting in Dutchess county New York about 80 miles from New York City but that seems to be a thing of the past. And I found them in places not often considered prime habitat like some of the Western states.

All you really need to enjoy the Uplands is a sense of adventure, a good dog, a shotgun, and a few shells.

In some parts of the states, or the British Isles the term may vary slightly: Upland, walked up, or rough shooting. They can be practiced in different ways.

In the cornfields of South Dakota, it is not uncommon for a group of hunters to work down the cornfields while others stand at the ends as stops. Similarly in the U.K., hunters will walk in line hoping to push grouse or ptarmigan depending on elevation off the hills or moors, most often with the help of dogs. While shooting driven grouse in Great Britain is exceedingly expensive, walked up days following well trained pointers is quite reasonable, and very exciting sport. A red grouse covey bursts into the air like wild quail on steroids. They are very fast birds, very strong and extremely sporting. Ptarmigan, closely related to Britain's red grouse, are even more so as you will be hunting at higher altitude—often cold and windy—where fitness definitely plays a role.

We had a snipe bog in Ireland that was grand sport when they were in. It was small, and I would only hunt once every 10 days or two weeks, but if I hit it right in a fairly short period of time I would put up a wisp (read : covey) or two.

Once I got very lucky: I put up a wisp of snipe and

▲ Quail rig at Gilchrist plantation. Berettas at the ready. Hunters right height to watch the pointing dogs working; the Berettas are well protected in the rack on the hood.

▲ Ptarmigan are closely related to Britain's red grouse. Both birds are very strong flyers, and present difficult shots whether you're hunting them in Alaska, as in these photos, or on high ground in Scotland. Photo courtesy of Crystal Creek Lodge and Brian Grossenbacher.

shot a brace, reloaded my shotgun, and as I did a straggler got up and I shot it as well. My Labrador, a superb retriever, came back with all three snipe in his mouth. I have never seen anything like that before or since.

I have had great Upland shooting for perdiz in Argentina with Chuck Larson from Burnt Pine Plantation; and similar sport with him on a number of upland species in South Africa.

The British Isles

I have used both pointing and flushing breeds to do walked-up woodcock shooting in Britain and in Ireland. This is great sport. They are often found in slightly more open areas than in the US, but that is not always the case. If you are shooting them where it is a bit more open, one of the keys to be successful is to wait for them to make their two or three zigs and zags after which they will most often straighten out and

present a more reasonable target otherwise you might shoot at their zig while in fact they zag.

"No man who has ever carried a gun forgets his first woodcock to the day of his death. You may forget your first salmon or even 'the first kiss at love's beginning', but never your first woodcock: and you may fish, shoot and hunt in any and every land and have the best of sport, but of many days in your sporting diary … the good days with the woodcock will be marked with the whitest pencil and be forever fraught with the pleasantest recollections." J. J. Manley in *Notes on Game Shooting*, 1880.

Wild bird shooting is sport to be treasured and few wild game birds deserve the respect or show the mystery of a woodcock. Compared to a pheasant who is a short distance sprinter, seven or eight seconds of wing beating and he is spent, woodcock fly across the North Sea from Scandinavia to the British Isles and American woodcock pile up in Cape May New Jersey before, when wind conditions are right on a full moon, make the harrowing flight across the Chesapeake Bay. It is also a bird steeped in literature especially amongst the giants from Russia. Turgenev and Tolstoy both described shooting woodcock.

Shooting woodcock is a truly wild sport for the purest. I always feel a twinge of guilt when I shoot one, and often on driven pheasant or partridge days, even when it is permitted, will let the 'cock' fly by. Still whenever one is out on a shoot and beaters yell 'cock' adrenaline flows. In America there are state and federal imposed limits on migratory birds. In Europe this does not occur and without all the research that needs to be done, one has to use judgment in shooting this small treasure. I did it on my property by limiting the number of days that we shoot rather than the bag. To my mind a reasonably big bag of 15 to 30 woodcock to a group once a fortnight is probably more fun and of less population damage than shooting say five birds a man five days a week for two weeks.

I have shot woodcock in Canada, America, England, Ireland both north and south, and in Scotland as far northwest as the Isle of Lewis in the Outer Hebrides. But in my wildest dreams, I never would have imagined that I would wind up owning such a wonderful woodcock shoot as Tressady almost as happenstance. When we bought the place, we were told that it was capable of providing good shooting of perhaps 15 to 25 birds per outing. I must admit, that I presumed that number to be high. On my first year on the estate with a keeper, we shot most typically 25 woodcock in a day and our best was 41 over pointers to three Guns. The number of flushes was great. Early on, I have returned from a half hour outing with a keeper where without the benefit of a dog we flushed 13 woodcock and four snipe in an hour. The copse which we hunted was primarily willow spread amongst agricultural land and no doubt the presence of cattle in the fields added much to the invertebrate life which snipe and woodcock favor. This is a satellite wood of perhaps 3 acres total and half an acre of actual woods that we hunted. We had limited ourselves to this small bit of ground because I was about to have my friends from the roving syndicate from London's Brooks's club up to shoot in a few days and I did not want to disturb the main

areas, but rather get a feel for the birds about. Had we a spaniel with us, I would have presumed two or three times as many birds would have been flushed—it was just that casual an outing.

I must admit that the woodcock beat me. I am quite a good shot most days, but being a tall driven bird specialist I am used to moving my feet planting them and having plenty of time to assess my most difficult target. The woodcock shooting I experienced that day was the antithesis of this. It was snap shooting and no warning and coupled with too much choke only a couple of birds came down. We picked them ourselves and unlike pheasant or partridge that I can take or leave as table fare, I always look forward already to that delicious, rich dark meat, that woodcock provide. (I just have to make a mental note to forget that I am eating biologically processed worm.)

The quick reflexes necessary for tackling this challenging game bird on uneven ground while off balance need to be honed and practiced. Work on it, or alternatively go out with pointers which allow one to get set, at least a bit, before the shot. (Woodcock tend to hold quite well for fast working pointers which elicit, I presume, predator-prey response).

The vast majority of the birds that we see in the Highlands are European migrants which have made the exhausting flights from Scandinavia and the ex-Soviet Union. No one knows how many birds winter in Britain each year and I have seen Game Conservancy estimates pushing a million. For the last few years, The Game Conservancy has been doing an in-depth study on the migratory habits of woodcock by tracking them. I am told that there are relatively few resident birds in Britain. Where we lived north of Inverness, I did see at least a few woodcock flying across the road on summer evenings, so there must be some breeding going on locally.

That said, and while it is possible for woodcock to come in some years in good numbers in October, it is most typically following the full moon of November that they become abundant in our area. Going out to lamp for fox in the evenings I have often seen four or five woodcock in the air simultaneously during their nocturnal movements. (They tend to go from woods to pastures for their night feeds). Even Tolstoy describes evening shooting of woodcock as they travel from their woods—"roding"—to their evening fields. It is exciting shooting as it is difficult to see them and normally one only glimpses them for a moment a blacker shadow across a dark sky. Fly fishermen who fish after dusk and are aware of bats flying around them will have an advantage in terms of visualizing what this night time flight is like. Roding is often accomplished down known flight paths, often improved by natural or man-made paths in the woods experienced gamekeepers know where to place the guns for best sport. Anyone who thinks this type of shooting is unsporting or easy has not tried it: try shooting at a shadow some time.

When I first came to Tressady, I tried organizing a couple of days of driven woodcock shooting, but had to relent simply because it was way too dangerous. I have never seen woodcock fly as low coming out of cover on Tressady. Whether it was because they are recent migrants and tired from their journey across the North Sea, whether it was the deep bracken that slows them, or whether it is just their nature to fly between waist and shoulder height for a good bit of their travel before rising I do not know but at Tressady these birds flew so low that only shots behind can be taken and it is nearly impossible shooting. I did shoot driven woodcock near Ashford in Ireland on the grounds that once belonged to the Guinness family and was considered in the time of the Guinness's *the* great woodcock shoots of the world. They had planted trees and cover especially for woodcock which drew them like magnets to an area that was otherwise quite barren—mostly peat bog I presume.

*Hugh Gladstone who kept records of such things noted that a record bag of woodcock shot by one man in one day was 109. Apparently the Gun could have shot more but he ran out of cartridges.

Having started three driven pheasant shoots from scratch and having reworked a good duck shoot to make it outstanding, it was rather amazing to have had a first class woodcock shoot fall in my lap.

To the Dogs:

The choice of dogs is as personal as it gets. Pointers, especially English pointers and setters, have been bred in America for generations, specifically for upland hunting. Today one has the choice of the continental breeds including the German Shorthaired Pointer, the

▲ Champion Cowboy's Footsteps won the Canadian Open Shooting Dog Championship. When he retired from competition, I sold him to Japan as a stud dog.

Drahthaar, the German wirehaired pointer, and other breeds that can also be multitasked to follow blood trails on big game, retrieve waterfowl, et cetera. Cocker spaniels, Springer spaniels, and Sprockers which are a hybrid of the first two if from proper working stock, are a joy to hunt over.

▲ Dusty with pheasant. Labs are renowned water dogs but make excellent upland hunters if properly trained.

In some ways the retrievers are the easiest to train, and possibly hyperactive spaniel the most difficult. There is an old saying in Britain that a lab is born half trained and a spaniel dies half trained. British cockers and Springers had the same progenitor. Sprockers now come from litters where cockers and springers are purposely mated. They exhibit hybrid vigor, are very popular in Britain, and are truly great dogs. Indeed, it is said that a lot of the dogs that win cocker championships are actually sprockers. I've only had one spaniel—a sprocker—in my life, Wellington, and he has proved a very easy dog to work. He grew up with six labs, never thought of himself as a small dog, and loves retrieving ducks in the water.

Pointers come in close ranging dogs, medium ranging, and big ranging which are best followed on horseback and are the paradigm for field trials and hunting quail or the prairies of Canada, et cetera. In many situations you need a dog to cover ground to find wild birds. While a lot of people want dogs to hunt close, if your pointer is well trained and can hold the game you will find more birds if he is not underfoot. But this is purely a personal decision.

▲ An English pointer is *the* classic quail dog. Setters are great too, but need to be shaved or clipped so as not to overheat.

As I write this, I am 70. But just as when I was 12, the anticipation of upland shooting in the autumn stirred me each year.

▲ The author's dog, Wellington, crossing the stream with a pheasant. Photo courtesy of Charles Sainsbury Plaice.

▲ Woodcock are brilliant birds to hunt, and hold much better for the dogs than ruffed grouse do. Photo courtesy of Nancy Whitehead.

CHAPTER 6
America's Golden Era

Most of us will never be able to afford a new Purdey, a fabulous Beretta SO10, an incredible Hartmann & Weiss, or other shotguns of the hand-built and bespoke genre. One should consider that there are some great firearms to cherish and to shoot on the second-hand market, though, and those from America and Italy are worth examining.

While the Winchester was "The Rifle That Won the West," and Colt was "The Great Equalizer," we must not forget America's shotgun heritage. America produced six gun makers whose side-by-side shotguns have stood the test of time. Today, they are extremely desirable and collectible.

When I was younger and demand for these fine guns hadn't yet peaked, I toyed with the idea of finding one gun from each of the six in mid- to high-grade configurations (obviously not the Parker Invincible) to form the heart of a collection. The truth is, though, I'm a shooter and a hunter, not a collector, so this idea went to the backburner. Considering how much these guns have appreciated in value that decision was a mistake, both aesthetically and financially.

I will deal with each of America's famous six gun makers alphabetically and briefly. For the gunmakers for which I have them, you will find details on the organizations and associations that specialize in each gun. Because this is brief, and because each of these makers deserves a specialist's book, there are some details from other sources that you'll find either conflict with mine or are vague. If you disagree with something I've written here, you might be right, but please don't write to me and break my chops. This is what was possible within the scope if this volume. Also, because of the natural constraints on this project, I am not including much, if anything, on blackpowder guns, hammer guns, or on Damascus barrels. All are of interest, but *tempus fugit*.

A. H. Fox

Ansley H. Fox produced a gun he claimed it was the finest gun ever made. A bold statement, especially when one considers the quality that Boss, Purdey, Westley Richards, Greener, et al, were crafting at the time. Be that as it may, his gun was indeed fine.

Fox's desire for building a great gun had roots in boxed-pigeon shoots, of which he was an enthusiast. Pigeon shooting has always been hard on guns. With big purses on the line, pigeon shoots then as now tried to cram as much powder and shot into a cartridge as possible; 1¼-ounce flyer loads are the max, but I'm not convinced this has always been adhered to by men who would do almost anything to win. Smokeless powder was still quite new at the turn of the twentieth century and a big deal, as it offered the possibilities for more efficient and lethal loads. But these powders generated higher pressures than their blackpowder predecessor. While some shooters were happy fitting new fluid steel barrels to actions originally designed for blackpowder, this left much to be desired. Indeed, in going from one weakness or another, these actions literally came apart.

Ansley Fox actually began manufacturing shotguns in the mid-1890s. His company then was called the Fox Gun Co., of Baltimore, Md. The A.H. Fox Gun Co. of Philadelphia was founded in 1907 (some sources have it as 1906), though it had short prior incarnations as the Baltimore Gun Co. There is some evidence that suggests Fox merely worked for the Baltimore arms company, rather than manufacturing his gun under that aegis, based on patents granted in 1904 and 1905, to the Philadelphia Gun Co. The latter guns are marked "Philadelphia Arms Co., Makers,

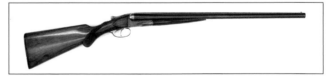

▲ A wonderful A.H. Fox 16-gauge Special. Photo courtesy Julia auction house.

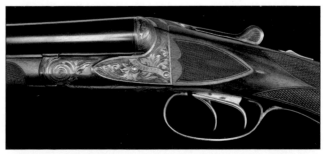

▲ Close-up of the A.H. Fox 16-gauge Special. Photo courtesy Julia auction house.

Philadelphia, PA" on the rib and "FOX" on the sides of the receiver. Outwardly, the gun looks quite similar to the Parker design, but its locks are much more closely aligned with those of Ithaca and Lefever. As Michael McIntosh wrote in his book, *The Best Shotguns Ever Made in America: Seven Vintage Doubles to Shoot and to Treasure*, "The entire Fox lock consists of only three parts: the hammer, with an integral firing pin; the sear, carefully milled from the finest drop-forged steel; and a piano-wire coil mainspring." The simplicity of the design was breathtaking.

▲ An A.H. Fox FE-Grade custom upgrade. Note the semi-pistol grip. Photo courtesy Julia auction house.

The early A.H. Fox guns were made in five grades, which ran in ascending order from A to F. The simplest was priced around $50 and came with plain walnut and little engraving. Grades B and C cost about $75 and $100, respectively, were stocked with better walnut, and sported better and more elaborate engraving. The D-grade, about $200, came with Circassian walnut and extensive engraving, while the F carried the princely sum of $500 and sported exhibition-grade wood and very fancy engraving inlaid with gold. Automatic ejectors were an optional extra, and one could purchase extra barrels and fore-ends, castoff stocks, and other custom add-ons.

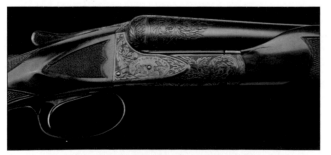

▲ A scarce A.H. Fox XE Grade. Note the beavertail fore-end and lack of a ventilated rib. Photos courtesy Julia auction house.

Around 1910, a field-grade Fox gun, the Sterlingworth, hit the market, but soon thereafter the company went bankrupt. A successful businessman named Godshalk bought the business in 1911 and made few changes to the gun. What he did do that was significant was add 16- and 20-gauge guns by 1912. Next came a single-barrel trap gun in 1919 designed specifically to compete with the Ithacas, Parkers, and L.C. Smiths in that market. A catalog from the early 1920s showed Fox doubles available in nine different grades, while the trap guns were only available four. The 1920s also saw the addition of a 12-gauge waterfowl gun with 3-inch chambers and an optional Fox-Kautzky single mechanical trigger.

▲ A beautiful, early A.H. Fox B-Grade. Photo courtesy Julia auction house.

The Great Depression signaled the death-knell to Godshalk's company, but there was a savior on the horizon in Savage Arms, which had moved production to a plant in Utica, New York. While the great economist Lord Keynes was noted for saying that prices are "sticky upwards," the Depression was one of the few exceptions; Fox prices actually went down across the various grades. The other effect of the Depression was that the highest-grade guns were eliminated or curtailed. World War II put the kibosh on shotgun production, though a few guns were made in 1945 and 1946 when Fox functionally ceased to exist. (There is evidence that Savage made a few guns from leftover parts into the 1960s. For those who own an original Fox shotgun or considering investing in one can obtain a factory letter authenticating the configuration most of these shotguns (though not the Savage incarnation), from John Callahan. Contact him for details on the services he offers and the fee that he charges (which is not exorbitant), by writing to P.O. Box 82, Southampton, MA 01073. The A.H. Fox Collectors Association (www.foxcollectors.com; 509-570-6042 is another good resource.)

The Ithaca Gun Company

The Ithaca Gun Company, like many of the early American gun manufacturers, had a number of incarnations, partners coming and going, and factories moving, but with the similar objective of improving designs as powders and metallurgy improved. W.H. Baker, one of the company's founders, was also an important designer of boxlock actions. Guns were manufactured under his own label, but he will always

be best known for his immense contribution to the Ithaca Gun Company.

We will start our journey in 1892, when a hammerless double was designed for Ithaca by Fred Crass. The Crass Ithaca was available in six grades ascending from 1 to 6. The No. 1 cost $50 and the No. 6 cost $200. It was available in 10-, 12-, and 16-gauge. Nearly 77,000 were manufactured before the design evolved to the Lewis model of which there were almost 30,000 produced. The next Ithaca in line was known as the Manier model, coming into existence in 1906.

It was Emile Flues who really brought the Ithaca gun into the twentieth century. Among his many achievements was a superfast lock time of just faster than 1/600-second—that's fast even by today's standards. The lowest-rank Ithaca Flues model was the Field, with the others being numbered 1 through 7 and having a number of variations. One of these options was a choice of barrels, including fluid steel or Krupp, and a pigeon gun was offered.

Probably the most famous single-barrel trap gun was the Ithaca introduced in 1914, especially in the beautifully engraved Sousa grade. When I was a teenager, I shot with a friend of my parents who owned one of those incredible guns (he had an amazing collection, including a Winchester Model 21 Grand American with 20- and 28-gauge and .410-bore

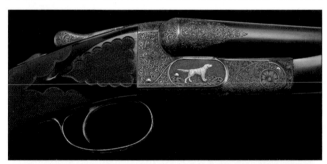

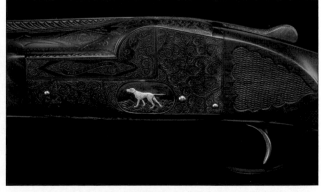

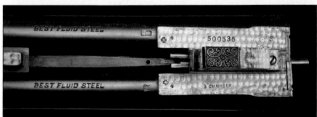

▲ The *pièce de résistance*, a one-of-a-kind Ithaca NID Sousa, grade 12-gauge magnum double-barrel shotgun. Exceptional firearm for a collector. Note the ivory bead and engravings. It was designed for three-inch cartridges. Photos courtesy Julia auction house.

▲ A very rare Sousa-grade Ithaca Kick. Photos courtesy Julia auction house.

barrels—quite rare), and I had the opportunity to shoot the Sousa at the trap field a number of times. I coveted that gun. There were also a few Sousa-grade double-barreled guns made. While John Philip Sousa was a very famous composer and conductor, he was also president of the ATA and an avid, competitive trap shot.

In 1921, Frank Knickerbocker created a design for the single-barrel trap gun that superseded the earlier models. The "Knick," as it was known, became the favored gun of most of the serious and illustrious trap competitors of the day, including many champions of the Grand American competition. The gun was never inexpensive, especially in higher grades; in 1975, the Sousa grade cost $5,000, quite expensive at the time, especially for single-barrel shotgun designed for one particular type of competition.

▲ A gorgeous Ithaca $5,000-grade single-barrel trap. Note the high Monte Carlo-styled comb.s Photo courtesy Julia auction house.

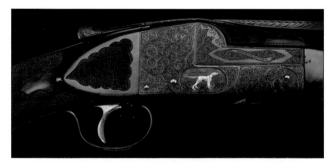

▲ A nicely restored, exceptionally rare Ithaca Knick Sousa-grade single-barrel trap gun. Photo courtesy Julia auction house.

▲ An Ithaca Knick Grade 7 single-barrel trap gun. Photo courtesy Julia auction house.

In 1924, 20-, 16-, and 12-gauge guns were upgraded and chambered to handle the modern 2¾-inch shells, and the greater pressures from those shells required another redesign. Called the "New Ithaca Double" (or "NID"), it debuted in 1925. This is a gun you want to buy if you are in the market for a classic Ithaca. In 1926, this gun was also offered in .410-bore, and, when in 1932 the Western Cartridge Company developed the 3½-inch 10-gauge Magnum shell, it was Ithaca that built the shotgun designed around this waterfowling cartridge.

▲ An Ithaca NID Grade 4 single-barrel trap gun. Photo courtesy Julia auction house.

▲ A near mint Ithaca Field-grade 12-gauge NID. Photo courtesy Julia auction house.

In 1935, Ithaca Field-grade guns sold for about $40, the No. 2 grade a whopping $62 and change. For about $11 extra, one could get the Magnum 10. Higher-grade guns came with ejectors and ran from about $100 for the Model 3 up to $380 for the Model 7 or, for the huge sum of $800, the same as a Sousa special. Few during the Depression had that sort of money. But while recessions come and go, and thankfully depressions are few and far between, there will always be some wealthy individuals. Indeed, as one man's fortune fades, another soars, so a few were built on order.

▲ A near-mint Ithaca 10-gauge Magnum Field grade, the bee's knees for waterfowlers. Photo courtesy Julia auction house.

The Ithaca Gun Company, LLC, was based in Ithaca, New York, from 1883 until 1986. It moved twice within the state between 1986 and 2005, when it was purchased by Ithaca Guns, USA of Upper Sandusky, Ohio. In 2007, according to www.ithaca-gun.com, "Ithaca Gun Company acquired the assets of Ithaca Guns USA, LLC, and continues moving forward in Ohio, bringing modern techniques and ideas to gunmaking." The current lineup is made only of pump-actions, save for the recent addition of a 1911 pistol.

For those looking to buy an Ithaca double, pick one after serial No. 400,000. The New Ithaca Double starts with those numbers and dates from 1925. These were simply stronger guns, more likely to survive the test of time and recoil. Grades 3 and higher in 28-gauge and .410-bore are extremely rare and desirable. Grade 5E is rare in 10-gauge as well. While many books can give you good price guidelines, when the extreme rarity rears its head, you'll need expert advice, ideally from an honest expert—not every gun trader or horse trader is both honest and expert.

▲ An Ithaca 5E All Option gun. Photo courtesy Julia auction house.

Lefever

The Lefever Arms Company was established in 1885, in Syracuse, New York, and went out of business in 1948, the year of my birth. (I swear that was purely coincidental.) The shotguns were made in Syracuse until 1916, when Lefever was acquired by Ithaca. To make it slightly more confusing, Dan Lefever seems to have left the company in 1901 to form sequentially incorporated companies, which had the significant involvement of his sons: D.M. Lefever and sons, Syracuse 1901; D.M. Lefever, Sons & Co., Syracuse 1901-'02; D.M. Lefever Gun Manufacturing, Defiance, Ohio 1903-'04; and, finally, D.M. Lefever Co., Bowling Green, Ohio 1905-'06. The last was dissolved when Lefever senior died. That said, it seems the original Lefever Arms shotguns made in Syracuse until 1916, when the Durston family

which owned it sold it to Ithaca Gun Company, are, perhaps, the most important.

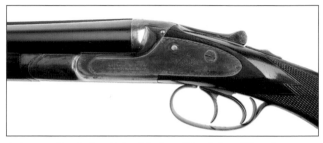

▲ An exceptionally fine, high original condition Lefever GE-grade 20-gauge. Photo courtesy Julia auction house.

In its final incarnations, the New Lefever manufactured in Ohio were produced in many grades, including the very rare Uncle Dan and Optimus grades. First produced in 1887, the Optimus grade, made with Whitworth steel barrels, beautifully engraved, and magnificently stocked, won awards at the 1893 exposition in Chicago.

The New Lefever was a pure boxlock, no longer with false sideplates. New Lefevers were available in seven grades, the lowest starting around $60, and a choice of steel or Damascus barrels, while ejectors cost an extra $10. Their No. 4 AA stocked with a better grade walnut cost a hefty $300. Because of the short-lived existence of D.M. Lefever and its variations, there are thought to be fewer than 2,000 boxlock guns in existence, so certainly the rarest of Lefever's designs.

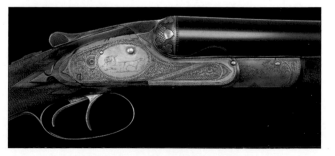

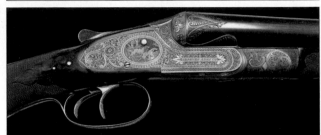

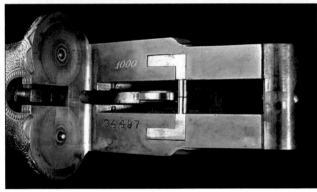

▲ A rare Lefever $1,000-grade. It is beautifully engraved with checkering on the triggers. Note the doll's head. Photo courtesy Julia auction house.

Approximately 60 percent of all Lefever guns were manufactured in 12-gauge. Curiously, 25 percent were made in 10-gauge. All were boxlock with sideplates, importantly *not* sidelock designs (the guns from Syracuse also sported sideplates, a better tableau for engraving).

▲ A unique Lefever Optimus presented to President Benjamin Harrison. Everything about this shotgun is interesting, from the pointer honoring the setter to the dogs' low-set tails. Adorned with a unique trigger guard and modern checkering, this old shotgun is in great condition. Photo courtesy Julia auction house.

World War I wreaked its havoc on fine gunmaking, as the country's manufacturers focused on the war effort, most understandably. Truly fine Lefevers became a thing of the past. That said, in 1921, Ithaca/Lefever (Syracuse) introduced the boxlock Nitro Special, and, in 1934, the Lefever Grade A.

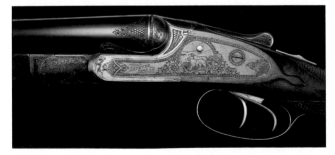

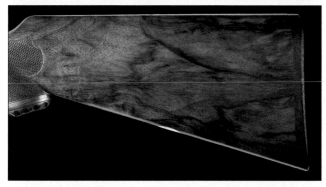

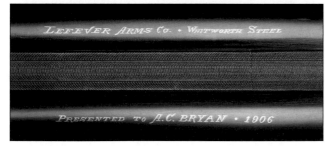

▲ An exceptionally fine Lefever Arms Company Presentation-grade ejector gun. Note the lovely engravings on the trigger guard, the interesting checkering pattern of the wood, and the intriguing stippling on the rib. Photo courtesy Julia auction house.

Lefevers with automatic ejectors were designated with the letter E in the serial number. Ejector models up through grade DE can be bought for not unreasonable money. Grades A and above are quite collectible and expensive, with the Optimus guns going for over $60,000 (assuming superb condition), and its $1,000-grade, of which only one is known to exist, once sold for $250,000. Again, a number of the most desirable Lefever guns including those from his Ohio

companies, have been degraded by sawing off part of the barrels at one extreme, and faking upgrades at the other. The Lefever club noted below is a good source of reference in regard to serial numbers etc., but a gunsmith who specializes in American classics should be consulted before buying anything.

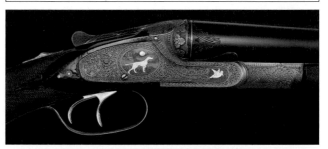

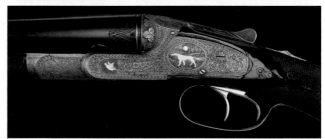

▲ An Optimus-grade Lefever. Note the pointer and woodcock in gold, as well as the setter and quail on the reverse side. Photo courtesy Julia auction house.

Dan Lefever designed America's original hammerless double-barrel gun. It was inspired by Greener's award-winning hammerless breechloading double-barrel shotgun, which was displayed at the Centennial Exposition in Philadelphia, in 1876. Lefever's first version was completed in 1878 and exhibited at the St. Louis Bench Show and Sportsman's Association that year. He won both the gold medal of the best American gun and for the best gun in the world. In 1884, Lefever struck out on his own. He had a number of partnerships that did not last, and then he formed the Lefever Arms Company of Syracuse. He created a fantastic gun called the Automatic Hammerless. It was a dramatic improvement on previous guns, for instead of the common form of choking (both of Lefever's time and today), he used a gradual barrel taper not unlike Greener's, the forerunner.

▲ A Lefever special-order GE-grade with original 27-inch barrel. Notice the slight difference at the cap of the semi-pistol grip, which makes this more of a Prince of Wales-style grip. Note the ivory front bead here as well. Photo courtesy Julia auction house.

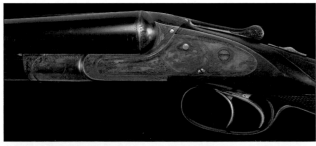

▲ A high original condition Lefever E-grade. Photo courtesy Julia auction house.

Parker—*The* American Maker

Charles Parker began his gunmaking career building rifles for the Union Army during the Civil War. As the war drew to a close, he shifted his interest to side-by-side shotguns. In 1868, production began in earnest, and, by that time, he and his brother John had bought out his previous partners and formed Parker Brothers. I will not delve into the early blackpowder and hammer guns they made, instead beginning with what I would call a "modern gun," one that can be used today.

One of Parker's shrewdest moves was hiring Charles King away from Smith & Wesson to help him come up with appropriate designs. The King-designed gun was put into production in 1882, and except for small changes in 1910, was basically the Parker shotgun as we know it now. Early guns were available both in hammer and hammerless models. The hammerless model came into existence in 1889, though hammer guns were available until 1920 and in common production until the early days of World War I.

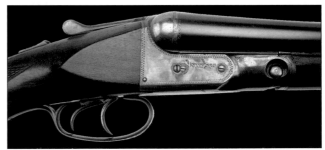

▲ An extremely fine high original condition Parker VHE 12-gauge. Photo courtesy Julia auction house.

A huge number of grades and variations were available, over 20 if one includes both hammer and hammerless. In 1902, ejectors became available, and guns with that option were marked with an "E;" whereas "H" designated hammerless guns. The top grade generally available was the AA Pigeon which was offered in both hammer and hammerless versions. The superb Parker Invincible was offered in 1929-1930 for about $1,500, a king's ransom during the Depression. There are various stories about the numbers of these actually made—some even thought just one, and a few experts believed none at all—but there are three on loan and displayed at the NRA Museum. I doubt there are any more, but it's not impossible.

The lowest normal Parker grade would probably be described as the VH, which sold for nearly $40 in 1912, when other serviceable and economy-minded shotguns could be purchased for about $10. Parker's low-end gun was the Trojan, which joined the production line in 1915 and sold for less than $30.

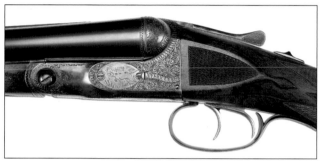

▲ A nicely restored Parker DH with engraving. Photo courtesy Julia auction house.

In 1910, James Hayes made some changes to the bolting and cocking systems. The production guns from 1917 on included these redesigned systems. Production of Parker's single-barrel trap gun also began in 1917. The single-barrel trap was based on an original design, rather than being the modification of the double. These were not inexpensive, with the SC, the lowest grade, costing $150, the most expensive SA-1 selling for $550, and with the two other grades falling in between. All were offered with ejectors as standard—truly a custom gun. Each was made to the owner specifications, from stock dimensions to choking.

At one time or another, Parkers were offered in every common and uncommon gauge, with the rarest Parkers being 10-gauge with 3½-inch chambers, 28-gauge, and the .410-bore. For much of the Roaring '20s, Parker did well, selling 5,000 or so guns a year, but once the Depression hit, production

fell to a few hundred. In 1934, Remington Arms bought Parker lock, stock, and barrels, as it were, from the patents to the factory. Even though production then rose to a couple thousand a year, in 1937, Remington chose to move the machinery to its factory in Ilion, New York, where reasonable numbers continued to be produced until Remington switched to wartime mode in 1942.

Because of their desirability, Parker guns have been upgraded (read: counterfeited), with refinished models sold as original. As with everything in the collectible market, *caveat emptor*.

From 1984 until 1989, Parker Reproductions were produced at the Olin-Kodensha plant in Japan. Experts say the guns were so faithful to the original design, the parts were largely interchangeable. I am not an expert on this, but I did, however, own one of these guns in 20-gauge. It was a joy to carry in grouse and woodcock coverts. It had a beautiful piece of wood, and I felt less guilty about taking such a fine-looking gun into the alders than I would have done with an original Parker in anything close to the 100 percent condition of my copy. Stupidly, I traded that gun toward some other pair of guns, and I have long suffered seller's remorse. Today, even these reproduction guns are collectible, with prices rising accordingly. The Parker Gun Collectors Association (www.parkerguns.org) is an excellent resource for those interested.

▲ A Parker DH trap gun with vent rib. Photo courtesy Julia auction house.

L. C. Smith—America's only Golden Era Sidelock Double

In 1880, Lyman Smith purchased W. H. Baker and Company from Baker and Leroy Smith. Lyman continued with the Baker-designed guns, but as Baker had left the company and Lyman Smith needed to update his shotguns, he turned to Alexander Brown, who had joined the company in 1878. The Brown-designed Smiths began production in 1884 and were stamped "L. C. Smith." These were hammer guns, but displayed racy, almost modern lines. It was, however, Brown's locking system that distinguished his from the other guns of the era.

▲ A near-mint L. C. Smith Field-grade 16-gauge with a straight grip. Photo courtesy Julia auction house.

Developing the hammerless *sidelock* gun separated L. C. Smith from all the other American makers. Indeed, it was the only sidelock produced in the American glory days of shotgun innovation. The shotguns were offered in six grades numbered 2 to 7, and I have no idea why they were not numbered 1 to 6, so don't ask. The higher the grade, the better the wood and the finer the twist used in the barrels. Early Grade 2 guns sold for around $80, while the very upmarket Grade 7 brought a hefty $450. The L. C. Smith Company was based in Syracuse, New York, and all the guns made in that factory had Damascus barrels.

Brown found his real brilliance in developing a typewriter capable of upper and lower case, and Lyman Smith, being no one's fool, saw the opportunity to make some serious bucks. Long story short, Brown's typewriter invention eventually became Smith-Corona. And so, with wealth on the horizon, Lyman Smith sold his shotgun company to the Hunter Arms Company of Fulton, New York, in 1890. With the change of ownership, came a different stamp—"HUNTER ARMS COMPANY, FULTON NY"—which was marked on the rib. The guns remained largely unchanged under the new owners, and though fluid steel barrels were soon offered, many continued to be purchased as hammerless guns with Damascus barrels.

▲ A near-mint L. C. Smith Field-grade 16-gauge with a Prince of Wales grip. Photo courtesy Julia auction house.

The Hunter Smiths came in even more grades than their predecessors, the lowest being 00, which sold for under $50. As with all the makers of the time, as grades went up, so did the quality of the barrels;

at the top end, they were produced in Nitro steel or Damascus to the customer's requirements. A top-of-the-line A3 was among America's most expensive shotguns, costing around $750.

A single trigger was developed in 1904. Early offerings were in 10- and 12-gauge, but 16- and 20-gauge shotguns appeared around the turn of the century. Both the 16- and the 20-gauge guns command premiums amongst collectors. Guns made after 1913 had their grades on the right barrel near the breech and the Hunter Arms company markings on the left barrel. Hammer guns were available as late as 1918. Hunter Arms also added two boxlock shotguns, known as the Fulton and the Fulton Special, the latter a slight upgrade of the former. These were designed for the less well-heeled market at $35 or less. Double triggers and extractors were standard, but ejectors and their proprietary single trigger were available. While dismissed by some collectors, these are well-made firearms, worthy of consideration, especially if someone wants to shoot their great-grandfather's guns.

▲ A scarce L. C. Smith Specialty 20-gauge. Photo courtesy Julia auction house.

The Trap Grade, designed especially for that sport, wore trap shooting engraving patterns and had a base price of about $70. I presume this double-barrel gun might also have found favor in the live-pigeon ring. The middle and higher grade Smiths, as always, were offered with better steel and wood. In 1918, the Hunter Arms Company added the L. C. Smith single-barrel trap gun, known as the "one-barrel trap gun," probably to distinguish it from the company's side-by-side trap gun. Again, these dedicated trap shotguns were expensive for the time; the lowest-grade Specialty sold for about $125, while the one-barrel trap gun fetched $350 in the Monogram grade. The Eagle and the Crown grades fell between the two. It won many competitions, including Olympic medals.

Hunter did make lovely L. C. Smith side-by-side guns in 20-gauge and .410, but as far as anyone knows, only a single 28-gauge was made, unless I completely misread the literature. Numerous variations including skeet models were available.

▲ An exceptional L.C. Smith Field-grade 410-bore. Photo courtesy Julia auction house.

The fine gunmakers that weren't destroyed by the Depression took it on the chin during World War II. At the end of the war, the hard-pressed Hunter Arms was purchased by Marlin; subsequent guns produced by that company are marked "LC SMITH COMPANY, INC." Marlin stopped producing the Smiths in 1950 or 1951, depending on whom you believe. In 1968, there was a short-lived revival, when Marlin brought the gun back in Field and Deluxe Field models, which sold for $350 and $400, respectively. The Deluxe Field was available only in 1971, in a very small run. Both latter-day Marlin manufactured Smiths had extractors (no ejectors), double triggers, and ventilated ribs. These were fairly plain guns, and I remember handling them at the old Abercrombie & Fitch store on Madison and 45th Street. Overall, these late Smiths were not a huge success. Americans were moving towards over/unders, and the Belgian Brownings and Berettas were making their marks. By 1972, this diminished incarnation, a shadow of its former self, faded to oblivion.

For more information, visit the L. C. Smith Collectors Association, www.lcsmith.org.

The Winchester Model 21, The Last of The Great Side-By-Sides

When I was a lad, perhaps 12, I used to shoot with Joe Cox at his preserve in Pawling New York. At first, Joe sent me out with guides. When I got older, for whatever reason he liked me, and I would hunt with him.

Joe shot a Model 21 Winchester. If memory serves, that custom gun cost around $1,000 in the early 1960s, a heck of a lot of money at the time. Joe had shot a lot, and extremely well, with an old-fashioned longbow and recurve, a rifle, and shotgun. Indeed, he had made safaris to East Africa and shikars to India for tiger. He was one of my heroes. He believed the Model

21 was the best shotgun he ever owned, at once well-made and endlessly reliable.

▲ A scarce Winchester Model 21, 16-gauge two-barrel set. Note the extensive engravings. Photo courtesy Julia auction house.

The Model 21 was first offered for sale in 1931. It took brave men and a brave company to create a new shotgun in those dark days of the Depression. The principal designer was a fellow named George Lewis. What he and the company designed was a thoroughly modern boxlock taking advantages of the technology and metallurgy advancements occurring during the first decades of the twentieth century. As Cox correctly pointed out to me, the 21 was incredibly strong. Heat-treated steel was machined to form the action, and chrome molybdenum steel was used for the barrels. While we might take that for granted now, it certainly was not commonplace in 1930. While I will not go through all the steps of joining the barrels, it should be pointed out that Winchester dovetailed the barrels into its own version of what the English nomenclature calls "chopper lump," or what the Europeans would describe as "demi-bloc," quite different from the monobloc design found on most double-barrel shotguns today.

While John Olin wasn't in the picture for the launch of the Model 21, he bought the company some months after production began, and he was a great fan. Olin

Industries already owned Western cartridge, and for those of you old like me, you might well remember the boxes marked "Winchester Western." Olin was more than just a man who ran gun and cartridge companies, he was a shooter, a hunter, and an enthusiast. His Nilo Farms—Nilo is Olin spelled backwards—was a place where he hosted hunts and ran some of the best Labrador retrievers in the world, winning numerous U.S. national field trial championships.

▲ A Winchester Model 21, Grade 4 in 410-bore. Photo courtesy Julia auction house.

The Model 21 was offered in skeet and trap variations, as well as various game guns, including a specialized duck gun to handle 12-gauge 3-inch loads. The Standard grade was in production from 1931 to 1959, in variations, with the Deluxe grade only coming into play after 1942. In 1941, Winchester did away with extractors to offer only ejectors, and in '44 it did away with double triggers in favor of its excellent single trigger. Beginning in 1960, only custom guns were offered, these in three grades, the simplest being the Custom, the most elaborate the Grand American, and the Pigeon in between.

Curiously, while 21's barrels are rust-blued, the frame is salt-blued, thus the difference in color between the two. The 21 was offered in the four standard gauges plus .410-bore, although few of the .410s were manufactured. I can only imagine what my parents' friend Fritz's three-gauge, three-barrel Grand American would be worth. When he purchased it in the 1960s or early 1970s, I recall him telling me it was the only one that Winchester had made. As I had seen it and handled it, its existence is definitely bona fide. I have never seen it mentioned in any literature. Unfortunately, his daughter and only child was not a shooter and it must have been sold from the estate at some point, for no one's seen nor spoken of it again.

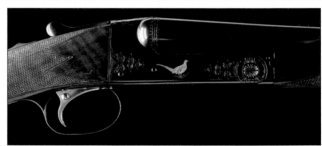

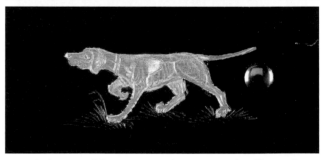

▲ A Winchester Model 21, custom-grade 20-gauge with gold engravings. Photo courtesy Julia auction house.

CHAPTER 7
British Shotguns

*I*n the 1800s, when the British Empire was at its peak, English gunmakers also ruled supreme. Roughly a dozen were located on or near Saint James's in London walking distance to Buckingham Palace. These included Rigby, Boss, Grant, and Woodward. The only British gunmaker still in Saint James's is Wm. Evans although Beretta, the great Italian gunmaker, has opened a gallery at the corner of St James's and Jermyn Street.

St James's made tremendous sense as it was close to most of the great gentlemen's clubs of London including White's, Brooks's, and Boodle's. While these were originally gambling clubs where gentlemen could also stay, eat and imbibe; they were largely the domain of the landed gentry and upper-class Brits. Undoubtedly if someone did well at a card game they might feel inspired to go out and buy a new gun. Alternatively, I'd imagine that there must've been at least a few occasions when duels were called for, so having gunmakers close at hand served a multiplicity of purposes.

More than any other group of guns, British guns, especially the British Best, have always been highly sought after which meant that their prices have stayed strong, often appreciating, if purchased wisely, on the second-hand market.

London is one of the great cities of the world and quite possibly offers the best shopping for peripatetic sportsman. I did a story for *Garden and Gun* magazine a dozen years back as a walking tour taking people from Mayfair through St. James is to Pall Mall stopping off at fishing shops, boot makers etc. in addition to the requisite visits to the gunmakers.

Purdey

We shall begin our tour of the English companies at Purdey's on South Audley Street. Purdey's was founded in 1814, a year before the Battle of Waterloo. Royal patronage followed shortly thereafter. In 1838, Queen Victoria purchased a pair of their best guns. She granted them a Royal Warrant, which I believe has also been granted by each subsequent monarch. (The Royals are dedicated shooters and sportsman.) Current shotguns show the same degree of fine craftsmanship that has always synonymous with Purdey. Indeed, Purdey set the benchmark against which all other

London gunmakers were, and still are, judged. In some ways, their best guns now are even better. They have embraced CNC technology as well as CAD/CAM technology. They let the machines do what they do best, and this is complemented by fantastic hand-finishing. (Boss and some other most significant makers believe that everything should be completely handmade and bespoke. There are pros and cons to both.)

▲ Modern Purdey hammer gun. Photo courtesy of Purdey's.

The history of British firearms has been closely linked to Purdey for over 200 years. Even term Express rifle, it has generally been agreed, was coined by James Purdey the Younger as he likened its performance to an express train, traveling fast and hitting hard. Purdey side-by-side and over unders have been very desirable both amongst affluent shooters and collectors.

James Purdey the Younger was similarly instrumental creating their London best sporting guns. He employed the Beesley action designed by Frederick Beesley in 1879. Beesley, a Purdey stocker, also designed a self-opening system which he patented 1880, and then he sold the patent to Purdey. The Purdey self-opening SxS shotgun is available in 12, 16, 20, 28, and .410 bore with each built on a dedicated action.

The first Purdey breech-loading OU action were produced in 1923 but it wasn't until 1948 with Purdey's purchase of James Woodward & Sons that the Purdey over-and-under started to shine as they based their over under on the better Woodward 1913 design/patent. Ernest and Harry Lawrence modified the Woodward ejector mechanism and redesigned other aspects. Many are still in evidence.

In 2004, Purdey reintroduced their "bar in iron

hammer ejector gun." It is a throwback to the Victorian period. I have shot Purdey live pigeon hammer guns. In fact, one of the few guns that I wish I had purchased in my life but did not was a side-by-side hammer gun designed for the live pigeon ring which my friend Gary Herman had for sale when he owned Safari Outfitters. I went 25 straight the first time I use it at trap, and trap is my weakest discipline. Piotti and other Italian makers also offer high quality modern hammer guns. They are quite special to shoot.

If Purdey's has a problem it is probably in the very complicated design of its mechanism. There are almost too many parts. It opens itself up to problems especially with the triggers which can be affected even by subtleties in shrinkage or expansion of the wood.

Purdey's all-Damascus gun is available in side-by-side or over-and-under models. Engraving makes no sense on a Damascus gun as each sports a distinctive pattern on the receiver.

▲ Classic Purdey side-by-side. Photo courtesy of Purdey's.

The Purdey Sporter is a collaboration with an Italian maker—Perugini Visini. Finished in England it has features of a clay gun with ventilated ribs, a trigger-lock action, plus Teague choke tubes if desired. Like many of the English collaborations with Italian makers, they are nice guns, but I'm not sure that they are worth the extra charge above purchasing the equivalent gun directly from Italy. The other Anglo–Italian or –Spanish collaborations are skipped as only Purdey is sufficiently significant to mention. The Purdey Sporting Clay shotgun, also a trigger lock, is just off the press, as it were. To date, only a few have been made. Unlike

the Purdey Sporter, it is completely made in Britain, but comes with a price tag of circa $100,000.

William Evans and Churchill's also do partnerships with continental gunmakers that I would put into the same category—guns made in Italy or Spain but finished in Britain.

Boss

▲ A beautiful pair of over under London Best Guns in an oak and leather case with two sets of barrels for each gun. Note both the single trigger and the ribless barrels for which Boss is justifiably famous.

It used to be a short walk from Purdey's on South Audley Street, indeed less than half a block, to the recent home of Boss on Mount Street. Boss gave up their expensive Mayfair shop and now does business from their factory in Kew Garden, Richmond. They differ from most the other big-name London makers in that they only make guns. They do not sell shooting suits, dog whistles, or cufflinks like some. They make best guns and only best guns and take pride.

Boss is unique among English gunmakers. First,

along with Woodward, they were better known for their over-and-unders than their side-by-side shotguns. Also, they made, at least in relative terms, a great number of single-trigger shotguns. They have had the rare U.K. reputation for making a single trigger that worked. (Messrs. Browning, Beretta, and others who are making mass-produced boxlocks rarely have problems with single triggers. Few custom makers adapted them well enough to the intricacies of a complicated bespoke sidelock.) Boss over-and-unders have a special place in the hearts of collectors and shooters. The Boss over-and-under has often been imitated. (Even the great German company Hartmann & Weiss make a fabulous shotgun based on the Boss design.) This is because of a design that allows for an especially shallow and elegant profile.

Quite possibly the most desirable and expensive of all the London guns. This Boss over-under with its ribless barrels will be very quick and the double triggers give you an instant choice of choke.

Decades ago I went to Boss when they were on Dover Street but they were no longer manufacturing guns—rather just repairing customers' firearms. It was

a sad dreary shop then. It basically ceased trading but then was revived by my friends Keith and Graham Halsey, and their partner Andreas Heechen.

Boss was founded in 1812 by Thomas Boss who had done his apprenticeship under his father at the famous Joseph Manton gunmakers. (It was fairly common practice for very talented gunsmiths to do an apprenticeship and then strike off on their own.) After his death in 1857, the company was managed by his widow, two nephews Edward and James Paddison; and Stephen Grant, who would go on to form his own company which is now part of Atkin, Grant and Lang.

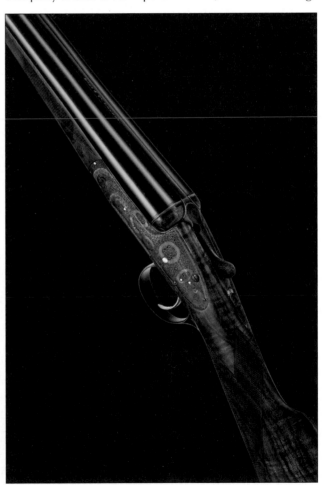

▲ This classic Boss side-by-side features a single trigger, beautiful walnut and case-coloring. Simple elegance.

The Boss over-and-under was designed by John Robertson who bought the family business in 1891 but kept the original name. Robertson's design and construction produced an elegant shotgun. It featured the Boss Single Trigger also designed by Robertson. Indeed, it was John Robertson's time with Boss starting in the 1890s which was assuredly the most significant period for the company from the point of view of the developing their modern sporting shotgun. The distinctive Boss rose and scroll is credited to John James Sumner, the third of four generations of Boss Sumner engravers.

In the last couple of years Boss was sold by my friends the Halseys to an acquaintance of mine Arthur DeMoulas who is doing a tremendous job of building London best guns. While they are most famous for their over unders, it should be noted that they do make lovely side-by-side as well. The bees' knees for day of driven grouse shooting, Boss are quite treasured by collectors. They should be. Best English guns have always been expensive.

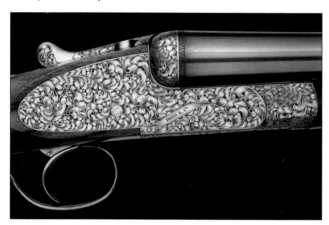

▲ This engraving shows artistry on metal.

Boss & Co Ltd
The Caxton House
110 Kew Green
Richmond
Surrey
TW9 3AP
Phone: 44 (0) 20 8948 2781

William & Son

From Purdey's, it was only a five-minute walk across Berkley Square to William & Son or Holland & Holland, both on Bruton Street. (The latter store is now closed.)

The William & Son signature classic Side-By-Side is a self-opening model. I have seen a number and my

friend David Nolan shot his pair, very well indeed, during our three driven days together in Yorkshire a few years ago. As Paul West from William & Sons points out, "The William and Son gun does have a H&H style self-opener but it is not a copy of a H&H as the sizes and shapes are different." Continuing, "We have a team of craftsman who work for us in their own workshops. They are all London trained and we have worked together for 30 years. The guns are entirely English in production as are component parts. We look to deliver a new gun in 18 months." 18 months is very quick by U.K. standards.

▲ William and Son side-by-side shotgun. Photo courtesy of William and Son.

Action: William & Son self-opening sidelock SxS ejector comes in gauges from .410 to 12 bore
Barrels: from 25- to 3-0inch chopper lump, 2 3/4-inch chambers, choke-bored as required
Stock: deluxe walnut, to individual measurements
Engraving: scroll engraving as standard; custom engraving available.
Weight (approximate): 12-bore/28-inch, 6 lbs. 10 oz.; 16-bore/28-inch, 6 lbs.; 20-bore/28-inch, 5 lbs. 10 oz.; 28-bore/28-inch, 5 lbs. 6 oz.; .410/28-inch, 4 lbs. 12 oz.

Over-and-Under "Sporter" Shotgun

The Sporter is a new addition to the William and Son's line. It is a trigger plate action but unlike most "sporters" offered by U.K. makers, it is built in Britain. It comes with hand engraving on its round body shape with distinctive scalloped action.

▲ William & Son over-and-under shotgun. Photo courtesy of William and Sons.

Gauges: 12 and 20
Action: Trigger plate
Barrels: from 25 to 32 inches
Stock: Deluxe Walnut, to individual measurements
Engraving: Large scroll engraving standard

William & Son
While guns are not shown on the website, I have included it in case contact details change in the future. There is no telephone number associated.
Email: info@williamandson.com
Website: www.williamandson.com

Holland & Holland

Arriving on the scene in 1835, Holland & Holland quickly established itself. Harris Holland founded the company, but it was really the addition of his nephew, Henry, in 1867 that led to many of their great innovations. From about 1870 on it has been regarded as one of the three great gun companies of London. Henry had more than forty patents to his credit, from the famous "Royal" action of 1883 to the most useful rifle cartridge the world has ever seen, the .375 H&H.

Holland and Holland's main retail operation and gun shop was located for decades at 33 Bruton St. in fashionable Mayfair. Unlike the other London best makers, they also maintain shops in Dallas (relocated recently from NYC) and in Paris.

▲ The Holland & Holland gunroom in Dallas. Photo courtesy of Holland & Holland.

I was always disappointed that my friend Capt. Jeremy Clowes, who was the logical successor to Malcolm Lyell, was passed over for Roger Mitchell as managing director, mostly because Mitchell did not have Jeremy's gunmakers/shooting background when Roger came to the position. H&H was until recently in the capable hands of Daryl Greatrex. Roger did grow into the job, but it was an unusual transition.

In early 2021, Beretta bought Holland & Holland!
Holland & Holland introduced the "Royal" hammerless side by side in 1894 with hand-detachable locks added in 1908 and the self-opening system in 1922. While metallurgy et cetera has changed, the design is virtually the same. Its simple locks give superior reliability than more complicated designs of a number of London Best makers. The "Royal" Over-and-Under has undergone three redesigns. The current ejectors, cocking and single trigger systems are based on a 1990s rethink.

The demand for sporting clay guns for those who desired a British rather than Italian, American, or Belgian platform led Holland and Holland to create the Sporting Over Under in the 1990s. I was at Casa de Campo shooting when Roger Mitchell was there with an early model on display. A number of my friends bought the gun, and basically to a man each had to send it back to England a number of times to get the trigger to work. It was a detachable trigger plate model reminiscent of Perazzi. In those days the Perazzi design worked and to be blunt, the Holland and Holland model left much to be desired. To be fair, the fit and finish of the stock and barrels was beautiful. Today and actually for a number of years now the trigger has been greatly improved.

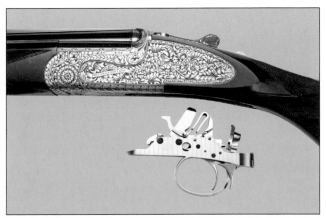

▲ An interchangeable trigger plate action sporting over-and-under. Photo courtesy of Holland & Holland.

The 'Round Action' model, introduced in 2002, harkens back to their 'Dominion' which they stopped making in the 1960s. It is a much less expensive alternative to the 'Royal' though only time will tell if it maintains value on the second-hand market. It must be a strong design as they offer a double rifle on basically the same action.

Holland and Holland new contact details:

011 +44 20 7499 4411 is the London number for Holland and Holland. The gunroom is located at their North London shooting grounds: gunroomuk@ hollandandholland.com 011+44+1923 825349 Holland & Holland Shooting Grounds Ducks Hill Road, Northwood United Kingdom HA6 2ST

Holland and Holland does still have premises in Dallas Texas.

Phone: 212-752-7755

6821 Preston Rd Dallas, TX 75205

▲ The Holland and Holland Royal is the epitome of British craftsmanship and the dream gun for many sportsmen.

William Evans

One can walk from Holland and Holland via Bond Street and Piccadilly to St. James's and arrive at Wm Evans in just over 5 minutes. They use some of Britain's Master Gunsmiths—each a specialist—actioner, stockmaker et al starting with actions that are built on the Holland & Holland patent. They produce best quality guns at reasonable prices by London standards. Crowned heads, Maharajahs, and top shots and mere mortals have been welcomed at their establishment. (Once here it is worth side trips to Lobb's bootmakers, Lock the Hatters, and Beretta, all on the other side of the street.)

Their guns are not made in house but rather almost in the style of the Italian Guild system, but they do keep a close eye on all aspects. By doing it this way they claim that they are able to be a bit less expensive than the other London makers.

WILLIAM EVANS LONDON

William Evans Ltd
67A St. James' Street
London
SW1A 1PH
Phone: +44 (0)20 7493 0415
Email: info@williamevans.com

Rigby

It is a short cab ride from Mayfair to Rigby's new location at 13–19 Pensbury Place. As Guy Bignell, the long-time head honcho at the renowned Griffin and Howe, pointed out just a couple of years ago, "Paul Roberts took over Rigby in 1982 and operated it until 1997. He made numerous shotguns of Italian heritage and placed the Rigby name on them. . . . As far as I know, since my friend Michael Lüke of Lüke & Ortmeier Group, took over John Rigby & Company, they have not made any shotguns."

This has now changed for the better as Rigby has recently reintroduced its impressive rising bite side-by-side shotgun.

Depending on whom you believe, Rigby is either the second or third oldest gunmakers in continuous operation in history. Beretta, without doubt is the oldest, and Rigby is certainly the oldest firm in the English-speaking world. But the date, 1735, often attributed to the origin of Rigby actually predates the birth of the first John Rigby—there were three John Rigby's in a row owning/running the company. This simply does not make sense. It is possible that the first John Rigby bought an established firm in Dublin and the date actually represents the founding of the original company, a.k.a. Rigby's predecessor. It is also possible that the date is apocryphal. It might even just be a simple typographical error from an early catalogue. The official founding date of the company is 1775.

Physically, Rigby has been all over the place, not unlike the Irish diaspora itself. Originating in Dublin where it was noted for its duelling pistols, fowling pieces, and target rifles, it established operations in London during the 1800s. At the cusp of the twentieth century the company ceased trading in Ireland to focus entirely on

British clients, though all three John Rigby's were born in Dublin. The first was a soldier which probably had much to do with his interest in duelling pistols. For a short period, it was operated through different ownership out of Paso Robles California, this being Rigby's nadir.

They have recently (January 2019) introduced their Rising-Bite side by side. It is available in 12-, 28-, 32-bore, and .410. This sidelock ejector features Rigby's signature dipped edge lock plates, chopper lump barrels, English straight-hand grip, hand-chequered butt, inlaid with a silver oval. It sports "Rigby Scroll" pattern engraving and carved folding leaves on fences. Engraving and wood upgrades are available.

London showroom, workshop, and museum:
John Rigby & Co. (Gunmakers) Ltd.
13–19 Pensbury Place
London SW8 4TP
Phone: +44 (0) 207 720 0757
Email: rigby@johnrigbyandco.com

Watson Bros Gunmakers

In the same general London area as Rigby one will find Watson.

Thomas Watson purchased the company and premises in Pall Mall of Durs Egg a Swiss born gunmaker in 1875. Durs Egg, established in London in 1772, became gunmaker to George IV in 1820. Watson's reputation grew and in 1885 his sons Arthur and Thomas junior succeeded him establishing Watson Brothers, thereby continuing the gunmaking traditions established by their father at 29 Old Bond St., London W1. They attracted royal warrants from the Sultan of Turkey and Shah of Persia. Over the following century they built circa 17,000 guns.

In 1989, Michael Louca, a Purdey trained barrel maker, bought the nearly inactive Watson Bros Gunmakers. Under Louca, they now specialize in innovative designs including a round-body self-opening over-and-under with a wider gape than found commonly on OUs that allows for faster reloading. It is distinguished by a very shallow frame. While inspired by Woodward and with some influence by Boss, Louca completely redesigned ejector system, and various other aspects set it apart as a truly new design. His design allows for a significantly lighter gun that handles as quickly as a side by side for those not shooting heavy loads—great for grouse or traditional driven partridge presented over hedgerows. Unlike a number of British makers, all guns are manufactured by hand without CNC machines in their near Tower of London premises. Michael Louca trains the superb craftsmen in the correct apprenticeship from a bygone era.

Watson Bros also offers a heavier High Pheasant model for tall bird enthusiasts and even offer true left-hand opening lever for southpaws.

Address: 41 Tower Bridge Rd, London SE1 4TL, U.K.
Phone: +44 (0) 20 7378 970

Near London
Atkin, Grant and Lang

While they all started as separate companies in the late nineteenth century, they merged into a single company circa 1960 (In 1925 the company of Stephen Grant and Joseph Lang was merged). To the best of my knowledge they were never known for making over unders but they were very well known, both separately and as the merged company for making sidelever guns, which I find a joy to behold. (Boss made some sidelevers as well, a friend of mine has a lovely pair in 16-gauge, but these companies were best known for that design.) Currently this company is also receiving accolades for buying used British guns and then rebuilding them with modern materials to a very high standard, but still being able to sell these "refurbished" for much less than a new London best gun.

Separately: Joseph Lang started London in 1821.

Stephen Grant opened in St James, London in 1866. His guns achieved Royal Warrants from the Prince of Wales in 1871 subsequently from Queen Victoria, and the Czar of Russia.

Henry Atkin like his father before him worked for James Purdey. In 1877 he opened his first premises in Haymarket, London using the name "Henry Atkin" (from Purdey's).

They have recently started to manufacture a round-bodied over-and-under sideplate shotgun.

Address: Broomhill Leys, Windmill Road, Markyate, St Albans AL3 8LP, United Kingdom
Phone: +44 (0) 1582 849382

E. J. Churchill

A short train ride to the countryside west of London will bring you to Churchill, an upstart among the English gunmakers. This is true of both the old company and the new. In 1891 Edwin John Churchill formed the gun company. Eight years later Robert Churchill, a well-known shot, known for his style— The Churchill method of shooting, and author of the classic *Game Shooting*, joined the firm. In 1980, the company—which at that time also incorporated Atkins, Grant, and Lang—went out of business. (I believe the kinder term is "ceased trading.") In 1997, Churchill was relaunched in formal conjunction with the West Wycombe shooting grounds. The small and well-run factory, of which I was given a guided tour about 20 years ago by Chris Batha, is housed in what used to be squash courts and staff quarters. One of the principals, Sir Edward Dashwood, is considered one of the finer shots in England. And it is on his magnificent estate and well-known pheasant shoot that the new factory is situated.

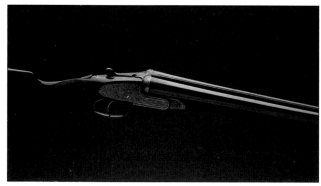

▲ A Churchill side-by-side. Photo courtesy EJ Churchill.

E. J. Churchill has been synonymous with fine handmade English shotguns since 1891 if one is being open-minded in regard to years of inactivity. They still uphold practises of traditional craftsmanship throughout their bespoke range shotguns.

From Chris Batha who represents them in the USA, sent me the following missive which I have taken the liberty of editing for space:

"The finest of all the Churchill guns was the 'Premiere' which exhibited all of the qualities expected of the highest grade English sporting gun—style, grace, balance, durability and innovation.

These qualities were no more obvious than in the manufacture of the pinless sidelock, which provided a firing mechanism impervious to the weather, whilst allowing the engraver an uninterrupted surface to indulge his art.

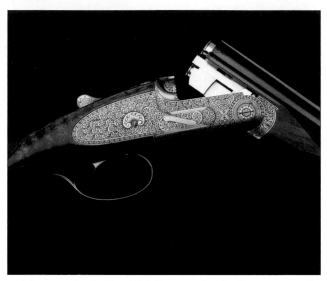

▲ A fine example of a Churchill-built over-and-under. Photo courtesy of E. J. Churchill.

Today E. J. Churchill Gunmakers still upholds these qualities throughout its range of 'best' hand built guns. The 'Premiere' side by side is the supreme example of classic English gunmaking. Available with square or round bodied action with graceful proportions, and superb balance and finish. The 'Premiere' over-and-under blends the practical benefits of a single sight plane with the elegant lines of a classic game gun. Both the square and round bodied action versions incorporate innovations such as replaceable trunnions, improved single trigger and enhanced ejectors.

These guns are entirely bespoke so specification can be discussed with the client."

E. J. Churchill Shooting Ground
Park Lane, Lane End
High Wycombe
Buckinghamshire
HP14 3NS
Phone: +44(0)1494 883227
Email: reception@ejchurchill.com

Birmingham
Westley Richards

Westley Richards of Birmingham is a highly regarded maker of Best Guns. More than anything else, they are well known for their famous droplock design. The hand-detachable locks were a follow-up to the company's famous Anson & Deeley boxlock, which was patented by John Deeley in 1897, when he was managing director of Westley Richards. The droplock was designed by him and his successor, Leslie Taylor. A hinge plate on the underside of the action is released by a small catch in its knuckle. When this drops down—ergo the term droplock—two plates, each carrying its own lock, are revealed. The elegant simplicity of the Anson & Deeley action is apparent. It works reliably, as it has very few moving parts. It is also a very strong action. Major Sir Gerald Burrard, a noted firearm authority and author, declared this "probably the strongest of all boxlock actions."

▲ A pair of Westley Richards hand-detachable-lock shotguns. Photo courtesy of Westley Richards.

Westley Richards normally adds a doll's-head extension. Patented by the founder's son in 1862, it is a very sturdy, reliable method of securing the barrels to the breech face. The extension from the barrel drops into the corresponding circular head carved in the breech. Any forward movement of the barrels off the face on firing is prevented. Since the firm's founding in 1812, many important patents were created. Among these, the Anson forend latch and the Deeley ejector system are two of the most important. Their single trigger, patented in Leslie Taylor's name, was actually created by Allen Lard, an American. While the British single trigger is historically unreliable, theirs has always been considered one of the best designs.

In 2008 Westley Richards moved into a new factory/showroom in Birmingham where they have been based for roughly two hundred years. Westley Richards founders' philosophy was "to build as good a gun as can be made" and remains their credo. Steven Harridence kindly opened the shop for me on a weekend when they were closed and gave me the royal guided tour. Very impressive indeed.

Droplock

Since its introduction in 1897, the Westley Richards hand detachable lock design has been unique and highly respected for its simplicity and strength. They are very simple with only six component parts—lockplate, cocking lifter, hammer, mainspring, sear and sear spring. They are virtually impossible to replace incorrectly.

▲ A Westley Richards 12-gauge round action sidelock. Photo courtesy of Westley Richards.

Sidelock

Westley Richards offers a hand detachable sidelock in 12-, 16-, 20-, and 28-gauge and .410-bore. It comes with assisted opening and true round-body action with a Birmingham touch.

Westley Richards & Co. Ltd
130 Pritchett Street
Birmingham
B6 4EH
England
Phone: +44 (0)121 333 1900
Fax: +44 (0)121 333 1901
Email: sales@westleyrichards.co.uk; retail@westley-richards.co.uk

Westley Richards Agency
5247 Gulf Breeze Parkway
Gulf Breeze, Florida
32563
United States of America
Phone: +1 850 677 3688
Fax: +1 850 502 5332
Email: info@westleyrichards.com

WW Greener was one of the most influential inventors and gunmakers of the modern era. William Wellington Greener, the son of William who founded the company in 1829, who took over the company in 1869 made many famous contributions to gunmaking including the cross bolt system which added great strength to their actions. He was instrumental in developing the modern choke. By 1900 he had 450 employees producing a thousand handmade guns a year—the biggest fine gun maker in British history. His book *The Gun and Its Development* was an important work in its day and of significance even now. WW1 led to the demise of the company as a maker of great guns as they joined the war effort and afterwards made less expensive and less desirable firearms.

For various reasons the company functionally went out of business in 1965 but in 1985 was given new life by WW's great-grandson Graham Greener and his three partners Ken Richardson, Richard Tandy, and David Dryhurst. David Dryhurst had started working at Greener in 1958, but as they ceased to exist he went on to work on his own. Fortunately he had a great apprenticeship with some Masters from the old company. He and Tandy have sterling reputations as gunmakers.

They now offer The Facile Princeps, (reintroduced in 1998) based on the original Greener design, plus sidelock SxS and sidelock over unders. Most of their guns are presentation or exhibition quality and have a commensurate price tag. They have even made a few hammer guns. Interestingly they made a number of pairs as a limited edition which were offered with both steel and Damascus barrels. Elaborate engraving and superb wood are available. Today shotguns can be ordered in all gauges from 10 to 32.

From a recent email by company director Graham N Greener:

1. "Currently we are making Presentation or Exhibition grade double barrel sporting rifles and shotguns in the following bores, calibres and types:
2. Facile Princeps type ejector shotguns in 20 bore and .360 Express rifles
3. Side-lock ejector shotguns in 10, 12, 16, 20, 28, 24, and 32 bores
4. Over-Under ejector shotguns in 20 bore only
5. Greener is also making a couple of exhibition shotguns with Anson & Deeley actions however, these are not finished yet so there are no photographs available. Visually these will look the same as the Facile Princeps guns but with different engraving."

W W Greener (Sporting Guns) Limited
The Mews, Hagley Hall, Hagley
Stourbridge, DY9 9LG, United Kingdom
Phone: +44 (0)1666–510351

SCOTLAND BOUND
John Dickson and MacNaughton
Historic Scottish gunmaker John Dickson & Son, one of the pioneers of the round bodied action, recently closed its Edinburgh shop and now operates out of its Perthshire factory. It is a shame as they had been in Edinburgh for nearly 200 years. Amongst its most famed clients was Lord Byron.

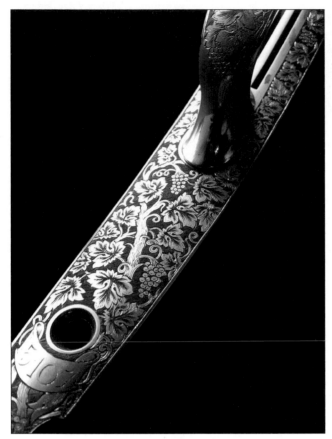

▲ The round action bar in wood design is both classic and strong.

They continue to build high quality shotguns in Dunkeld. Their shop on Frederick Street, Edinburgh was a fixture for sportsmen for 80 years with a sign embellished "John Dickson and MacNaughton." In January 2017, the company proclaimed: "It is with regret that we announce the closure of John Dickson & Son. The business closed ending 211 years of Dickson gunmaking in Edinburgh, eighty of these years at their present location."

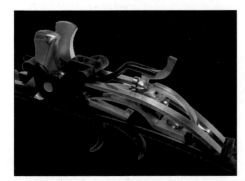

▲ The trigger plate action has been employed in Scotland for a very long time and with great success on their superb side-by-side shotguns.

▲ Notice the difference between the Dickson and MacNaughton versions of the trigger plate.

In 1806, John Dickson, age 12, apprenticed to gunmaker James Wallace on Edinburgh's High Street. Dickson in 1838 began building firearms on his own. John Dickson and Sons has incorporated a number of other Scottish gunmakers including Thomas Mortimer and Daniel Fraser. When the firm was bought by American Charles Palmer in 1999 it brought John Dickson & Son under the same ownership as James MacNaughton, a longtime rival. Dickson and MacNaughton had a patent dispute in the late 1880s over the trigger plate action. Mr. MacNaughton patented his in 1876 and Dickson in 1880. The courts sided with Mr. Dickson.

▲ The round action is strong, functional, and elegant. The engraving is strong yet tasteful.

Read more at: www.scotsman.com/business/edinburgh-gunmaker-john-dickson-son-closes-after-200-years-1-4338240
Dickson & MacNaughton
John Dickson & Son
Address: The Steading, House Home Farm, Dunkeld PH8 0HX, U.K.
Phone: +44 1350 728763

David McKay Brown

David McKay Brown apprenticed with Alex Martin Ltd. Glasgow. Alex Martin was taken over by John Dickson & Son, Edinburgh famous for its round body design during his apprenticeship and he completed training in the Edinburgh workshop. In 1967, he established his own company. In 1974 his first round action guns under his appellation were completed. He continued to specialize in the elegant and strong round body action until he recently sold to Buchan.

The approximate weights for side by side:

While typical SxS are light 12 bore, their SxS with 28-inch barrels weighs circa 6 lbs 6 ozs and the .410 only around 5 lbs 4 oz. For high bird specialists, it can be made heavier with longer barrels, straighter stock dimensions for increased elevation, and chokes designed for extreme range with larger shot sizes. It can even be made to a wildfowler's specification for use with non-toxic shot.

O/U strength is increased by thicker action walls, supporting joint pins and buttresses. It is augmented with the slender curving fences. Recently they also developed an over-and-under gun for committed high bird masters. It is fitted with 31- or 32-inch barrels and choked for patterns employing larger shot at longer range. It weighs 7 lbs 8 ozs or a bit more.

Precision screw in chokes can be fitted if required, but personally I would stick to fixed chokes.

Standard 12 bore OU weighs roughly 6 lbs 14 ozs with 28-inch barrels while the 28 bore is a dynamic 6 lbs 2 oz.

The company of David McKay Brown was first established in the town of Hamilton and recently moved to its present address in Longside when acquired by Buchan.

Buchan Guns & McKay Brown
Ugie Lodge
Mill of Rora
Longside
Aberdeenshire
Scotland AB42 4UB
Office #: 011 +44 1779 821978
Grant Buchan Mobile: 011 +44 7557 133668
Email: grant@buchanguns.com
Email: info@mckaybrown.com
Email: admin@buchanguns.com
Website: www.mckaybrown.com
or order the guns in America through Guy Bignell at
  Griffin and Howe bignell@griffinhowe.com.

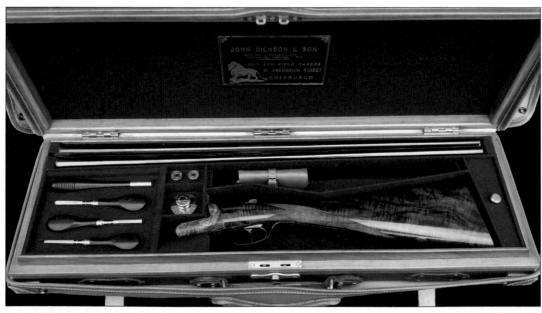

▲ John Dickson round-action 20 gauge, cased.

CHAPTER 8
Italian Shotguns

▲ This gullwing gun by Beretta displays all the hallmarks of the true work of art.

I wrote an article in 1994 that appeared in the March/April 1995 issue of *Shooting Sportsman* titled "The Italian Revolution." Some things have changed since then: For example, Caesar Guerini has become a much bigger player in the field; Fausti and other companies have appeared on the American market, and one company, Famars, proved to make beautiful, but unreliable and poorly manufactured shotguns for a largely unsuspecting public–including me. With that as a prologue, I shall revisit the subject.

Addictions are curious. I've had several in my life: women, English setters and British Labradors, African safaris, fly fishing, European bird shoots, and Italian guns. Each burns brighter than the others for a while, and then reestablishes itself elsewhere in the random, often-changing hierarchy. But of them all, only shotguns have had any investment value.

There is good value for the money in the new market as well as in the used. And the used market, back in the 1990s, made these guns a relative steal; the best of the Italian guns now do well at auction. A second reason is that I feel these guns are simply amongst the best made in the world, and this is especially true of (alphabetically), Beretta's SO line, Bosis, Fabbri, Piotti, and the Rizzini R1.

The Italian gunmakers have set the standard for the art: Firearms cut by fully-automated computerized machines to tolerances not perceptible to the human eye and then finished and embellished by the greatest engravers the world has ever known—Fracassi, Galeazzi, Torcolli, Pedretti, Pedersoli, and Terzi, to name only a few.

The Italian revolution, as I like to call it, in firearms making is evident in written works, as well. In Jack O'Connor's *The Complete Book of Rifles and Shotguns: With a Seven-Lesson Rifle Shooting Course,* published in 1961, Italian guns take up less than a half-page of text, and the only makers mentioned are Beretta, Franchi, and Bernardelli. More recently, Bob Brister, in his exceptional work *Shotgunning: The Art and The Science*, says a considerable influence has been felt from Italian gun makers, especially Daniele Perazzi and his former partner Ennio Mattarelli, an Olympic gold medalist in trap. In *The Double Shotgun*, written by Don Zutz in 1978, the Italian gun is described as eclipsing all others. And not to be outdone, Michael McIntosh even has a chapter entitled "The Italian Renaissance" in his 1989 book, *Best Guns*. So, let's take a look, alphabetically, at some of the best of the best from Italy.

Battista Rizzini

From Marcheno, Italy, Battista Rizzini has been in business since 1965, and its firearms have been imported by a number of companies over the years. Its game guns, especially the round bodied over/under, have a devoted following in Britain, as they are a well-made gun at a reasonable price. While most of these guns are mass-produced, some are hand-engraved and have other custom upgrades available. www.rizziniusa.com

Beretta

The company dates its own formation to 1526, making it the oldest continuously operating gun manufacturer, indeed, *the* oldest continuously operating company in the world. Founder Bartolomeo was a master barrel maker in Gardone, Val Trompia, and fifteen generations of his family have followed in his footsteps over the last five centuries.

One of the unique aspects of Beretta is that the company has employed virtually every aspect of firearm

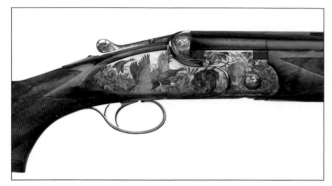

▲ The gullwing closed. While certainly ornate the artistry is unmistakable—a true collector's item.

design, from matchlock, wheellocks, and flintlocks to external hammer percussion blackpowder guns and, finally, the modern shotguns we know today. And though the maker is best known today for its well-made mass-produced firearms, Beretta is capable of creating some lovely and highly coveted shotguns in its custom shop.

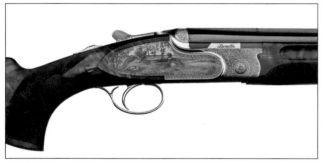

▲ The Beretta SO10 is one of the finest guns ever produced. It combines fine handling, the pinnacle of gunmakers art and the reliability for which Beretta is renowned.

Beretta's high-end production revolves around its sidelock over/under SO series, side-by-side model 452, and its double rifles. The SO6 is available in a number of grades, including the exquisite EELL. Its SO10 now sports demi-block barrels in all four gauges. All these guns come from the maker's custom shop with an endless array of options, including custom

▲ The S06EELL has one of the strongest locking systems around. As it is a true sidelock, there is a large surface for engraving artistry to be employed, but also looks great plain.

engraving signed by the master of your choice. Just expect to pay extra. www.beretta.com

Beretta Galleries in New York, Dallas, London, and other cities are an important destination for shotgun cognoscenti and aficionados.

Bernardelli

Vincenzo Bernardelli opened his shop in Gardone more than two centuries ago. Since then, his name has become synonymous with a wide variety of side-by-side shotguns at affordable prices. Today, the company makes everything from slug guns to over/unders and even includes external hammer pieces. Its most popular line is the Roma boxlock based on the Anson & Deeley system, some with false sideplates. Other models include the Hemingway with its short and light barrels ideal for woodcock or quail hunting; the Las Palomas for the pigeon ring; and the Brescia and Italia hammer guns. Of course, all are available with a variety of options, including stock, choke, grip, ejectors, triggers, and so on. Note, these guns are not to be confused with those from Pietro Bernardelli, generally considered to be inferior products. www.bernadelli.com

Bertuzzi

▲ Photo courtesy Guy Bignell/Griffin and Howe of Bertuzzi gullwing.

Yet another well-known maker from Gardone, Bertuzzi produced a wide range of shotguns, including boxlock and sidelock side-by-sides and boxlock over/unders. The Bertuzzi brothers worked out of a small shop roughly the size of a two-car garage, and in that shop a few artisans created 30 or 40 guns each year. Though no longer in business, every Bertuzzi when they were being made could be ordered with intricate and exquisite engraving from the engraver of your choice.

▲ Photo courtesy Guy Bignell/Griffin and Howe of Bertuzzi.

Bosis

Luciano Bosis produces a small number of guns each year. Side-by-sides are based on the Anson & Deeley-style boxlock, sidelocks are based on Holland & Holland's. Bosis's over/unders are hugely coveted guns. They show more handwork, perhaps, than the more recent manufactured Fabbris. The quality overall is certainly close to Fabbri. www.bosis.com. Do not confuse this short review of Bosis guns with a reflection of quality. They are amongst the best and if you can afford them are definitely worth consideration.

Caesar Guerini

They are manufactured in Marcheno, Italy, and, since 2003, have been imported into America as Caesar Guerini USA. They are well-made production guns in the mid-price range and are popular both amongst clay guys and game shooters in the appropriate models. The company does produce more shotguns than most Italian manufacturers. www.gueriniusa.com

Desenzani

Enrico Desenzani worked at Franchi in the 1930s, before going off to create his own fine line of side-by-sides. These, too, were based on Anson & Deeley and H&H actions, as is true of so many of the Italian masters. Though only a handful of guns are produced each year, their exquisite quality has given them a loyal following among the cognoscenti. www.armidesenzani.it

Fabbri

Most of Fabbri's innovations have more to do with manufacturing and milling than with action design (although some aspects of Fabbri's actions are unique). It is the synergy between the theoretical aspects of design and the perfect execution that separates Fabbri from most the other custom gunmakers in the world.

Ivo Fabbri, who started in the design studio at Fiat, began his gunmaking career in 1963. His profound understanding of metallurgy and design, along with his engineering background, combined in his creation of machining techniques for building firearms to amazing tolerances.

Fabbri is undoubtedly one of the five greatest over/under gunmakers of modern times. The flawless mechanisms of the company's guns are complemented by perfect handling characteristics, excellent fit and finish, and embellishment most often by one of several famed engravers. The highest praise for Fabbri is that the company's guns are the top choices amongst the best live-pigeon shots in the world, where serious money is often on the line. www.fabbri.it

Fausti

They were established in the year of my birth, 1948, with a factory in Marcheno, Italy, and have been imported since 2009 by Fausti USA in Fredericksburg, Virginia. While it began with Stefano Fausti, the company is now very well managed by his three daughters, Barbara, Elena, and Giovanna. In general, Faustis are relatively high-end guns, not expensive on the order of a British best gun, but most are between $8,000 and $30,000. At least for that price one does get hand engraving on most models, with some of the lower un-engraved but still hand finished. I viewed the guns briefly at an SCI convention in Vegas one year, and while not field-tested, my quick once-over told me the wood-to-metal and metal-to-metal fit seemed good and the handling characteristics excellent. Fausti also produces a hammer model with case color hardening. www.faustiusa.com

Ferlib

The Ferlib factory has been operating since 1952, and the founding owner, Libero Ferraglio, has been making shotguns since 1949. The firm's strength lies in its ability to market guns at reasonable prices. www.ferlib.com

Fratelli Rizzini (F. Lli Rizzini)

Fratelli Rizzini is a gunmaker of significance that was instrumental in spreading the fame of the Italian gun trade around the world. Indeed, more than a few authorities consider F. Lli Rizzini's sidelock R1 side-by-side the pinnacle of the gunmaker's art. More impressive, whereas most makers in Italy have used English actions, primarily Holland and Holland, as their foundations, Rizzini developed and patented its own sidelock, single trigger, automatic ejector model. These very original guns are renowned for their mechanical perfection, execution, and elegant lines. Additionally, the company has master engravers for the final embellishments. Only a few dozen guns are created each year, with an understandably long delivery time. (Do

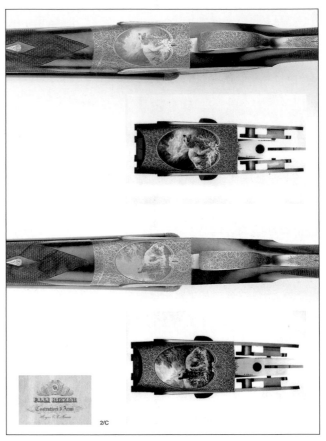

▲ Some Cognoscenti believe the Rizzini R1 is the greatest side-by-side in the world.

not confuse these with the B. Rizzinis, noted earlier and which are produced en masse.)

In their workshops, the Rizzini brothers oversee just a few talented craftsmen. Brother Guido was the mastermind of the company, and it was he who was directly responsible for most of the maker's patents. www.fllirizzini.it They are imported into America by William Larkin Moore and have been for a long time.

Marocchi

Marocchi is a well-known and respected name amongst the Italian gunmakers and has been manufacturing guns since 1922. Today, the company has a large full-time staff and many subcontractors making the firm a big one by Italian standards. Though it has produced many types of firearms over the years, including an award-winning compressed-air rifle, it is primarily known for its excellent line of over/under competition shotguns. www.marocchiguns.com

The Guild System

The finest Italian gunmakers have always come from the Val Trompia region of north-central Italy, a bit east of Milan, with Brescia as its southern pole and Gardone its northern. This area beneath the Alps survives largely on the guild system, which dates back to the Middle Ages.

A guild is a loose grouping of manufacturers and craftsmen (e.g., barrel makers, engravers, and so on), who work together to produce a finished product. In this manner, a small maker can exchange his services with those of the other guild members, thereby allowing him access to the best components.

It should be noted that, in many cases, several engravers collaborate on a single gun. One engraver might do the scroll and contours, while another does the Bulino work on the sideplates. On my beautifully engraved, mechanically defective Famars, Sabatti did the deep-chiseled engraving, while the artist Terzi performed the Bulino work.

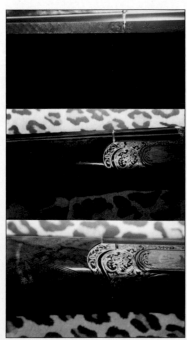

▲ Three images showing the separation of the barrels, the rib, and the large gape in the forend metal. Famars, a.k.a. Abbiatico and Salvenelli, is now under new ownership. Hopefully their problems are behind them.

Perazzi

▲ A lot of handwork goes into finishing a Perazzi. No machine produces the end result that hand checkering does.

The Perazzi competition guns are among the best on the market. The detachable trigger assembly houses the locks, and all one has to do is press the safety forward to pull out the works. Some prefer the leaf springs that are not terribly difficult to interchange, while others prefer the coil springs. Interchangeable stocks allow shooters to alter fit at will. (A long, hex-like screwdriver slips through a hole in the recoil pad, making stock swapping relatively painless.) There must be 30 American and European style dimensions available, perhaps more. Certainly, one can also opt to have a custom stock made.

▲ Author shown shooting a pair of SCO sideplate Perazzis. His loader Bully is one of the fastest in the business, shooting at famed Haddeo. Photo courtesy of *The Shooting Gazette* and Charles Sansbury-Claice.

Much credit for the mechanics of these fine guns goes to Daniele Perazzi, but some also to Olympic gold medalist and Daniele's one-time partner Ennio Mattarelli (mentioned above), who took the early Mirage model to gold-medal victory at the 1964 Tokyo Olympic Games. He helped to design the Mirage and establish it in the competition shooter market. Live pigeon, trap, and skeet shooters flocked to the gun.

While most shooters view Perazzis as some of the greatest competition guns of all time, few realize the great beauty of the company's higher-grade guns, where one often sees shimmering artistry in steel and wood and a large selection of fine English scroll, deep-chiseled relief, gamebird scenes, and so on. At the very top, one can have them engraved by master engravers who sign their work. They have recently added a ribless model á la Boss to their lineup, which makes for a very fast, classical shotgun. The ribless model lightens the barrels and is preferred by many game shots.

▲ An elegant engraving pattern on a Perazzi SCO.

The SHO sidelock edition, which was produced only for a limited time, is a true collector's gun, as is the DHO, Perazzi's one very successful attempt aesthetically, if not financially, at a sidelock side-by-side. But that was many years ago. Several decades ago now, it also developed a small-frame over/under game gun; the 28-gauge gun is trim and slick. The one that I field-tested in the mid-1990s had a single trigger that was both selective and non-detachable. www.perazzi.it

▲ Whereas Perazzi competition guns tend to be embellished, beautiful high-end engraving is available both for competition and game guns.

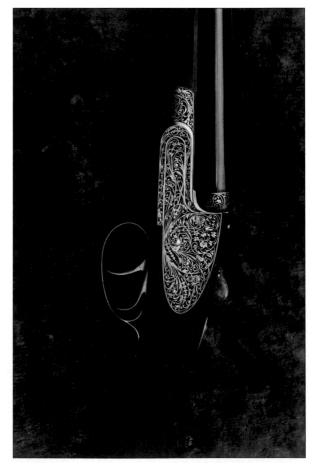

▲ A classic Rizzini sideplate.

▲ A pair of Piottis. Photo courtesy of William Larkin Moore & Sons.

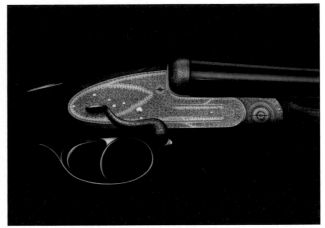

▲ I've always considered side lever shotguns to be especially beautiful. Boss, Grant, and other British makers offered them, but it's most unusual to see in modern Italian makers like this Piotti.

Piotti

The Piotti brothers have long been known for building some of the world's best guns, guns that have been favored by many top European pigeon and target shooters (a Piotti shotgun helped take a gold medal in the 1972 Olympics), as well as by well-heeled game shooters in Europe, Britain, and America. Though the company does make Puma and Westlake boxlocks, it is in its sidelocks that it really shines. The King, the Monte Carlo, the King Extra, the Lunik, and the Monaco models differ primarily in the quality of wood, finish, and engraving.

Piotti is noted for ensuring that through every aspect of its gunmaking its quality standards are maintained. I have read about, but have no idea whether it's apocryphal or not, the company's unique way of testing its buttstocks to make sure they won't crack: After the stock has been headed, it is banged a few times against a concrete floor. Piotti's theory is that if it's ever going to split, it will do so then, thus saving the stockmaker time and the owner inconvenience. www.piotti.com

Renato Gamba

Renato Gamba is another well-established firm from Brescia that works in part of the guild system. This maker's line of guns is broad and includes double rifles, boxlock and sidelock game guns, and over/under competition guns with removable trigger mechanisms. Guns range from the mid-priced to the expensive, with engraving always a critical factor in cost. www.renatogamba.it

Zanotti

This is one of the older names in the Italian gunmaking world as the family's gunmaking dates back to 1625. However, it was Fabio who, in the early part of the twentieth century, brought the name to the forefront with a number of mechanical and aesthetic innovations to his well-known model 34 and Thomas side-by-sides. It was one of the earliest of the Italian gunmakers to be recognized abroad, as its guns won a number of international competitions.

Fabio died in 1971, leaving the company to his son Stefano. In 1984, Zanotti merged with Renato Gamba. In recent manufacture, one will see guns labeled Fabio Zanotti da Bologna, Renato Zanotti, Stefano Zanotti, Zanotti & Gamba, or Zanotti 1625, and that does not include the most recent variations. One can order sidelocks, side-by-side boxlocks, over/unders, or even hammer guns. Most are based on Fabio Zanotti's designs. www.renatogamba.it

CHAPTER 9
Tested Shotguns

Beretta
DT11

▲ DT11 Black Edition. Photo courtesy of Beretta.

I read somewhere that more Olympic medals have been won with Beretta shotguns than that of any other manufacturer. I have not been able to verify this, but I have no reason to doubt it. Beretta has always won more than its share of trophies in all shotgun disciplines. The DT11 has significantly increased the count.

In 2012, the DT11 replaced the DT10 which had been introduced in 2000. Ferdinando Belleri headed the team of designers and engineers who redesigned the DT10 into the DT11, making more than mere cosmetic changes. The DT11 is a premium hand-finished gun, combining the best of ultramodern production methods with Beretta's custom-shop finishing. Indeed, the DT11 comes out of the same custom shop that builds the SO guns. These are state-of-the-art guns are assembled by hand by well-trained craftsmen, ensuring both the integrity of the gun, and that final component that makes a great gun great. For a company that makes a huge number of shotguns is important to realize that it builds just 15 DT11s per day.

The DT11's tri-alloy Steelium barrels has a new bore profile that is truly innovative, with a nearly full-length transitional taper instead of a forcing cone—think of the Greener Chamberless Shotgun. This reduces perceived recoil—you get a softer push—and improves patterns.

▲ DT11 Trap International. Photo courtesy of Beretta.

The trap version generally employs tight fixed chokes with a bore diameter going down to 18.4mm. The Sporter model goes to 18.6mm (a modest backbore) with interchangeable chokes. Either gun can be ordered with fixed or optima HP choke tubes. These extended and flush mounted choke tubes have a long

parallel wall and slow transition that produces beautiful patterns.

▲ DT11 Sporting. Photo courtesy of Beretta.

Ed Anderson, a Master Class shot, shoots Improved Modified and Full. After a lesson I took with Anthony Matarese, he suggested I order a DT11 with 32-inch barrels. I did so with a new DT11 Black (see more below) as, at age 70 and being less strong than I once was, I need a gun a little bit lighter and quicker.

These 12-gauge shotguns are designed specifically for sporting, skeet, and trap, plus an All Competition Shotgun (ACS), which has both an adjustable rib and stock plus the ability to change the gun's balance via weights in the buttstock. Skeet, Trap, and Sporting models have 3-inch chambers; the International Trap model has 2¾-inch chambers. Each version is also available with a clever new adjustable-stock system called the B-Fast. This is the best adjustable stock I've shot in that almost any conceivable cast and drop the shooter desires can be executed. This is facilitated with hardware of exceptional quality.

The DT11 has barrels available from twenty-eight to thirty-four inches, depending on the version. It sports an oil-finished walnut stock and uses a new, improved combination safety and barrel selector. Its canted top-lever works for both right and left-handed shooters, though obviously it opens to the right. A left-handed stock is available, as are custom stock dimensions.

▲ DT11 X-Trap B-Fast. Photo courtesy of Beretta.

The early DT11s with thirty-two-inch barrels came in between eight and three-quarters and nine pounds. Now they come in about eight and one-half pounds (with the buttstock weights in the ACS version, you make it heavier and change the gun's overall balance). The early DT11 models at nine pounds lends itself to a "gun-up mount" (pre-mounted gun) for most, but that is often preferred these days. Beretta re-jigged the action of the DT11 to put more weight between the hands. Some shooters say the gun feels more solid than the DT10. Many shooters love their "old" DT10s. Some of the more recent DT11's are lighter than the earlier shotguns.

DT11 features what is commonly referred to as the "Kersten crossbolt fastening system" previously used on the DT10, but now with a 3mm-wider receiver (there are minor differences with a true Kersten but no point getting that technical). The detachable trigger group (that's what the "DT" stands for), with various stout leaf springs, has pulls coming in from the factory at a crisp 3½ pounds, give or take. Some competitors opt to have it slightly heavier, while some might tune it lighter. With this cross bolt, you should hold the lever to the right until after the barrels are closed and then release it. This is actually true on most shotguns, but particularly important on this design. The gun will stay tight longer.

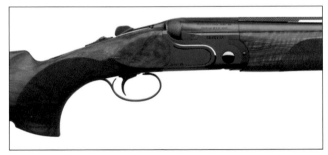

▲ DT11 Black Edition. Photo courtesy of Beretta.

The tri-alloy barrels are made by a new process that is a combination of deep drilling followed by hammer-forging, and, finally, vacuum stress-relieving to a mirror finish. "Beretta refined the Steelium process to elongate the forcing cones. There is no sudden forcing-cone constriction in front of the chamber as the shot pellets travel into the barrel. Steelium Pro has basically turned the bore into a continuous forcing cone that gently flows to the muzzle. The DT11's bore size is 0.767 in front of the forcing cones and then gradually tapers to 0.725 behind the chokes (0.725-inch = 18.4mm) only for the trap version. For the Sporting

barrels, the internal bore diameter is 18.6 mm = 0.732-inch." Steelium Pro complements the long, slender, Optima-Bore HP screw-in chokes. This combination diminishes perceived recoil, muzzle flip, and shot deformation.

▲ Forcing cones. Photo courtesy of Beretta.

Beretta barrels have a great reputation, which is consistent with the company's attention to its metallurgical processes (there's a dedicated laboratory within the factory). Barrels and other components are regularly subjected to X-ray and other analysis. Indeed, Beretta houses its own branches of the Italian proof house. This scientific approach has always impressed me, as does the great care Beretta takes with ensuring barrel regulation via hand soldering laser aligned barrels.

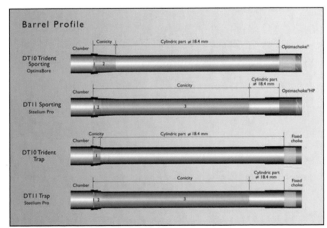

▲ Beretta barrels. Courtesy of Beretta.

The ventilated top rib is 10mm wide and parallel in the trap model, but tapers from 10mm to 8mm for the other models. Side ribs are also vented, to reduce both weight and heat haze. The ACS has a B-Fast rib that is adjustable for point of impact.

Now to the important part: how it shoots. In three words: *like a dream*. I did add a bit of weight to the buttstock not to make it heavier, with weights provided with the shotgun, but to change the balance. This worked very well for me. The long thirty-two-inch barrels on my test gun sliced through the air like a rapier. (You don't want to reduce the weight the front too much or add too much to the back for any gun, or muzzle flip will be exaggerated and you never want the barrels so light that they get whippy. The balance point should be around the hinge pin–give or take depending on individual preferences.) The combination of boring to reduce perceived recoil and the overall weight of the gun, made the recoil not just manageable, but psychologically negligible. This was also aided by a superb trigger. It wasn't just how quickly, and perhaps more important, accurately, I could get on the first target, but also how quickly and decisively I could move to the second bird. The choking and improved bore definitely worked, as the clays were turned to powder. The palm swell and well-designed radiused grip gave excellent control and comfort. For a top-of-the-line gun for serious competition, one cannot do better.

One final word: For me, the big recent additions to the Beretta lineup of fantastic guns are the Black models, which all feature reduced weight. The truth is, while I find the DT11 to be a great gun, I am just not strong enough at 70 to shoot it for long periods the way I once would have. I find the DT11 in the Black version, perfect for me—fast but not whippy. I can adjust the weight and balance to perfection for my style and preferences—and all shooters using this gun have the same option. Whether you shoot sustained lead or pull away or combination of both, this gun is a dream to shoot.

▲ DT11 Sporting.

Manufacturer:	Beretta
Model:	DT11 Sporting
Action:	over/under
Stock:	walnut
Barrel:	30, 32 in.
Chokes:	Optima-Bore HP
Weight:	9 lbs.
Bore/Gauge:	12
Capacity:	2
MSRP:	$8,999–$13,450

The DT11 Black Sporting

Well, I finally bit the bullet and bought the clay gun of my dreams.

The DT11 dominated the last Olympics with ten of the fifteen medals available to win in shotgunning sports. But at 70, I'm no longer strong enough to handle standard DT11. Lucky for me, the recently introduced DT11 black comes in at about three-quarters of a pound lighter . . . eight pounds give or take depending on barrel length, stock choice, density of wood. etc.

I picked the model with the adjustable stock. Besides being able to get a custom fit it myself, this configuration also allows me to shoot more than one game with the same gun–I generally have it set up for sporting clays at 60/40 but I could use it for trap or boxed pigeon simply by raising the comb thus raising the point of impact.

I have spent a lot of time with the gun on the patterning board, indeed, much more than I normally would. Ed Anderson set the cast as I desired one-quarter inch at the face, but as it is so easy to change drop, I decided I would work on that on my own.

As delivered it shot dead on–50/50 which is the way a lot of shooters like their guns set. I prefer 60/40 as mentioned above and it took just a few moments to add the wafers to the right height to get that point of impact.

The gun was a little bit short for me with the originally installed pad—the thinnest Beretta makes. Beretta offers four different thicknesses of recoil pads and I bought the 2 thickest, so I was quickly able to correct the length of pull. (In the summer, I will shoot with the

▲ The author test-fires a DT11.

Stepping up to top-of-the-line Fiocchi's, Federal's or Winchester's AA's gave what can only be described as brilliant patterns. The gun shoots slightly narrower patterns than one would normally expect for the given choke designation. For example the width/diameter on IC is about what one would expect on a modified barrel. But I think this is not so much a factor of mislabeling as it is the lack of flyers that tend to inhabit the outer three inches of a patterning plate.

▲ The DT11 black sports a very well-designed full grip, which competition shooters require.

1.1-inch pad and in the fall or winter when wearing more clothes can switch easily to the .9-inch pad.)

The gun throws amazing patterns. With all the different chokes the point of impact on both barrels is identical or at least so close that I can't see any difference. Beyond that the patterns this gun throws are astonishing. Normally, I don't get too excited about new terms and names for barrels or chokes or what have you, but Beretta has devised the absolute paradigm for pattern perfection. There are hardly any flyers and drastically reduced barrel scrub deformation because of the Steelium barrel design.

I have shot it with inexpensive shells purchased on special at Gander Mountain and Dicks and these gave beautiful patterns although some of the Rio cartridges were misshapen /unable to be chambered and one was completely missing a primer, can you believe it?

Now to its handling: We all develop muscle memory in our shooting. A lot of this is directly linked to the gun we shoot with–weight, fit, and balance all contributing factors. In the 1980s and 1990s, I primarily shot with two competition guns. A light K-80 that had been custom choked and tuned for me by the late great Ken Eyster, and a Perazzi Sporting Clay Gun that was a gift from Daniele Perazzi. When I moved to Ireland I sold the Krieghoff and regret it to this day as I won a sporting clay championship with it at Casa de Campo one year, and a number of other events both in sporting and skeet. I had sub-gauge tube sets from Briley for the gun and that was reason enough to keep it. But I sold it as I just didn't see myself doing much clay shooting at that point. I did shoot the Perazzi often when in America. It required a bit of time to adjust to the new gun. Sometimes you have to go down to go up. But the gun is quick. The barrels, as I mentioned before, slice through air like a knife through butter and do so without getting whippy which is what often happens if the barrels are too light compared to the butt stock—this most often occurs when the balance is just too far back.

I was going to go and take another lesson from Anthony Matarese, not only one of America's greatest shots but also one of its greatest coaches. When I mentioned to Anthony that I was having a bit of a problem adjusting to the gun when I first started shooting it, he said that is a common occurrence. He went on to say that it took him a year to switch to his new DT11 and be completely happy with it but one must remember that he was shooting an autoloader up to that point. But he did win the World Championship in 2016 with his DT11. Strong and young. . . . I now shoot My DT11 Black better than I shot any gun; at least at the super veteran stage of life.

The fit and finish of the gun are outstanding. The checkering is sharp and crisp. The radius of the pistol grip is a little tighter than I would like but that is easily remedied. Remember, I am used to shooting a Prince of Wales, a.k.a. semi pistol grip as found on the old Belgian Browning's. I used to the Prince of Wales grip because I shoot more driven game than clay targets and have done so for the last twenty years.

Carbon fiber is the secret ingredient that makes this gun light. It is used in the rib, and in the trigger housing. Besides being light it is durable and looks fine on the shotgun.

▲ The gun is perfectly balanced between my hands. Notice the left hand and finger placement. Right-hand forefinger is correctly placed on the trigger.

Detachable triggers are great. You can carry a spare and should the unthinkable happen and you have a problem, in a matter of seconds the problem is fixed. If you're serious tournament shooter, while not inexpensive, I always think an extra trigger is a great idea. (A

tool kit comes with a gun which allows one to change springs etc.)

The chokes that came standard with it are beautifully designed extended chokes that are color-coded as well is marked. But Beretta also makes flush chokes and even longer extended chokes specifically for this gun. I have switched to the matching black chokes which I prefer as it is one fewer things for my left eye to notice at the front of the gun. While the normal DT11 shooters often go to titanium choke tubes to reduce weight in the barrels, simply because the gun is heavy, as light as the Black DT11 gun is, it's probably better to balance the gun as you desire by adding weight to the butt stock; titanium chokes are not needed.

Remington

Model 1100 Competition Synthetic
The gas piston-operated Remington 1100 is near and dear to my heart. After all, it was my second autoloading shotgun (my first was a Browning Auto-5), and, amazingly, it was purchased with Green Stamps collected by my mother, I believe from A&P stores, when I was about 13. Can you imagine going back to a time and a world where one could redeem points at a supermarket for shotguns?

One didn't have many choices with this gun back then. It came with a plain barrel in Full choke, which I still have. I did have, at some point, a ventilated rib added aftermarket by the old Abercrombie and Fitch.

▲ A close-up of the Remington 1100 Sporting. With the help of my friend Charlie Conger, who won the New York State Sporting Clays championships twice and worked for Remington for a number of years, we adjusted the comb for me and the length of pull in a couple of minutes.

I believe it was made by Simmons, but I would hate to have to swear to it after all these years. To make the stock long enough for me over the years as I grew, I added recoil pads with extra spacers, and I had the comb heightened with moleskin. I tweaked the added height off to the side a bit to give it some cast.

When I got a bit older, but still a teenager, I purchased a skeet barrel with a ventilated rib for my 1100, and I still occasionally shoot that gun for skeet. Indeed, it is the only gun I bought before I was 25 that I still own. I broke my first 25 straight at skeet, and my first 25 straight at trap with its full choke barrel. I recall that, at some point, it was the gun of choice for most of the serious skeet competitors in 12-gauge. It made sense. An autoloader, especially one gas-operated, does have much less felt/perceived recoil than a fixed-breech gun. (Think push versus punch in terms of perceived recoil.) So, while many national champions use over/unders with multiple barrel sets or tubed over/unders, in the sub-gauge events, the Remington 1100 was and probably still is the choice of many American skeet champions in the 12-gauge event.

Some people have occasionally complained about ejection problems with this gun, but there are two little holes under the fore-end ring and, if they are cleaned out occasionally with an old-fashioned pipe cleaner, I find that is all it takes to keep the shells cycling. I have shot it with light 1-ounce target loads and 1½-ounce magnum loads. Obviously, once in a while the action needs to be removed and properly cleaned. Not a difficult job by gunsmithing standards. You should know whether you can handle it or need to give it to a gunsmith.

Over the years, the Remington 1100 has been offered in many different gauges, including 28-gauge and .410-bore for skeet, a Magnum model with 3-inch chambers for waterfowling, a Youth model with scaled-down stock and barrel length, a slug gun, Ducks Unlimited Special Editions, and the list goes on. Some had relatively short runs, others were produced for decades. Certainly, it must be the most successful American design and manufactured autoloader.

On top of all this, the gun shoots very well. I don't know whether it is the balance, the shape, or some combination thereof, but it is just an easy gun to shoot well, for both novice and champion. Some individuals

▲ I am seen here with my Remington 1100. Note the adjustable composite stock.

shoot over/unders better than autoloaders at sporting clays, and for other shooters, the autoloader is the preferred gun. If you are a person who prefers autoloaders, this is one you simply must try.

If the gun had one fault, it was aesthetic, not functional. Plain Jane wood coupled with stamped checkering was common on most models. The new competition synthetic model's receiver is nickel-coated, and many of the internal parts are nickel-Teflon-coated, the latter to ensure greater reliability and smoothness of the working parts. The stock is a dark synthetic, and, overall, if handsome is as handsome does, this gun is gorgeous.

If Beretta's DT11 is my choice of over/under for competition, this is my first choice in an autoloader for sporting clays.

The Model 1100 Competition Synthetic I've been shooting for a while is, without doubt, one of the finest auto-loaders ever designed with the competitive shooter in mind. The new design is simply faster in the hands than the old, and while the pistol grip looks too severely angled, it actually fits the hand very well and gives great control.

One of the first days I shot the gun, my friend Charlie Conger, who field tests guns for Remington amongst other hats he has worn for that company, wound up on the same skeet field as I did. We had a patterning board close by, and Charlie quickly adjusted the height and cast of the shotgun's comb so the gun fit me like a glove. (With the ability to adjust cast, a lefty can set this up with cast on.) Also, because the stock can be adjusted so quickly for height and point of impact, it would be no trick at all to shoot it one day at skeet or sporting clays and have it set to shoot fairly flat, and the next day raise the height of the comb so that the gun shoots high and put in good scores at the trap field.

While the 1100 has always been known as a soft-shooting gun, I was not prepared for just how true that was with the Competition Synthetic. Between the recoil-reducing stock system and the gas operation, this must be one of the most pleasant 12-gauge shotguns of all time.

This new gun really is made with the serious competitor in mind. The trigger on the gun I tested is great, and a good trigger goes a long way toward improving how one shoots. The 30-inch barrel is over bored, the forcing cones have been lengthened, and extended Briley choke tubes are standard. There's a 10mm ventilated rib, and a center bead is also standard. While it does weigh a bit over eight pounds, it is a very quick gun.

Manufacturer:	Remington
Model:	1100 Competition Synthetic
Action:	semiautomatic
Stock:	synthetic
Barrel:	30 in.
Chokes:	five extended Briley
Weight:	8 lbs. 2 oz.
Bore/Gauge:	12
Capacity:	4+1
MSRP:	$1,305

Versa Max

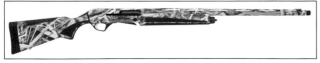

▲ The Versa Max has one of the most reliable systems for cycling cartridges from 2¾ inches standard to 3 ½-inch behemoths.

Gas and inertia autoloaders have existed for a long time. Shotguns that are gas fed are cycled by the pressure of the gasses expended by the fired shell, rather than inertia as found on, for example, the Browning Auto-5. Gas has historically been siphoned through ports, commonly two, placed under the barrel at the barrel ring where the gas enters a cylinder forcing back the piston. Via a rod, the piston unlocks and pushes back the bolt, ejecting the spent cartridge while the next cartridge is carried up and placed in front of the bolt for chambering now you are ready to go (an oversimplified, but sufficient explanation). This is how the gun cycles, something that transpires in a fraction of second.

Today, the challenge faced in autoloader design is to create a system that enables the shotgun to cycle a light game or target load and then a heavy load without jamming and while maintaining the soft-shooting characteristics for which most appreciate a semiautomatic in the first place. Various manufacturers have designed different mechanisms to deal with cartridges at the light and heavy extremes of the scale with equal reliability. Some have worked better than others, but it was Remington that completely changed the gas system when it introduced the Versa Max in 2010.

Rather than placing the gas ports far up the barrel, Remington bored eight ports along the chamber. The idea was simple: "elegant" is the way a scientist would describe it. A long cartridge case would cover all but three ports when the gun was fired, whereas a 2¾-inch case would leave all the ports exposed, thus allowing the maximum amount of gas to escape through the ports and work the action. A 3-inch shell leaves four ports exposed. As the 3½-inch shells generate more energy than the 3-inch and more again than the 2¾-inch, the correct amount of gas was siphoned to work the action regardless of the cartridge being shot, and that allows one to shoot a 1-ounce target load followed by a 3½-inch maximum power turkey load and back to the target load without unloading, reloading, switching rings, or jamming the action because of a failure to eject.

I have shot the Versa Max with 1-ounce target loads and 3½-inch HEVI-Shot, and the gun performed flawlessly, even alternating heavy and light loads and regardless of whatever order randomly used, and the gun cycled perfectly.

Replacing the large piston and linkage long associated with previous designs are a pair of small pistons placed close to the breech and housed on the underside of the barrel. The gas ports are just at the front of the chamber.

▲ 3½-inch loads produce very significant recoil. A gas-operated system that takes some of the punch out is extremely helpful, especially when coupled with the first class recoil pad.

One problem with autoloaders is that, if they aren't cleaned properly, at some stage the fouling from fired shells negatively affects ejection. This Versa Max design will work past the point where earlier models will not, but that doesn't mean that you should not maintain and clean your gun as needed. What it does mean is that it gives you a little extra breathing room.

Proper cleaning and maintenance is required for all shotguns, especially autoloaders, but this gun is much easier to deal with than most and it comes with an excellent instruction book and some tools. With a wrench provided in the toolkit, it takes only a few minutes to remove, clean, and finally replace the pistons. Similarly, this is the easiest trigger mechanism I've ever seen on an autoloader to take out and put back in; a single pin does it. Whether you purchase the camo Versa Max like I did or the plain black version, you will find Remington's Trinyte blacking on the barrel exterior and the trigger mechanism offer significantly better resistance to rust and saltwater corrosion than the normal bluing.

Remington provides shims and plates that allow the length of pull to be adjusted from 14¼ to 15¼ inches. This is great! For instance, if you hunt sea ducks or in colder, northern climes, you will need a shorter stock than you'd use for, say, dove shooting in shirtsleeves or for skeet practice in a light clays vest, and this stock lets you make that adjustment. Out-of-the-box stock dimensions will work for the mythical "average shooter," but realize that the gun that fits you and shoots where you look will always allow you to perform to your best abilities in the field.

Remington's Versa Max offers a number of recoil-reducing features. A soft-rubber comb offered real dampening to the recoil felt at the face. The soft butt-pad ameliorated some of the effects of tremendous recoil from 3½-inch magnum loads. The over-molded forend and pistol grip help keep a secure grip, and the oversized, well-placed safety (located at the rear of the trigger guard), made for easy handling, even when wearing heavy gloves for waterfowling. Also regarding glove use, the trigger guard is large and well-proportioned. The gun weighs 7¾ pounds unloaded, which works well for a shotgun designed to handle 3½-inch cartridges; you wouldn't want it any lighter.

▲ The softgel top of comb insert helps ameliorate the effects of heavy loads on one's cheek and neck.

I have shot a lot of waterfowl with this gun over the last few seasons, primarily mallard, but also Canada geese and teal— one extreme of size to the other. I find the 3½ inch loads offer a great advantage in lethality on big birds like Canada geese. At the same time, I see no reason to beat myself up on a duck as small as a teal, especially at close range and if they are decoying well, so comparatively light 2¾-inch cartridges were perfect for small bird waterfowling. My Versa Max has performed admirably across the spectrum of shotshell power and payloads and a wide variety of hunting conditions.

While the gun comes with five different choke tubes, I generally leave the Modified choke in and it seems to do the trick for most flying things that I shoot. I do put on the Predator choke when coyote hunting.

I fiddled with the gun a bit to get it to fit me. The correct length of pull with all the clothes I had on was just about 14¾ inches. I like some cast, and a quarter of an inch does nicely. Once I made these changes, not terribly time-consuming, the gun shot where I looked, and I must say I really enjoy shooting it from a blind.

While it is a long gun overall, it still weighs less than most of my sporting clay or skeet guns. I found it both quick and precise, and it tamed recoil from even the heaviest magnum, allowing me to get back on target quickly for second and third shots.

Set up as it is in camouflage, and being drilled and tapped for an optical sight, the Versa Max accommodates turkey season as easily as it does duck and goose season. All you need to do is pick the right cartridge, shoot it as is or add an optical dotted sight, and you are all ready to go. It's actually like getting two guns for the price of one. (Good thing, for this is not an inexpensive gun.) I have also used it a few times to shoot clays just to get a feel for the gun, and I must admit I shot better scores than I expected with it. Now if I could just talk Remington into adding a rifled barrel for slugs to go along with the drilled and tapped receiver, it would be phenomenal value for money!

Manufacturer:	Remington
Model:	Versa Max
Action:	semiautomatic
Stock:	synthetic
Barrel:	26, 28 in.
Chokes:	up to five flush-mount pro chokes, depending on model
Weight:	7 lbs. 8 oz.–7lbs. 11 oz.
Bore/Gauge:	12
Capacity:	3+1
MSRP:	$1,066–$1,765

BERETTA

690 Field III, 692 Sporting Black Edition

Recently, both the 690 and 692 have had some modifications to make them even better handling guns in the normal version.

For game shooters, the 690 Field III deserves a close look. It comes with oil-finished, higher-grade wood and twenty-six- or twenty-eight-inch barrels with three-inch chambers.

The 692 Sporting and International Trap Black Editions and the 690 Black editions have many of the same features as the DT11, including balancing systems on the barrels, forends, and buttstocks plus carbon-fiber ribs and side-porting to reduce weight. Both are much less expensive than the DT11, but still offer a first-class clay gun for serious competitors.

Manufacturer:	Beretta
Model:	690 Field III
Action:	over/under
Stock:	wood
Barrel:	26, 28, 30 in.
Chokes:	5 OptiChoke HP
Weight:	20-gauge 6 lbs. 3 oz.; 12-gauge 7 lbs. 6 oz.
Bore/Gauge:	20, 12
Capacity:	2
MSRP:	$3,475

Manufacturer:	Beretta
Model:	692 Sporting Black Edition
Action:	over/under
Stock:	walnut
Barrel:	30, 32 in.
Chokes:	5 OptiChoke HP
Weight:	7 lbs. 8 oz.
Bore/Gauge:	12
Capacity:	2
MSRP:	$5,250–$5,750

1301 Tactical

With its aluminum receiver and gas-operated action, Beretta's 1301 Tactical should prove to be a coyote-killing machine. An extended tube can be bought aftermarket, and its addition enables the installation of a secondary Picatinny rail. (As Beretta points out on its website, "NOTE FOR U.S. CUSTOMERS: In conformance to federal law, the magazine-extension tube is available only as an after-market accessory that the customer may purchase separately and install.") An oversized charging handle, bolt release, and safety are standard.

Beretta's tactical shotgun should work for almost any shooters' requirements, as the stock is adjustable for length of pull with provided spacers. Drop and cast are also adjustable. For added flexibility, the receiver offers a MIL-STD 1913 Picatinny rail. The gun comes with an 18½-inch barrel, three-inch chambers in 12-gauge, and a fixed Cylinder choke. This also makes for a great home defense gun.

Manufacturer:	Beretta
Model:	1301 Tactical
Action:	semiautomatic
Stock:	synthetic
Barrel:	18½ in.
Chokes:	fixed Cylinder
Weight:	7 lbs. 2 oz.
Bore/Gauge:	12
Capacity:	5+1
MSRP:	$1,075

A300 Outlander Turkey

The Beretta A300 Outlander Turkey is a reliable solution for shotgunners who want a Beretta and all its legendary reliability, but in an economical package. It comes with a twenty-four-inch barrel, a three-inch chamber, and Realtree Xtra camo on its stock and hardware. Fitted with TruGlo fiber optic sights and drilled and tapped for optic attachment, this shotgun also comes with sling attachment studs and a reversible safety.

Manufacturer:	Beretta
Model:	A300 Outlander Turkey
Action:	semiautomatic
Stock:	synthetic
Barrel:	24 in.
Chokes:	3 (F, M, IC)
Weight:	7 lbs. 9 oz.
Bore/Gauge:	12
Capacity:	3+1
MSRP:	$900

A400 Xtrema Max 5

Beretta A400 Xtreme is always a great choice for hunters pursuing large birds as thus semiauto is just as suitable for bagging a tom as a goose. The 3½-inch magnum is largely tamed by Beretta's third-generation Kick-Off dampening system that uses hydraulics built into the stock to reduce perceived recoil by about 60 percent. This very popular A400 autoloader is now available and left-handed versions as well.

Manufacturer:	Beretta
Model:	A400 Xtreme Max 5
Action:	semiautomatic
Stock:	synthetic
Barrel:	26, 28, 30 in.; left-hand models are available in 28-inch only
Chokes:	3 Optima-Bore HP
Weight:	7 lbs. 8 oz.–7 lbs. 12 oz.
Bore/Gauge:	12
Capacity:	2 + 1
MSRP:	$1,900; left-hand $1,950

Benelli

828U

At 6½ pounds in 12-gauge, and even with its recoil-reduction stock that Benelli calls its "Progressive Comfort System," I would be judicious before going to the heaviest loads. Still, a very nice feature of the stock is its shim set, which allows a virtual custom fit for drop and cast.

One of the reasons the gun is so light is that it does come with an alloy receiver in a choice of engraved nickel or anodized finishes. The top tang safety is automatic, which I find a pain on the clay field, but which makes sense to those who primarily shoot game. The trigger assembly drops out for easy cleaning. Currently, 26- and 28-inch barrels are available. Choke tubes and AA grade Walnut stock are standard.

Manufacturer:	Benelli
Model:	828U
Action:	over/under
Stock:	walnut
Barrel:	26, 28 in.
Chokes:	five Crio Choke (C, IC, M, IM, F)
Weight:	6 lbs. 8 oz.
Bore/Gauge:	12
Capacity:	2
MSRP:	$2,499–$2,999

Performance Shop SBE II Turkey Edition

This autoloading turkey gun, available in both 20- and 12-gauge, comes from Benelli's Performance Shop. While a top-of-the-line turkey gun, it is easily adapted to predator hunting and comes with many cool features, including a custom-tuned trigger, a very tight custom Rob Roberts choke tube for turkeys or predator, and a pre-sighted Burris FastFire II optic. These guns are test-fired at the factory for accuracy and reliability—and with a price tag of more than three grand for the 12-gauge, should be.

Manufacturer:	Benelli
Model:	Performance Shop SBE II Turkey Edition
Action:	semiautomatic
Stock:	synthetic
Barrel:	24 in.
Chokes:	Extra-Full turkey
Weight:	7 lbs. 2 oz.
Bore/Gauge:	12
Capacity:	3+1
MSRP:	$3,399

Performance Shop M2 Waterfowl Edition

This waterfowl-specific model comes as a 20- or 12-gauge with a 3-inch chamber and will meet the needs of the most dedicated waterfowl hunter. It comes standard with Benelli's ultra-reliable Inertia Driven system, lengthened forcing cones, polished action and a custom-tuned trigger group. The large bolt handle is

well suited for gloved hands. According to the Benelli website, "Waterfowl Edition models are test-fired with a computerized pattern analysis to ensure consistent and even patterns." Most impressive.

Manufacturer:	Benelli
Model:	Performance Shop M2 Waterfowl Edition
Action:	semiautomatic
Stock:	synthetic
Barrel:	28 in.
Chokes:	three Rob Roberts Triple Threat
Weight:	20-gauge 5 lbs. 14 oz.; 12-gauge 7 lbs. 8 oz.
Bore/Gauge:	12
Capacity:	3+1
MSRP:	20-gauge $2,399; 12-gauge $2,699

Vinci Tactical

This autoloader wears an 18½-inch barrel and has a four-round capacity including one in the chamber. It features a Picatinny rail on the receiver, but does not have one on the bottom of the fore-end, which is a shame. That said, once again one can go the Brownells route and add one. This handy defense or smoothbore old-style Foster slug gun shoots 12-gauge 2¾-inch and 3-inch cartridges. Buyers can choose between the standard stock and a pistol grip. Either should make a great coyote or pest-control shotgun.

Manufacturer:	Benelli
Model:	Vinci Tactical Shotgun
Action:	semiautomatic
Stock:	synthetic
Barrel:	18½ in.
Chokes:	three (IC, M, F)
Weight:	6 lbs. 11 oz.
Bore/Gauge:	12
Capacity:	3+1
MSRP:	$1,499–$1,599

Blaser

F16

The Blaser F16 from Germany is a quality over/under with a loyal following. Blaser offered to send me a four-barrel set to field test and return, but time constraints precluded an in-depth analysis. Nonetheless, here are the goods on this gun.

Blaser states that it's lowered the F16's center of gravity with a redesigned and shallow boxlock action. In theory, this should make for a fast gun, but without the above-mentioned field test, it would just be conjecture on my part. Much of the design almost gives it the look of a round action.

The F16 features a Triplex bore. (Everyone and their mother seem to give a new name for how they bore their barrels these days. Why everyone cannot just use the term "over bored" for their barrels or give a diameter .740, for example, I don't know.) The F16's trigger is set at about 3½ pounds, light for some shooters, and heavy for others, but acceptable to most. From what I've seen on gun store shelves, fit and finish seem to be excellent. Three versions are offered, Game (Standard, Grande Luxe, and Heritage grades), Sporting (same three grades), and the designed-for-women Intuition in Game and Sporting versions. The Game gun has a 14¾-inch length of pull—this is longer than standard—and a choice of 28- or 30-inch barrels. The Sporting version comes with 30- or 32-inch barrels and the ability to change the gun's balance via the Stock Balancing System, and its trigger is adjustable for length of pull.

Manufacturer:	Blaser
Model:	F16 Game
Action:	over/under
Stock:	walnut
Barrel:	28, 30 in.
Chokes:	Blaser flush
Weight:	7 lbs. 11 oz.
Bore/Gauge:	12
Capacity:	2
MSRP:	starting at $3,795

Browning

A5 Sweet Sixteen

Browning has reintroduced its Sweet Sixteen, but it is dramatically different from the old Belgian version. What it does share with the original is its lightness— just under 6 pounds—making it most pleasant for a day carrying it in the uplands.

Manufacturer:	Browning
Model:	A5 Sweet Sixteen
Action:	semiautomatic
Stock:	Turkish walnut
Barrel:	28 in.
Chokes:	three Invector-DS (F, M, IC)
Weight:	5 lbs. 13 oz.
Bore/Gauge:	16
Capacity:	4+1
MSRP:	$1,699.99

Maxus All-Purpose Hunter—Mossy Oak Break-Up Country

The Maxus All-Purpose Hunter, in Mossy Oak Break-Up Country features a Dura-Touch camo finish composite stock, an aluminum alloy receiver, and a magnetic HiViz fiber optic front sight. Its Dura-Touch Armor Coating, which provides a good gripping surface even when wet, ensures this 3½-inch-chambered gun can take on the toughest conditions a waterfowler could find himself in. It's also a flexible gun: Browning's Power Drive gas system cycles a wide range of loads from 2¾- to 3½-inch magnum loads. The Lightning Trigger offers a particularly fast trigger lock time for an autoloader.

Manufacturer:	Browning
Model:	Maxus All-Purpose Hunter— Mossy Oak Break-Up Country
Action:	semiautomatic
Stock:	composite
Barrel:	26 in.
Chokes:	three Invector-Plus
Weight:	7 lbs. 1 oz.
Bore/Gauge:	12
Capacity:	4 +1
MSRP:	$1,739.99

BPS Rifled Deer Hunter

Southpaws looking for a pump gun that doesn't eject hulls towards them should consider the BPS. Like Ithaca, shells feed and eject from the bottom. It is available in 3-inch 20- and 12-gauge with a 22-inch rifled, thick-walled slug barrel ideal for sabot slugs. A top tang safety, walnut stock, sling swivel studs, and top cantilever scope mount round out the package.

Manufacturer:	Browning
Model:	BPS Rifled Deer Hunter
Action:	pump
Stock:	walnut
Barrel:	22 in.
Chokes:	screw-in tubes
Weight:	7 lbs. 4 oz.–7 lbs. 10 oz.
Bore/Gauge:	20, 12
Capacity:	4+1
MSRP:	20-gauge $839.99; 12-gauge $829.99

725 Citori Field

The 725 Citori is one of the most popular over/unders around, and recently Browning has added Sporting and Field versions chambered for 28-gauge and .410-bore. With the 725, Browning designed a lower-profile action, considered an improvement over previous Citoris. The Sporting version has ported barrels in 30- or 32-inch configurations. The Field version comes with shorter barrels, your choice of 26- or 28-inch. Both feature a glossy, though understated, oil finish.

Manufacturer:	Browning
Model:	Citori 725 Field
Action:	over/under
Stock:	walnut
Barrel:	26, 28, 30 in. (30-in. 12-gauge only)
Chokes:	Invector-DS
Weight:	6 lbs. 7 oz.–7 lbs. 8 oz.
Bore/Gauge:	12, 20, 28, .410
Capacity:	2
MSRP:	$2,469.99–$2,539.99

Manufacturer:	Browning
Model:	Citori 725 Sporting
Action:	over/under
Stock:	walnut
Barrel:	28, 30, 32 in.
Chokes:	Invector-DS
Weight:	6 lbs. 4 oz.–7 lbs. 10 oz.
Bore/Gauge:	12, 20, 28, .410
Capacity:	2
MSRP:	$3,069.99–$3,199.99

Cynergy Ultimate Turkey Mossy Oak Break-Up Country

The Browning Cynergy Ultimate Turkey Mossy Oak Break-Up Country is an over/under that should be equally at home on turkey or wildfowl, assuming one uses the correct amount of choking. It is chambered to handle the devastating 3½-inch load—just realize that means it's a killer on two sides. You get terminal ballistics, but with the price of recoil that's more apparent in a fixed-breech gun.

This Cynergy features a stock which is adjustable for drop. Vector Pro lengthened forcing cones coupled with Extended Ultimate Full Turkey and Spreader choke tubes make this a useful gun in various situations. It is also supplied with three flush-fit Invector-Plus choke tubes (F, M, and IC). Since this is intended for turkeys, a Marble Arms Bullseye rear sight with a fiber-optic front sight are included, though they can be supplanted with a short 1913 rail suitable for a small red-dot optic. (Note: For waterfowl, you'll want to remove the rear bull's-eye sight.)

Manufacturer:	Browning
Model:	Cynergy Ultimate Turkey Mossy Oak Break-Up Country
Action:	over/under
Stock:	composite
Barrel:	26 in.
Chokes:	five Invector-Plus chokes
Weight:	7 lbs. 6 oz.
Bore/Gauge:	12
Capacity:	2
MSRP:	$900

Maxus Rifled Deer Stalker

This deer-specific slug gun sports a cantilever scope mount, rifled barrel, aluminum alloy receiver, a composite, matte black stock, a special thick-walled, 22-inch barrel designed exclusively for slugs, and 3-inch chamber. It sports an adjustable stock for length of pull, cast, and drop. The gas-operated semiauto boasts Browning's Power Drive, which reduces recoil and improves cycling across a range of ammunition power levels and payloads, and includes Browning's removable Lightning Trigger, which the company says has a lock time of just 5.2 milliseconds and is up to 24 percent faster than other comparable semiautos.

Manufacturer:	Browning
Model:	Maxus Rifled Deer Stalker
Action:	semiautomatic
Stock:	synthetic
Barrel:	22 in.
Chokes:	Invector-Plus
Weight:	7 lbs. 3 oz.
Bore/Gauge:	12
Capacity:	4+1
MSRP:	$1,519.99

Silver Rifled Deer Matte

A bit more economical, the Silver Rifled Deer Matte also has a 22-inch rifled barrel for sabot type slugs and a cantilever scope, but this 3-inch gas-operated semiauto gets a walnut stock, and a lightweight aluminum alloy receiver.

Manufacturer:	Browning
Model:	Silver Rifled Deer Matte
Action:	semiautomatic
Stock:	walnut
Barrel:	22 in.
Chokes:	Invector-Plus
Weight:	6 lbs. 12 oz.
Bore/Gauge:	12
Capacity:	4+1
MSRP:	$1,199.99

Gold Light 10-Gauge Mossy Oak Break-Up, Shadow Grass Blades

Did someone say 10-gauge? Browning's semiautomatic Gold Light 10-Gauge in Mossy Oak Break-Up Country or Shadow Grass Versions has a receiver made of aluminum alloy and a gas-operated action that reduces recoil. It will cycle all 10-gauge loads up to the massive 3½-inch cartridge. It has a magazine capacity of four, and this plus one in the chamber for five is legal in most places for snow geese in the spring. It can, of course, be plugged for the rest of the waterfowl season. The stock is a weather-resistance composite.

Manufacturer:	Browning
Model:	Gold Light 10-Gauge
Action:	semiautomatic
Stock:	composite
Barrel:	26, 28 in.
Chokes:	Invector-Plus flush
Weight:	9 lbs. 10 oz.
Bore/Gauge:	10
Capacity:	4+1
MSRP:	$1,739.99

Caesar Guerini

Invictus I Trap

The Invictus I Trap model is available as an over/under with 32-inch barrels, an Unsingle with a 34-inch barrel, or a combination of the two. A left-handed model is available for a surcharge of a couple of hundred bucks. Perhaps the nicest feature of this gun is its weight system that allows one to change the balance of the gun to suit individual preferences.

Manufacturer:	Caesar Guerini
Model:	Invictus I Trap
Action:	over/under
Stock:	wood
Barrel:	32 in. double-barrel; 34 in. Unsingle
Chokes:	five MAXIS double-barrel; three MAXIS Unsingle

Weight:	8 lbs. 15 oz. double-barrel; 9 lbs. 5 oz. Unsingle
Bore/Gauge:	12
Capacity:	2
MSRP:	$8,895; combo $11,675

Invictus I Ascent

The unique Invictus I Ascent model is designed for those who like to address their targets with a very upright shooting and head position. It features a medium-profile adjustable comb that is also adjustable and a mid-height 10mm that tapers in width from 10mcf to 8mm. Minimal engraving and a hand-rubbed oil finish stock make this a handsome piece. It is available in left-hand stock configuration for southpaws.

Manufacturer:	Caesar Guerini
Model:	Invictus I Ascent
Action:	over/under
Stock:	wood
Barrel:	30 in., 32 in.
Chokes:	six MAXIS competition
Weight:	8 lbs. 6 oz.
Bore/Gauge:	12
Capacity:	2
MSRP:	$7,950; add $235 for left-hand

Invictus V Sporting

With all the improved durability inherent with the Invictus system's modular locking surfaces and how the barrel and action lock together when closed, the Invictus V Sporting gets the addition of Caesar Guerini's DPS2 trigger system that improves trigger pull weight, its take-up, and its lock time. It is reported to be an ultra-crisp trigger. The V Sporting also gets full-cover sideplate game scene engravings in deep relief in the Italian Ornato style.

Manufacturer:	Caesar Guerini
Model:	Invictus V Sporting
Action:	over/under
Stock:	wood
Barrel:	30, 32 in.
Chokes:	six MAXIS competition
Weight:	8 lbs. 1 oz.–8 lbs. 3 oz.
Bore/Gauge	12
Capacity:	2
MSRP:	$8,975; add $235 for left-hand, $335 for adjustable comb

Gold Edition Ellipse Curve

Recent additions to Caesar Guerini's lineup are the 20- and 28-gauge limited-edition Gold Edition Ellipse Curves. The Ellipse Curve is a round-body action, which the company says makes a more responsive, better handling shotgun. This trim gun in its limited-edition makeup boasts upgraded engraving with gold accents and a high-grade hand-rubbed oil walnut stock.

Manufacturer:	Caesar Guerini
Model:	Gold Edition Ellipse Curve
Action:	over/under
Stock:	wood
Barrel:	28 in.
Chokes:	six MAXIS competition
Weight:	6 lbs. 5 oz.–6 lbs. 10 oz.
Bore/Gauge:	20, 28
Capacity:	2
MSRP:	$7,795

Century Arms

Catamount Fury II

The 12-gauge Catamount Fury II is a gas-operated autoloading shotgun from Century Arms that uses five- or 10-round detachable magazines. Designed for self-defense and certainly a candidate for Three-Gun competition or predator hunting, it has a 20-inch barrel and Picatinny rails both top and bottom for lights, optics, and other accessories, and uses both 2¾- and 3-inch shells.

Manufacturer:	Century Arms
Model:	Catamount Fury II
Action:	semiautomatic
Stock:	synthetic
Barrel:	20 in.
Chokes:	three (F, M, C)
Weight:	8 lbs. 7 oz.
Bore/Gauge:	12
Capacity:	5+1, 10+1
MSRP:	$350

CZ-USA

712 Green G2
CZ-USA has introduced a number of new shotguns in the low to mid-priced range in recent years. Its 712 Green G2 gas-operated semiauto 12-gauge is one. It comes with a Turkish walnut stock and a green anodized receiver, pretty sharp-looking.

Manufacturer:	CZ-USA
Model:	**712 Green G2**
Action:	semiautomatic
Stock:	Turkish walnut
Barrel:	28 in.
Chokes:	five (F, IM, M, IC, C)
Weight:	7 lbs. 5 oz.
Bore/Gauge:	12
Capacity:	4+1
MSRP:	$499

712 Synthetic Camo G2
The 712 Synthetic Camo G2 12-gauge has a polymer stock with Mossy Oak Shadow Grass Blades pattern that CZ touts as being weatherproof. An excellent, economical choice for waterfowl hunters, it could certainly see use for predators as well.

Manufacturer:	CZ-USA
Model:	712 Synthetic Camo G2
Action:	semiautomatic
Stock:	synthetic
Barrel:	28 in.
Chokes:	three extended
Weight:	6 lbs. 11 oz.
Bore/Gauge:	12
Capacity:	4 + 1 shells
MSRP:	$679

Lady Sterling, Southpaw Sterling
CZ's Lady Sterling over/under with 28-inch barrels comes with an adjustable comb, a shorter length of pull, and a steeper pitch to the buttstock to better fit a woman's physique. The Southpaw Sterling has cast-on for lefties and gets longer, 30-inch barrels. The longer barrels will make this gun attractive to left-handed shooters seeking a well-balanced, competent gun for sporting clays that won't break the bank. Both guns handle up to 3-inch 12-gauge shells.

Manufacturer:	CZ-USA
Model:	Lady Sterling
Action:	over/under
Stock:	Turkish walnut
Barrel:	28 in.
Chokes:	five (F, IM, M, IC, C)
Weight:	7 lbs. 8 oz.
Bore/Gauge:	12
Capacity:	2
MSRP:	$1,321

Manufacturer:	CZ-USA
Model:	Southpaw Sterling
Action:	over/under
Stock:	Turkish walnut
Barrel:	30 in.
Chokes:	five (F, IM, M, IC, C)
Weight:	7 lbs. 8 oz.

Bore/Gauge:	12
Capacity:	2
MSRP:	$999

Redhead Premier

The Redhead Premier over/under comes with a single selective trigger, Turkish walnut stock, and five choke tubes, all within $50 either side of $1,000 across four gauges. The .410-bore will come with 28-inch barrels, the other three gauges have the choice of 28 or 26 inches. CZ says this is an all-purpose gun, I say it's a bargain.

Manufacturer:	CZ-USA
Model:	Redhead Premier
Action:	over/under
Stock:	Turkish walnut
Barrel:	26, 28 in.;.410 28 in. only
Chokes:	five flush-mount (F, IM, M, IC, C)
Weight:	6 lbs. 14 oz.
Bore/Gauge:	12, 20, 28, .410
Capacity:	2 shells
MSRP:	$959 (12 and 20); $1,057 (28 and .410)

Sharp Tail

CZ's Sharp Tail side-by-side has color case-hardened finish and is available in 12, 20, 28, and .410. It is offered with sideplates, 28-inch barrels, and extractors rather than ejectors. A new action replaces leaf springs with coil springs, and the one-piece receiver houses independent floating firing pins and coil-spring operated hammers. Expect this one to be durable, and that says a lot for a shotgun in this price range.

Manufacturer:	CZ-USA
Model:	**Sharp Tail**
Action:	side-by-side
Stock:	Turkish walnut
Barrel:	28 in.
Chokes:	five flush

Weight:	6 lbs.–7 lbs. 5 oz.
Bore/Gauge:	12, 20, 28, .410
Capacity:	2
MSRP:	$1,022–$1,229

Fabarm

Axis RS 12 Sporting Black, Axis RS 12 Sporting Q.R.R.

Their Axis RS is a 12-gauge sporting over/under offered in right- and left-handed models and with the choice of 30- or 32-inch barrels. It comes with five interchangeable choke tubes, an adjustable trigger, and a black satin-finished receiver. A variation called the Axis RS Q.R.R. with a tapering rib designed to allow for changes to point of impact. It, too, is available for righties and lefties and boasts 3-inch chambers plus an adjustable comb. These aren't inexpensive shotguns, but certainly choices to consider for those who have been bitten by the sporty clays bug and are looking to upgrade from their first clays guns and get serious about competition.

Manufacturer:	Fabarm
Model:	Axis RS 12 Sporting Black, RS Sporting Q.R.R.
Action:	over/under
Stock:	wood
Barrel:	30, 32 in.
Chokes:	five Exis HP
Weight:	8 lbs. 4 oz.
Bore/Gauge	12
Capacity:	2
MSRP:	$3,215 Sporting Black; $3,695 Q.R.R.

XLR5 Waterfowler Banshee

Fabarm introduced its XLR5 Waterfowler Banshee with a modern gas-operated design. The Tribore HP barrel and accompanying choke tubes are designed for non-toxic loads. The spacious trigger guard and safety are designed for gloved hands. Some protection against salt water is incorporated in the design. The gun's full-coverage Kryptech Banshee camouflage works in a variety of environments and work just as well for turkey season as it does for waterfowl.

Manufacturer:	Fabarm
Model:	XLR5 Waterfowler Banshee
Action:	semiautomatic
Stock:	synthetic
Barrel:	28, 30 in.
Chokes:	four
Weight:	7 lbs.
Bore/Gauge:	12
Capacity:	4+1
MSRP:	$1,695

F.A.I.R.

Iside Prestige Tartargua Gold

This is a new Italian gunmaker (Fabbrica Armi Isidoro Rizzini) on the American scene. Iside is the name of its side-by-sides line. The Iside Prestige Tartargua Gold features case-colored receiver in a number of gauges and styles. The boxlock boasts sideplates for a larger engraving surface. The pushbutton forearm release is a nice touch, and the guns have automatic ejectors and wood buttplates. The Tartargua Gold comes in 3-inch chambered 12- and 20-gauge; or 2¾-inch 16- and 28- gauge plus .410-bore. Barrels across all gauges are offered in 26¾, 28, or 30 inches.

Model:	Iside Prestige Tartargua Gold
Action:	side-by-side
Stock:	wood
Barrel:	26¾, 28, 30 in.
Chokes:	five
Weight:	6 lbs. 2 oz.–6 lbs. 10 oz.
Bore/Gauge:	12, 16, 20, 28, .410
Capacity:	2
MSRP:	$2,999

Fausti USA

Aphrodite

Women continue to prevail among new offerings by Italian makers, and Fausti now offers its round-body shotgun designed specifically for the fairer sex and aptly named Aphrodite. It is nicely laser engraved and has a round Prince of Wales grip and automatic ejectors. The 12-, 20-, and 28-gauge and .410-bores are on a boxlock action with a choice of 26-, 28-, or 30-inch barrels across all gauges. Interchangeable chokes are standard on all but the .410, which gets fixed chokes. I viewed this gun at the annual SCI convention and was impressed with the high-grade, hand-oiled walnut stock on the sample.

Manufacturer:	Fausti USA
Model:	Aphrodite
Action:	over/under
Stock:	AA+ walnut
Barrel:	26, 28, 30 in.
Chokes:	five C, IC, M, IM F; .410-bore fixed M/F
Weight:	5 lbs. 14 oz.–7 lbs. 6 oz.
Bore/Gauge:	12, 16, 20, 28, .410
Capacity:	2
MSRP:	$4,199–$4,789

Italyco

The Italyco round-bodied over/unders are part of Fausti's boutique lineup. This model comes with a choice of single or double triggers and with a choice of extractors or ejectors. It comes with a classic Prince of Wales grip with grip cap, a very nice touch indeed on this oil-finished medium grade walnut stock. It comes in all four major gauges plus the .410-bore, a selection of barrel lengths, and choice of fixed or interchangeable choke tubes.

Manufacturer:	Fausti USA
Model:	Italyco
Action:	over/under

Stock:	4A Turkish walnut
Barrel:	26, 28, 29, 30 in.
Chokes:	fixed, multi-choke
Weight:	5 lbs. 14 oz.–7 lbs. 6 oz.
Bore/Gauge:	12, 16, 20, 28, .410
Capacity:	2
MSRP:	$8,960–$12,600

Franchi USA

Affinity Catalyst

This inertia-driven semiautomatic 12-gauge is a light-weight at less than seven pounds, and that makes this a nimble, responsive gun for upland birds or skeet and sporting clays. It chambers 3-inch shells, boasts A-grade walnut in a satin finish, comes with three chokes and a wrench, shim kit, and a fiber-optic front sight—all for under a grand. Its dimensions are dimensions designed for the female form.

Manufacturer:	Franchi USA
Model:	Affinity Catalyst
Action:	semiautomatic
Stock:	walnut
Barrel:	28 in.
Chokes:	three (IC, M, F)
Weight:	6 lbs. 9 oz.
Bore/Gauge:	12
Capacity:	4+1
MSRP:	$999

Instinct Catalyst

Another designed-for-women shotgun is Franchi's Instinct Catalyst, an over/under with drop, pitch, cast, and length of pull most females will find better suits their anatomy than other guns built for the mythical "average" male. Like its sister Affinity semiauto, this double-barrel chambers 3-inch 12-gauge shells and wears an A-grade walnut stock and 28-inch tubes. The action employs and automatic safety upon opening.

Manufacturer:	Franchi USA
Model:	Instinct Catalyst
Action:	over/under
Stock:	walnut
Barrel:	28 in.
Chokes:	three (IC, M, F)
Weight:	6 lbs. 14 oz.
Bore/Gauge:	12
Capacity:	2
MSRP:	$1,599

H&R 1871

Pardner Turkey

Harrington and Richardson's break-open single-shot hammer guns are favored by many deer hunters, but the company also makes a smoothbore model in camo known as the Pardner Turkey. While it comes with a number of options, the most interesting fact is that one can get it in 10- or 12-gauge, both with 3½-inch chambers, at the very low price of $250.

Manufacturer:	H&R 1871
Model:	Pardner Turkey Gun
Action:	single shot
Stock:	hardwood
Barrel:	24 in.
Chokes:	two (XTF, F)
Weight:	6 lbs. 12-gauge; 9 lbs. 10-gauge
Bore/Gauge:	10, 12
Capacity:	1
MSRP:	$250

Ultra Light Slug Hunter, Hunter Compact, Hunter Deluxe, Hunter Thumbhole Stock

According to the company, its rifling uses six oval lands and grooves without sharp corners, much like traditional rifling, to impart a stabilizing spin on your slug that resists distorting the sabot jacket. The Hunter and Hunter Compact have American hardwood stocks, while the Deluxe and Thumbhole are of laminated hardwood. All have a Monte Carlo comb that promotes rapid alignment with scopes, and scope mounts are included. The 12-gauge Hunter comes with a factory-mounted and bore-sighted 3-9X scope. The Compact is a 20-gauge-only and has a 22-inch barrel, two inches shorter than all the others.

Manufacturer:	H&R 1871
Model:	Ultra Light Slug Hunter
Action:	single-shot
Stock:	hardwood
Barrel:	24 in.
Chokes:	N/A
Weight:	5 lbs. 4 oz.
Bore/Gauge:	12, 20
Capacity:	1
MSRP:	N/A

Manufacturer:	H&R 1871
Model:	Ultra Slug Hunter Compact
Action:	single-shot
Stock:	hardwood
Barrel:	22 in.
Chokes:	None
Weight:	7 lbs.
Bore/Gauge:	20
Capacity:	1
MSRP:	N/A

Manufacturer:	H&R 1871
Model:	Ultra Slug Hunter Deluxe
Action:	single-shot
Stock:	laminated hardwood
Barrel:	24 in.
Chokes:	N/A
Weight:	8 lbs. 8 oz.
Bore/Gauge:	12, 20
Capacity:	1
MSRP:	N/A

Manufacturer:	H&R 1871
Model:	Ultra Slug Hunter Thumbhole Stock
Action:	single-shot
Stock:	laminated hardwood
Barrel:	24 in.
Chokes:	N/A
Weight:	8 lbs. 9 oz.
Bore/Gauge:	12, 20
Capacity:	1
MSRP:	N/A

Ithaca

Deerslayer II, Deerslayer III

The Ithaca Deerslayer II is a dependable, pump-action, bottom-ejecting dedicated slug gun. The action is machined of one piece of steel. The Deerslayer II is available in 12- and 20-gauge, as is the heavier Deerslayer III in 12-gauge with its fluted, heavy barrel. Ithaca claims the Deerslayer III is capable of four-inch groups at 200 yards, which makes shooting at that range an ethical proposition. Other features include sling swivel studs, Pachmayr 750 Decelerator recoil pad, a matte blued finish on barrel, gold-plated trigger, a fixed barrel, and fiber optics rifle sights. The shotguns are drilled and tapped for a Weaver rail.

Manufacturer:	Ithaca
Model:	Deerslayer II
Action:	pump
Stock:	walnut
Barrel:	24 in.
Chokes:	N/A
Weight:	6.8 lbs.–8 lbs. 6 oz.
Bore/Gauge:	12, 20
Capacity:	4+1
MSRP:	$1,150

Manufacturer:	Ithaca
Model:	Deerslayer III
Action:	pump
Stock:	walnut; optional thumbhole
Barrel:	26 in.
Chokes:	N/A
Weight:	8 lbs. 2 oz.–9 lbs. 8 oz.
Bore/Gauge:	12, 20
Capacity:	4+1
MSRP:	$1,350

Krieghoff International

Essencia Game Gun

While not new, the Essencia sidelock is one of the best-looking round-body side-by-sides on the market. It harks back to the days of the early Rigby shotguns. Double triggers, H&H-style ejectors, fixed chokes at Improved Cylinder and Modified, checkered butt, and a choice of Prince of Wales grip or a straight stock are all standard features, and the gun comes in a Krieghoff leather trunk case. The color case-hardened receiver is beautifully done and also sports English scroll engraving. The stock's oil finish makes for a very traditional shotgun anyone would be proud to take afield.

Manufacturer:	Krieghoff International
Model:	Essencia Game Gun
Action:	side-by-side
Stock:	Turkish walnut
Barrel:	28, 30 in.; the .410 is only offered with 28 in. barrels
Chokes:	fixed (IC/M)
Weight:	6 lbs.-6 lbs. 12 oz.
Bore/Gauge:	12, 16, 20, 28, .410
Capacity:	2
MSRP:	$19,895–$37,450

K-20 Parcours

Krieghoff's relatively recent addition is the graceful K-20 Parcours, a nod toward accommodating the FITASC crowd. A variant on the tried and true K-80, the Parcours has a receiver designed for 20- and 28-gauges. The hand-oiled walnut is a nice touch on this nimble gun, and Krieghoff's crisp, adjustable mechanical trigger is one of the best. The K-20 Parcours 20-gauge uses 30- or 32-inch barrels, while the 28-gauge is available only with 30-inch barrels. Chokes are fixed Modified and Improved Modified chokes.

Manufacturer:	Krieghoff International
Model:	K-20 Parcours
Action:	over/under
Stock:	Turkish walnut
Barrel:	30, 32 in. 20-gauge; 30 in. 28-gauge
Chokes:	fixed (M/IM)
Weight:	7 lbs. 8 oz.
Bore/Gauge:	20, 28, .410 (sporting model only)
Capacity:	2
MSRP:	$11,395–$11,495; additional gauge-fitted barrels $4,695

Mossberg

500 Slugster

The Mossberg fully rifled 500 Slugster comes in a number of 12- and 20-gauge configurations. Some have rifle sights, one a cantilever scope mount. All have wood stocks, but one of the 20-gauge models can have its wood dressed in Mossy Oak camo. Two have a height-adjustable comb add-on.

Manufacturer:	Mossberg
Model:	500 Slugster
Action:	pump
Stock:	wood
Barrel:	24 in.
Chokes:	N/A
Weight:	6 lbs. 12 oz.–7 lbs. 4 oz.
Bore/Gauge:	12, 20
Capacity:	5+1
MSRP:	$419–$514

930, 935 Pro-Series Waterfowl

Mossberg offers two dedicated 12-gauge waterfowling autoloaders, the 930 and the 935 Pro-Series Waterfowl. The 930 is designed for 3-inch loads, while the 935 will chamber up to 3½-inch shells. Both wear synthetic stocks and hardware in full-coverage Mossy Oak Shadow Grass. For semiautos intended for waterfowling, these are long guns with their 28-inch barrels.

Manufacturer:	Mossberg
Model:	930, 935 Pro-Series Waterfowl
Action:	semiautomatic
Stock:	synthetic
Barrel:	28 in.
Chokes:	three (F, M, IC)
Weight:	7 lbs. 12 oz.
Bore/Gauge:	12
Capacity:	5+1
MSRP:	$874–930; $959–935

930 Snow Goose

Perhaps Mossberg's most interesting offering is the 930 Snow Goose model which is available in Kryptek's white Yeti camo pattern or in an all-black synthetic with an extended magazine that will hold 12 cartridges. Such capacity does make sense, I suppose, for those who shoot snow geese in the spring; currently New York has 25 birds per day limit for its spring season. For about a thousand dollars, you get a rather unique, very purpose-built, 12-gauge 3-inch shotgun.

Manufacturer:	Mossberg
Model:	930 Snow Goose
Action:	semiautomatic
Stock:	synthetic
Barrel:	28 in.
Chokes:	three (F, M, IC)
Weight:	8 lbs. 4 oz.
Bore/Gauge:	12
Capacity:	12+1 shells
MSRP:	$964 black; $1,022 Kryptec Yeti

Maverick HS12 Thunder Ranch Over/Under

This is a tactical shotgun that should fit the bill for many predator hunters, especially as Picatinny rails are mounted both on the receiver for sights and below the barrel for easy installation of lights and other accessories. This over/under is inherently reliable and very reasonably priced. Short-barreled and nimble, it should find favor with predator hunters who work in teams, with one man on a rifle and another on a shotgun to take care of the up close and personal work.

Manufacturer:	Mossberg
Model:	Maverick HS12 Thunder Ranch
Action:	over/under
Stock:	synthetic
Barrel:	18½ in.
Chokes:	fixed (C)
Weight:	6 lb. 4 oz.
Bore/Gauge:	12
Capacity:	2
MSRP:	$594

Versa Max Sportsman Turkey Camo

Remington's Versa Max Sportsman Turkey tames recoil through its unique gas system and SuperCell recoil pad. Fitted with a short 22-inch vent rib barrel to make it handier, this autoloader is drilled and tapped to mount optics. This one chambers up to the big 3½-inch 12-gauge shells, it comes with both rifle sights and interchangeable HiViz fiber optic sights. It comes in full-coverage Mossy Oak Duck Blind or Obsession camo patterns.

Manufacturer:	Remington
Model:	Versa Max Sportsman Turkey Camo
Action:	semiautomatic
Stock:	synthetic
Barrel:	22 in.
Chokes:	2 (M and Turkey Xtra Full)
Weight:	7 lbs. 12 oz.
Bore/Gauge:	12
Capacity:	3+1
MSRP:	$1,222

Versa Max Tactical

Remington's Versa Max Tactical is probably the No. 1 choice for a gun that can pull double duty on turkeys and predators plus would make an unbelievably efficient home-protection or Three-Gun competition firearm, thanks to its ability to chamber up to 3½-inch 12-gauge rounds. This auto-loader has all the outstanding reliability for which the Versa Max has become known, plus it comes with a Picatinny rail on the receiver, forward barrel-clamp side rails for accessories, and an extended magazine that will hold eight 2¾-inch rounds. You'll get an Improved Cylinder and Tactical Extended ProBore chokes, and the nickel- and nickel-Teflon-plated bore and internal components offer extreme corrosion resistance. Length of pull as well as drop and cast are adjustable on this shotgun.

Manufacturer:	Remington
Model:	Versa Max Tactical
Action:	semiautomatic
Stock:	synthetic
Barrel:	22 in.
Chokes:	fixed (C)
Weight:	7 lbs. 12 oz.
Bore/Gauge:	12
Capacity:	8+1
MSRP:	$1,456

11–87 Sportsman Cantilever Slug

This 11–87 20-gauge model has the advantage over the 1100 as it shoots both 2¾- and 3-inch shells. The gas action, heavier steel receiver, and Super Cell recoil pad ameliorate the heavy recoil associated with slugs, and the cantilever scope mount and Monte Carlo stock work well with high scope mounts. This model comes with a fully rifled barrel and sling swivel studs.

Manufacturer:	Remington
Model:	11–87 Sportsman Cantilever Slug
Action:	semiautomatic
Stock:	synthetic
Barrel:	21 in.

Chokes:	N/A
Weight:	7 lbs. 8 oz.
Bore/Gauge:	20
Capacity:	4+1
MSRP:	$899.37

Model 870 Express

This model is about as classic as it gets, when it comes to a pump shotgun. It is available in 12- or 20-gauge, with matte blue hardware, hardwood or synthetic stocks, a variety of barrel lengths, and RemChoke choke tubes, and two options in full-cover Camo. This shotgun is about as flexible as you can get.

Manufacturer:	Remington
Model:	Model 870 Express
Action:	pump
Stock:	hardwood, synthetic
Barrel:	18¾, 21, 26, 28 in.
Chokes:	RemChoke (M)
Weight:	5 lbs. 12 oz.–7 lbs. 8oz.
Bore/Gauge:	12, 20
Capacity:	4+1
MSRP:	$417–$468

870 Express Super Magnum Turkey/Waterfowl

Remington's Model 870 Express Super Magnum Turkey/Waterfowl is a dual-purpose shotgun that handles up to 3½-inch 12-gauge rounds and wears Mossy Oak Bottomland camo. A 26-inch ventilated rib barrel with HiViz fiber-optics sights makes it useful for most turkey hunting or waterfowl situations, especially as the pump is supplied with extended waterfowl and turkey RemChokes. It is drilled and tapped for optics, a bonus for turkey hunters.

Manufacturer:	Remington
Model:	Model 870 Express Super Magnum Turkey/Waterfowl
Action:	pump
Stock:	synthetic

Barrel:	26 in.
Chokes:	RemChoke
Weight:	7 lbs. 4 oz.
Bore/Gauge:	12
Capacity:	4+1
MSRP:	$629

870 SPS Super Magnum Turkey/Predator with Scope

The model 870 SPS Super Magnum Turkey/Predator is pre-mounted with a TruGlo red/green dot optic in a Mossy Oak Obsession camo-wrapped package designed for turkey and predators at relatively long distance. It sports a short, maneuverable 20-inch barrel and handles 2¾-, 3-, and 3½-inch 12-gauge rounds. A black padded sling and Wingmaster HD Turkey/Predator RemChoke are included, and the thumbhole stock has over-molded grip panels.

Manufacturer:	Remington
Model:	Model 870 SPS Super Magnum Turkey/Predator with Scope
Action:	pump
Stock:	synthetic
Barrel:	25½ in.
Chokes:	Wingmaster HD Turkey/Predator RemChoke
Weight:	7 lbs. 2 oz.
Bore/Gauge:	12
Capacity:	4+1
MSRP:	$710

Model 870 SPS SuperSlug

Avid, serious slug hunters should consider the new 12-gauge Model 870 SPS SuperSlug. The fully rifled barrel has an extra-heavy, 1-inch diameter contour, and its 25½-inch length is pinned to the receiver to control vibration for shot-to-shot consistency. It accepts 2¾- and 3-inch 12-gauge slugs. Five longitudinal flutes reduce weight while simultaneously bolstering barrel rigidity. The ambidextrous ShurShot pistol-grip thumbhole synthetic stock sports Remington's SuperCell

recoil pad and the receiver is drilled and tapped; a Weaver rail and sling swivel studs are included.

Manufacturer:	Remington
Model:	Model 870 SPS SuperSlug
Action:	pump
Stock:	synthetic
Barrel:	25½ in.
Chokes:	N/A
Weight:	7 lbs. 14 oz.
Bore/Gauge:	12
Capacity:	4+1
MSRP:	$829

V3 Field Sport

The V3 Field Sport from Remington is a 3-inch, gas-operated autoloader that function equally well and reliably with 2¾- or 3-inch shells, handling both light and heavy loads with ease. It is one of the most pleasant 12-gauges one can shoot. Remington's oversized trigger guard makes waterfowling or predator hunting with heavy gloves practical, while the gun's light-contour barrel is equally at home on the sporting clays course or an upland bird hunt.

Manufacturer:	Remington
Model:	V3 Field Sport
Action:	semiautomatic
Stock:	synthetic
Barrel:	26, 28 in.
Chokes:	RemChoke
Weight:	7 lbs. 4 oz.
Bore/Gauge:	12
Capacity:	3+1
MSRP:	$895

Savage

Model 212, 220

Savage firearms are dependable, accurate, and reasonably priced. The 12-gauge Model 212 and 20-gauge Model 220 with a 22-inch rifled barrel and a two-round detachable box magazine and come with the Savage AccuTrigger, which is super; I have Savage's 17HMR with this trigger. Since this is a bolt-action, do consider the 20-gauge, which will have significantly less recoil than the 12.

Manufacturer:	Savage
Model:	212, 220
Action:	bolt
Stock:	walnut
Barrel:	22 in. rifled
Chokes:	N/A
Weight:	7 lbs. 7 oz.–7 lbs. 8 oz.
Bore/Gauge:	12, 20
Capacity:	2
MSRP:	$704 12-gauge; $619 20-gauge

SKB

200HR Target

SKB's Model 200HR is a side-by-side target gun with stocks available cast for both right- and left-handed shooters. Offered in 12-, 20-, and 28-gauge, and .410 bore, as well as in two-barrel 28-gauge and .410-bore sets, the gun has a trigger-plate action with non-selective single trigger. It comes with a raised ventilated rib, which I don't like on side-by-sides (though they may be useful for clay target shooters), and 28- and 30-inch barrels, which I do. (32-inch barrels are optional on the 12-gauge). A full set of flush-mount choke tubes, reduced barrel weight, Pachmayr recoil pad, and Schnabel fore-end are standard.

Manufacturer:	SKB
Model:	200HR Target
Action:	side-by-side
Stock:	wood
Barrel:	28, 30 in.; 32 in. only available for 12-gauge
Chokes:	five (F, IM, M, IC, S)
Weight:	6 lbs. 4 oz.–8 lbs.
Bore/Gauge:	12, 20, 28, .410
Capacity:	2
MSRP:	$2,500–$3,600

90TSS Sporting

The 90TSS Sporting over/under features an adjustable comb, as well as an adjustable buttplate that works for both right and left-handed shooters. This 12-gauge boxlock comes with 30- or 32-inch barrels, an improved mechanical trigger, 10mm vent rib, automatic ejectors, and a barrel selector built into the safety. Its 3-inch chambers might encourage cross-over hunting use for some.

Manufacturer:	SKB
Model:	90TSS Sporting
Action:	over/under
Stock:	wood
Barrel:	28 in., 30 in., 32 in.
Weight:	7 lb. 12 oz.–8 lb. 12 oz.
Bore/Gauge:	12, 20
Capacity:	2
MSRP:	$1,800–$1,900

90TSS Trap, Trap Combo

The 90TSS Trap over/under has buttplates that allow length-of-pull adjustments from 13½ to 14¾ inches, as well as adjustable combs, making this a good choice for women and growing youth shooters. Barrels are available in 30- or 32-inch lengths, and if you opt for the combo, you get a 34-inch top-profile single barrel.

Manufacturer:	SKB
Model:	90TSS Trap, Trap Combo
Action:	over/under
Stock:	wood
Barrel:	30, 32 in.; 34 in. top single available in Combo
Chokes:	five
Weight:	8 lbs. 10 oz.–8 lbs. 14 oz.
Bore/Gauge:	12
Capacity:	2
MSRP:	$1,800–$2,750

Stoeger

M3000 Turkey Gun

The Stoeger M3000 Turkey Gun has a short 24-inch barrel and comes with three interchangeable choke tubes, Improved Cylinder, Modified, and an Extra-Full Turkey. This inertia-driven auto-loader is chambered for 2¾-inch and 3-inch 12-gauge cartridges, has a stepped vent rib, fiber-optic front sight, and is available in Realtree Max-5 or APG full-cover camo, in addition to all-black. A great gun for coyotes and the like, both turkey and predator hunters will find the Steady Grip version is great for long sits.

Manufacturer:	Stoeger
Model:	M3000 Turkey Gun
Action:	semiautomatic
Stock:	synthetic
Barrel:	18½, 24, 26, 28, 30 in.
Chokes:	three (IC, XFT, M)
Weight:	6 lbs. 1 oz.–7 lbs. 8 oz.
Bore/Gauge:	12
Capacity:	4+1
MSRP:	$599–$679

Syren USA

Elos Sporting

Caesar Guerini has seen the rise in women shooters, one of the fastest expanding parts of the market, and introduced the Syren XLR5 line specifically with women in mind. Stock dimensions were specifically created with the physical attributes of women in mind. The Elos Sporting is a fairly lightweight gun, just under eight pounds in 12-gauge, that has 30-inch barrels chambered for 3-inch cartridges. The length of pull is adjustable; it's equipped with five competition choke tubes, and has a 10mm vent rib. A nice touch is Guerini's TRIWOOD finish in the Turkish walnut stock, a treatment that enhances grain and increases water resistance.

Manufacturer:	Syren
Model:	Elos Sporting
Action:	over/under
Stock:	Turkish walnut
Barrel:	30 in.
Chokes:	5 EXIS HP
Weight:	7 lbs. 14 oz.
Bore/Gauge:	12
Capacity:	2
MSRP:	$2,650; add $125 for left-hand stock

Tempio Trap

Syren's Tempio Trap is a competition over/under trap gun for which an unsingle barrel can also be ordered. The gun's Dynamic Tuning System sports the type of rib which is now so popular adjusting the point of impact. The Monte Carlo comb adjusts for drop and cast, and the gun has lengthened forcing cones. You get upgraded wood and gold-accent engraving, making this model as pretty as it is functional.

Manufacturer:	Syren
Model:	Tempio Trap
Action:	over/under, unsingle
Stock:	Turkish walnut
Barrel:	30 in; 32 in. unsingle
Chokes:	three or five MAXIS competition
Weight:	8 lbs. 5 oz.–8 lbs. 6 oz.
Bore/Gauge:	12
Capacity:	2
MSRP:	$6,495; $9,330 combo; add $235 for left-hand stock

XLR5 Waterfowler

The XLR5 Waterfowler is a gas-operated autoloader available in left-hand and right-hand versions, again designed for women and capable of handling both 2¾- and 3-inch 12-gauge loads. Full-coverage soft-touch Realtree Max-5 camo on the wood stock and five choke tubes are standard.

Manufacturer:	Stoeger
Model:	XLR5 Waterfowler
Action:	semiautomatic
Stock:	wood
Barrel:	28 in.
Chokes:	5 INNER HP
Weight:	7 lbs. 1 oz.
Bore/Gauge:	12
Capacity:	5
MSRP:	$1,795; add $189 for left-hand stock

TarHunt

RSG-12 Professional

The RSG (Rifled Slug Gun) from Randy Fritz, TarHunt's founder, is a premium bolt-action, two-lug, control-feed slug shotgun. It is considered among the most accurate of its kind. Fritz joined benchrest bolt-action rifle know-how with a top-of-the-line rifled shotgun barrel. The gun features a glass-bedded action drilled and tapped for standard Leupold or Weaver bases, McMillan fiberglass stock, a heavy Shaw stainless steel barrel threaded into the action and the barrel is ported. It is renowned for its crisp trigger. This is as close to rifle accuracy as you're going to get in a slug gun, but at a price.

Manufacturer:	TarHunt
Model:	RSG-12 Professional
Action:	bolt
Stock:	synthetic
Barrel:	23 in.
Chokes:	N/A
Weight:	8 lbs. 12 oz.
Bore/Gauge:	12
Capacity:	2
MSRP:	$3,495; add $130 for left-hand build

RSG-20 Mountaineer

For those looking for a lighter bolt-action from TarHunt, the Mountaineer 20-gauge is worth considering. A muzzle brake and the custom 2½-pound Jewell trigger are standard equipment. It is drilled and tapped for standard Leupold or Weaver bases and chambered for 3-inch slugs.

Manufacturer:	TarHunt
Model:	RSG-20 Mountaineer
Action:	bolt
Stock:	synthetic
Barrel:	23 in.
Chokes:	N/A
Weight:	7 lbs. 4 oz.
Bore/Gauge:	20
Capacity:	2
MSRP:	$3,495; add $130 for left-hand build

Thompson/Center

Encore

With its famous interchangeable barrel system, the T/C Encore allows the user to switch from centerfire rifle to a muzzleloader or even to a shotgun. The scope mounts to the barrel. The Pro Hunter Shotgun Slug sports a long, fluted, fully rifled barrel, synthetic stock, and is available in both 12- and 20-gauge.

Manufacturer:	Thompson/Center
Model:	Encore Pro Hunter XT
Action:	single-shot
Stock:	synthetic
Barrel:	28 in.
Chokes:	N/A
Weight:	5 lbs. 8 oz.
Bore/Gauge:	12, 20
Capacity:	1
MSRP:	$892

Weatherby

Element Waterfowler Max-5

This budget-minded autoloader is offered in 12- and 20-gauge. It works on an inertia system, and features a slim body and receiver profile, one that should prove nimble in the tight quarters of a duck blind. Drop and cast adjustments, fiber-optic front sight, vent rib are standard, as are over-molds at the fore-end, and pistol grips are standard, which are a great help in wet weather. It is supplied in full-coverage Realtree Max-5 camo.

Manufacturer:	Weatherby
Model:	Element Waterfowler Max-5
Action:	semiautomatic
Stock:	composite
Barrel:	26, 28 in.
Chokes:	four (F, M, IC, Long Range Steel)
Weight:	6 lbs. 4 oz.–6 lbs. 12 oz.
Bore/Gauge:	12, 20
Capacity:	4+1
MSRP:	$849

SA-08 Synthetic, SA-08 Synthetic Compact

Prefer a gas-operated autoloader? Weatherby's SA line might be the answer for you. The Synthetic (12- and 20-gauge) and Synthetic Compact (20-gauge only) have an easily removable trigger system which, after a day of shooting, especially in salt water environments, can be a bonus. The Compact model has a short 12½-inch length of pull, and shorter 24-inch barrel, which should appeal to younger or more slightly built shooters and youth shooters just beginning to hunt.

Manufacturer:	Weatherby
Model:	SA-08 Synthetic, SA-08 Synthetic Compact
Action:	semiautomatic
Stock:	composite
Barrel:	26, 28 in.; Compact 24 in. only
Chokes:	three (IC, M, F)
Weight:	5 lbs. 12 oz.–6 lbs. 8 oz.
Bore/Gauge:	12, 20
Capacity:	5+1
MSRP:	$649

SA-549 Turkey Xtra Green

Weatherby's SA-549 Turkey Xtra Green takes the company's gas-operated semiautomatic action and adds a pistol grip, top-side removable Picatinny rail, and full-coverage Realtree Xtra Green camo. An extended, fluted Extra-Full choke is included. It is available in 12- or 20-gauge.

Model:	Weatherby SA-459 Turkey Xtra Green
Action:	semiautomatic
Stock:	synthetic
Barrel:	22 in.
Chokes:	one (XTF)
Weight:	6 lbs. 4 oz.–6 lbs. 12 oz.
Bore/Gauge:	12, 20
Capacity:	5+1
MSRP:	$799

Winchester

SXP Turkey Hunter

Pump guns generally cost far less than autoloaders, and while I would not want to put a lot of 3½-inch loads through one, for the few shots each turkey season likely to be taken, Winchester's Super-X Turkey Hunter in 12-gauge should be considered. The 24-inch barrel is back-bored to .742-inch, and the Invector-Plus Extra Full Turkey choke is good for long-range patterns. Winchester uses Inflex Technology recoil pad to soften recoil. Rifle sights are fully adjustable for windage and elevation. Also available in a 3-inch, 20-gauge, both versions come in Mossy Oak Break-Up Country.

Manufacturer:	Winchester
Model:	SXP Turkey Hunter
Action:	pump
Stock:	synthetic
Barrel:	24 in.
Chokes:	Invector-Plus Extra full Turkey choke
Weight:	12-gauge, 6 lbs. 10 oz.; 20-gauge, 6 lbs. 4 oz.
Bore/Gauge:	12, 20
Capacity:	4+1
MSRP:	$519.99

Super X Pump Long Beard

This is Winchester's top of the line turkey gun, with interchangeable combs to accommodate iron sights or optics, length of pull spacers, fiber optic sights, and an Inflex Technology recoil pad. The gun is drilled and tapped for optic, sports Mossy Oak Break-Up Country camo, and comes with an extended, camouflaged, and fluted Extra-Full turkey choke tube. In 12- or 20-gauge, the 12-gauge can be had with either 3- or 3½-inch chambers.

Manufacturer:	Winchester
Model:	Super X Pump Long Beard
Action:	pump
Stock:	synthetic
Barrel:	24 in.
Chokes:	one (XTF Turkey)
Weight:	12-gauge, 6 lbs. 14 oz.–7 lbs.; 20-gauge, 6 lbs. 14 oz.
Bore/Gauge:	12, 20
Capacity:	4+1
MSRP:	$559.99

Super X3 Universal Hunter

This is a lightweight autoloader with a drop-out trigger group that makes for easy cleaning. In Mossy Oak camo, this predator gun will work on waterfowl and turkey as it is drilled and tapped for optics, and the back-bored barrel and Active Valve gas system ease recoil while improving accuracy and reliability. It is offered in 12-gauge 3-inch and 20-gauge 3-inch.

Manufacturer:	Winchester
Model:	Winchester Super X3 Universal Hunter
Action:	semiautomatic
Stock:	synthetic
Barrel:	26 in., 28 in.
Chokes:	three Invector-Plus (F, M, IC)
Weight:	6 lbs. 10 oz.–7 lbs.
Bore/Gauge:	12, 20
Capacity:	4+1
MSRP:	$1,239.99

SXP Waterfowl

Lots of choices in this dedicated line of economically priced waterfowl guns, including 3½- and 3-inch 12-gauges and a 3-inch 20-gauge. Barrels are either 26 or 28 inches, and full-coverage Mossy Oak Shadow Grass Blades works in a wide variety of waterfowl habitat. Chrome-plated chambers and barrels and Invector-Plus choke tubes are standard, as is an aluminum-alloy receiver, TruGlo fiber optic sights, and sling swivel studs.

Manufacturer:	Winchester
Model:	SXP Waterfowl Hunter
Action:	pump
Stock:	synthetic
Barrel:	26, 28 in.
Chokes:	Invector-Plus
Weight:	6 lbs. 8 oz.–7 lbs.
Bore/Gauge:	12, 20
Capacity:	4+1
MSRP:	$459–$499.99

CHAPTER 10
Have Guns, Will Travel

For more than fifty years, I have travelled America from Alaska to Florida, and the world from Argentina to Zambia, with sporting weapons. I have never lost a firearm on a flight. If one employs a little common sense, allows sufficient time for foreign bureaucrats (most often customs officials or police) to process paperwork, and extra time at airports for check-in and security verifications, travel need not be unduly traumatic.

Sounds simple—but then there's reality.

A few years ago, flying from the U.S. on Virgin Atlantic to Scotland, I decided to bring some ammunition with me. At check-in I met the duty manager, who was actually quite nice and helpful but who informed me that I would not be allowed on the plane with my ammunition in the hold. He said they'd contacted Virgin Atlantic's U.K. office, which told them it had to be packed separately from everything else, in a locked hard-sided container. Merely being in a hard container inside a locked duffle bag, the way I had brought it to and from Africa dozens of times, was no longer acceptable.

The duty manager took pity on me and had the ammunition locked in the airline's safe, saving me the hassle of disposing of ammunition away from airport and likely missing my flight in the process. Rules change.

Baggage Woes
Flying to Johannesburg from Heathrow one August, I was charged the exorbitant sum of $1,000 one way for my rifle case by Virgin; leaving the Republic of South Africa (RSA), I was not charged anything extra for this case. I booked all my tickets from my home in Scotland over the internet, and Virgin flying from America has or had a blanket allowance of two bags regardless of weight, plus a gun case. Had I booked my ticket from New York to Johannesburg as a single flight with a long stopover in London on my way to Johannesburg and returned to London as part of a New York originating booking, I would have been allowed the two bags plus my gun case on all the legs of the flight.

For anyone considering travel to Africa with guns,

you'll need to research your bag numbers and weight maximums carefully before you book your flights. For instance, the current baggage allowance in standard economy of one bag with maximum weight of 23 kilos (fifty pounds) on most airlines plus five kilos (eleven pounds) of ammunition (5 kg is an international regulation on all flights as best I can make out) is plainly insufficient for a long sporting trip. My two rifles and their case probably touch the scales around thirty pounds, which is normal. Going over the weight can cost heavily. Airline weight limits, number of bags, and the occasional free sport bag—British Airlines allows one gun case free—all vary depending on the airline, and these allowances frequently change. Upon booking, immediately print out your airline's luggage policy and bring it with you to show at check-in if there is a dispute. (Travelers from and to the U.S. will find more information here: www.tsa.gov/travel/transporting-firearms-and-ammunition.)

In 2007, American Airlines prohibited firearms in checked baggage on flights landing in the U.K. The other U.S. carriers did not follow suit, but since the decision to allow firearms as baggage is one of both origin and destination, you must verify both ends before booking. Some airlines are actually quite good about accepting firearms, although they may have a surcharge to add a gun case. For those flying *within* South Africa, only South African Airlines and its subsidiaries are allowed by law to transport guns, so, if you are flying into Johannesburg or Cape Town and beyond, you need to be aware of this; you can fly *into* RSA on any international carrier. Regardless of your destination, you should confirm with the airlines in all circumstances upon making the booking that you will be travelling with firearms and, simultaneously, that shotguns are confirmed on the flight. To do this with some airlines requires a phone booking, while others allow booking flights with firearm baggage online.

Paperwork and Processing
Each airline and each airport, even for passengers travelling within the U.S., seems to have their own procedures, protocols, and regulations when it comes

to flying with firearms. At New York's JFK and most airports, a police officer comes to inspect the gun and, if travelling abroad, the U.S. Customs form 4457 is reviewed. The officer then either accompanies the permit holder to a special screening area or calls for a special baggage handler to do so. In the U.K., visitor permits are checked by customs officials or police, depending on airport, once the government official gives the go-ahead, they are then brought by *Securicor* baggage handlers to the airplane. In London-Heathrow, they generally look at the permits but do not check the firearm serial numbers for internal flights. *Securicor* can take anything from ten minutes to forty-five minutes to arrive, at least in my experience, and I therefore add at least an hour of extra time to check-in when I do travel with guns and know this will be the process. I also allow at least two and preferably three hours for international connections. Landing or departing from Bristol, for instance always seems to include a police inspection to double-check licenses and serial numbers even on landing for flights within the country where serial numbers and licenses would have been checked on departure, from, for example Heathrow. At Inverness airport, guns are screened by machine and paperwork is rarely if ever checked (although a form does have to be completed at the counter).

The U.S. Customs 4457 is required for Americans on all international flights. I always try and get mine at a small nearby airport having international service by making an appointment in advance, rather than waiting for departure day at a big international airport like JFK. If you must complete it at check-in, allow at least an extra hour.

For travelling abroad, you will, of course, need a passport. Make a copy of the first pages in case of loss to speed replacement. For countries that require visas, they often also require a minimum of six blank pages, no idea why. The U.S. passport service will add pages, but this takes a few weeks unless you pay for expedited handling. Note: 4457 forms must now be filled out online and mailed to the airport DHS from which you are departing.

U.K.

Clearing sporting guns at U.K. international arrival halls is straightforward if paperwork is in order. Foreigners coming to the U.K. must also have a U.K. Visitors Permit. Additionally, if you are visiting Northern Ireland to shoot, a separate license from the Ulster (Northern Ireland) Constabulary is required. For foreign visitors transiting through the U.K. without visitors permits, there are expediting services licensed to take possession of the guns for lawful transport to the next airport for connections.

Africa

South Africa has changed from a country where customs officials would fill out paperwork on the spot and in minutes for visiting sportsmen, to one where, in an ever-expanding bureaucracy, one can wait up to five hours to have paperwork completed. The best way to ease the pain here is to use an expeditor who will have your licenses pre-issued and will meet and greet you on arrival in the country. While this service costs somewhere between $50 and $100, it is worth every penny. Police will still need to check serial numbers, but the time required is reduced to about five minutes.

It is important if you are travelling to other countries from RSA to make sure that you have an RSA multiple-entrance permit and that it's good for the entire duration of your travel. It also is important to have a small amount of money to tip baggage handlers here. They carry the guns from the police to the airlines and expect a gratuity. I find $10 to be sufficient.

If at all possible, make sure that any paperwork regarding your personal travel and travel with firearms is completed well in advance when heading to any foreign destination, especially those on the Dark Continent. (Namibia is the exception in Africa, where all one needs to show is a letter of invite from the hunting company for speedy entry.) Have contact phone numbers and emails on your cell phone before travelling in case you cannot find your "meet-and-greet" contacts or need help recovering firearms lost in transit.

Most African countries, except Namibia, require gun licenses, and these must be arranged by the hunting companies in advance. Namibia, Zimbabwe, and RSA allow permits to be issued on arrival, but you will need a letter of invite from the hunting company (bona fide).

Added Insurance

Whether your firearm is worth $1,000 or $100,000, having it lost in transit is traumatic. I find a little travel insurance can at least help heal the wound to the pocket if not the heart and memories attached to the lost treasure.

I have used Sportsman's Insurance Agency, discounted through memberships in SCI, NSSA, NSCA, and others. When my rifle was stolen in RSA at Falaza, its agents were very helpful, needing only to see a police report. I had a great experience with them and I do suggest insuring firearms when travelling.

Sportsman's Insurance Agency, Inc.
1364 North U.S. 1, Suite 503
Ormond Beach, FL 32174
Toll Free: 800-925-7767
Phone: 386-677-2588
Fax: 386-677-3292
www.siai.net
Contact Chuck Sandnes csandnes@siai.net or Keren Sandnes ksandnes@siai.net.

Global Rescue is another reputable insurance company. It has short and long-term plans. If you are travelling from Ohio to Montana, their policies may not be worth it—but its agents will arrange to medivac you out of the middle of nowhere via helicopter if needed. Policies are very reasonable for service provided. I would never consider going to Africa or anywhere in the third world or back and beyond, a pack trip, for example, without it. You can see what the company offers at www.globalrescue.com.

Finally, in addition to the insurance your air carrier can provide, check your homeowners and rental policies. You might be surprised at what losses some of these will cover when you travel, though you'll have to balance the ability to issue a claim against the size of your deductible.

Packing

One would think that with heightened airport security, bags would not get misrouted or pilfered—well, if one were to think that, then one would be wrong! *Never* pack valuables in checked luggage. That includes watches, cameras, laptops, expensive eyewear, etc. I try to make a practice of photographing everything I pack, which can help identify recovered lost luggage and aid in replacing stolen belongings.

◄ Binoculars and other small items are best put in carry-on luggage as they are too easily pilfered. This great case from Negrini is ideal for road trips or once one has reached the final destination.

Lost baggage is a pain no matter who and where you are, but it's especially troublesome if you're traveling, say, initially to Johannesburg and then many hours by plane or vehicle to camp. If you are travelling with two bags, split your clothes between them, preferably with a complete set of day clothing in each, that way if one bag gets lost, you're not stuck with a suitcase of nothing but pants and sneakers. If you are only allowed one bag but are travelling with a buddy or wife, the shared bag concept can still apply, as this again helps assure that everyone in your party will have a clean change of underwear, shirts, pants, socks, and shoes upon arrival. Even when all your baggage does arrive as planned, I suggest you open them at your arrival airport and verify the contents you started with are still there. TSA-approved locks and airline tracking apps are both a help these days.

General and Airline-Specific Guidelines for Travel with Firearms

Each airline's rules for handling firearms differ, with various restrictions or fees. Check your airline's website and read their rules for accepting and handling checked firearms and recheck a day or two before the flight to make certain that the rules haven't changed. It is smart to print out these rules and bring them with you to push under the gate agent's nose in case they tell you something different when checking in.

▲ A thoughtfully packed hard gun luggage case. Photos courtesy of International Case Co. LLC/Negrini Cases.

Checked firearms must be packed in a locked hard case and be partially disassembled. Only you may have the key or combination to the case. If possible, physically accompany your guns through the screening process.

All airlines now have a five-kilogram limit (eleven pounds) on the transport of cartridges per passenger. Current guidelines require that locked metal or hard-plastic containers are also necessary for ammunition transport. My own suggestion here would be for an aluminum or hard plastic case that meets the requirements but does not add much weight of its own.

As airline transport of ammunition requires a separate case, it is often not worth the hassle for shotgun cartridges, as the eleven pound limit is small—absurdly small if you are, say, going to Argentina for doves. If, however, you would also be shooting a bit of waterfowl or quail and want to bring some special ammo for such hunts, for instance 3½-inch 12-gauge tungsten or some upland 28-gauge loads, doing so can offset the trouble of procuring what you need on arrival at your destination.

One carry-on bag is universally permitted, although sometimes you'll also be charged for it. It is here that I carry all valuables, my cameras, laptops, prescription medicine, jewelry, etc.

Falaza: A Cautionary Tale

The day after I finished hunting with John Abraham at his concession the Limpopo region where I hunted fruitlessly for a kudu, we made the long drive with the hunting vehicles and our trackers to Hluhluwe. We were staying at a resort lodge called Falaza, which was across the road from the area where we were to hunt nyala. The lodge itself primarily attracted photographic tourists, but was used by a number of professional hunters pursuing the species in Natal. We were taken by one of the managers to our three chalets, one for my wife and myself, one for John, and one for the videographer we had with us filming the hunt.

The first thing I did upon arrival was ask if the lodge had a gun safe in which I could store my rifle. I was told by a member of their staff there was not. The chalets themselves were clean and well laid out, and the food was good. There were two armed guards—one carrying a rifle, one carrying a shotgun—patrolling the property, which was fenced. There were also some surveillance cameras present on the perimeter of the property. There were no locks on the doors and there were no small safes built in as is so common in hotels and motels these days for storing small valuables. Had there been, I would have taken the bolt out of the rifle and placed it inside the safe, rendering the gun inert.

The night after I shot my second nyala, the four of us were having dinner in a private area of the compound. We weren't there long, perhaps an hour. During that time, thieves cut through the compound's fence and went straight to our three chalets (and not bothering with the chalets of the photographic tourists at all). My rifle and ammunition and a few other items were stolen. John did not have his rifle with him, as no dangerous game was present in the area, but the criminals did steal his wallet and other valuables. Many items of value were also taken from the videographer. Fortunately, I had my passport and wallet in my jacket and Renata had hers in the purse she carried with her.

After the burglary, we were told by the bartender that the lodge did indeed have gun safes. I am very cautious when it comes to guns, as I have lived most of the last twenty years in Scotland and Ireland, where one is responsible for one's firearms at all times and they must be stored in safes. They are periodically checked by the police. Indeed, to prevent losing one's license, it is the owner's responsibility to remove the bolt or fore-end of the shotgun, rendering it harmless, and carry it with them, should one go to lunch or dinner and leave the guns unaccompanied in one's vehicle. Found otherwise, one can find serious trouble with the police if they want to press the issue.

I never received any sort of apology or acknowledgment from the owners of Falaza. Neither has John, who had been bringing them clients for many years. Though in truth, Abraham should have known that there was a gun safe and should have used them on previous safaris to abide by the laws and regulations of RSA. The only things I ever received from Falaza were veiled threats from their attorney, who at some point wrote to me to say they were close to finding the rifle and that they had offered a reward. That soon went quiet. Then he said that the owners were looking into paying me from their insurance but nothing came of that. I did pose ten questions for the owners, sent to their attorney, about the training of their security team; but never received a response to that from either the attorney or the owners. At some point they also wrote and told me that another reason that they hadn't refunded some of the loss of my rifle was that John Abraham had never paid them for our stay or for the trophy fees, even though I had paid him.

All in all, at least from my perspective, the situation was handled in a very unprofessional manner. But what was really worrying was that it could have occurred while Renata and I were asleep in our tents, in which case we likely would have been injured or killed by panga-carrying thugs (pangas are like machetes). That idea is not as far-fetched as you might think: the owner's son had

been attacked and nearly died near the entrance to Falaza, approximately a year before our arrival. I only learned of this shortly before we left.

While I cannot say to a certitude that this was an inside job, it is rather curious that I was lied to by a member of the lodge's staff about the availability of gun safes, and that only our three tents were targeted.

I have hunted the Danakil desert of Ethiopia, as well as the mountains. I have hunted the Sudan, I have hunted Moyowoshi, Masailand, and near Ruaha National Park in Tanzania. I have hunted Mulobezi in Zambia twice, the Luangwa once. I've hunted Namibia. I have hunted Botswana five times, and I have hunted South Africa eight times—and still this is not a complete list. Never before has this kind of brazen theft happened to me. Certainly, Africa can be a dangerous place, and cities are more dangerous than the bush, but at an upscale resort with visible security, this should not have happened.

All I can say is do everything you can to be sure your guns are safeguarded, and if you find yourself in a situation where you have to leave them unattended, be sure to take the bolt or fore-end with you. The worst part of the entire crime is the fact that, undoubtedly, my rifle will now be used for poaching; the .338 Trophy Bonded bullets which were stolen are certainly capable of killing a rhino. Totally disgusting. I would never under any circumstance return to Falaza again.

The Hard Case for Hard Cases

It is important to use an appropriate firearms hard case when traveling. I prefer metal cases, because I think they make it harder for careless baggage handlers to damage guns. However, there are times when weight limitations are an issue and a molded plastic case will be preferable. Whether you travel a few miles or tens of thousands, and whether you travel by vehicle or plane, no other piece of equipment is as important to safeguarding your treasured shotguns as is your choice of cases.

One of the earliest metal cases that withstood

▲ Ready for travel. Photo courtesy of International Case Co. LLC/Negrini Cases.

▲ An Americase hard case. It's practically indestructible.

abusive airline baggage handlers was by the maker Kalispell. Today, that brand has been eclipsed, at least in my mind, by a few companies. My favorite cases these days for carrying side-by-side or over-under shotguns come from Negrini and Americase, which offer models for single and double-barrel shotguns and rifles.

Negrini has been making cases for a number of gunmakers for many years. Today you can buy them and pair them with your shotguns. I have a wonderful old Perazzi case, the interior of which has basically dissolved. My Negrini takedown case is the perfect replacement. It is better looking than the original shell plastic and offers more protection for the gun. I also have Negrini's long double-gun case which I use for international travel and when I'm transporting a pair of long guns. It works equally well with rifles or very long shotguns like the Versa Max waterfowling gun from Remington without needing to take the guns apart, handy for the short run from my house to a duck marsh, for example.

The other case that I have a lot of experience with is Americase. I have a double shotgun case of this brand that has traveled with me in the back of a four-wheel-drive for hundreds of miles at a time on over a dozen occasions and has seen more airplane rides than that. The model that works with pairs of side-by-sides will not fit an over under, so I have one of each. Both are so stout that it would take a baggage handler dropping it from the top of an airplane to dent it. Even in that case, my guess is the guns would be protected, though I'm prone to remember the old TV commercial warning, "Don't try this at home."

The downside compared to some brands is that the Americase is heavy and you'll need to be moderately fit to carry it for any distance (certainly not something a small or older individual who doesn't work out wants to do). The good news is that a pair of shotguns in the Americase double case is still light enough to meet airline guidelines.

There are other good molded cases and metal ones but these are the two companies above with which I have the most experience.

◀ The Mud River Truck Seat Organizer, another good way to keep all of your guns and gear in order. This holds two shotguns plus four pouches for gear and accessories for you, your dog, and your guns. Installs quickly and easily. www.boytharness.com. Photo courtesy Mud River.

CHAPTER 11
Clay Bird Shooting Locations

Casa de Campo–The Caribbean's Best Shooting Facility

▲ Targets are thrown from three levels of the tower. In the early days of the competition they ran a one- and three-man flurry off the tower from all levels. I have won both events. Photo Courtesy of Casa de Campo.

▲ Mr. José Pepe Fanjul shooting. He has made the top game shot list both in U.K.'s *Fieldsports* and *The Field* magazine.

I started going to Casa de Campo, near the town of La Romana on the southeastern coast of the Dominican Republic, in the late 1970s for polo. It was one of the few places I could get into excellent and quite fast medium-goal matches by renting horses for the game. The Maharajah Jabar Singh, a famous player and excellent coach, did a great job of running the club and producing professional polo players. In those days, the 7,000-acre resort was owned by Gulf & Western and was the favorite toy of the company's colorful chairman, Charlie Bludhorn. I returned to the resort often through the early 1980s.

One day, while I was working a polo pony, I noticed a flyer shoot underway in the pigeon ring. (In those days, the equestrian complex and the shooting grounds were contiguous; now they are miles apart.) I went over and introduced myself and was invited to join in. That was my first meeting with Pepe Fanjul, who, along with his brother Alfonso, were the resort's new owners. His devotion to the shooting sports is legendary on many continents.

Pepe Fanjul's pet project was to create a complete shooting facility. Today, Casa has not only the normal array of skeet, trap, five-stand, and wobble-trap layouts, it also has two flyer rings with Barnabee boxes.

The sporting clays course with dozens of stations is one of the best anywhere and provides challenging variations of each shot so that novice and expert alike can test their skills.

Every April, for over thirty years, Casa has hosted the Sugar Invitational Shoot. The courses for this tournament have presented relatively few long targets, yet most years only a few shooters have managed scores in the mid-80s or low 90s. (90s are generally only shot by master class or professional shooters.) This speaks much for the creativity of the original course designer, founding shooting center director, and former resident instructor Michael Rose. "It took over two months to design the course at Casa de Campo," Rose said. "We had to do it via helicopter, because the jungle was so thick we couldn't begin to see the potential by walking the grounds."

The red-and-white high tower is the heart and heartbreaker of the course. It was built to withstand 150 mph hurricane winds and soars so far above the ground it requires a light to ward off low-flying planes. Birds are thrown from forty, eighty, and one hundred ten feet above. The most infuriating are launched from the top and approach both directly overhead and at extreme right and left angles. (The hard right is a forty-five- to sixty-yard target, depending on where it is taken and the vagaries of the wind.)

Rose was arguably one of the most famous bird-shooting coaches of our time and, as former head instructor at the famed West London shooting grounds and gunfitter for Purdey's, taught many of the royals to shoot. He retired from Casa de Camp a few years back, but private lessons on the sporting clays course are available under the guidance of one of the many well-trained instructors employed there. Rental guns and ammunition are available at the shooting center pro shop.

Casa de Campo boasts one of the most unusual partridge and pheasant shoots in the world. Indeed, it is one of the few driven partridge shoots in the Americas. Partridge and pheasant are shot at Rancho Peligro, less than a ten-minute helicopter ride or about a half-hour drive from the resort. Driven mallard are also on offer. Wild doves are shot over sorghum plots, and quail shooting is available over well-trained pointers.

I have enjoyed extended stays at resorts from Gleneagles, in Scotland, to Sun City, in South Africa, and I know of no other that offers the shooting sportsman such an array of pursuits: Casa de Campo has four world-class golf courses, tennis (with ball boys provided), polo, casual horseback rides on the beach, squash, a fitness center, beautiful beaches, all the usual water sports, many fine restaurants, an artists' colony, and all manner of accommodations from fully staffed (cook, butler, maid and so on) villas on the beach to simpler but still very nicely appointed hotel rooms, many with nearby swimming pools. A superb marina has also been built.

In addition to the sporting clay course, there is a five-stand setup, three trap fields, a skeet field, the two live pigeon rings, and, amazingly, colombaire shooting on demand. Casa was one of the first venues at which I shot a sporting clays round using a golf cart to go from station to station. Such a vehicle saves a great deal of time on this long course, and on days when it is warm, makes for a much more pleasant experience. Indeed, golf carts are supplied with all rooms, so that hotel guests can get almost anywhere in the resort as they wish.

Jake Pike, who was trained to the highest levels in Britain, now manages the shooting and all the shooting aspects at Casa de Campo. The shooting today is even more varied than it was under Michael Rose's original leadership, especially with the addition of live bird shooting. It is a testament to the vision of José Pepe Fanjul.

Jake Pike
Shooting Director
J.pike@ccampo.com.do
Phone: 829-599-8739 (cell)

Phone: 809-523-3333 ext. 5145
Email: tiendashooting@ccmpo.com.do
www.casadecampo.com.do

Orvis Sandanona

Conveniently located five minutes from the town of Millbrook, New York, and about ninety minutes north of Manhattan and easily reached from the Taconic State Parkway, Sandanona is the oldest licensed shooting preserve in the America. Fortunately, one does not need to be a member to shoot here. It is sort of run as a combination private and public club in that some activities are for full members only (bird hunts), and the sporting clays membership, which is quite reasonable, gives one a discount. But one does not need to be a sporting clays member to enjoy all the clay shooting the club offers. In addition, it holds shooting clinics, dog handling clinics, wingshooting schools, fly fishing schools, and a Game Fair every September that is always a huge success with some of the premier gunmakers from America, Italy, and Britain in attendance.

As it is owned by Orvis, it is quite natural that Sandanona has a first-class pro shop. It had an excellent chief instructor/ gunfitter in James Ross for many years. In the spring of 2020 the new Chief Shooting Instructor was Paula Moore, an NSCA level III instructor and a competitor with many wins. Sandanona offers private shooting lessons, and the occasional morning or afternoon sporting clays clinic concentrating on a particular target. If live birds are of more interest, the club has an Upland membership, and offers tower pheasant shoots and flighted duck releases.

Open 363 days a year from 9:00 a.m. to 5:00 p.m. (lunch is available most days), one can take advantage of shooting the club's twenty-stand sporting clays course, skeet, five-stand, flurry setups, patterning boards, and more. Reservations are recommended, as they have trappers on call. One has the choice of scooting around the course from a golf buggy or walking it; fitness and time both play a part here.

I won the Davidoff spring shoot in 2014 here with an 88x100 against a field of over 100; next closest was five birds back—but who's counting?

Sandanona Shooting Grounds
3047 Sharon Rd.
Millbrook, NY 12545
Phone: 845-677-9701
Email: sandanona@orvis.com

The Homestead

There is a small cadre of shooting friends from around America who call themselves the "Green Jackets" and have an annual sporting clay competition at the Homestead resort in Virginia. While I've been invited many times by various friends who are members, I've only made the pilgrimage once, as their shoot takes place in October and I am more often in some far-flung destination shooting live birds. That said, I really enjoyed the experience.

The Homestead (now an Omni Hotel) has always been one of the classic famous American resorts, dating back to 1933. David Judah is a well-known coach and has been the manager at the Homestead for decades. In addition to two sporting clays courses, there are four skeet fields, trap, and five-stand layouts. Both group and private lessons are available through

one of the resort's many NSCA certified instructors. The U.S. Open Sporting Clays Championship was held there in 1992.

Other outdoor activities include fly fishing, falconry, horseback riding, hiking, carriage and hayrides, plus kayaking and canoeing. For those who do not have an outdoor bent, there are excellent dining and spa facilities.

The Omni Homestead Resort
7696 Sam Snead Highway
Hot Springs, VA 24445
Phone: 800-838-1766
N.S.C.A. shooting instructors are available for group and private lessons. Reservations required; call 540–839–7787 for information or an appointment.

The Griffin & Howe Shooting School at Hudson Farm

▲ Hudson Farm Main House. Courtesy of Griffin & Howe.

An easy one-hour drive from New York City and only minutes off Interstate 80 is the Hudson Farm. Set in the rural countryside of Andover, New Jersey, this private shooting club is established on the largest privately owned piece of land in the state. "The Farm" consists of 3,800 acres of beautifully landscaped farmland with several ponds and lakes. There are two sporting clay courses, a pheasant flurry field, trap field, many live pheasant release points, and multiple duck presentations from multiple blinds. For the lucky few who are members or their guests, delightful accommodation is available.

Griffin & Howe calls Hudson Farm home, hosting many charity events through its consummate Shooting School. "Rain or shine instruction" is available utilizing enclosed shooting areas. While Hudson Farm is a private shooting club, The Griffin & Howe Shooting School is available to the public 364 days a year, offering shotgun and rifle instruction on The Farm's beautiful sporting clays course and new state-of-the-art long-range rifle facilities. Throughout the summer the public is welcomed to shoot the 20-station sporting clay course on various days most frequently combined with a charity event.

▲ Courtesy of Griffin & Howe.

Pre or post-shooting private luncheons may be served in the unique setting of the Griffin & Howe Gunroom. The gunroom has hundreds of some of the finest sporting firearms available, together with affordable brands displayed for one's viewing pleasure. Shooting attire and all accessories are also to be found at this location—truly one-stop shopping! It is also home to a 6,000 square-foot Griffin & Howe custom rifle manufacturing and gunsmithing facility, which provides a "try it before you buy it" approach.

Since the inception of the Griffin & Howe Shooting School in 1935 (the oldest shooting school in America), the company has offered discriminating sportsmen and sportswomen professional and comprehensive shotgun instruction and gunfitting. It has one of the very few

NSCA Level III Instructors, (there are only four in the Tri-State area).

For the avid wing or clay shooter, few things compare with the satisfaction of a successful day in the field or at the range, and few things can match the frustration of missing a bird that should have been an easy shot. "Anyone can have an 'off day,' but when the problem occurs again and again," as the former head honcho Guy Bignell is quick to point out "it's time to consider a lesson with the Griffin & Howe Shooting School. Clients are tutored combining the elements of the Stanbury and Churchill styles of shooting." This starts with the fundamentals of correct shooting posture and stance, proper gun mounting (greatly assisted by a gun that fits the shooter), and the ability to focus on the target. Instructors then discuss and review their client's goals and lay out a plan to achieve them. While the Griffin & Howe instruction program has been designed to enhance the shooting skills of upland bird and waterfowl hunters, the basic principles help many sporting clay shots as well.

In pre-Covid 2019, I gave half-day clinics at The Hudson Farm in driven shooting techniques for tall birds. There are sessions for shooters new to the game and for advanced shots. The techniques taught works equally well for any long range pass shooting including dove and duck.

270 Stanhope Sparta Road
Andover, NJ 07821
Phone: 973-398-2670
griffinhowe.com/contact/shooting-school

The Greenbrier

The Greenbrier has been a gun club since 1913. In addition to a number of skeet and trap fields, it has a good-quality and extensive sporting clays course. This rural area of West Virginia offers much to interest sportsmen, from upland shooting to trout fishing. Indeed, trout fishing is available both on the property and as guided trips off-site.

The resort provides great food and accommodations, plus all sorts of add-ons in case one's better half is not a shooter. These include everything from spas to golf and tennis to horseback riding. I do find their rates both for skeet and sporting clays to be steep, but it is what it is.

Today, it's much easier to get to Greenbrier as there are Amtrak runs from Washington, D.C. It is a very long drive from most of the Northeast, but once you arrive it is worth the journey.

The Greenbrier
101 Main Street, West
White Sulphur Springs, WV 24986
Phone: 855-453-4858
www.greenbrier.com/Activities/Activity-Collection/Gun-Club

A.I.M. at M&M Hunting and Sporting Clays

▲ Matarese is both a great shot and a great coach—a rare combination. Courtesy of Anthony Matarese Jr.

Anthony Matarese was originally coached by the legendary Dan Carlisle, but, as Anthony pointed out to me, he's gone on to develop his own style. I have taken lessons from many of the top British and American coaches, and Anthony is very impressive both as a coach and, obviously, a talented shot, having won a World Championship in 2016. The fact that he has tremendous mental discipline and a great eye for targets is obvious, but he also has the benefit of having been brought up at his family M&M Hunting & Sporting Clays property in Pennsville, New Jersey. The facility is quite close to Philadelphia, and not too bad a run from New York, Baltimore, or even Washington, D.C.

As Anthony's middle initial is I, it is appropriate he created the acronym A.I.M. Shooting School for the method he uses. According to his website (www.clayshootinginstruction.com), the method of the A.I.M. Shooting School is "based on being in 'control' of every target by learning how to 'connect' with each different type of target presentation. A.I.M. Shooting School uses a base technique with a few core principles that can be tailored to allow the shooter to approach a target in the most efficient manner. Shooters learn how to balance the science of shooting with the "feel" part of the game."

In addition to individual instructions by Anthony or his two associates, Diane Sorantino, who won the women's division of The World Championship in 2018 on a course designed by the great George Digweed; and Dan Krumm, you can be assured that you will learn the correct methodology and fundamentals that are the foundation of any serious success in shooting. One of the real strengths of A.I.M. is the mental game part of coaching, and there are even specialized seminars and clinics for this.

Again, from the website but something to which I can also personally attest: "Anthony is considered by many to have one of the best mental games in the world. Anthony is known for consistently performing well under pressure. Learn the mental system that has contributed to his consistent performances."

Private, semi-private, and group instruction is available from Matarese and his two Associates. Check their website or call for more information.

Phone: 609-685-0704
Email: anthony@clayshootinginstruction.com

Brays Island Plantation

▲ Life at Brays Island offers traditional Southern hospitality at its best. Photo courtesy of Brays Island.

I shot at Brays Island in the early 1990s, and was invited back down this year but couldn't make it as I was slaving away on this manuscript. Truly disappointing. While Brays Island is a private residential community, it is occasionally open to invited guests of exhibitors attending the annual shooting expo. Brays is located about 60 miles southwest of the Charleston Airport and 50 miles north of Savannah, Georgia, which makes getting there a snap.

The sporting clays course was recently updated by the highly respected course designer Marty Fisher. It has been expanded from 12 to 15 stations. The shooting grounds also offer skeet, trap, and five-stand, plus rifle, pistol and archery ranges. The club pro shop offers full-time instruction, apparel, shotguns, and supplies, as well as gun cleaning, storage, rentals, and repairs. In addition to the clay sports, one can also hunt quail, pheasant, and partridge on foot, by horseback, and even by old fashioned mule-drawn hunt wagon. Brays 5,500 acres includes 3,500 acres of pristine woods, marshes, and fields that promise a fine hunting experience. Other opportunities include deer, dove, and turkey in season. There are over 30 pointing dogs in the large kennel, and Brays has a full-time dog trainer and many guides on hand. Brays has a wide range of fishing opportunities, plus an equestrian center, golf, tennis, a gymnasium. In addition to being a club where one can shoot upon occasion without membership through lessons or various competitions and expositions held

at the club, there is also the opportunity to purchase land. According to Paul Burton, "Befriending an owner at Brays may give you the opportunity to experience the shooter's dream, but becoming an owner there will assure that you live the dream!"

Brays Island
115 Brays Island Dr.
Sheldon, SC 29941
Phone: 1-843-846-3100
Email: pburton@islc.net

Vero Beach Clay Shooting Sports
This is the new name for the facility once known as the Indian River Trap & Skeet and located about 20 minutes from downtown Vero Beach.

Since the early eighties, I have tried to spend a week or two in Florida to break up the midwinter blues. Until recently that meant Palm Beach, chosen because my two close friends in Florida call that home. In 2019, for a change of pace, I decided to try Vero Beach for my winter vacation. It was a good choice. Far less social than Palm Beach, and in my old age so am I. (As one friend calls it, "post-social" as opposed to antisocial.)

It was a similar run from Vero to my friend's ranch near Okeechobee where for decades I have had the privilege of shooting wild quail with him. The sport, as always, was sublime.

On the second day in Vero Beach I was taking the elevator up to my room at the hotel when a gentleman entered carrying a cased shotgun over his shoulder. I smiled and asked him if he was down for the competitions. He said he was shooting the Caribbean Cup which kicked off the Florida season at the nearby Vero Beach Clays. He told me it was only a twenty minute ride and definitely worth the trip.

Vero Beach has a wonderful feel to it as there are very few commercial buildings in the town. And as one drives out of Vero proper and over the bridge one passes numerous gated communities but within 10 minutes one arrives in a more rural South. Soon one is passing boat sales and horse farms. The final few miles to the shooting club is on a dirt road. Very cool. Indeed, the adjacent property is a tree farm called Hammond Grove. Driving into the facility one could tell everything was well-planned—necessary as the

▲ The guide and the hunter move forward while a staunch pointer stands statuesque. Game shooting is important at Bray's, though harder to partake for non-owners than clays. Photo courtesy of Brays Islands.

Caribbean Cup has hundreds of attendees, many of whom are master class shots.

The office was very rudimentary. Outside, however, were schematics for the planned new clubhouse. This was part of an overall upgrade due to a change of ownership. Mick and Emma Howells, originally from Britain, established in 2005 Indian River Shooting Sports on the grounds of the old Indian River Trap and Skeet Club. The new owners are Dan Lewis and Murry Gerber, who purchased the facility in December 2018 and also own Elite Shotguns with stores in many states.

Emma told me how the trap and skeet club was quite run down and needed a major cleanup in addition to a major refurbishment. There were few better people to undertake the task than Mick. Mick had already won major World Championships including English sporting and Fitasc both as an individual and team Gold. It is now under new management.

Sporting clays is the heart of the facility. While it is set on fewer than 30 acres, it maximizes the utility of the grounds while taking advantage of the natural beauty of the property. The attractiveness of the facility has been enhanced by the removal of hundreds of non-native invasive Brazilian pepper trees plus additional plantings of appropriate species. The course is basically a large circle with all the shot fall heading safely towards the center. As one makes a cycular permutation one finds well-designed stands where one can either shoot on one's own with the time delay or trap for each other if shooting with friends. It is a prepaid card system that does not require a professional trapper to accompany the shooter or group. I must admit I prefer the system.

Depending on the day, there are 24 to 28 stations. They are broken down into two categories: the blue which shows competition quality targets and the red which offers slighter softer targets. In many cases a station will have four traps and one can choose from the menu to shoot the red or the blue presentations. When I shot here this past March with my friend Scott Hurley we generally shot the blue course but at some stations shot both presentations. Approximately 100 new traps have been purchased and incorporated into the sporting clay course.

The five stand, which presents an interesting and testing array of targets, is covered which is a definite advantage should a shower pop up. There are also trap and skeet fields. While they primarily hold NSCA competitions, plans are in the work to bring back ATA events.

If you going to be in the area for a while, it is probably worth getting a membership, which is $250. Without a membership a round of sporting clays costs $48 and with membership $38. Both are good value for money. Similarly, cart rentals are $20 and $15 respectively. Members see a host of discounts including on shotguns. As the folks from Elite now own this there will be a large selection of shotguns including Beretta, Kolar, Browning, Caesar Guarini and on and on.

In addition to the Caribbean Cup they also offer a number of NSCA shoots over the course of each year. Most interestingly they have seen the increased interest in women's shooting and have tailored both lady days and clinics specifically for women with just a few women to each NSCA instructor—and on these days all the instructors are female.

From late January to mid-February there are two other international shoots in addition to the Caribbean Cup in the Treasure Coast area: Krieghoff Classic at the South Florida Shooting Club in Palm City and the Gator Cup at Quail Creek Plantation in Okeechobee so many shooters come down and shoot the circuit. (Florida has a very active sporting clay winter season and a list of the tournaments can be found on http://www.floridaclays.com/ or contact FloridaSportingClaysAssn@gmail.com. They cover all things competitive in Florida—at least from a shotgunners point of view.)

5925 82nd Ave.
Vero Beach, FL 32967
Phone: 772-978-0935
Email: info@verobeachclayshooting.com
https://verobeachclayshooting.com

I have not personally shot the following but picked them due to great reputations and geographic diversity:

Dallas Gun Club

The Dallas Gun Club has all manners of targets including skeet, trap, sporting clays, and Helice. While it is a

▲ The clubhouse at Dallas Gun Club. Photo courtesy of Dallas Gun Club

membership club, if you are interested in shooting at the venue there are many registered events where the public is welcome to compete. Lessons are available in all disciplines and the famous competitor Todd Bender gives frequent clinics.

Phone: 972-462-0043
Email: richard@dallasgunclub.com.

Forest City Gun Club

This historic club was founded in 1883 and has been in continuous operation since then. It is a large club with a forty-acre lake and grounds of nearly a square mile. In addition to twenty-six skeet fields, it also offers trap and sporting clays.

The club has had a variety of locations over the years. In the 1880s it shot on Hutchison Island, not at clay pigeons but its precursor, glass balls. More than 20 years ago the club hosted the World Skeet Shooting Championships, and the old fields were torn up and 26 new ones were built.

While the waiting list for membership is long, you can use the facility during a sanctioned competition.

9203 Ferguson Avenue
Savannah GA 31406
Phone: 912-354-0210
Email: zac@forestcitygunclub.com
www.forestcitygunclub.com

Nemacolin Woodlands Resort

Located in Farmington, Pennsylvania, 70 miles southeast of Pittsburgh, the resort's Field Club is offers

more than 30 stations on three separate sporting clay courses. Five-stand, a wobble trap field, and tall towers are available, as is instruction. There is also fly fishing and fly-fishing instruction, and upland bird hunts during the preserve season.

▲ Nemacolin has more than 30 stations on three separate sporting clays courses.

1001 Lafayette Dr.
Farmington, PA 15437
Phone: 866-344-6957
www.nemacolin.com/shootingevents

Oak Tree Gun Club

This California facility was opened in 1973 as a private club and had such Hollywood celebs including Charlton Heston and Roy Rogers as early members, plus the well-known actor and skeet shooting champ Robert Stack and my pal John Milius. It is now a public facility. Originally it was just a skeet and trap range. It has expanded greatly and now offers sporting clays and even international varieties of skeet and trap. It has two extensive pro shops, including a Beretta gallery. Both classes and private lessons are available. It is a great facility in Southern California and very reasonably priced.

23121 Coltrane Ave.
Newhall, CA 91321
www.oaktreegunclub.com
Phone: 661-259-7441

Grouse Ridge Shotgun Shooting Club

This range is located about an hour from Anchorage in the town of Wasilla and is one of the largest shotgunning facilities in the state. It is best known for its sporting clay course, but also offers FITASC, five-stand, skeet, and trap. It is open both on a membership and non-membership basis. The Alaska State Sporting Clays Championship took place here in 2015, and the range regularly hosts regional and state championships. It even boasts a popular restaurant.

Phone: 907-376-2473
Email: grouse@mtaonline.net
grouseridge.com

The South Florida Shooting Club

This range is located in Palm City, not terribly far from Palm Beach. While it is primarily a private membership club, it offers many ATA, NSSA, and NSCA tournament so there is ample opportunity to enjoy the facilities. It even has a Helice field. Lessons are also available.

Phone: 772-597-5852
Email: kristen@southfloridashootingclub.com
www.southfloridashootingclub.com

Quail Creek Plantation

This is a fantastic facility that holds The Gator Cup, one of the more important sporting Clay and FITASC tournaments in the country, amongst other competitions and offers both clay shooting, upland hunting, and more. The facility is currently up for sale, but hopefully it will stay the shooting facility that is open to the public. I visited it recently and was most impressed. It is convenient to shooters from Palm Beach to Vero Beach and all points in between (via a 45-minute run from the two towns mentioned).

www.quailcreekplantation.com
12399 Northeast 224th St.
Okeechobee, FL 34972
Phone: 863-763-2529

Sport Abroad

Whenever I travel, and that is possibly too often, I do try and keep my eye in by shooting at local grounds. Should this tome make a second or third edition, I will add Canada, Australia and New Zealand to cover most of the English-speaking world. If you are fortunate

▲ While staying at the Vineyard Hotel in Cape Town, with Table Mountain as the backdrop from the window of my room, I was able to go to a number of venues to shoot clays.

enough to travel to Britain or to South Africa, these are worthwhile shooting facilities to try.

While I was off big game hunting before and after this trip and did not have a shotgun with me it was easy enough to rent. Wherever you travel, it is a good idea to check out places to shoot and learn to break different targets from different presentations. Constancia, Stellenbosch and Franschhoek are near Cape Town, worth the trip for the wine, and Hermanus which is also not a long drive is famous for whale watching. Cape Horn is stunningly beautiful in a very raw, wild sense.

The website for RSA's clay competitions and clubs is www.ctsasa.co.za/clubs, and it will steer you in the right direction. Below are a number of clubs in the Cape—both Eastern and Western—that are worth trying especially if you are holidaying in the area. The main website of the governing body for clay pigeon shooting in the country is www.ctsasa.co.za/.

Complete Contact Details
Clay Target Shooting Association of South Africa
PO Box 812
Great Brak River
6525
South Africa
Phone: +27 (0) 86 111 4581 (Telephone hours: 08h00 to 15h00 Monday to Friday)
Fax: +27 (0) 86 684 1973
Email: ctsasa@netactive.co.za

For something a little different, Tigger 2 Charters in Cape Town offers fantastic boat cruises along the magnificent Cape Coastline and offers many activities including clay pigeon shooting from the deck of their yacht. Not only are you able to enjoy some exciting South African clay pigeon shooting, but you will enjoy the picturesque surroundings and luxurious relaxation that these cruises have to offer. The area code for RSA is 27. If you call once you are there you would dial 0214180241 or 0828524383. If you're calling from abroad, you add 011 for international +27 for RSA and drop zero before the rest of the number. This is not a serious clay shooting venue but would make for a fun outing and something unique to do, especially if you're traveling with your family.

▲ The Cape of Good Hope is the most southwestern point in Africa. While shooting is the most important aspect of our sport, when in distant lands one should stop and smell the roses, metaphorically speaking.

The sporting venues below offer more traditional clay shooting and competitions:

Hermanus Skietklub
Name: Elna van der Merwe
Number: 073-510-1122
Email: hermanusskietklub@gmail.com
Province: Western Cape

False Bay Gun Club
Name: Charles Montgomery
Number: 082-431-9256
Email: charles@suburbanguns.co.za
Province: Western Cape

Greyton Gun Club
Name: J R Sedgwick
Email: douglas@greyton.co.za
Province: Western Cape

Elgin Sporting Clays
Name: Zoe Smith
Number: 082-339-4998
Email: info@elginsportingclays.com
Province: Western Cape

Morgenrood Kleiduif Klub
Name: Julius du Preez
Number: 082-338-2487
Email: joubertsdal@barvallei.co.za
Province: Western Cape

Outeniqua Clay Target Club
Name: Peter Sullivan
Number: 082-498-1797
Email: peters@compute.co.za
Province: Western Cape

Swartland Skietklub
Name: Hans Hanekom
Number: 082-8927-369
Email: hans@swartland.co.za
Province: Western Cape

Valley Gun Club
Name: Anton van den Berg
Number: 071-451-0486
Email: valleygunclub@paarlonline.co.za
Province: Western Cape

Great Britain, a.k.a. United Kingdom
Great Britain is the home of sporting clays as most Americans know it. Many of the very best shots have come from there, amongst whom George Digweed stands at the top. The last time I checked George had 30 world championships to his credit.

Britain offers fantastic clay shooting opportunities as they have been set up to teach both game and competitive shooters since the inception of the modern aspects of our sport.

Below are shooting grounds in no particular order:

West London Shooting School

Since 1901, it has been an institution of shooting tuition and gunfitting where Purdey's and other London best have sent clients. The great Percy Stanbury whose books are very much worth reading taught here, and his method has been followed by acolytes including Michael and Alan Rose.

Less than twelve miles from central London, this shooting ground boasts one hundred traps, a lodge, and restaurant. Chief instructor Alan Rose, now semi-retired, learned his trade from the legendary Percy Stanbury, and their contingent of instructors will definitely help you shoot better. Personally, I found Alan's brother Michael a better instructor, but both are excellent.

West London Shooting School
Sharvel Lane
West End Road
Northolt
Middlesex
UB5 6RA
Phone: +44 (0)208 8451377
www.shootingschool.co.uk

Holland & Holland Shooting Ground

Hertfordshire

Holland & Holland has an excellent ground with a comfortable lodge quite close to London. Indeed, they used to run an interclub shoot with the best London clubs: Whites, Brooks's, Boodle's and others competing in a very gentlemanly arena. One year they invited me to lead a team from my New York club. Great fun especially as they provided transportation to and from the grounds so that we could imbibe to our hearts delight during dinner. Their current chief instructor is Chris Bird, though I have not shot with him so I cannot comment.

I shot with them when Rex Gage ran the show and then with Ken Davies who wrote their book *The Better Shot . . . with Holland and Holland*. I must admit I found Davies a reasonably good instructor but slightly goofy in that he wore deer stalker's, which is fine if you're stalking or trying to look like Sherlock Holmes but inappropriate for bird shooting. I did not find him as useful an instructor as Rex Gage.

Holland & Holland Shooting Grounds
Ducks Hill Road, Northwood, HA6 2ST
011+ 441923 825349 grounds@hollandandholland.com

West Kent Shooting School

It is set close to Royal Tunbridge Wells. The sporting course gives a good selection target combinations and they do have a one-hundred-foot tower that can present reasonably tall birds.

West Kent Shooting School
New Hay Farm
Old Hay
Paddock Wood
Kent
TN12 7DG
Phone: +44 (0)1892 834306
www.westkentshooting.co.uk

Lady's Wood Shooting School is better known for game shooting instruction then for competitive clay shooting. Its 40-yard high tower offers realistic practice the tall bird shooters. It is conveniently situated near Junction 18 of the M4 or Junction 14 of the M5.

Lady's Wood Shooting School
Mapleridge Lane
Horton
Bristol
BS37 6PW
Phone: +44 (0)1454 294546
www.ladyswood.co.uk

Ian Coley Shooting School

Situated in the Cotswolds, it is not a bad run from Heathrow Airport assuming one does not get stuck in traffic. Ian Coley was Britain's Olympic coach for many years. Sporting three high towers and many other stations, it offers a multitude of target presentations. Instruction is available.

Ian Coley Shooting School
Nr Andoversford
Cheltenham
Gloucestershire
GL54 4AX
Phone: +44 (0)1242 870391
www.iancoley.co.uk

E. J. Churchill Shooting Ground

E. J. Churchill on Sir Edward Dashwood's West Wycombe estate is not too far a run from London and quite close to Heathrow. This is also the home of the gun company. I visited the gun shop with Chris Batha years ago but did not shoot the course. It does include high towers and a large layout of targets that are suitable both for the clay shot and also for individuals wanting to tune-up before heading to the hills to shoot driven grouse.

They have a good team of coaches. Their three high towers can throw targets over 50 yards high and they also offer many disciplines including Skeet and English Sporting. It is located about 30 miles from London.

E. J. Churchill Shooting Ground
Park Lane
Lane End
High Wycombe
Buckinghamshire
NP14 3NS
Phone: +44 (0)1494 883227
www.ejchurchill.com

Hopetoun Clays

It is situated on the 6,500-acre estate in Scotland but a mere half-hour drive from Edinburgh, and even less than that from Edinburgh Airport. Stewart Cumming, a top FITASC shooter, manages the facility which has a fine reputation.

Hopetoun Clays
Hopetoun Estate
South Queensferry
EH30 9SL
Phone: +44 (0)1313 319940
www.hopetounclays.co.uk

Hazel Bank Shooting Ground

Hazel Bank Shooting Ground
Hazel Bank
Knaresborough
North Yorkshire
HG5 0QQ
Phone: +44 (0)7852 785590
www.hazelbankshooting.co.uk

Auchterhouse Country Sports

Auchterhouse, voted Scotland's favorite shooting ground, runs everything from small competitions to national and even international events. They boast skeet fields, DTL (the English equivalent of trap), doubles trap, Sporting stations and a high tower and other facilities.

Auchterhouse Country Sports
Burnhead Farm
Auchterhouse near Dundee
DD3 0QN
Phone: +44 (0)1382 320476
www.auchterhousecountrysports.co.uk

The Royal Berkshire Shooting School

It is about an hour's drive or only about half an hour by fast train from Paddington station in London. Specializes in corporate entertainment, but has a number of instructors plus a gun shop, store etc.

Hook End Lane
Pangbourne
Berkshire
RG8 8SD
Shooting School
Phone: 01491 672 900
Email: info@rbss.co.uk

Bisley Shooting Ground

Founded in 1895, Bisley is famous for its long-range rifle shooting competitions, but also offers a tremendous number of clay shooting opportunities for beginners and for expert shots. They run a number of competitions and have both membership and non-membership packages. Again quite close to London in

Surrey, Bisley Shooting Ground is worth the trip simply for its historic significance. Its English Victorian clubhouse was built in 1865 on Wimbledon Common. The headquarters were dismantled and moved to Bisley in 1895.

Bisley Clay Pigeon Shooting Ground
Bisley Camp, Brookwood, Woking GU24 0NY, U.K.
Bookings & General Enquiries
Phone: +44+(0)1483797017
Email: office@bisleyshooting.co.uk

Bisley at Braidwood

Bisley has sister shooting grounds in Scotland located on an estate in the Scottish Borders near the Eildon Hills. It is one of Scotland's most complete shooting grounds. A comfortable clubhouse has an informal café, as well as a restaurant.

Bisley at Braidwood
Braidwood
Midlem
Nr Selkirk
TD7 4QD
01835 870816
Bookings and General Enquiries
Phone: +441835870280
Email: braidwood@bisleyshooting.co.uk

Barbury Shooting School

Located in Wiltshire, this venue offers shooting practice seven days a week, and often puts on competitions in various disciplines.

Phone: 01793 940420 or 07872 666154
Email: enquiries@barburyshoot.com
Barbury Shooting School is a ten-minute drive from Junction 15 of the M4
www.barburyshootingschool.com

North Wales Shooting School

It is a very complete facility offering Olympic Trap (covered), Down the Line, plus a number of skeet and sporting clay layouts not to mention high and low towers.

It offers the shooter the ability to go round on one's own through an automated system.

www.nwshootingschool.co.uk
North Wales Shooting School, Sealand Manor, Deeside, Flintshire CH5 2SB.
Phone: 01244 812219F. 01244 822650E.
Email: info@nwshootingschool.co.uk

Bywell Shooting Ground

Bywell Shooting Ground in Northumberland it is fairly close to the Duke of Northumberland's famous Alnwick castle and estate. It is also a well-known gun shop with a wide variety of interesting shotguns primarily from British and Italian manufacturers. At their clubhouse refreshments are available and there are good parking facilities. They have run national and international competitions here.

Bywell Farm
Felton
Northumberland
NE65 9QQ
Phone: 01670 787 827
Fax: 01670 787 093
Email: info@bywellshootingground.co.uk
www.bywellshootingground.co.uk

Coniston Shooting Ground

Located in the beautiful Yorkshire Dales, Coniston is attached to a hotel and has many other sporting opportunities available. One can stay at the hotel and shoot but that is not required.

The Coniston Hotel which also has a spa, would make for a good family outing. The serious shot will find a large selection of twenty sporting presentations plus a Compak, DTL (down the line/trap), and skeet stands.

The Coniston Hotel Country Estate and Spa
Coniston Cold
Skipton
North Yorkshire
BD23 4EA
Phone: 01756 748080
Fax: 01756 749487
Email: info@theconistonhotel.com
www.theconistonhotel.com/activities/shooting-ground

Willow Farm Shooting Ground

They offer English sporting, skeet, compak, and DTL from Tuesday to Saturday for practice and lessons. Every Sunday, there are either a seventy- or one-hundred-bird sporting competition with a Compak Pool Shoot. There are classes from beginners to competitive AA shots.

Nestled in the beautiful Kent countryside, offers the ideal surroundings to spend a day shooting.

Willow Farm Shooting Ground
Reading Street
Tenterden, Kent
TN30 7LA
Phone: 01233 758703
Email: info@willowfarmshootingground.co.uk
www.willowfarmshootingground.co.uk

A1 Shooting Ground

Offering clay pigeon shooting for every ability level, A1 Shooting Ground is not far outside of London city center.

Claudio Capaldo, the ground owner, is a very well-known coach who has acted as National Team coach in many Continental, World as well as the 2004 Olympic Games

A1 Shooting Ground offers traditional English Sporting, Olympic Trap and most interestingly for a venue near London, Helice.

A1 Shooting Ground
A1 Barnet Bypass
Barnet EN5 3GZ
Phone: 02084419986
Email: CLAUDIO@A1SG.CO.UK

Loch Lomond Shooting School

It is about half an hour north of Glasgow, Scotland, and not too far to run from Edinburgh.
Loch Lomond Shooting School
Tullichewan Farm
Upper Stoneymollan Road
Balloch G83 8QY
Phone: 01389 711190
lomondshooting.co.uk

Grimsthorpe Estate

In the East Midlands, Grimsthorpe offers instruction, practice rounds, plus registered and FITASC and English sporting competitions.

Grimsthorpe Estate Shooting Ground
Scottlethorpe Grange
near Edenham
Bourne
Lincolnshire
PE10 0LN
Phone: +44 (0)1778 591128

Other facilities worth Googling are: Southern Counties, renamed but reopened www.dorsetshootingschool.co.uk

East Yorkshire parklodgeshootingschool.co.uk

The Joe Neville Shooting School
Jackhill Farm Nottingham Rd, Tansley, Matlock, DE4 5FR
Phone: 01629 582859
Mid Wales, near Wrexham www.midwalesshooting-centre.com

Southdown in West Sussex southdowngunclub.co.uk

David Olive's Apsley (I shot with him once in the early 1980s when I was doing an article for *Town & Country*) www.apsleyshootinggrounds.com

Doveridge in Derbyshire www.doveridgeclaysports.co.uk

Mike Reynolds's Mid-Norfolk www.norfolkshooting.co.uk

West Midlands Shooting Ground, Shropshire www.wmsg.co.uk

CHAPTER 12
Where to Go Shooting Live

efore I continue to a long general reference for North America's best wingshooting venues, allow me to describe a recent quail hunt with my great and good friend Peter Horn, passionate hunter, conservationist, and Beretta's Vice President Emeritus.

Pine Hill Plantation

▲ Damien with quail. Photo courtesy of Peter Horn.

Few things in life are as enjoyable as Southern hospitality or hunting bobwhite quail. When you put the two together, life is glorious. And so it is at Pine Hill Plantation.

Rod pointed and Thriller backed, English pointers which were frozen like statues. This gave Peter Horn, my shooting companion on the left of the line, Steven Coe, the guide in the middle, and your humble scribe plenty of time to move forward in safe formation. It wasn't our first point of the morning, but it was one of the most exciting, as a covey of wild birds more than 20 strong exploded just as we got into position.

I have shot quail for fifty years, give or take (God, I'm old), and yet, unlike the BB King song, the thrill is not gone. My first go during college was a humdrum affair at a very commercial preserve near Palm Beach,

where the birds flew like chickens. My second hunt was at a plantation in Georgia. When the first flush of wild quail appeared, I nearly stroked. The distinction was so great between the two that I was completely unprepared for the amazing sight of whirling wings, seemingly loud as thunder, as they broke cover.

▲ Peter Horn awaiting duck.

While I'm no longer as taken aback as I was all those years ago, the adrenaline still rushes. Since my first go at reared quail, I have seen many non-wild birds that flew well; I think it is the initial acceleration that wild birds display that puts them in a league of their own.

At Pine Hill, even the reared birds flew like rockets. Hiding in the wire grass or food plots scattered between the tall pines, the birds were often unseen until flushed. I watched the ground carefully at all times on this shoot, as it had been unseasonably warm that year and snakes were active. While I had not seen any, there had been reported sightings. Make no mistake; though close to towns like Tallahassee and Thomasville, this is a wild place, where one is far more likely to see an alligator than a man in a three-piece suit.

Peter fired two shots in his quadrant, and I did the same in mine, and in quick order the dogs had picked up the three quail we'd shot. Peter is a great sportsman and friend (one of my few), with whom I've shared adventures from Ethiopia and the Sudan to Hungary. We'd flown from JFK down to Tallahassee, leaving winter behind and arriving in Florida's autumnal splendor. Because of a short connection in Raleigh, we'd chosen not to bring our own quail guns, but didn't sweat it, as we knew Beretta shotguns were the loaners at Pine Hill.

Peter and I arrived about the right time for supper. There were delicious appetizers to munch while we were drinking at the bar. We were sent menus to choose our courses in advance of our trip; being Yankees, we both knew we wanted fried chicken for the first night. We were joined for dinner by Pine Hill's owners, Doug and Jackie Coe, with whom we would be sharing our newest adventure. Doug and Jackie enjoy sharing their passion for history, tradition, and wingshooting. It is part of what makes Pine Hill so special. We shot as a foursome, Jackie and Doug astride as Peter and I rode in comfort in the wagon.

A unique aspect of Pine Hill is that there are four manor houses. Of Georgian tidewater architecture, each is separately staffed with a first-rate chef and a housekeeper to look after guests requirements. It is one of the very few lodges that make the cut to be part of the Beretta Trident program, and it was Orvis Lodge of the Year in 2013.

Before dinner that first night, Steven Coe, our hunt master, stopped by to introduce himself. Steven is twenty-seven and has been hunting in South Georgia with his father, Doug, since he was five, guiding from age seventeen. He has a degree from Auburn in forestry.

Doug, Jackie, Peter, and I drove out to the quail field in a four-wheel-drive vehicle, where we met Herman, our wagon driver, Damian (a.k.a. "Junior"), our assistant huntmaster, and Steven. As Herman was driving the wagon, the Coe's Lab, Cam, sat beside him, with Peter and me perched comfortably behind.

Within five minutes, we were on our first covey. The first brace of dogs was "put down" to run, as were all of Steven's dogs, English pointers. Each dog hunted well. They ranged out nicely, chewing up the ground. It is amazing how good dogs will vary their range depending on how they are hunted—from the ground or from horseback. My setters Buck and Rose would put on the afterburners and really range out as soon as I sat on a horse, yet hunt closer when I was afoot.

Blue and Betty kept finding covey after covey. They backed each other well. It was a joy to watch. The

▲ Herman the mule team driver, a horse, and three asses, two of which were mules.

▲ Shooting at quail while more erupt beside me. Photo courtesy of Peter Horn.

quail were a mixture of wild birds and reared quail. The wild birds, in general, did not hold as well or as long. Strangely, I think this is when bigger-ranging, faster dogs have the advantage in that they create more predator/prey response so that the quail, fearing the worst, tend to want to sit and hide, rather than fly away—at least until men appear.

What I found fascinating was the way the guides used the pointers to pin the birds down, while Steven had Cam wait for us to get into position. Once we were ready, the Lab went in and flushed the birds. This really worked nicely.

▲ Jackie Coe on horseback.

Pine Hill plantation in southern Georgia is a bit south of the private plantations that have made the Albany, Georgia/Northern Florida region so famous for wild quail. Though quail is king, Pine Hill is much more than just quail. Here, one can entertain privately or corporately with quail shooting, clays, skeet, and bass fishing, or dove and turkey when in season. Wild duck coincides with much of the prime quail season.

The four lodges of Pine Hill have wonderful views of the unnamed 90-acre lake on whose banks they have been built. There's a large kennel of dogs—almost exclusively English pointers—which they run, as should be, in braces. Interestingly, many of their dogs came from field trials, where they didn't quite have what it

takes to be champions. They are perfect for this work, though, as they are steady to wing and shot, which has the practical advantage of allowing one to take low shots with drastically less concern about hitting a dog (one still has to be on one's toes, as few hunting dogs are 100 percent steady to wing and shot).

▲ Doug Coe and I walking in on point. Photo courtesy of Peter Horn.

The shoots take place in an interesting fashion. There is a morning hunt and an afternoon hunt. Some guests do one session or the other but most do both. A half-day hunt generally covers over 100 acres, though if scenting conditions are less than ideal, they cover more ground. Pine Hill hunters never cover the same ground twice during their visit. Lunch is often taken in the field, normally something simple but hearty, a pulled-pork sandwich, for example.

After breakfast—this day, great pancakes with bacon on the side—on one's first day at Pine Hill, one will be taken to watch a safety video on quail shooting. It is one of the best I've seen—short, clear, and to the point. Then one gets into a vehicle and driven to the quail fields. There, the day's shooters disembark and join their guides, known as hunt masters, and the mule drivers who drive wagons set up specifically for quail hunting. In these wagons, the seats are elevated to give the hunters a good view of the terrain, dog boxes are set behind, and on each side is a well-designed gun

Six Thousand Acres of Bird-Hunting Heaven

Pine Hill Plantation hunts quail over approximately 6,000 acres and can accommodate private group of four to 36. A morning duck hunt can be added to a day of quail hunting for a nominal charge. The most common ducks are ringnecks, teal, and wood ducks, though in colder weather there are the occasional mallard or canvasback in the mix.

You'll need a preserve hunting license, and remember your Federal duck stamp if you opt for duck hunting. Birds will be dressed, packaged, and frozen, then placed in soft coolers on the day of your departure.

From late March through mid-May, Pine Hill Plantation offers some of the best Eastern wild turkey hunting that South Georgia has to offer. It can be combined with excellent bass fishing.

Each lodge at Pine Hill has Wi-Fi and cable TV. Additional services can include transportation to and from Bainbridge, Georgia, or Tallahassee, Florida airports.

rack to make grabbing one's gun a breeze as needed, while otherwise protecting them in a fashion that prevents shotguns being scratched. This does matter.

Before the dogs got too tired or overheated we returned to the buggy and Steve or Jr. gave them a ton of water to drink so that they could cool down. He then picked them up and put the next brace out to run. (Before I go on, I would like to point out that the guides take great care of their dogs at Pine Hill, always making sure they had plenty of water to keep cool and picking up the pointers before they could overheat. A hose was set up at the back of the wagon, from which the dogs drank greedily.)

The second brace was as good as the first. It seemed there were hardly 15 minutes that would go by without a covey being pointed. They only allow two shooters on each point and three birds to be taken from a covey—unless all four barrels connect. Occasionally singles were shot, but most often this was while following up on cripples. It was a great and exciting day in the field made more enjoyable by the shared companionship of good sportsmen. Everyone was safe

and a good shot. (Being a safe shot is all that really matters.) At some stage on the first morning, as we walked back to the wagon, Doug pointed out to Peter and me, "It is what we call a 'gopher' tortoise and an Eastern diamondback rattlesnake that co-hibernate. The gopher tortoise gets its name because it digs a hole in the sandy soil a bit like a gopher does."

▲ Dog work at Pinehill Plantation is superb. Photo courtesy of Peter Horn.

What really sets Pine Hill Plantation apart from most other commercial quail plantations in the South is its habitat. Doug and Jackie manage over 6,000 acres of long-leaf pine forest quail habitat using the same wildlife science practices as some of the most exclusive private plantations. Their success at this ensures you will be challenged with exhilarating covey rises and shooting.

"Pine Hill Plantation's ecosystem is ideal for wild bobwhite quail habitat and is formed from a combination of long-leaf pine forest, wiregrass understory, and its location close to the Gulf of Mexico," Doug pointed out as we drove to our field. "With its proximity to the Gulf of Mexico, there is dew in the pine forest most every morning, even during long, hot, summer draughts. The dew condenses beneath the pine forest canopy onto the wiregrass and drips down to the base of the wiregrass where it acts like a little drinking fountain for the birds.

"In summer, the forest understory gets very thick, providing excellent brood habitat that is protected from avian predators. Additionally, the summer environment is insect-rich, providing high-protein intake for the quail population. In winter, the climate is mild, allowing the quail to require less feed for energy and be exposed less to predators."

Doug continued, "In addition to Mother Nature's ecosystem, Pine Hill Plantation employs habitat management practices including periodic controlled burns, trapping for mammalian predators, and broadcast supplemental feeding."

My last night at Pine Hill came all too soon. Complementing the excellent dinner was good companionship and lots of laughter; great camaraderie, especially when it's unexpected, is always a bonus. A perfect end to a wonderful experience, and one I recommend highly. But don't take my word for it: Pine Hill is one of just thirteen sportsmen's experiences to make the grade in the Beretta Trident Program.

Beretta's Trident Program—Highlighting Excellence

The Beretta Trident Program (contact Ian Harrison: iharrison@Berettausa.com; cell phone 347-899-1463) is a unique, quality rating system that reflects an objective assessment of the complete guest experience at a sporting venue. The program requires venues offering wingshooting and shotgun sports to undergo a detailed and specific assessment of every area that can impact the guest experience. A "Trident" is awarded to designate the venue's level of excellence. It is estimated that only 5 percent of sporting venues worldwide qualify.

The program ultimately provides consumer confidence in the quality of the field sports, accommodations, and guest services when making a reservation with a Beretta Trident Sporting Venue. From the professionalism of the staff and the knowledge of the guides to the performance of the dogs, everything is evaluated. Qualifying venues co-market and leverage Beretta's brand to differentiate themselves from their competitors.

The first venues to earn the prestigious Beretta Trident rating were upland bird destinations in the United States. Trident properties offer everything from traditional South Dakota pheasant hunting or a mixed bag in the Hill Country of Texas, to plantation quail hunting in Georgia or big-game hunting in Spain. Today there are many venues in the Beretta Trident Program, each offering the discerning sportsman or sportswoman a destination to meet their dreams.

Three of the other Beretta Trident premier facilities specializing in upland birds and shotguns sports are:

Highland Hills Ranch

▲ One of the great professional hunters in the history of Africa was John Knowles of Zambia. While no one hunted harder, he believed in a comfortable camp stating "any fool can be miserable in the bush." After a hard day of hunting, what could be better than returning to Highland Hills Ranch?

Considered among the finest hunting facilities in the North America, Highland Hills Ranch sits on 3,000 acres in North Central Oregon and provides some of the best and most diverse wingshooting you will ever experience. Go for the HHR "Grand Slam" of pheasant, chukar, gray partridge, and valley quail. From creek bottoms to mountain ridges and everything in between, you'll find the game and the terrain that suits you. The lodge may be as good as the hunting and that's saying something. The rustic, 10,000 square-foot hand-hewn logs blend seamlessly with the glorious natural setting. The professionally trained staff, exceptional service, incredible cuisine, and five-star accommodations ensure an adventure you will never forget. A wine cellar full of Pacific Northwest vintages and culinary excellence completes each day. It's all an experience that stands up to its setting.

▲ This photo exemplifies one of those great to be alive moments which I find more common, while still rare, while enjoying outdoor pursuits than anywhere else. Photo courtesy Highland Hills Ranch.

Joshua Creek Ranch—The area around San Antonio is known for its pleasant climes, its varied vistas and topography, its wildlife habitat, and the hospitality of area ranches. It's also becoming—or in the case of Joshua Creek Ranch has become—renowned for its upland birds, including pheasants, chukars, and bobwhite quail. Joshua Creek has more than 10 areas with well-spaced shooting butts and pegs, some suitable for beginning shooters, others suitable for experienced shots looking for real challenges.

Cheyenne Ridge Signature Lodge

▲ A classic Western lodge.

The pheasant hunting at Signature Lodge is done in the traditional South Dakota fashion—block and drive. It is common to put hundreds of birds in the air on

a quarter-mile drive. The lodge itself has thirty-three single occupancy rooms, while the culinary program is run by an award-winning chef, with meals served in a formal dining room. All meals are accompanied by fine wine pairings, and premium top shelf liquors and some of the best non-Cuban cigars found anywhere.

▲ The traditional way of hunting pheasant out West.

The Orvis Stamp of Approval

Before there was the Beretta Trident, there was Orvis Endorsed. In a letter to me, Reid Bryant, Wingshooting Services Manager with The Orvis Company, Inc., explained the parameters for Orvis Endorsement on the hunting side:

"The concept of the endorsements stemmed from a wonderfully organic perception that Orvis, as an authority in the bird hunting space, would be able to recommend guides and destinations to our customers. The Perkins family is an avid and authentic group of wingshooters and, having travelled and shot extensively, they find that customers seek both their and Orvis' opinion about where to go. From that need, there grew a bigger conversation about Orvis' service to the customer: in essence, could we formalize a protocol for evaluating lodges and guides, in order that we could ensure a premium experience, and Orvis-caliber service, to our customers? What culminated from that conversation is the Endorsed Partnership.

"In essence, the ELOG program is a marketing/licensing agreement. In exchange for a nominal annual fee, Orvis promotes a partner via catalog and web and provides them with resources garnered from an assessment of industry best practices. This is not a pay-to-play program, as we rigorously curate the part-nership, with regular assessment and reassessment of partners. I do not know that we have done a great job clarifying that we do not maintain this program as a money-making venture; to the contrary, it is a service to our customers and an opportunity for us to ally the Orvis brand with the best operators on the ground and in the business, for mutual benefit. It is, in essence, a reinforcing loop, with the quality of each represented brand serving to heighten the perceived quality of all associated partners, and Orvis, of course.

"On a nuts-and-bolts level, we basically endorse lodges that have a put-and-take preserve type model (and wild birds or in some cases both), hunting grounds (wherein we endorse the cover, guides, dogs, and experience, but not the lodging/food service), and guides/outfitters. The guides and outfitters are gener-ally smaller operations that make use of a wild bird resource. For this reason, these guides are operating on leased private land or public land, often with a range of cover that occupies a region, rather than a specific, defined location. Typically, the guides will offer suggestions for lodging/food, but we do not endorse that. We endorse the guide, any contract guides under them, and their dogs (as well as the guided experience).

"Because wild birds are inherently unpredict-able, guides have to remain nimble, have to man-age their resource, have to scout extensively, and have to communicate to clients that success is not a foregone conclusion. For this reason, the service they provide has to offset any limitations on the part of the resource, and in order to be endorsed, they must operate in the 'best-of-the-best' resource areas. For this reason, you will see that our guides work in the historic wild bird meccas, namely the upper Midwest, northern Maine, Saskatchewan, Arizona, Nebraska, South Dakota, etc. They are a phenom-enal group to a man, and a network of guides unpar-alleled in the world. If you consider North America to offer the last, best, and most diverse opportunity for wild bird hunting, these guys are the most expe-rienced out there. Their collective knowledge and experience is without parallel, and I don't know that the wingshooting world truly recognizes what 'rare birds' they are.

"Hope this helps. By all means, ask any more ques-tions, and thanks."

J. Reid Bryant
Wingshooting Services Manager
The Orvis Company, Inc.
www.orvis.com

The following is a sample, alphabetically by state, of the many North American wild-bird lodges and outfit-ters qualifying for Orvis Endorsement.

Alaska

▲ Loading up the floatplane for a day of shooter. Photo courtesy of Crystal Creek Lodge and Brian Grossenbachers.

Crystal Creek Lodge

While an Orvis-Endorsed fly-fishing lodge, Crystal Creek (www. rystalcreeklodge.com; 907-357-3153), also offers some great wild bird shooting. The willow

▲ Photo courtesy of Crystal Creek Lodge and Brian Grossenbacher.

ptarmigan season starts on August 10 and goes into early October. Wildfowl species include mallard, widgeon, greenwing teal, gadwall, and pintail, plus various species of diving ducks, occasionally sea ducks, and Canada geese.

Eight guides take hunters, normally two at a time out from the lodge which is only three miles from King Salmon, Alaska, also the location of the nearest airport. Hunters will head out either by plane (Havilland Beaver) or by boat. Most guests spend four to seven days at the lodge and typically hunt in the morning and fish in the afternoon. The fishing is for salmon and trout. The limit on ptarmigan is eight birds per day, with the same limit on ducks and a possession limit of 24, and a limit both daily and possession of eight geese. In Alaska, a state small-game license plus

Alaska waterfowl stamp and federal duck stamp are required.

German wirehair pointers are used for the ptarmigan hunts and Labradors for the waterfowl. Ptarmigan hunts take place in open tundra/glacial moraines and short willow thickets. Waterfowl hunting occurs both on the tundra and on coastal ponds. The typical temperature range during the hunt is 40° to 60°F, but rain is common, with precipitation occurring about 50 percent of the time.

Crystal Creek Lodge offers a full service luxury wing-shooting, fishing and adventure experience. Typically there are 14 to 16 guests at the lodge at any given time. They provide virtually all equipment necessary from waders to fishing rods and even upland strap vests. (Obviously, do bring your normal hunting clothes and boots.) Non-shooting companions can visit nearby national parks to view brown bear, walrus, and other animals not found in the lower 48.

As Orvis-endorsed wingshooting guide and lodge owner Dan Michels points out, "Crystal Creek Lodge is primarily a fly fishing lodge that caters to bird hunters. We recommend that people reserving a trip have a strong interest in fishing as the primary activity, and bird hunting a secondary activity. There is fly fishing for nine species of salmon and trout, plus float trips, on a great variety of rivers and streams to fish in the world-famous Bristol Bay region of Southwest Alaska."

Arizona

Classic Bird Hunts

In the winter months, Mark Nissen and his Classic Bird Hunts (www.classicbirdhunts.com; 414-915-9072) operation moves from its fall base in Wisconsin (see the Wisconsin entry) to Arizona where he hunts Mearns, Gambel's, and scaled quail behind pointing breeds. It is all wild hunting; preserve hunting does not even enter the vocabulary here. With two full-time and two part-time guides, he operates on over a million acres of primarily public land, but also offers hunting on the 30,000-acre Babacomari Ranch in Arizona. Dove shooting is also available in season, and this tends to end the days afield, a nice juxtaposition to a long day walking.

▲ Warm clothing can make all the difference when it comes to having a pleasant day afield. Courtesy of Crystal Creek Lodge and Brian Grossenbacher.

▲ Photos courtesy of Classic Bird Hunts.

▲ Hunting wild birds in the Southwest. Photos courtesy of Classic Bird Hunts.

As you'd expect, this is foot hunting mostly behind pointing dogs, but occasionally Labs come into play. The typical day starts hunting at 8:00 a.m., with a break for lunch and then hunting until half an hour before dark.

"The day can be finished by hunting doves at sunset, if dove season is open," explained Mark. "We cater our hunts to the client's wishes and physical fitness. The more miles walked the more birds are moved. On average years, four to eight coveys are moved per day. Better years see six to12 coveys, while on down years we'll see three to five." Limits are 15 quail per day of which eight may be Mearns. A general hunting license is required, as is a state migratory bird stamp if hunting doves.

"Hunting is conducted in a variety of desert habitat," said Mark. "Mearns are found primarily in hilly, grassy, live oak areas. Gambel's and scalies are at lower altitudes, less hilly and with less grass. There is rocky terrain throughout. Average highs will be in the mid-60s. Be prepared for any type of weather, as we have

hunted on days with highs near 80 or on cold days where lows are a chilly 20 degrees.

"Lightweight, comfortable hiking/hunting boots are critical. Dress in layers, as most mornings it's near freezing, and typical afternoons will be in the mid-60s and sunny. Snake boots are not necessary—we have seen one snake between December and February in sixteen years of hunting."

Unlike his Wisconsin hunts, Mark's operation in Arizona offers all-inclusive hunts, with lodging and meals included. Standard hunts include lunch. Client dogs are welcome, and pet-friendly lodging is available. There's a maximum of two hunters per guide. Activities for non-hunters include winery, cavern, and mine tours, artist communities, Native American and old west history exploration and more.

The nearest commercial airports are Tucson, a

one-hour drive, and Phoenix, a three-hour drive. Private smaller prop planes can fly into the ranch if prearranged, while larger private prop and jets can fly to Sierra Vista.

Maine

Libby Camps

Libby Camps (www.libbycamps.com; 207-435-8274), has been well-known and -respected for many decades. Nine full-time and part-time guides take clients hunting on 3½ million acres of private forest land for a ruffed grouse and woodcock during the season which runs from October 1 to November 15. They hunt the area by walking and working their dogs—Brittany spaniels, English setters, English pointers, black Labs, and cocker spaniels—on the edges of grown-up logging roads, edge cover of recently forested areas, and seven- to fifteen-year-old clear cuts. Clients are allowed to bring their own dogs, and there are both kennels for them and dog friendly rooms, the best of all worlds. A typical stay is four nights with three days hunting.

A typical day starts early with breakfast at 7:00, with hunters usually arriving at the first covert by 9:00. They'll hunt one or two coverts in the morning and one or two in the afternoon. Walking miles each day is necessary for this type of hunting. Hunters average about twelve opportunities per day. There is a four grouse and three woodcock limit per day. "I would say an average kill day would be about four to six birds total between two hunters," said Libby Camps owner Matt Libby.

The terrain is mostly gradual rolling hills with short steep grades. Much of the walking is over old logging roads, but when in the woods, the walking is quite difficult over blowdowns and through thick spruce/fir stands and raspberry bushes. The weather by season, roughly, is usually in the upper 20s to low 40s in the morning, getting up to 50s to 70s in the afternoon. You can have bright sunshine, pouring down rain or even snow, sometimes all in the same day. Because of all the walking, Matt says, "Good waterproof boots that you can walk all day in" is the most important single piece of equipment to have.

Libby Camps serves family-style meals in the main lodge and packs sandwiches and soup for lunch. The occasional meal of freshly shot grouse at lunch can be arranged for those that want to take the time. There are nine private guest cabins spread out around the main lodge where everyone gathers for meals and telling tall tales. Cabins are log and range from nearly new to 125 years old. All are comfortably appointed with full bathrooms, propane lights, and wood stoves.

A Maine small-game hunting license is required; a three-day license is available.

The lodge does have a sense of humor: To my question, "What's the nearest town?" they replied, "Ashland—if you can call it a town." The nearest commercial or private airport is Presque Isle, Maine.

Grouse Haven Wing-Shooting

Grouse Haven (www.grousehavenwingshooting.com; 207-491-9856) is owned and operated by Michael Browning, who wrote to me saying, "Ruffed grouse and woodcock are my passion, and after you visit Grouse Haven, hopefully you'll be even more passionate about grouse and woodcock hunting." Like Libby camps, woodcock and grouse can be hunted together from October 1 through November 15, but Browning continues guiding grouse hunters through December on over 3,500 acres. He and his clients follow pointing dogs walking logging roads or through alders intermixed with poplars and balsam fir.

The mornings start with a light breakfast, then hunting, a short break for lunch, and hunting until sundown. If conditions and weather are favorable, hunters will often have 10 to 15 flushes on grouse and the same for woodcock, although Browning says in some areas the grouse are "very skittish and require an experienced wing shooter."

Most guests stay for three days, and there is a maximum of three clients to one guide going down the logging roads or hunting the fields. Full-day hunts run from about 8:30 in the morning until 4:00 p.m., and half-day hunts that run until just past the noon hour are also available and make sense for those who want to get half-day's hunting in before heading home.

Two good places to stay nearby are Wilson Lake Inn, 15 minutes from Grouse Haven, or the Comfort Inn, which is a little closer and is dog-friendly. The nearest town is New Sharon, and the nearest commercial

▲ Woodcock and ruffed grouse are challenging and wily gamebirds.
Photos courtesy of Michael Browning.

airports are Portland and Bangor, with a private airport at Augusta.

A small-game hunting license is required.

Montana

Hoover Outfitting

Hoover Outfitting (www.hooveroutfitting.com; 406-490-6864), offers wild birds hunts for sharptail grouse, Hungarian partridge, and pheasant in wild country with great guides and great accommodations. While Hoover also guides for migratory birds, waterfowling takes place only in October, when clients can jump-shoot ducks. Hoover has access to over 100,000 acres of private hunting land. Two full-time guides take clients hunting behind both flushing and pointing dogs. This is not a preserve operation. In addition to wild bird hunts, Hover also offers guided fishing and big-game hunts.

A typical day is spent hunting sharp-tailed grouse and Hungarian partridge. "Often, guests enjoy watching sharp-tailed grouse dance," wrote owner Chad Hoover. "We have one of the largest populations of sharp-tailed grouse in North America. Hunters consistently have opportunities to fill their daily bag limit."

"Northeastern Montana is very remote and unpopulated," he continued. "We hunt one of the largest contiguous wild prairie ecosystems in the country. Prairie habitat and the top hunting areas are those that produce snowberry and buffalo berry, as well as harvested grains. The land consists of medium terrain. The landscape has both rolling hills and occasional breaks with aspen lined draws, and transition areas near grain crops.

"September weather is usually cool and comfortable in the mornings, with very warm afternoons. October is generally mild with occasional cool weather. Guests typically hunt three days. Hunts are two hunters per guide unless other arrangements are made, and we hunt both morning and afternoon. We offer a full breakfast and excellent supper at our headquarters each day. Lunch is a hearty meal in the field.

"The best local hotel is the Cottonwood Inn at Glasgow, Montana. (The Glasgow International Airport is the closest fly-in point.) Our lodging headquarters is located 45 minutes from town. It includes a very comfortable large cabin that can sleep 6 individuals."

Nebraska

▲ Photo courtesy of Pheasant Bonanza.

Pheasant Bonanza

Pheasant Bonanza (www.pheasantbonanza.com; 888-366-4868), specializes in combining waterfowl hunts in the morning with upland hunts in the afternoon on its 2,500-acre property.

As Trent Leichleiter, club manager for the last decade points out, "Pheasant Bonanza is where gourmet meals, premier lodging, service, and a staff that builds personal, long-lasting relationships with guests. Our guides personally connect with each guest, which is made possible because of the small hunter-to-guide ratio. Hunters return because of the relationships they build with staff and dogs.

"We begin our day by shuttling our hunters to the fully enclosed and heated duck blind on the Missouri River. After shooting ducks at first light, our guide cooks a gourmet breakfast in the blind. After the morning flight ends, we shuttle hunters back to the main lodge for lunch and relaxation before their afternoon pheasant hunt. If a waterfowl hunt is not desired, then it can easily be substituted with a morning pheasant hunt. In the hunter's spare time, they are more than welcome to take advantage of our sporting clay course, trap and skeet ranges. After the hunt, hunters return to the lodge to rest and clean up before dinner and drinks. The rest of the evening is spent around the campfire with friends, family, and staff."

Eastern Nebraska's beautiful rolling hills, with its CRP grass and milo strips and occasional patch of timber with creek beds comprise most of the hunting terrain. Cool mornings and warm afternoons in September and October are typical, with colder November days and an occasional light snow. Winter shoots can be cold in December and January, with a high possibility of at least a few inches of snow on the ground.

The wild bird season runs as follows: Mallard ducks from early October through mid-December; goose from early October through roughly the end of December and then again for a couple weeks in late January and early February; and dove from September 1 through the end of October. There is preserve shooting for pheasant and quail from September 1 to April 1.

Pheasant Bonanza employs four full-time guides and 12 part-time guides. For the dogs, Trent said, "We mainly use German shorthaired pointers and Labrador retrievers. We also have a few English pointers and German wirehaired pointers. Ideal dog teams would be two to three pointers and one or two labs. We like our pointers steady to flush; steady to shot usually gives crippled birds too much time to run away. Guests are more than welcome to bring their dogs along. They can bring them out to hunt as well. Dogs are rarely allowed to be kept in the lodge, but they are more than welcome to stay in our kennel."

Licenses are required, including a pheasant/quail habitat stamp and a CSA permit. Prices are the same for resident and non-resident. For waterfowl you'll need a habitat stamp, HIP number, federal waterfowl stamp, Nebraska state stamp, and a non-resident or resident hunting license.

"Lodging is on site at Pheasant Bonanza," said Trent. "Our brand-new lodge is three stories with 15 total rooms. Twelve have double queen beds and three have single kings. The entire lodge is wheelchair accessible, with handicap showers and an elevator. The basement houses our restaurant, dining area, pool table, big screen TVs, and conference rooms. We have a full-time chef who will cook breakfast, lunch, dinner, appetizers, and desert for guests. The menu includes everything from prime rib to signature pheasant dishes to beef and bison burgers."

Tekamah, Nebraska, is the nearest town to Pheasant Bonanza. Omaha or Sioux City, Iowa, are the closest cities of size, and the nearest commercial airport is Eppley Airport in Omaha, about 50 minutes away. For those who fly their own planes, Blair Municipal Airport in Blair Nebraska is approximately 30 minutes away, and Tekamah Municipal Airport is approximately fifteen minutes away.

▲ Photo courtesy of Pheasant Bonanza.

Pheasant Bonanza has a pro shop that can outfit you from head to toe, including gloves, boots, jackets, coats, chaps, and logo wear. "We would recommend bringing an insulated and waterproof pair of boots," said Trent, "especially when there is snow on the ground and it is cold. People usually warm up after they begin walking through the field, even when it's cold. A quality pair of gloves is recommended as well."

Sporting clays, trap, skeet, five-stand, deer hunting, turkey hunting, and coyote hunting are also available, and for non-shooting companions, Silver Hills Winery and golf courses are just a 15-minute drive.

Wind River Wingshooting

Kyle Waggoner has been manager/owner/head guide/cook/bottle washer at Wind River Wingshooting (www.windriverwingshooting.com; 307-438-3439), formerly 3 Corners Outfitting Company, for over 10 years. Wind River offers exclusive wild bird hunting on some of the finest leases in the three-corner region of Nebraska, Colorado, and Kansas, and, with a recent expansion, now Wyoming. Experienced local guides follow pointing dogs through the prairies and croplands of the region, including pastures, CRP, grain stubble, and shelter belts that compose much of the region's bird cover. Rolling hills and flat agricultural ground make for fairly easy walking and open shots. That said, the birds can get up a good head of steam. Also, many miles can be covered in a day, so a certain a degree of fitness is definitely a plus.

Generally, a high-desert grassland weather pattern is expected. Precipitation tends to be the exception during the bird hunting season, but winds can be strong. Early season can see some high temperatures and bright sun, and late season can be quite chilly, particularly at night. Late-season snows are not uncommon.

Meals and accommodations are available from Wind River's base camp in Laird, Colorado. "This location offers easy access to all four states that we hunt," said Kyle Waggoner, owner and head guide." Most hunters fly into Denver, though DIA International and Imperial Municipal are generally the most convenient airports. The Balcony House in Imperial, Nebraska, is a good place to stay, though client dogs are not allowed. Kyle does have kennels available and will look after hunters' dogs for his clients.

Pheasant, bobwhite, and prairie chicken are the main species pursued, but dove hunting is also occasionally offered. State small-game licenses are required for each state. Days begin with a hearty breakfast around 7:30, and one is hunting by around 8:30. Lunch is in the field and followed by more hunting in the afternoon. Cocktails and dinner in the evening hours are filled with tales of adventure. Remember to bring reliable guns and comfy, well-worn in boots, as you will be covering a lot of ground.

South Dakota

Tumbleweed Lodge

Tumbleweed Lodge (www.tumbleweedlodge.com; 605-875-3440) offers a great combination of upland shooting and waterfowl for wild birds. And while South Dakota is justifiably famous for its wild pheasant population, Tumbleweed Lodge also offers shooting for sharp-tailed grouse, greater prairie chicken, and wild Hungarian partridge. Add mallards and greater Canada geese, if you time it right, then you're in for a great all-around experience.

Located six miles from Harrold, South Dakota and served by Pierre Regional Airport, this outfitter was ranked in the Top 10 Greatest Hunting Lodges in the World on the Outdoor Channel series "Outdoor's 10 Best." The beautiful, 18,000 sq.-ft. accommodations include a 2,200 sq.-ft. gazebo with a state-of-the-art salt water Jacuzzi and steam room. The lodge also has a "Wild Bill Hickok" cigar and poker room themed in South Dakota Deadwood style. Multiple large fireplaces and den settings make for great reading downtime. Two chefs on staff provide some of the best Midwest-style country cuisine, and a complimentary top shelf bar and fine table wines are available to complement any meal.

The wild bird season starts with sharptail grouse, greater prairie chicken, and Hungarian partridge on the third Saturday in September and runs until January 3. Pheasant begins the third Saturday in October and also run until January 3.

Tumbleweed employs twenty-six part-time guides throughout the hunting season. "All are professionals in their full-time jobs and take vacation/time off to enjoy the passion of working their dogs and meeting folks from throughout the world," explained Michael Bollweg, co-owner and manager. And with 12,000 acres of prime habitat to hunt, you're not terribly likely to bump into other parties.

Pheasants are hunted using the South Dakota classic walk-and-block method, mostly behind flushing dogs. Prairie grouse species are hunted without blockers and most often pointing breeds. Labradors are the primary upland retrieving dog, and you'll find German shorthairs, English pointers, Lab crosses, German wirehairs, Drahthaars, and wirehaired pointing Griffons.

The daily schedule depends on the time of the year you hunt. The first half of the season is as follows: breakfast at 8:00, hunt pheasants and Huns until noon, break for lunch, then return to the fields at 2:30 for either additional pheasant hunting or an afternoon prairie grouse hunt. This is followed by dinner at 7:00. In the second half of season, the afternoon hunt may be replaced with waterfowl hunting on the bluffs of the Missouri River. Normally, two to three hunters are taken out with each guide.

Three-day/four-night and three-night/two-day hunt packages are most common. September hunts can be combined with walleye and smallmouth bass fishing. An eight-station sporting clay course, as well as an automated trap thrower, are available for those wanting a quick tune-up . Non-shooting activities including touring and seeing the history of South Dakota and the state capital of Pierre only thirty-five minutes away. Otherwise guests can relax and take advantage of all the amenities the lodge offers.

Central South Dakota is part of the prairie pothole region. Glaciers once covered the land here and when they receded, they left slightly rolling terrain and glacial rocks sprinkled across the countryside. Farming and ranching make up the dynamics of land development, with no urban influence.

This is one of the few areas in the Upper Midwest where guests can target four species, the "Grand Slam" of the Dakotas: Pheasants, Huns, sharp-tailed grouse and prairie chicken. Grouse species are targeted in the windswept native grass prairies and alfalfa fields. Pheasants are found along creek bottoms, grasslands, sorghum and corn plots, and shelterbelts of plum thickets and Eastern red cedars. Huns can be found across both areas.

Highs in the early season through October can range from the 50s to upper 70s with a few rare 80s. Lows will range from the upper 30s to mid-50s. November to

December highs can range from the mid-40s to upper 50s, with lows in the teens to low 30s. Accumulating snowfall, albeit minimal, begins in mid- to late November. Occasional showers occur earlier in the season.

The non-resident upland bird license is $125, for all non-migratory species. A non-resident preserve license for $78 covers pheasant and Huns only. A non-resident waterfowl license is $85.

Texas

Greystone Castle Sporting Club

▲ Dove shooting offers great, challenging sport with generous bag limits for a wild North American bird. Photo courtesy Greystone Castle.

Greystone Castle Sporting Club (www.greystonecastle. com; 800-399-3006), Orvis Lodge of the Year in 2011, 2014, and 2015, offers wild bird hunting for dove, both mourning and white wing, from opening day in September until October 15, while turkey hunting takes place from April 1to May 15. Greystone Castle also offers hunts for trophy whitetail deer and operates a preserve for pheasant, quail, chukkar partridge, Hungarian partridge, and mallard from Oct 15 through March 31.

Upland hunts take place on the club's 6,500 acres, and the club normally employs five to seven full-time guides plus one or two part-time guides. Depending on the species sought, hunts take place either walking behind pointing dogs, or from blinds etc. They use English pointers, German shorthair pointers, setters, Labradors, and English cockers.

A typical day begins with a gourmet breakfast followed by a warm-up on clays. The mallard hunt starts at 9:00 am, followed by lunch at noon. Relax and nap until 2:45 (sounds good to me) "when you head out for a traditional upland walk-up hunt. Evening offers appetizers, open bar, and gourmet dinner followed by lodging in a private suite," said the Club's Jennifer Miller. "Upland hunts range over open grassy areas, planted millet/sorghum fields, hilly areas, and mesquite trees. Mallard hunts are over ponds in a dry blind. Turkey hunts are call-and-stalk or blinds over wooded terrain. Dove hunts are over sunflower/millet/ sorghum fields.

"The weather by season: Texas is usually beautiful in the fall and winter with highs in the 50° to 70°F range for upland and mallard hunts. In winter, snow and ice are possible. Dove season is typically hot, in the 80 and 90s, and turkey season is perfect in the 60s to 80s. Rolling hills with grassy areas mixed with heavily wooded oak and mesquite trees perfectly describes the landscape.

"Our 2,500-square-foot pavilion offers a perfect space for entertaining. With a custom horseshoe bar and huge outdoor fire pit, there is lots of room for conversation. The game room offers a pool table, dart boards, and game tables, as well as a LaserShot shooting game. A heated pool, 12-person hot tub, and steam room are perfect for relaxing after a long day afield. Meals are prepared by our Executive Chef, following gourmet Texas cuisine and making use of much of the game offered on Greystone. We offer over 15 types of beer and a highly rated Bordeaux wine in addition to our heavily stocked bar of Scotch, whisky, rum, vodka, and tequila.

"Upland and mallard hunts are three hunters per guide, dove hunts are up to five hunters per guide, and turkey hunts are one to two hunters per guide. All hunts are half-day hunts, offered in the morning and afternoon. A typical group comes in, hunts the afternoon, stays overnight, hunts the morning, and departs after lunch. We also have day hunters and trips that are much longer.

"We offer twenty-six private bedrooms in six separate lodges. All have either a king- or queen-size bed. We also have a sporting clays course, exceptional whitetail deer, exotics, and bass fishing, and a corporate conference room for executive retreats and additional activities, including spa services, can be booked for non-hunters.

"Licenses are required, resident or non-resident bird license plus applicable upland stamp, migratory bird stamp, banded bird stamp, duck stamp. The nearest commercial airport is DFW or Love, while the nearest private airports are Mineral Wells, Eastland, or Stephenville."

Wisconsin

Classic Bird Hunts

Mark Nissen's Classic Bird Hunts (www.classicbird-hunts.com; 414-915-9072), has been running for over thirty-five years, providing hunting for strictly wild birds—ruffed grouse and Woodcock in Wisconsin, before he moves Southwest and guides for quail in Arizona (more details in that section).

Ruffed grouse hunting takes place from mid-September through December, though serious snowfalls can interrupt this. Woodcock closes early in November.

Two full-time and three part-time guides hunt with their clients over one million acres of national, state, county, and private lands. (This is a guide-only service; no lodging is available). This is foot hunting behind pointing dogs, mostly Brittany spaniels, English setters and German shorthairs, and the hunters tend to work the walking trails over this mostly flat, wooded land while the dogs do the hard work in the adjacent cover. There is a maximum of two hunters per guide. The weather obviously changes with each month, from highs near 70°F in mid-September to cooler highs near 30°F in December.

Cable, Wisconsin, is the base of operation. Getting there is not overly difficult, with most clients flying to Minneapolis/St. Paul, a three-hour drive, or the other commercial airport of Duluth, which is only an hour and a half away. Private planes can fly into Cable or Hayward, Wisconsin, just minutes from the hunting coverts.

The typical day starts with a hunt beginning about 8:00 a.m. There will be a short break for lunch after which the hunt continues until dark. That said, Classic Bird Hunts caters to the client's wishes and physical fitness. Obviously the more miles walked, the more birds will be found, but amazingly, Mark wrote telling me that, "On an average year, from the end of September through early November, expect 20 grouse and 20 woodcock flushes per day." That's certainly unheard of in most other grouse and woodcock areas.

▲ Photos courtesy of Classic Bird Hunts.

Wyoming

Brush Creek Ranch

Brush Creek Ranch (www.brushcreekranch.com; 307-327-5284), is not your run-of-the-mill hunting camp. Set on 30,000 pristine private acres in the heart of the Platte River Valley in southeastern Wyoming, the Lodge & Spa at Brush Creek Ranch offers guests the opportunity to experience the grandeur and adventure of the American West in sophisticated style. Brush Creek Ranch, voted the No. 1 Resort in the USA by Conde Nast Traveler in 2014, 2015, and 2016, was founded in the late 1800s and remains a working cattle ranch as in days past. Its historic ranchlands include, according to Matt Anderson, Director of Outfitting and Activities, "The A Cross/Sanger Ranch, Upper and Lower Encampment Ranches and TZ Ranch and includes high mountain desert, from rolling hay meadow, creeks, and rivers, to sage-covered hillsides and mountain foothills, all surrounded by majestic mountain peaks of the Snowy Range."

For wild upland hunts you jump in a pickup after breakfast at the lodge and transport to hunt area where you'll spend approximately three hours. Hunts can be customized to the physical ability of the hunter, from those in moderate physical condition to hunters in excellent condition. Upland hunts take place walking behind well-trained pointers.

High-mountain desert can include a variety of weather from August 1 through the end of October. Generally, August is quite warm throughout, with mornings slightly cooler and highs in the 80s expected in the afternoons. The climate and humidity tend be dry. In September and October, mornings can be crisp and cool, with temperatures in the 30s and 40s often warming up into the 50s, 60s, and 70s in the afternoon. At any time in September and October, periods of snow can be expected. Sometimes, storms blow in mornings or afternoons that can include rain, hail, or snow, depending on the month, as well as thunder and lightning. Often these storms are short-lived and clear quickly.

▲ Courtesy of Brush Creek Ranch.

Brush Creek Ranch includes 5-star in-house chef staff and wine cellar, with nightly entertainment during season. Tower shoots and mock driven shoots off cliff faces are also on offer. For those new to hunting, all hunting gear and accessories can be provided, including over/under shotguns, ammunition, shooting vests, hearing protection, shooting glasses, sunscreen, refreshments, and snacks.

Wyoming has daily upland/small game licenses. Waterfowl hunters also need federal duck stamp and HIP stamp.

There are more opportunities for preserve than wild hunting, but if you can get on Brush Creek's limited wild hunts you can experience: sage grouse, daily limit of two, possession four during the brief, late-September season; blue grouse, daily limit of three and nine in possession during the season which runs September 1 through November 30; waterfowl daily limits of six ducks and four geese with a season that runs from late September until early January. The preserve season runs from August 1 through October 31 with pheasant, chukar, and Hungarian partridge available.

The dog work here is exceptional, with pointers and setters steady to wing and shot, and retrievers trained to walk at heel and flush on command and retrievers trained to quarter and flush in walking shotgun range. Obviously, retrievers are trained on blinds and marks for waterfowl hunts. Vickie Lamb is the Wingshooting Manager. She's been at Brush Creek Ranch for the last few years, with a thirty-year background in hunting, dog training, guiding, and the shooting sports.

Brush Creek Ranch hunt packages are all inclusive for lodging. The nearest commercial airports are Laramie, Wyoming, about 1½ hours' drive, and Denver, about a three-hour drive. For those coming in on their own planes, Shively airport in Saratoga is only fifteen miles away.

"Brush Creek Ranch provides spectacular bird hunting in some of the most breathtaking private acreage available in the West, with exceptionally trained sporting dogs, expert guiding and hardy birds that provide challenging shooting for the most discriminating bird hunter," Matt wrote to me. Even though hunting gear and accessories can be provided, clients should bring any personal clothing items they are particularly comfortable using while hunting, especially boots.

Brush Creek is also known for its world-class fly fishing, boasting over twenty miles of superb private water and options of wading or float trips. Cast-and-blast packages are available, and they can be a great combination, plus a multitude of shooting ranges (including trap, five-stand, sporting clays, rifles, and pistols), and multiple 3D archery ranges and a full selection of traditional and compound bows. Brush Creek hosts a wide variety of activities for the whole family, such as horseback riding, roping course, zip lines, paintball, hiking, biking, yoga, a full-service spa, arcade, fitness center, full-court basketball, lawn games, and much more.

Canada, New Brunswick

The Ledges

The Ledges (www.ledgesinn.com; 877-365-1820), was written up in my second book, *The World's Best Shoots*, by Vic Venters, well-known writer, firearms authority and book author. While this outfitter primarily hunts woodcock (September 15 to November 15) and grouse (October 1 to December 31), the Lodge also has a three-hundred-acre pheasant preserve to hunt from September 15 to December 15. And while it goes almost without saying, I will say it nevertheless: people go to New Brunswick not for a preserve hunt for pheasants, but because of its outstanding reputation for wild upland birds.

The Ledges has two full-time and two part-time guides with endless areas to hunt, most on private land, but some Crown land as well. Clients hunt old farms and alder flats over well-trained pointing dogs, mostly English pointers, English setters, and Brittany spaniels. Guides pick up their hunters at The Ledges after breakfast, complete with a boxed lunch. Sportsmen hunt a full eight- to nine-hour day, depending on the client, their desires, and fitness. The weather fluctuates every day, so bring many layers and some rain gear. Temperatures range from -4° to +12°C (about 24° to 53°F).

Although New Brunswick's woodcock bag limit is eight per day The Ledges have a camp limit of five woodcock and six grouse. Success depends on the vagaries of weather, population fluctuations, and the abilities of the shooter. That said, this is one of the best places to hunt these game birds in the Northeast of North America. A small game license for grouse and a migratory stamp for woodcock are necessary, which the outfitter can arrange.

The nearest commercial airport is Fredericton, New Brunswick, while the nearest private airport is Miramichi.

Generally two hunters share a guide, and most guests hunt for at least three to five days.

"We are a small lodge that only takes in six hunters at a time," explained owner Caroline St. Pierre. "We provide top-quality hunts for wild woodcock and grouse, over well-trained pointing dogs. Our guides all work hard at finding good coverts, and we rarely hunt a covert more than twice in a season. Our food is second to none, and Cedar Lodge is cozy and private. We work hard to make The Ledges a lodge everyone wants come back to every year."

In the first two weeks of October, Atlantic salmon fishing can be combined with upland hunting.

Dogs are allowed in the rooms but not on the beds, which seems perfectly reasonable to me.

Adventures Abroad

Although thousands of Americans make the long journey to Argentina and other South American destinations, great shooting can be had in the British Isles without spending a fortune. Long seasons (and often no bag limits), make it a great choice, and spouses who do not shoot can sightsee. They even speak the same language—kind of—and Brits are very hospitable. Heck, you can even drink the water, and flights are generally shorter and less expensive than travelling to South America. Another bonus: The British pound sterling is the weakest it's been in 30 or 40 years, which makes traveling there more appealing than ever for Americans who want to get a taste of the U.K.'s great varied sport from woodcock and grouse to wood pigeon and wildfowling.

Britain Without Breaking the Bank

Shooting in Britain has a number of reputations, much like myself—some deserved, some not. One of these is for being expensive. While this certainly can be true, it doesn't have to be. Spending a week on a legendary grouse moor or a week of big days in the West Country is probably more money than most of us spent on our first car. But if one goes to less-famous shoots where smaller bags are the norm, one can have an exciting day and probably walk away with change for £500. Woodcock, pigeon, and waterfowling should run half that, perhaps less, depending on the size of the party, area, reputation of the guide, etc., far less than the cost for a day in Cordoba or Entre Rios.

Pigeon shooting in the U.K. is an exciting and testing endeavor that is much less expensive than a dove shoot in South America, and while shooting thousands of rounds a day is certainly unlikely, shooting hundreds is certainly possible, and, if timed right, probable. Wood pigeon fly like a dove on steroids: faster and stronger.

Duck shooting, aka "flighting," is a splendid sport, on a windy evening exhilarating. It's done very differently in the British Isles, where shooting after sunset is legal, as is feeding the ponds to attract birds.

Roding or walking up woodcock is also exciting. Woodcock over pointers generally produces bigger bags, legally, than woodcock hunts in America. U.K. woodcock are a larger bird and a stronger flying. With these, like any migratory bird, luck and conditions play a part.

At our former estate, Tressady, in the Northeast of Scotland, while there was a small resident population of woodcock, the majority of the birds would come in after the first full moon in November. I had one friend in for a shoot, and after walking for hours we'd put up only three or four birds. The next day a commercial group came in and shot over 40. Here today and gone tomorrow, or vice-versa as it were. *C'est la guerre.*

A couple exceptions to the generalities: In Scotland, it is common for estates to rent out a lodge with sport by the week, often six days of sport and six or seven nights of lodging so that they have time to turn the house around for the next group. Also, shooting, and indeed salmon fishing, does not occur on Sundays in Britain; the Republic of Ireland does not have this constraint.

There are great lodges if you look for them, some where one can salmon fish, do walked-up grouse, woodcock, and occasionally ptarmigan, and perhaps add stag or roebuck stalking into the mix. Some lodges provide cooks, while others will give the names of recommended cooks, or one may choose to self-cater. There are some excellent agents who specialize in Scottish "lets," or short-term whole lodge rentals, and I recommend George Goldsmith very highly, as I used him almost exclusively when we did rent out Tressady. Five to ten couples can often have excellent accommodation for perhaps £1,000 per couple per week plus the cost of food, wine, booze, and sport. Sometimes less expensive lodges are on offer, and more exclusive and expensive properties may even provide a butler and a housekeeper, but charge a wee bit more. Scottish sport is a never-to-be-forgotten experience and often less expensive than many top lodges in America would charge for similar accommodation or sport, so now let's take a more in-depth look at wingshooting as only the U.K. can provide.

Pigeon

Wood pigeon are often described as the "poor man's grouse." It is a bird for everyone. Farmers will often let locals come in to shoot the birds that raid their crops. Pigeons tend to eat very well indeed, going to peas when they are ripe, beans when they are perfect, rape later in the year, etc. But referring to them as the poor man's grouse does not really do them justice. While they are easier to hit if they are decoying well, just like settling mallards compared to pass shooting birds; they often produce more challenging shots and more angles than most driven grouse in August. Swinging hard on birds shying from decoys at distance or pass shooting pigeons present some of the toughest shots around; think of super-charged doves. They move very fast and very deceptively. As soon as they stop flapping their wings, they drop considerably. Many of England's premier shots spend much of the off-season keeping their eye in by pigeon shooting. Best of all, unlike our feral pigeons which are essentially rats with wings, "woodies" produce delicious table fare.

I have shot them from Hampshire in England, north to Scotland, and West to Ireland. There are a number of ways to shoot pigeons. The most common and most successful way is to shoot out of a blind over a crop upon which the birds are feasting. This takes scouting. One normally sits in a makeshift blind. Move little and slowly; fieldcraft is necessary, or birds will flair out of range. Decoys are placed by the guides, and placement is important just as it would be for decoying ducks. Pigeon magnets are becoming very popular for attracting the birds. It is the same sort of idea as motorized duck decoys, but in addition to a stationary bird with flapping wings, normally three decoys are placed on a motorized rotor that goes in a circle. The motion allows birds to see the setup from a long way.

The second most effective way to shoot them is on a windy stormy evening in a wood that is their roost. This is most commonly done by a cult of pigeon shooting aficionados, and less commonly by professional guides for clients.

The most difficult shooting is pass shooting them on their flight lines from their roosts to the fields or on the return journey. This will generally produce the longest shots and the fastest birds. It will probably not put the number of birds in the bag that the other two methods will.

Though all three require field craft to determine the best place to set up, you do not need to bring much gear with you, as the professionals will be supplying the decoys, the blinds, and most—at least the good ones—will have done their due diligence in terms of scouting locations. All you will need is an appropriate neutral-colored hat, camo if you prefer, a camo sweater, shirt, or jacket depending on weather, perhaps a face mask like a bowhunter would wear, and probably some water or coffee and a sandwich or snack if you plan on staying in the blind for more than a few hours.

I once was out with a great guide in Hampshire 30-odd years ago, the hunt arranged by an outstanding booking agent in America, Tom Spang, long since retired. I was shooting about a slab an hour for two hours. It was so much shooting, with a rented gun that didn't fit terribly well, that I called it quits even though the birds were coming in suicidally to the peas. It was a last-minute arranged shoot that I added to a trout fishing trip on the river Test, that most hallowed water, for a story that I was writing for *European Travel and Leisure magazine*, long defunct.

I also had my worst experience ever with a so-called pigeon guide. I was researching an equestrian feature for *Town and Country* in the late 1970s, back when it was still a real magazine with interesting articles, and had a couple of days to kill in Waterford. I asked at the hotel where I was staying if they could recommend someone.

This gent, and I'm using the term gent sarcastically, the hotel recommended came by and we had a drink at the bar. I had never shot pigeons before. I asked him what time we should go out, and he said he would pick me up about 9.30 a.m. I queried him, as that seemed kind of late. He said it would be perfect. I noticed him at the bar drinking away at nearly midnight as I headed to my room. Being American by birth and Germanic by nature, I was downstairs and ready to go at nine. He arrived around 11:00, just as I was about to head out on my own for a drive around the local countryside. Nonetheless, I went with him.

I think I saw all of three birds, and each was out of range. When he picked me up two hours later, he announced we should have been there earlier. I think drinking was his main sport, and taking foreigners for a ride simply a fringe benefit.

Guides, of course, come in all arrays of talent and dedication. There was a great guide in County Wicklow, Paul Carberry, near my better half's property, where we would send friends or clients who wanted wood pigeon shooting. He tended to average about 50 birds per man per day over the course of the season. Most of Carberry's clients came from Italy and France. Obviously some days were better than others, and also some fellows shoot better than others, but this is very inexpensive shooting, and, if you hit it right, it will be good enough to last in your memories for a very long time. £300 per gun per day give or take is the most expensive shooting that I've heard of for wood pigeon and generally it runs about half that, but if you get a reputable guide it is worth every penny—and it is still much less than you would spend for a day shooting dove in Córdoba.

Pheasant

I have run four shoots with my better half: Humewood Castle, Tressady, plus two forestry blocks we rented from the Irish government. In addition to managing the shoots, I have worked as a picker-up, and even on rare occasions as a beater. I have worked with the Game Conservancy and with our own keepers to design drives. I have captained teams (led groups of friends and clients) to shoots across the British Isles, Eastern Europe, and Spain. Indeed, I have shot over 1,000 driven days to my own gun in Britain and Ireland, and hundreds in Spain. I do not mean this in any form of braggadocio, but rather to point out that I am experienced in ways of driven shooting that few Americans, indeed few Brits, are.

From a purely commercial aspect, and we did run our shoots commercially, bigger bags were definitely better. Let me be blunt: the fixed costs are largely the same. One pays beaters and pickers up, one provides them lunch, and one provides lunch for the shooting team, ideally with some decent wine. Add in elevenses—sloe gin, King's Ginger, fizz on occasion, and something to eat to put the cold and wet at bay, and there's over £1,000 in expenses; on big, or fancy corporate entertaining days, double that.

▲ Pierre Villere shooting his very fine pair of Arrietta shotguns. Spanish guns are generally based on the Holland and Holland system and offer great value in the secondhand market as demand has reduced and driven prices down. Photo Courtesy Charles Sainsbury Plaice.

I still lead a few trips every year for friends and clients to some of the best shoots in the world. The one real advantage of larger days is that it minimizes the likelihood that someone will have poor sport. A team of eight, booking an expected bag of 100 birds, will often have one or two shooters out of the action on a couple of drives, without sufficient birds to make up for it on others. (Hence, I presume, the term "the luck of the draw.") With an expected bag of 300 or more birds, one can certainly have a bad drive, but the odds are definitely in favor of being able to compensate on another.

Shooting the crème de la crème of Britain's shoots is expensive. VAT—value added tax—is currently 20 percent. So, a pheasant shoot that is charged at £35 per bird actually costs £42. (Some of the really coveted shoots are getting £40 to £50 per bird plus VAT.) Multiply this time an expected bag of say 300 or 400 birds, divided by a line of eight guns, and one is not talking about an inexpensive day afield. All that said, if one does go to one of the great shoots of Britain, shooting birds that are curling and slipping on the wind and at the limit of one's range, one will experience one of our sport's most hallowed traditions and greatest challenges. (If you're looking for a deal on these pricier estates, many estates, even the very good ones, will put on smaller days, often on the periphery of their lands with the idea of pushing birds back towards the center of the estate.)

▲ You have to love a shoot with a sense of humor. Photo Courtesy *The Shooting Gazette*.

A few years ago, I was invited by Ray Entwistle to join him as his guest at Fasque estate in southeastern Scotland. This is a fabulous estate and can provide very substantial and exhilarating sporting days. Ray had purchased a relatively small day, about 100 birds, at a Game Conservancy auction in Edinburgh. The landscape was brilliant, the keepering team professional and charming, the food excellent, and the birds very testing. (The last criterion, to my mind, is the most important.) In addition to pheasant, a few woodcock and wood pigeon were shot. But one does not have to purchase these at auction. There are a few booking agents who specialize in offering highly refined sport, yet still great value for money on small driven days.

I have a lawyer friend in Edinburgh who is a great sportsman. He has a roving syndicate of friends with the typical day costing £350 to £500 per man. The bags

tend to be about 100 birds, sometimes a bit more sometimes a bit less, and because he is so plugged in to the local shoots, he's able to select shoots where quality of sport is not adversely affected by the small bag. He generously provided the details of an agent who can help readers who want to pursue this option (see sidebar).

DRIVER ASLEEP PLEASE PASS WIDE AND SLOW
▲ One can take shooting seriously but one should never take oneself too seriously. Photo Courtesy *The Shooting Gazette*.

I will also go on record here as saying there is a British website that has been hugely successful in connecting shooters with shoots. The only problem as I can tell there is no vetting of the actual venues on offer—all shoots are welcomed to list. So, if you are a Brit, you can probably check with friends who shoot in the area, or perhaps even with a local gun shop to find out how good any particular shoot is. If you're reading this in America, it is highly unlikely you could distinguish the wheat from the chaff, which is why I suggest working with an agent. Also, the agent will be able to help you arrange visitor's shotgun certificates. You need shoot liability insurance most reasonably obtained from BASC (British Association for Shooting and Conservation) or the Countryside Alliance (CA) to be allowed to shoot at U.K. estates.

U.K. Guide Contacts

Pigeon Specialists

Phil and William Beasley, Oxfordshire
Phone: 01144+1869 278946
www.huntinguk.com/index.php/pigeon-shooting
.html

Jim Albone, Bedfordshire
Phone: 01144+1767 312152; 01144+7860
919909 (cell)

Tom Faulkner, Lincolnshire
Phone: 01144+7956626589

Luke Roberts, Adam Calvert Shooting,
Oxfordshire. Offers the unique service of
instruction along with guiding. I know them and
highly recommend them.
Phone: 01144+1235 834441
Email: Luke@adamcalvert.co.uk

Owen Beardsmore, www.cervus-uk.co.uk

Nick Elsdon, www.angliasporting.co.uk

Tim Tortonese, TCT Shooting Services
Phone: 01144+7900–317163 or
01144+1453–731389

Steve Nuttall, www.borderfieldsports.co.uk

www.pigeonalldaylong.com

Waterfowling

BASC; also, shoot liability insurance can be
bought from them, which is necessary to shoot.
Phone: 01144+1244 573 011
Email: wildfowling@basc.org.uk
www.basc.org.uk/wildfowling

Dave Campbell, www.solwayshooting.co.uk
/solway.htm

Hebrides Russell Hird, www.rjhsports.co.uk

Cornwall, www.hendrabarns.co.uk

Callum Isles and his ground centers on the Carse
of Stirling, decoying geese over stubbles, plus
access to a lot of ponds for morning and evening
flighting ducks.
Email: ck.isles@outlook.com

Peter Stephen recommends Scotland's Stuart
Waugh
Phone: 01144+7768 652294
Email: stuart.waugh@btconnect
www.malkempsonwildfowling.co.uk

Woodcock

▲ Considering how long the club has been going, relatively few people
are able to accomplish this feat. Not only must one shoot a left and right
on woodcock—difficult enough—but one must have two witnesses.

The vast majority of the birds shot in Britain and Ireland did their nesting in Russia or Scandinavia. Like the American woodcock, which piles up in Cape May waiting for favorable sconditions to fly across the Chesapeake, these birds migrate across the sea. I have heard tales, I have no way of knowing whether they are apocryphal or not, of crossings in unfortunate or changing weather conditions when huge numbers of birds drowned. Regrettably, it is all too plausible. (Unlike a duck, once they hit the water, woodcock are unable to again become airborne.)

The first significant fall of woodcock tends to reach Britain after the first full moon in November, but occasionally, and especially if the full moon comes towards the end of October, the following week can be prime as well. The shoots close to landfall get the birds first, and the birds will stay for a while assuming the ground is soft enough for them to find worms.

The first time I shot woodcock in Europe was in the early 1980s when a group of American friends owned Garynahine estate on the Isle of Lewis. The previous owners had planted pine forests on this very peaty land, at least where the soil was good enough, and my friends were trying to establish a driven pheasant shoot. While there were a couple of very good drives, most were fairly ordinary, as Garynahine just did not have the terrain to consistently show great birds. But I have never seen the number of woodcock come through a pheasant drive as I did at Garynahine. In two days, I shot 16 woodcock to my own gun, my own record, which I doubt I will ever break.

There are a few estates that specialize in driven woodcock. But one must always remember with woodcock that they are migratory bird, here today gone tomorrow, and it can be very hard to time.

Many great Russian authors, including Tolstoy and Turgenev, wrote about the joys of roding: standing in the breaks of the woods and shooting at last light, often past the gloaming, as the birds moved from the woods to the fields to feed. Don't let anyone tell you this is easy shooting. You are shooting at silhouettes against the dark sky. If one is waiting at the edge of the field with woods in front, one has to be very, very quick to take the birds before they drop below the tree line, where they often completely disappear from sight.

I had a great spot at Tressady for roding. I had to learn to mount to the bird as soon as movement was spotted and *then* determine whether it was indeed a woodcock. If one waited to be certain of the target before mounting and starting to move, it was too late to shoot.

Woodcock shooting over pointers is brilliant sport in the U.K. and very similar to the way we shoot in North America. The biggest difference is the terrain and cover. Sometimes a great place to look for the birds is in or near fields frequented by cows, as the dung seems to go hand in glove with good worm populations. Otherwise the walking can be fairly demanding, especially along hillsides often covered in heather, or while hiking towards river bottoms or alders equivalents.

The real key to successful shooting was not to shoot too soon. Woodcock zig and zag two or three or four times, but then tend to fly on a straight line, and that is the ideal time to shoot. Be patient. Over a pointer or close-quartering spaniel, this will usually occur well within range.

I am a Member No. 1241 of *The Shooting Times's* prestigious Woodcock Club. To become a member one must shoot a left and right in front of two witnesses. I've actually done this a few times, but only on the last occasion, in 2012, did I have the two witnesses required. Should you get lucky and do the same, Google *The Shooting Times* and submit the form.

Waterfowling

Goose shooting generally takes on two forms in the U.K. One is along the shorelines of estuaries, tidal waters, or large lochs, as well as on inland fields, similar to shooting in North America. Obviously, where water is involved, waders and or boats will probably be necessary, and local experience is required both for safety and for success. The BASC has list of goose hunting clubs, many of which will take on nonresident members, and often are able to assign knowledgeable guides (see sidebar).

The other main form that waterfowling takes is duck shooting on fed (baited) ponds in the evenings. While it is illegal here in America, it is common both in South America and in Europe to feed ponds. But even though the ponds are fed, they still cannot be shot too frequently, or the ducks will stop visiting them.

Often the same guide who takes you out for geese in the morning can take you out for an evening duck flight. It's a truly great combination. In general, rubber boots and some waterproof clothes are the key components of kit, as the Brits call their gear, for night flighting.

Grouse

If you are able to organize walked-up grouse as part of your sporting holiday in Britain, realize there is a little in the sporting field to rival it. Appreciate the glorious setting, its wildness, the aroma of heather, and the pointers working, and expect a serious adrenaline rush as the first covey explodes.

▲ Grouse are found amongst the heather. Grouse and its close relative ptarmigan are the upland's fastest birds. Photo courtesy George Goldsmith.

Do not equate "walked-up grouse" with "shooting over dogs." Dogs in this instance for shooting over grouse denotes pointing breeds, usually big running English pointers and setters ranging over the moors in search of grouse. Once a point is achieved, the handler selects a pair of "Guns" (U.K. nomenclature for shooters), to go forward to shoot. Pickers will normally work behind the team, so be sure you know where everyone is before contemplating a shot. Safety, as always, is paramount.

Walking-up, on the other hand, involves a large group of guns, six to eight is common, though sometime more, moving in formation, a straight line with the keeper in charge, with spaniels or retrievers quartering ahead.

A degree of fitness is required—this is not a walk in the park. It is often at altitude or at least up and down hills, often over difficult terrain. It's not Snake River chukar difficult, but significantly more so than walking after quail or pheasant on flat terrain.

A good strong stalking boot is more suitable than common Wellingtons, as ankle support is critical. If the boots are short, you might want to wear a pair of gaiters to keep seeds and midges at bay. A light gun that you can comfortably carry all day is preferable to something heavier. Check with the team captain, keeper, or agent ahead of time to see if there will be a break for lunch or if you should bring a sandwich with you. A traditional English game bag is ideal to carry some rain gear (a rolled-up poncho will often suffice), plus lunch, a flask, a bottle of water, and other necessities.

Grouse accelerate quickly. Just like the first time a covey of wild quail exploded in front of you, do expect to be startled; but then the learning curve is part of the joy of the day. When a covey does flush, try to kill the old birds, which are larger and darker than immature grouse of this season's brood. This will curry favor with the keeper, but do not be hard on yourself if you cannot see this distinction on your first few outings on a moor.

▲ Grouse tend to be found in rugged country requiring well-built four-wheel drives and ATVs. Photo courtesy George Goldsmith.

All forms of driven grouse shooting are at least slightly dangerous. Think about it. If you shooting at pheasants 40 yards overhead, it takes a complete moron to send pellets towards a neighbor—and yet it still does happen. When shooting at birds at eye level or sometimes below, it's an easier thing to do. That is why on driven grouse shoots, stakes are placed on butts to signify areas where one should not be shooting—and to limit one's ability to swing/shoot through the line but even these stakes cannot guarantee safety. If you are doing a driven day, be sure to visualize and memorize the actual line of the butts and note where the stops (flagmen) are; they are flagging birds to try and keep them over the guns. *Never* swing through the line of guns, be it a walk-up day or a driven. On a driven day, raise your gun, turn around, and take birds safely behind. On a walk-up day, the keeper will set the pace and try and keep the line as straight as possible, but it is your responsibility to pay attention and be safe. It is also important on a walk-up day to mind where you step, it is easy to take a tumble or twist an ankle.

Scottish Estates for Mixed Sport

The following are generally let by the week.

Black Corries Estate

The 30,000-acre Black Corries Estate, Glencoe, is situated 2½ hours from Glasgow Airport and offers fantastic mixed sporting weeks, including walked-up snipe, woodcock, and duck flighting. Add small driven days (walk and stand) of pheasant and partridge from late October through December. Walked-up grouse is normally available until about September 20. Black Corries Lodge sleeps up to 12 guests, including a daily housekeeper. From £500 per gun per week based on a party of 10 secures a sporting package including accommodations on a self-catered basis.

Flichity Estate

Flichity Estate will be offering a very comfortable five-bedroom, three-bath farmhouse with mixed shooting packages including pheasant, partridge, snipe, and duck flighting. This would be let on a self-catered basis, but a cook can be arranged. It is a good lower priced option for smaller shooting parties. Flichity is situated in Strathnairn, an hour from Inverness Airport.

Tressady

Tressady, a former sporting lodge of the Duke of Sutherland, offers wild and wonderful woodcock

The Field and Hunter

request the pleasure of your company at

The Macnab Challenge Dinner

at

Boisdale of Bishopsgate

on

Thursday 2nd December, 7.00 for 7.30pm

RSVP on enclosed card by 19th November   *Dress: withdrawing-room suits*

▲ To achieve a Macnab, one must shoot a brace of red grouse, a stag, and land a salmon all in a day. I did a double Macnab including a left and right on stag and joined the Macnab club in the first year of its inception in 2010.

shooting for two to four guns. Prices are from £250 per gun per day for the shooting only. Bag expectations will vary depending on falls of woodcock. Late November and early December is a prime time, but a few days after the full moon in November usually sees a good fall of birds. Accommodation available in Tressady Middle Lodge offering four bedrooms and three bathrooms from £950 per week, self-catered. The main house is available for larger parties. Duck flighting can often be arranged. For a decade this was my home—my all-time favorite—and I miss it.

Ardtornish Estate

Woodcock shooting on the west coast of Scotland can be superb. Ardtornish Estate, Argyll, is situated three hours from Glasgow/Inverness Airports where Headkeeper Simon Boult has first-class pointers and can offer limited days. Cost is £200 plus VAT per gun plus £150 plus VAT for the use of the pointers with that cost shared by up to three guns. A three-bedroom cottage, which is situated on the estate and overlooks the sea, is available for shooting tenants. The cottage costs from £500 per week. In season, red deer stalking for stags and hinds, salmon fishing on the River Aline, and trout fishing on the hill lochs are also available.

Glenmuick

This estate in Royal Deeside offers accommodation for up to 20 guests, along with traditional red deer stalking and driven grouse shooting. Driven days of 50 to 80 brace can be offered subject to grouse stocks. Glenmuick makes a great base for a large sporting gathering. The house is let on a self-catered basis with five hours of housekeeping included each day at a rental of £10,200 (included VAT) for the week for up to 20 guests. Cooks can be arranged. Driven grouse is from £150 plus VAT per brace. Pointers can be hired or grouse walked up without. Pigeon and wildfowling can be arranged nearby.

Invercauld Estate

Ptarmigan shooting is offered on a limited basis and Invercauld Estate in Royal Deeside can occasionally offer days on the high ground for smaller parties of three or four guns. This normally is charged around £250 plus VAT per gun. Both driven and walked-up grouse are available subject to counts and prior bookings Accommodation can be arranged in Lary or Glenmuick subject to availability, or smaller self-catering accommodations, pubs, and hotels in Braemar and Ballater. Pigeon can be had nearby.

▲ Cover of the *Sportsman's Guide,* 1881. Sportsmen would travel in the old days by train from London to Scotland to shoot grouse, ptarmigan, woodcock, black game, Capercaille, and waterfowl in the days when only wild game was shot. They would also stalk deer and fish for salmon.

▲ A covey of grouse flushes in front of hunter and his keeper/dog handler. Think wild quail on steroids.

CHAPTER 13
Gear–Chokes and Over-Boring

Chokes—For Briley, It is About the Choke Length and Sweet Spot

Briley is a well-established, well-respected company, with many employees and state-of-the-art equipment. It started, however, in the back of a garage with Jess working on a mill and Cliff Moller working on a honing machine. For his first three years at Briley, Cliff's job was to hone-in jug chokes, a process in which the diameter of the bore is actually widened, leaving the original choke diameter untouched. "It was an expensive way to do the work, and it was also fairly unpredictable going from one barrel to another. Sometimes the results were quite good and other times not at all, so the lengths of the diameter would have to be played with to get the barrels to pattern well. It was just an inherently incosnsistent way to work."

Chokes, it turns out, are actually pretty complicated. For instance, the length of the screw-in choke affects performance. In their early days, Cliff Moller reviewed the barrels of a lot of manufacturers and found a great variation between them. I had a conversation with him about this:

"Some were three inches and parallel, and some were only two inches in parallel length. It was as though the manufacturers were buying one length of sleeve and cutting it back. While you can do almost anything with screw-in chokes, you couldn't do a lot with the conical end of fixed chokes.

"On a custom basis, it is very difficult to modify the conical section of a fixed choke, because tapered reamers tend to chatter and cut eccentrically. However, some manufacturers, for example Browning, did produce a long conical section in their fixed-choked barrels (probably roller-forged). Most manufacturers traditionally used relatively short conical sections in their fixed-choked barrels."

Bore-to-diameter ratios are critical, when determining the manufacturing cost of a choke. The shorter versions are less expensive to manufacture.

"When you use a boring bar, you need to control the chatter of the tool," explained Cliff. "The farther you extend the cutting tool, the more it wants to vibrate. One uses the thickest bar possible to cut down on vibration."

In 12-gauge shotguns, chokes start to become expensive to manufacture when they are longer than 2.2 inches (a 3:1 bore-to-diameter ratio). As the length of the choke increases, the manufacturing difficulty increases exponentially.

As Moller pointed out, "During the development stage, we spent a lot of time determining what was the optimal length to make our chokes achieve their best performance. How long should it be? How long should the conical section be? How long should the restrictive section be? How much gap clearance should we allow?"

The gap clearance is the difference in diameter between the bore of the shotgun and the seat of the choke where they mate up.

"Another highly critical detail is ensuring that the choke counter-bore [the machined geometry where you screw in the choke] is absolutely lined up perfectly within .0015 total indicator run-out. [i.e., the counter-bore needs to be machined in line and concentric with the bore of the shotgun barrel.] "We discovered that a choke length of 2¾ inches was ideal. It features two inches of transition length (the conical section) and ¾-inch of restrictive diameter length (the choke). If the gap clearances are kept at a minimum, it produces the best and most consistent results.

"Another reason for designing a long choke is to compensate for any small error that might occur in the installation over a longer surface area," said Moller. "In other words, neutralizing most of the negative effects of error by minimizing them. Longer choke produces a longer transitional area before the restrictive diameter. It gives more room to compensate for the small error that might occur in the installation of screw chokes. That error should be no more than one and a half thousandths—a very close tolerance.

"Weird things can occur with silly conical or restrictive lengths. Restrictive lengths that are too long generate poor open patterns. Super-short restrictive lengths generate extremely inconsistent patterns. For example, if 2¾ is good, isn't 3½ better? No. It doesn't hurt, but it will not perform better 99.99 percent of the time. We do make chokes longer than 2¾ for other utilitarian purposes, such as color-coded extended chokes. This makes thing easier for fast changes of a great selection of chokes."

Harder Than Lead? Time for a Choke Change

George Trulock and his company Trulock Chokes (www.trulockchokes.com) is another force in the world of choke tubes and pattern performance.

Steel shot, tungsten, and especially HEVI-Shot and TSS need modern, recently manufactured choke tubes designed for them. Remember these are harder than lead. Indeed, twenty-five or so years ago when I had Briley put its Series 1 tubes in one of my Perazzis, I ordered steel shot-specific choke tubes as well. They were heavier and sturdier than their normal thin-walled choke tubes.

HEVI-shot patterns have excellent tight performance, a plus for turkey hunters. A number of manufacturers provide super-tight turkey choke tubes. Trulock is amongst them, and it recommends choke tubes between .690- and .660-inch for these heavier-than-lead loads and also suggests that some shot sizes work better with different choke constrictions than others. It is worth looking at their website, but these are guidelines are a great place to start before heading to the patterning board.

Following is what Trulock suggests for turkey choke constrictions, relative to bore size, for use with either Nos. 5 or 6 in lead.

- .670 first choice for .740-bore guns
- .665 first choice for .730-bore guns
- .660 first choice for .725-bore guns

Please note that a choke of a given exit diameter is usually going to give a different pattern when used in guns of different bore diameters. This must be confirmed with your gun and load at a patterning board. Each barrel, forgetting its actual bore, will behave slightly differently.

Choke Wisdom

Yes, You Need to Clean Them

Cleanliness is close to godliness is as true for "gun hygiene" as it is for personal hygiene. Chokes should be cleaned regularly as this is where the most plastic residue from wadding accumulates—and in

▲ A friend of mine choke bulged the barrel when he was lent the wrong choke tube. . . . Make sure you get the exact same choke that is designed for your model of gun, not just the make.

a worst-case scenario can lead to a barrel bulges or worse. To be honest I don't clean my barrels or my chokes every day, or every time I shoot. (I do clean rifles and pistols every time I shoot. To get good accuracy, one needs to thoroughly get rid of fouling and so on.) I do clean them any time it rains. Or anytime I feel that I have put enough cartridges through the gun that is serious cleaning is in order. Or if I discovered that the chokes weren't as well seated as I believed (not in tight enough—an exceptionally rare occurrence when I shoot as I do use a wrench to tighten them), which would lead to build up where the base of the choke meets the barrel—all too common with individuals who tighten using only their fingers. Plastic fouling and powder residue is far worse in screw-in chokes than in fixed-choke guns and builds up faster—and if it gets under a choke tube, especially choke tube that has not been sufficiently tightened—you can have real troubles. Also, whereas a buildup of fouling in a fixed choke gun might be annoying, it rarely produces serious problems. It does in screw-in choke tube guns. This occurs is when powder and plastic fouling gets between the choke and the choke counter-bore in the barrel.

Soaking the chokes in solvent and then using the gunsmith's equivalent of a toothbrush to get rid of residue is the right way to start. The solvent dissolves the fouling. Make sure the threads are clean, then use a little bit of oil and replace them into the barrels or if you've shot multiple choke tubes put the spares in your case. Again I cannot over-emphasize the importance of having choke tubes set fully and tight. Not so tight that you can't remove them. Chokes can rust in place, and then you have trouble…. That is why you want to oil them lightly.

If your choke tubes are clean, the threads are clean, the outside of the choke tube is lightly oiled, and properly tightened, you will avoid many potential problems.

Screw That Thing In

A choke tube wrench should be employed to make sure that the choke tube is properly seated. While you don't want to over-tighten the choke so you have difficulty getting it out, it must be in tight enough that it cannot shoot loose. It is a good idea to check chokes between stations to make sure that they are tight. As I wrote above, a light coating, and by light I mean light, of oil will lessen the chance of the choke being frozen. There are special brushes designed to clean the threads inside the barrel. Use them.

Frozen Chokes

Chokes that are frozen have to be pulled out by a professional gunsmith. It usually means pitching the choke tube. This is most frequently caused by rust, but can also be caused by not having any lubrication on the choke tube and tightening it so much that it freezes. A less common cause of frozen chokes is using steel shot with too much choke, for example improved modified or full. This causes the choke to expand, a.k.a. choke creep. This is not common but it does occur and what it does the choke will be "locked" in the barrel. Only give the problem barrels/chokes to a gunsmith who is familiar and competent with this type of work to safely remove it without damaging the barrels . . . much better to throw away the choke to than a set of barrels. As always an ounce of prevention is worth a pound of cure.

Choke Storage

Choke tubes should be stored in specially designed cases, ideally padded. Be careful not to drop a choke or even a choke tube case, as they can easily be damaged and once damaged must be discarded and replaced.

The 12-Gauge Gets Bigger

A long time ago I had a lengthy conversation with Briley's Cliff Moller about the practice of back-boring, something that's become so popular, many major brands offer their shotguns, especially those intended for competition, with back-bored barrels straight from the factory.

"Over-boring or back-boring: We have found that over-bored barrels produce excellent patterns for cylinder to light full chokes," said Cliff. "One has to work a little harder to get super-tight patterns from over-bored barrels. It is possible, just more difficult. On the other hand, under-bored barrels with small bore diameters (.718- to .723-inch) resist producing good open patterns in Cylinder or Skeet, but do generate tight patterns rather easily. There are other advantages to over-boring, including less recoil. Public enemy No. 1 of a competition shooter is recoil. If you want to end your career fast, develop a flinch. So, if you are fighting recoil and want tight patterns, use an over-bored gun and screw in your tightest Briley chokes. (I doubt you will outperform the efficiency of our chokes.) In games like sporting clays, skeet, and trap, over-bored guns are ideal for the vast majority of targets."

When asked about the internal diameter of forcing cones, that area of the barrel between the chamber and the bore that tapers to seal gases behind the wad and shot, Cliff said, "The standard forcing cone is five degrees. We believe that the ideal is between 2 and 2½ degrees."

They aren't big fans of longer cones for two reasons.

"First is safety. The barrel profile of O.D. (outer dimensions) begins to thin out, and if you extend the forcing cones, you start to compromise the safety of the barrel. Second is that we have yet to see any benefit of forcing cones longer than two degrees."

Choke is the tapered constriction of the gun barrel's

bore and, with the exception of Cylinder, is smaller by some dimension than the actual bore of the barrel. If the bore of the barrel is .730-inch and the diameter of the choke is .700, the constriction is defined as .030.

Constriction for a nominal choke varies among manufacturers. If the barrel is .740-inch and the choke is .700, you have now gone much tighter, to Full in fact. Standard chokes tend to range between .000 (Cylinder) and .045 (Full is generally .040). Special turkey chokes can be even tighter. Most chokes, both fixed and interchangeable, have a length between 1½ and four inches. Choke designs are usually either conical parallel or straight conical. The former has a cone that blends into a parallel section, stabilizing the shot charge as it exits the muzzle. The straight conical choke is a cone, and where it stops the shot exits the muzzle. The conical parallel is more common.

While .730-.729. 728-inch was standard for decades as the 12-gauge shotgun bore diameter, in an effort to improve patterns, back-boring (also called "over-boring"), has become common; .740-inch may become the new norm, though many manufacturers deviate from this some offering bores even slightly larger. The plastic shot cups and petals of today's wads, which maintain a gas seal, enabled this advance.

Tube Sets—From Heavyweight to Featherweight

▲ A perfect case for a competitor traveling by car or plane. Courtesy Americase.

In the 1970s, Claude Purbaugh started making the first sub-gauge tube sets for the skeet shooting community. In doing so, in a matter of minutes, a 12-gauge gun could be converted to 20- or 28-gauge or .410-bore.

In 1975, Noel Winters used a set of sub-gauge tubes in his Krieghoff to become the World Skeet Champion—shooting the same gun in all four events. (I understand that he did not use carrier barrels to keep the weight and balance close, as is sometimes the case today.)

▲ These excellent tubes are available both in custom configurations to your barrels and in drop-in models. They come with interchangeable choke tubes. Courtesy Briley.

The first sub-gauge tubes were an all-aluminum product and did not feature integral ejectors. The shooter had to remove the 12-gauge ejector from the gun and insert an extra set of ejectors in the appropriate gauge that were modified to match that specific set of tubes. This was especially cumbersome with spring-loaded ejector guns, such as those from Beretta and Perazzi. Stan Baker was one of the early pioneers in making interchangeable choke tubes. Jess Briley was another. Briley helped create the revolution and fostered the evolution in tube sets. His tubes were made from two materials, stainless steel for the chambers and aluminum for the barrels. The stainless chambers allowed the use of integral ejectors, which made it possible to change gauges quickly and easily. These tube sets also have interchangeable chokes.

The early sets were quite heavy—the .410 tubes weighed 1½ pounds. The newer tube sets only weigh ounces per set, not pounds. This was accomplished by replacing the stainless chambers with titanium and by intelligently creating high-tech barrel profiles, which reduce the mass of the barrel as the pressure decreases.

CHAPTER 14
Gear–Hearing and Vision

Hearing Protection

Nearly 40 years ago, I started as Founding Editor a number of magazines for a company called Harris Publications. Of course, they were all about shooting and hunting and included such titles as *Combat Handguns*. Now this was after the glory days of American outdoor magazines, when incredible shooters and hunters such as Jack O'Connor and Warren Page were at their zeniths. In this context and capacity, I went to the SHOT Show, which was in its infancy circa 1980. Big names reigned, with Jim Carmichael, John Wootters, Bob Brister, and a *pistolero* named Bill Jordan (no, not Realtree's Bill Jordan) at the forefront. At a big lunch sponsored by Winchester, my table included Jordan and Slim Pickens, who was best known for his acting role as the pilot in the *Doctor Strangelove* movie who rode the H-bomb to the ground, whooping and hollering all the way. Jordan and Pickens were having a competition for who could tell the best story. They were both so funny that both were declared winners. That was the good news. The bad was the conversation was often a shouting contest, since most had shot for many years without serious hearing protection. Indeed, for their generation, and to a lesser extent for my own, hearing protection was, at best, rudimentary. Cotton stuffed into the ears seemed to be the best option at the time.

Indeed, as a youngster on the skeet range, a bit of cotton was all that was available. Soon I discovered ear valves that were a soft-rubber doohickey with a metal insert. They were a vast improvement over cotton. Muffs were available for use at the rifle range, but were heavy and clumsy and too large for shotgunning.

Today's shooter is spoiled for choice when it comes to hearing protection (well, all gear, really). But first let us discuss briefly why ear protection is so vital.

Sensor neural hearing loss is damage to the inner ear. It is usually irreversible, even by surgery. The main cause is deterioration of "hair" cells due to extremely loud noise. For instance, when a blast from a shotgun is sent into an unprotected ear, these delicate hair cells that transmit sound to the auditory nerve are damaged.

It is generally thought that noise in excess of 90 decibels is harmful to hearing if experienced over time. The louder the sound, the shorter the prolonged exposure needed to cause damage. Gunfire often exceeds 130 decibels. Make no mistake: Gunshot, the noise and waves, causes hearing loss. Indeed, I now have tinnitus from all my years of shooting. I did my best to protect my hearing, rarely shooting without earplugs in those post-cotton days. Still, I must admit that there have been a few occasions when I was shooting reasonably high-volume days and the earplugs fell out, or an earplug fell out, and I might not have noticed it for twenty minutes in the heat of the battle. It all adds up. Ear protection prevents damage to hearing. Wear something.

Simple foam plugs provide a fair amount of protection for pennies, if bought in bulk. For a few bucks, non-electronic muffs from RidgeLine and others provide lots of protection. Those shooters who are serious are often seen with electronic devices: Amplified models as muffs from RidgeLine and electronic plugs (some are custom-fitted to the user) from Walker, EAR, ESP, and others. Their creators claim that sound waves are limited to a safe level by miniaturized circuitry, while sounds under 80 to 90 dB, such as speech, are actually amplified.

For those who like muffs, RidgeLine and ProEars deserve consideration. From the latter's website, you'll learn that "Due to the sophisticated, audiophile components extreme linear characteristics, wide 80 dB dynamic range and surface mount technology, Pro Ears provide the clearest, most natural sound quality ever found in hearing products. Every sound comes in crisp and clear, so natural it's like you are wearing nothing at all." From my own experience, this seems to be so.

To protect one's hearing, it is necessary that electronic devices shut down quickly when high noise levels are detected, but they also must recover just as quickly once the noise level drops to a safe level. Amplification increases the ability to hear accurately at distance. ProEars provides an adjustable range to increase hearing up to eight times with programmable units that allow the user to "gain sensitivity" by adjusting the muffs to fit their individual's specific needs. It is, using current technology, possible to hear a pigeon coming out of a box or clay being released from a trap arm while simultaneously protecting your hearing. (Actually, you hear the mechanics of the trap and the arm making its launch; if you can hear the clay, sign up for superhero status.) The wearer has independent volume controls on each cup to compensate for unique situations that call for one ear to be more or less sensitive. And because each ear cup features its own electronics, every ProEars provides true stereo for directional sound detection, very helpful to shooting flyers (a.k.a. boxed birds).

Let's take a look at some individual hearing protection brands and models making the grade today.

Walker's Game Ear

Walker's Game Ear (www.gmsoutdoors.com) products use technologically advanced circuitry for sound amplification and hearing protection. Their Digital Signal Processing (DSP) gives the wearer the clearest sound signal possible. I have limited experience with these, being a cheap SOB who uses either disposable plugs or non-electronic muffs depending on conditions. Walker's current lineup includes:

Razor Series—Slim Shooter Folding Muff

This model works on two AAA batteries, uses NRR23dB—HD Sound Output with rubberized cups, and is a good value at $70.

Game Ear Micro Elite

These are in the ear canal and have multiple modes. At $700 they are not inexpensive but it is a good design.

Pro Low Profile Folding Muff

The Low Profile model has a padded headband and soft PVC ear pads with a noise reduce rating of NRR 31dB. They costs only $16.

Champion

Champion (www.championtarget.com) molded foam plugs fit in the ear canal and are inexpensive and disposable. I generally use this type of earplug with muffs over them.

Molded Foam Plugs

Six-pair packs are $3.45 and 100-pair boxes cost $33.45

Ear Muffs

Electronic Champion muffs are available in standard or electronic versions. The electronic version at $43.45 are definitely a best buy. NRR 25dB

These muffs are light, comfortable, and provide superior hearing protection. Both standard or electronic versions are available. Adjustable fit and collapsible for compact storage. The electronic muffs amplify quiet sounds while protecting against harmful noise levels (NRR 25dB)

40974 Ear Muffs—Electronic; 25dB NRR. MSRP $43.45

Slim Ear Muffs

40972 Slim Passive Hearing Muffs-Pink; 21dB NRR. MSRP $18.45

Ear Muffs—Passive

40970 Ear Muffs—Passive; 27dB NRR. MSRP $18.45

Etymotic Research

Etymotic Research has been producing ear protection for three decades, but products specially geared for shooters for under a decade. In its wide range of offerings, the GunSport Pro (a.k.a. GSP-15) is amongst the most popular electronic earplug. It has two modes. The first allows normal hearing, but then shuts off when sounds amplify. An enhanced mode features five-times amplification on low-volume sounds, which makes great sense in some hunting situations. They retail for $299, but are ready to use without custom fitting. They do come with an assortment of ear tips, so you can find the one that fits you best. The company's website (www.etymotic.com) is good and I recommend you view it to find the right model for you as the selection is wide.

GunSport•PRO

These electronic earplugs are designed for gun sport enthusiasts in the field or at the range where enhanced awareness, clear communication, and blast protection are desired.

GSP•15 Electronic Earplugs

These are for gun sport enthusiasts who need protection from firearm blasts, but also need protection from loud continuous noise from vehicles, machinery, or repeated gunfire from nearby shooters. Improves distance detection up to 5X. MSRP: $299.

Beretta is now also offering a pair of electronic muffs that do a great job. They are both compact and comfortable. Add reasonably priced, which they are, and you have a great purchase.

E.A.R. makes a number of well-designed and industry-leading earplugs but they do require a mold to be taken for custom fitting.

Eye Protection

The eyes require serious protection, as they are amongst our most vulnerable organs—and I know this from personal experience. My wife, Renata, and I were invited by an old friend of hers to one of the great shoots of Great Britain, Cocking on the South Downs, about an hour and a half from London. The estate's most famous drive is called the "Chalk Pit," as the birds are driven over trees at the very top of the cliff face. Guns are placed on the road going up the chalk pit and also at the bottom.

I had drawn my favorite peg, on which I'd shot on a half-dozen occasions. It is in the far left corner and provides birds that are extremely challenging, with all sorts of angles, classic overhead birds, and long passing crossers (as there were no guns to my left, there was no one to poach).

We had already shot two drives, and while it was a cool humid day with a good breeze, I was starting to sweat. As I perspired, my glasses started to fog up. I remedied this at first by removing my hat. But I realized birds were flaring, so I put the Tweed cap back on. Once again the glasses fogged.

Now, I have been hit in the face on about three occasions by pellets—always a single pellet—out of roughly a thousand driven days, and I knew that the likelihood of being struck in the eye with a pellet was slim on a tall bird shoot. I decided to take off my glasses.

That was a huge mistake. I think because of the humidity and the wind coming towards me, I wound up getting burnt on the cornea by some hot powder that was blown back into my face. I completed the drive, and our host's wife brought in eyewash solution to lunch. (I had thought that I had just gotten something in my eye and hadn't realized at this stage that the cornea had been burnt.) The eyewash failed to help, and instead of going out to shoot after lunch, my wife was forced to drive me to the local hospital. They did not have much of an eye center and sent us elsewhere.

Long story short, I was quite lucky. While the cornea had been burnt, it wasn't over the pupil and after a week or two of treatment with a prescription ointment, the cornea healed. That said, I would never take that chance or make that mistake again.

I have had a number of shooting glasses in my life, starting with Ray Bans as a teenager. They are probably amongst the first glasses commonly used by shooters, as they rode very high on the face. They were available in prescription, and with hardened glass lenses to reduce the likelihood of being struck by a pellet. They were quite heavy but good quality. I had these in yellow for low light conditions and in light gray for brighter days. This was decades before companies started specializing in glasses for shooters, especially glasses for competitive shots who needed prescription lenses.

From there I went to Decot, but over fifteen years ago I switched to Randolph Ranger (www.randolphusa.com) glasses and have not looked back. In a word, they are superb. (Though I reached out to Decot a number of times for this book, they never responded to my emails.) That said, I think that Randolph produces a wider range of glasses for shooters now, some for those who need prescription lenses, and some that are available only to those who do not. Lenses come in more colors than one can shake a stick at. This includes three HIGH DEF lenses. I tend to use the lightest color HIGH DEF in lowlight conditions and the darkest in bright, but I also have a set of purple lenses I find very useful, especially with some backgrounds.

RE Ranger

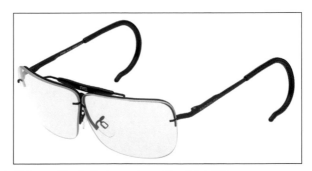

▲ RE Ranger Classic. Photo courtesy of Randolph USA.

RE Ranger is quite probably the dominant glasses brand in the clay shooting market. I often wear them when shooting pistols or rifles at the range, and in hunting situations as well.

As Ranger's Sarah Waszkiewicz, RE Ranger Specialist, points out, "Our frames are made from either Monel or Niclafor 1000 metals, which then receive plating color and a tough E-Coat process for durability. Our lenses are high impact polycarbonate made by Zeiss. All lenses contain a hard coating to increase the scratch resistance.

"The main differences between the styles are the different shapes of lenses offered and the curvature of the frames. The Classic frame is one of our original styles that has very little curvature or adjustability, while the Sporter acts as a typical pair of eyeglasses with colored clip-on lens. People can wear these as their normal eyewear and add the clip-ons when they are ready to shoot. This style can also hold a heavy prescription."

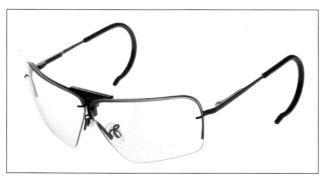
▲ Ranger Edge. Photo Courtesy of Randolph USA.

The Edge is an upgraded style from the now-discontinued XL model. The Edge has a sportier lens cut, an adjustable nose piece, and a smaller DBL (distance between the lenses).

▲ Ranger XLW with HD light lens. Photo Courtesy of Randolph USA.

The XLW model is the first wrap frame from Randolph. This model holds a wider lens for better eye coverage and also has an adjustable nose bridge. The XLW can hold a detachable optical insert. Prescriptions cannot be placed within the lens due to the high curvature of the lens.

▲ Ranger Falcon Pro. Photo Courtesy of Randolph USA.

The Falcon line is Ranger's first one-lens shield system. It comes in various frame colors.

"As for lenses, there are twelve lens color options for the Edge, Classic, and Sporter frames, 13 lens options for the XLW frame, and seven lens options for the Falcon Series," said Waszkiewicz. "All of our frames except the Falcons can be made with a prescription in some form," she added. "When making prescription optical lenses for the shooting community, it's important to use an Authorized Ranger Dealer. Typically, the frames will sit higher on a person's face compared to normal use eyeglasses. With that said, the optical expert must modify the optical center within the lens, in addition to adjusting for the distance between the pupils. This will allow for best visibility no matter where you look out of the lens."

Costa Del Mar

▲ These Costa Blackfin glasses are perfect for a cast and blast adventure.

Harking back to my early days with Ray Bans, I've always had a fondness for aviator-style glasses. Recently, I've taken to wearing a pair of Costas, and they are terrific glasses. Like Ranger, the lenses are straight from Zeiss. Some of the models come in glass, others in polycarbonate. The polycarbonate lenses meet safety requirements for shooting but the company does not market them for shooting as they feel that the frames do not. The glass models are not impact safe, but unless you're on a grouse moor or are shooting in the upland's where a pellet could ricochet off a tree (or a fellow shooter gets careless), I probably wouldn't sweat it too much (then again, I'm the guy who burnt his cornea). Statistically, getting peppered with a large number of shot is probably most common in a grouse butt or upland hunting, and in these conditions super-safe glasses are an advantage. Indeed, I had an old pair of glasses for Spanish partridge and grouse shooting that had metal protection on the side of the frames, thus protecting the eye from shot coming in from the side. Luckily, I shot with safe teams and have never seen an accident in either type of shooting, but this shooting can prove dangerous.

I guess this is a long way of getting to the point, which is that in some shooting circumstances, safety is more of a concern than in others. For example, if I'm shooting on a trap field, while burnt powder could get into my eye, the likelihood of being struck by an errant pellet approaches zero. So, if I am doing that type of shooting or are off on my own property walking through the woods in pursuit of game and want to use the same glasses I use for driving, I will go to my Costa South Point models with glass lenses. They are amazingly comfortable and the optics are, like Randolph, superb. I have the copper high definition lenses, which are excellent for shooting and driving. One should also remember that these are amongst the best fishing glasses in the world, so I will often be found wearing them on trout streams. Costa's Blackfin model is perfect for a cast-and-blast outing. They give great side protection, and fly casting in the wind one should have good eye protection from an errant hook.

I guess this is as good a point as any to mention that, in theory, polarized glasses slightly distort distance perception. I have not found this to be much of a factor when using my Costas. That said, if I were practicing seriously for competition or competing, I wouldn't want the psychological impact nagging at the back of my mind and would therefore probably go to my Randolph Rangers.

Heather Miller, Costa's knowledgeable head of PR and also an avid shooter with good gun dogs, points out, "Costa's 580 lens technology selectively filters out harsh yellow and harmful high-energy ultraviolet blue light. Filtering yellow light enhances reds, blues, and greens and produces better contrast and definition while reducing glare and eye fatigue. Absorbing high-energy blue light cuts haze, producing greater visual clarity and sharpness.

"The 100 percent polarization and UV protection are embedded directly into the lens.

"The lenses are available in either optically ground glass or super lightweight polycarbonate. Costa's copper lens is a great all around lens choice. The copper lens allows 12 percent light transmission and provides enhanced color and contrast in all conditions. Similarly, the Sunrise lens allows the most light to enter the lens and is best suited for low light conditions (e.g., early morning or late afternoon). The sunrise lens allows 27 percent light transmission.

"Prescription lenses are also available through authorized Costa optical retailers."

Like Randolph Rangers, Costa does pick its partners for prescription lenses. It is important to work with one of them.

▲ These Costa Southpoints are perfect for cast-and-blast holidays on bright days.

CHAPTER 15
Gear—Gun Cases and Luggage

Gun Cases

Americase—www.americase.com

Premium Series—These are among the most indestructible cases on the market. Utilizing fine quality hardware and materials, these handsome cases can be built to almost any length or width. A sturdy, anodized aluminum frame and extremely strong side panels yield a case that resists warping and dents. Closure of the case engages the wedge-lock gasket system, which seals out dust and resists water. They are available in single- and double-gun models, and for over/unders or side-by-sides. I have two of these cases, and while they're not the lightest cases in the world, have always found them to provide excellent protection for my firearms, especially when subjected to the rigors of air travel. MSRP: $392.14–$540.51

▲ This case holds two shotguns. Photos courtesy of Americase, Inc.

Ultra-Lite Series—This case line is 30 percent lighter than the Premium case line, but as they are made of aircraft aluminum they do offer excellent protection. These are riveted cases with premium velvet interiors, two key-locking flip latches, and two pad-lockable eyelets. The ends are reinforced with double-layer end caps for extra toughness and durability. Ultra-Lite cases are offered in different sizes and varieties for breakdown shotguns. MSRP: $390–$557.91

Extruded Skeet Tube Holder—This will be of particular interest to clay target shooters who compete in

sub-gauges events. It can be had for two, four, or six tubes and in 28-, 30-, 32-, or 34- inch lengths. Being made of extruded aluminum it is quite tough while fairly lightweight. MSRP: $63.96

Negrini—www.negrinicases.com

Negrini is so well-established that many of the best gunmakers in the world, including Beretta, Benelli, Blaser, Browning, Perazzi, Holland & Holland, and Krieghoff, offer its cases with their shotguns. It has been in the business for over 35 years making first-class cases for traveling sportsman.

When my ancient Perazzi case interior dissolved, it was basically a no-brainer to go to Negrini for its replacement. While very strong, these Italian cases are roughly one third the weight of most aluminum cases. Negrini gun cases are finished with plush padded interiors and recessed combination locks to protect firearms from the abuse of airline travel. One of the many aspects of the Negrini that I really appreciate is the fact that whereas they are lighter than metal cases, they are quite strong due to their own patented double wall construction with an ABS outer case welded to a thermoformed inner. This gives great shock absorption, necessary for travel. Upgraded luxury finishes include 100 percent Italian leather trim and handles up to full leather exteriors and interiors. Each gun case is fitted with hardened steel combination locks and hinges, and locks are recessed to prevent gun case damage on conveyor belts.

Negrini gun case interiors are designed with separate compartments for stock and receiver, barrel/s, and fore-end, as well as accessories. All materials used are certified to not corrode firearms. Many colors available, they carry a limited lifetime warranty, and are certified for international air travel.

Recently Negrini added the Uplander Series luxury shotgun hard case which is ultra-compact and ultra-light tipping the scales at less than 5½ pounds. It is designed for shotguns that are 20-gauge or smaller and will accommodate barrels up to 30½ inches. The Uplander is approved for air travel and features a new, patent-pending hand-detachable sling system to carry hands-free. It features a velvet hand-upholstered interior with separate compartments for your stock and receiver plus all accessories on one side, with separate storage for barrel and forearm.

"We are very excited to provide the lightest and most compact shotgun case the industry has ever seen!" says Jon Reddout, INTELCASE General Manager. "With the new quick-detach swivel mount, we've provided a comfortable hands-free solution that provides a sleek, stylish and air travel-certified case."

I also use Negrini's Rifle Luggage cases, which are obviously also very well suited for slug guns, waterfowl shotguns, or any other autoloader or pump you don't want to disassemble. They're great for putting in the back of the car, getting to my destination, and being ready to go upon arrival. They are rated highly for airline travel both for protecting valuable firearms and for complying with FAA and airline regulations. I recommend them highly.

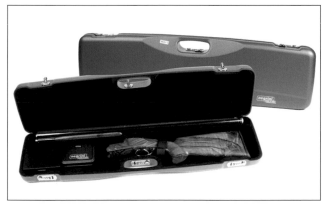

▲ Negrini is the preferred case of many top gunmakers. Photo courtesy of International Case Co. LLC/Negrini Cases.

Luggage

Orvis—www.orvis.com

Battenkill Rolling Magnum Duffle Case—This great bag is made of eighteen-ounce green cotton canvas and it is amazingly spacious. I have used mine for over ten years traveling from shoot to shoot. It has a lower compartment that zips separately and into which a double gun case fits perfectly. Before the laws got tighter, I would often fly with this bag with the guns on the bottom (obviously declared and in a locked case), but now I presume that guns have to be packed separately. It's still very useful, as city clothes can go in the bottom section and hunting clothes in the top. The fact

that it has wheels is a real bonus; I've carried this bag with guns and ammo in it and it weighs so much with two shotguns in a hard case in the bottom section that even a young Arnold Schwarzenegger would probably have to be in shape to walk down the street with it. It has worn quite well over the years. If you need a bag bigger than this, you must be related to my wife. MSRP: $479

▲ I have traveled the world with this case. Sometimes I put shooting clothes in the top, and city clothes in the bottom compartment. It holds a ton. Photo courtesy of Orvis.

Plano Molding—www.planomolding.om

Field Locker Mil-Spec Long Gun Case—Each of Plano's three Field Locker Mil-Spec Gun Cases—Single, Tactical, and Double Long Gun—have been certified by an accredited test facility as meeting military specifications for immersion, dust, vibration, and transit drop per MIL-STD-810G. Waterproof and dustproof, these cases are designed to be shotgun travel cases. Secure sealing with premium Dry-Loc gaskets and exact measurements ensure that the contents won't be adversely affected by water or dirty environments. Their advanced pressure-release valve, which equalizes pressure divergence caused by altitude or temperature, is an added measure of security.

Over-molded heavy-duty handles, reinforced padlock gates, and a pair of easy-glide enclosed ball bearing wheels to make the case incredibly mobile are all features appreciated by travelers. Internally, each case features double-density foam. Fully customizable, the foam layers can be configured for perfect fit with your particular shotgun. MSRP: $149.99

Red Oxx Manufacturing, Inc.—www.redoxx.com

I first saw Red Oxx products on one of Ivan Carter's Safari shows. They were handsome, so I ordered a duffel and a soft gun case. Sometimes looks are only skin deep. In the case of Red Oxx, they are great to bone. They are made in America, and the quality on every level from material used to hardware and zippers are first rate.

Safari Beanos PR5.5—This duffel bag is one *Outside Magazine* recognized as one of 2004's fifteen best outdoor products. It was designed for those flyers who need to keep within the 23-kg/50-pound weight limit when traveling. These bags are not super light, but this is because they are made tough, tough enough to provide great protection to your important possessions. They are realistically, nay reasonably, priced for the quality provided. In fact, I'd consider them a best buy.

While the company says this is the travel duffel bag to take out into the world for "your seven- to ten-day trip," it is an acceptable minimum on safari where laundry is done daily. If you are going waterfowling, you will probably need a second bag for waders and other large gear.

▲ Safari Beanos are tough as nails. Photo courtesy of Red Oxx.

The large number of pockets allow easy and quick access for the well-organized traveler. There zippers are terrific and the material is seriously tough.

These 1000 weight Cordura nylon duffels come in a number of colors—I prefer tan, but many are available from subdued to highly visible. MSRP: $230

Safari-Beanos PR6—If you need a larger bag than the 5.5, consider this model. The PR6 duffel is perfect for a long trip the field, for example the Safari or trip to Alaska. It is the original "Large" duffel in the Safari-Beanos Series and can hold up to seventy pounds of gear. MSRP: $240

Safari-Beanos PR5—Red Oxx designed this is a carry-on to go along with an expedition to carry valuables, cameras medicines etc. clothes you can't live without as it is the maximum size that will fit an overhead compartment. It also makes a great weekend bag. MSRP: $220

Tenzing Outdoors—www.tenzing.com

▲ A perfect day bag for accessories. Photo courtesy of Tenzing.

Tenzing UPSBB Upland Field Box—To my mind, the day bag is one of the most important pieces of equipment. Obviously, the bag I take to the sporting clay field is different from the upland waterfowl bag and a world away from a day bag for a safari, but they all share a certain commonality: holding must-have items.

Introduced in 2016, the Tenzing TZ UPSBB Upland Field Box has room for everything I need for a day of upland hunting, and this is my designated bag for upland hunts. Extra shooting glasses and gloves, reading glasses, soft earplugs, a canine first aid kit, dog whistles, a bore cleaner should something get stuck in my barrels, a small camera to record memories, some Band-Aids® and Neosporin® all live in this bag. I just add the appropriate ammo and a few other items needed for that day afield and I'm set to go.

The box is constructed of quality materials, and comes in blaze orange color with charcoal accents. Heavy-duty carry handles and a padded shoulder strap ensure safe and comfortable transport, while a molded bottom helps keep moisture out, especially important as I do leave cameras and other electronics in it. Indeed, Tenzing's engineers have flushed out an impressive degree of utility from this relatively compact bag with side pockets for shooting glasses and smartphones, while a versatile front main pocket with mesh dividers is perfect for items like maps, keys, and field gun-cleaning supplies. There's even a collapsible water bowl for dogs. Inside, a large main pocket zips open to provide ample space for shell boxes, radios, electronic collars, snacks, dog food, water bottles and more. Finally, an ingenious molded lid cradles a removable Pro-Latch storage box that allows immediate access to small necessities like choke tubes, wrenches, extra batteries, et cetera. MSRP $149.99.

▲ Kim Rhode is the USA's most decorated Olympic shot, having won medals in a number of shotgunning disciplines at a number of Olympics. Clearly she is well organized. The beauty of her Truck Vault is that it can be set up in a number of configurations, depending on your interests. It provides great peace of mind with its extra security. www.truckvault.com. Photo courtesy of Truck Vault.

CHAPTER 16
Gear–Upland

Shirts, Coats, Vests, and Other Tops

Beretta—www.berettausa.com

Beretta Gunner Field Jacket—New technology eliminates the oily finish and odor of waxed cotton, a longtime staple of British country sports, without compromising the fabric's performance. It is waterproof, thorn-proof, windproof, yet breathable. This jacket incorporates lightweight Beretta thermal padding for warmth. It sports an abundance of multifunctional pockets inside and out, some zipped for protecting valuables—you don't want to lose car keys in the alders—plus roomy front cargo pockets with elasticized cartridge holders that actually fit shells. You can machine wash this coat, but do *not* use detergent. MSRP: $279

▲ These shirts are ideal both for days afield or shooting clays, and make you look good to boot.

Beretta Waxed Cotton Strap Vest—This is top of the line. Its oil-free and odor-free waxed cotton adds a layer of waterproof protection for your shells and

▲ This jacket has everything desired by a serious upland hunter.

Beretta TM Roll Up Shooting Shirt

To my mind, this is a combination of a safari shirt and an upland shirt and has many of the best features of both. It is very lightweight and comfortable, and because it is moisture wicking, it will keep you dry through a long day afield. It sports a right-handed shooting patch with the Beretta trident logo embroidered on the left chest pocket. MSRP: $69

▲ Strap vests are gaining popularity because they can be worn both in warm weather and on crisp fall days over a wool sweater, down vest etc. Their design adds comfort to a long day afield.

game. The adjustable shoulder straps evenly distribute the load of a laden vest, and makes it a better fit regardless of ones height and girth. The roomy, waterproof game bag is accessible from the front or the back, but I really like using it from the front, making for more comfortable and convenient access for bird insertion. Spacious double front pockets feature elastic cartridge holders. The facing on the front pockets and the rear game bag has high-visibility blaze orange for safety. A zippered interior pocket is great for carrying a wallet or keys. It is washable so long as you don't use detergent. MSRP: $135

Beretta Retriever Field Vest—This vest continues Beretta's line of well-designed products with this take on a classic. It is made from military grade cotton twill and sports micro-ripstop blaze orange panels. There is enough high-visibility orange from all angles to provide safety and comply with state laws, and enough tan to prevent temporary blindness. Pockets are well thought-out, especially the two zippered security pocket on the chest. Good-sized pockets for carrying shells or grub are made even more practical with elasticized cartridge loops on the front pockets holding a box of shells. The game bag with waterproof, washable fabric (for cleaning up blood, etc.) melds into a mesh back yoke to keep it light and cool. MSRP: $149

▲ This classic vest works well on all but the warmest days.

Orvis—www.orvis.com
Foul-Weather Lined Sweater—This is a terrific wool sweater. It is extremely warm, which is surprising because it is so light. I presume that the windproof liner must have something to do with it. Often windproof layered clothing is too stiff, but that's not the case this time, as this cardigan is soft and supple. I will wear it on its own for a day in the uplands, assuming I am not going into briars, etc. and the suede quilted shooting patches provide the type of tacky surface needed to prevent buttstocks from slipping. I also wear it under the Orvis shell jacket or under a heavier outer coat, over a sweater, etc. It is also great on the clay fields in combination with a shell pouch, and perfect for casual wear in almost any circumstance. MSRP: $139

▲ I use this on cool days for shooting sporting clays or chasing my bird dogs. Terrific when used with a strap vest.

Upland Shell Coat—This Upland Shell is my go-to jacket. Besides the fact that is damn comfortable, there is a zippered inner pocket that holds my wallet safely and a clip inside one of the hand warmer pockets that secures my car keys. I wore it every day while on a plantation hunt in February, and it was perfect. The mornings were cold, but a heavy sweater underneath gave me more than sufficient warmth. As the day warmed up, I shed the sweater but kept the jacket. Because the model I chose was trimmed in orange, it gave me the visibility and safety I needed when shooting as part of a group. This coat breathes well, and the cloth is water resistant. I really liked the adjustable cuffs and the fact that the coat can be washed, if needed. It stood up well to briars and other tough habitat elements, and if you put a lightweight strap vest over it you have room for shells, birds, etc. MSRP: $198

![This coat breathes well, and the cloth is water resistant.]

▲ This coat breathes well, and the cloth is water resistant.

Tenzing Outdoors—www.tenzingoutdoors.com

TZ BV16 Upland Bird Vest Pack For hunters who take this sport seriously and hunt hard over miles looking for wild birds, Tenzing's TZ BV16 Upland bird vest, redesigned in 2016, definitely is worth considering. It blends the advantages of a blaze orange hunting vest with a hunting pack and will carry all the gear you need to take for a full day going from covert to covert or over the vast expanses of the plains.

It is a very comfortable pack, due in part to its thick "air-cooled" design and fully adjustable shoulder and waist straps. The shell is constructed of ultra-strong, 100 percent cotton Ripstop fabric. A large,

wraparound mesh game pocket has easy side openings, but it is the total of 13 pockets to carry everything from gear for yourself and your dogs, to perhaps a small emergency kit, that separates *this pack* from the "pack." Tenzing's optional two-liter or three-liter hydration bladders are designed to fit it as well. Shells are comfortably carried in 14 individual shotshell loops. MSRP: $219.99–$229.99.

Pants, Chaps, and Other Bottoms

Beretta—www.berettausa.com

Beretta Covey Waxed Cotton Chaps, Red Line Jeans— These are great. I live in blue jeans, and having these easy-on, easy-off waterproof chaps provides plenty of protection as I transition to the field. Beretta says they

▲ Chaps are great for when hunting wear protection from heavy cover is required and easy to get on and off.

are breathable, and while I never heard them exhale, I have no reason to doubt it. They are tough as nails and comfortable as can be, and the protection they provide to the back of the leg is a plus for those of us who attack heavy cover. They sport anti-abrasion panels "where you need them most and articulated knees for comfortable walking." Double-snap height adjustment and over-the-boot 18" gusseted out-seam cover flange for the leg zippers. As they are designed to be worn over boots, they allow sufficient length for almost anyone not named LeBron James. The outside pocket at the top of the leg is handy and useful. MSRP: $109

Combine the Wax Chaps with Beretta's Red Line Jeans "Comfortable All-American Fit" and you are ready to go. MSRP: $89

Beretta Thorn Resistant Pants GTX—These classic bird hunting pants protect you from the cold the wind the rain and even heavy cover often encountered in serious days afield. The Gore-Tex lining makes them both waterproof and windproof. Anti-abrasion inserts strategically located protect you from brambles etc. MSRP: $199

◄ These traditional shooting trousers are outstanding.

Orvis—www.orvis.com
Missouri Breaks Briar Pants—I ordered these this past autumn to replace other Orvis briar pants as my waist changed (and not for the better). One of the many things I like about Orvis is that they will hem to an odd length. These are good-looking and tough pants and have served me well from the Northeast in woodcock covers to the Deep South pursuing bobwhite quail. They are made from 100 percent cotton eight-ounce canvas poplin cloth and faced with dry wax-impregnated poplin for added protection against briars. They are washable, which is handy when traveling. Wide belt loops are great for strapping on the various paraphernalia we bird shooters tend to carry. MSRP: $129

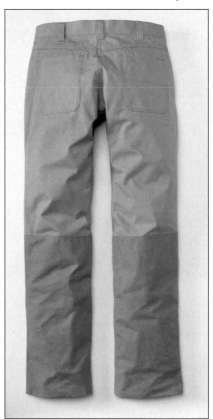

▲ I have worn these for a couple of seasons and they are still going strong. Photo courtesy of Orvis.

Outerwear Extras

Beretta—www.berettausa.com
Beretta Packable Hunter Hat—This sturdy but soft, pure wool, light felt fedora is water repellent, crushable,

and wrapped with a blaze orange pleated pug band. Stuff it in your pocket or gear bag and it springs back to shape. The brim is 2½ inches on the sides and three inches in the front and back, and the band in blaze orange is 1½ inches and really does add visibility. Most important, it looks and feels great and I wear it all the time. MSRP: $65

Footwear

Beretta—www.berettausa.com
Beretta Sportek Mid-2 Boots—I have put these through the mill since last February, and they've served me wonderfully well from local bird shoots to mountainous big-game hunts. They are extremely comfortable and take very little breaking in. They are available in a number of different heights, so select depending on your needs. The boots are also waterproof, lightweight, and offer superior traction with a Vibram Approach rubber soles. Ortholite high-performance insoles make them even more comfortable. MSRP: $169

Irish Setter—www.irishsetterboots.com
Part of the Red Wing Brands of America umbrella, Irish Setter has been one of the bigger names in boots for decades, and for good reason: It makes a great product and it makes them here in America. I have been using two of its boot models for the last few seasons and have been putting them through their paces, no pun intended, impressed with both pairs.

Havoc—This lightweight upland hunting boot has served double duty both for upland hunting and big-game hunting. It is a very rugged and waterproof leather boot. It was designed for tough hunting conditions, and I can attest to the veracity of the statement.

The Havoc uses Irish Setter's Flexlock, a design element in which the leather upper is hand-sewn to the sole, "providing out-of-the-box comfort and flexibility without sacrificing stability and support." CuShin Comfort tongue technology continues Irish Setter's proprietary nomenclature, this time referring to the tongue design, which, according to the company's website, is intended to reduce the pressure some users "feel on their shin from the top of the boot tongue. A four-way stretch nylon offers relief and flexibility while walking, and an internal padded waffle mesh maintains premium comfort." While I have never suffered from that problem, I can say is that these are a very comfortable boot.

The uppers are handcrafted from Trout Brook Leather, something the company named after the stream that flows outside the back of the tannery in Red Wing Minnesota. I can attest to both the quality and toughness of this hide. The Havoc also employs a GORE-TEX membrane that prevents water from getting in, while also allowing sweat to evaporate. MSRP: $224.99

Rutmaster 2.0—This is a waterproof, insulated camo rubber boot that first made its name amongst bow

▲ These are great for deer, turkey, and waterfowl hunting with excellent ankle support and insulation. Photos courtesy of Irish Setter.

▲ Excellent classic boots for the upland hunter. Photo courtesy of Irish Setter.

hunters. Unlike many rubber boots, it is tight at the ankle for good support and to prevent blistering when walking. I have found this boot to be particularly useful on cast-and-blast trips where waders were not needed and for wildfowl hunts where a high rubber boot is sufficient. It's also great for deer hunting from a stand, depending on the severity of cold temps.

Irish Setter's ExoFlex technology made the Rutmaster easy to slip on and take off, yet provides much more support than other, looser-fitting rubber boots. It comes with ScentBan bacteria-killing/odor-blocking technology, obviously more of a concern to deer hunters than bird hunters, and the Mud Claw RPM sole provides superior grip on slippery ground. PrimaLoft Gold is their insulation, which keeps feet warm in dry or wet conditions. MSRP: $149.99–$179.99

Just for Turkey Hunters

Avian-X—www.avian-x.com

▲ Turkey hunters need all the help they can get to bag these crafty birds, and the laydown hen should be in your arsenal of tricks. Courtesy of Avian-X.

Avian-X LCD Laydown Hen Turkey Decoy—Hens play the predominant role in determining spring gobbler behavior and spring turkey hunting success. From the first gobbling of the breeding season through the end of the nesting period, toms are constantly on the look-out for receptive hens.

The Avian-X LCD Laydown Hen provides turkey hunters with a powerful and convincing tool to fool lovesick gobblers. Depending on the circumstances,

it can be used on its own, adjacent to, or in a simulated breeding position with an Avian-X LCD Jake or undersized LCD Strutter. This decoy excels during late morning and mid-day hunts by accurately simulating a dusting hen. It starts with a realistic, soft, and quiet Dura-Rubber body. Detail comes from deeply textured and highly intricate feather lines. The body form, high head, and wing positions of the LCD Laydown Hen realistically mimics the breeding position of a hen turkey. As she is squatting for the mating ritual, she displays that she is highly receptive. The Avian-X LCD Laydown Hen is finished with incredible detail and a no-flake paint job that will last for many seasons. A drawstring bag is provided for safe and easy carrying afield. MSRP: $79.99

Flextone Game Calls—www.flextonegamecalls. com

Flextone Aluminum Tramp Stamp Turkey Call—Turkey hunters often find inclement weather disrupts hunting, especially wind. When it blows, it can wreak havoc on the best turkey hunting tactics. Traditional slate calls often aren't capable of punching a loud yelp through the wall of sound the wind creates, and so won't be heard by distant gobblers. To address this situation, Flextone engineered solutions for this problem with its Flextone Tramp Stamp Aluminum pot call, designed specifically to cut through howling winds. The durable Magnum Hickory Striker coupled with the aluminum surface produces high-frequency yelps that, they say, "drive even the most stubborn gobblers insane." Toms answer this call with a frenzy of gobbling, then strut-in, spitting and drumming. It sports Realtree Xtra Green camo pattern on the pot for maximum concealment from approaching gobblers. MSRP: $21.99

Zink Calls—www.zinkcalls.com

Z-Pak Z-Series Mouth Turkey Call Combo Pack—The very best turkey callers have mastered every type of call and use them, at times, throughout every season. But the majority of these masters won't be caught watching the first birds of the morning drop off a limb without a diaphragm call loosening-up in their mouths. It's the most versatile call in the turkey hunter's arsenal, but also, perhaps, the most difficult to master. The Zink Calls Z-Pak Z-Series Mouth Call Combo Pack contains three unique turkey calls—hand-built and stretched one at a time with 365-day-a-year turkey passion. The double split-reed Z-Yelper produces a classic two-note yelp with a mild rasp. The Z-Cutter brings more rasp, while retaining a crystal clear front end. Rounding out this selection of mouth calls is the Z-Combo, featuring the popular "combo-cut," but built around a two-reed design that is much easier to blow. Producing a nice, clear, front-end finished with raunchy rasp on the backside; the Z-Combo replicates mature hen vocalizations. MSRP: $19.99

A Useful Tool for Birds Big, Small, Upland, and Waterbound

Conceived to be compact and highly portable dove hunting field box and seat, Plano Molding's (www.planomolding.com) 1812 Hunting Stool will also earn devotees from the world of waterfowling or folks using pop-up blinds. Anyone who appreciates the dual functionality of a comfy seat atop a useful carryall will find a new favorite in the clever 1812 Hunting Stool. The sturdy, stealthy Magnum 1812 Field/Ammo Box serves as the 1812 Hunting Stool's core and superstructure. The oversized 1812 Magnum Can keeps shotshells, sandwiches, and other necessities at hand throughout the hunt. A latched, quick-access storage compartment is molded right into the can's lid for immediate access to choke tubes, wrenches, and other small items. The 1812 Magnum is finished with a brass bail latch and a heavy-duty molded handle. A hardwearing but lightweight ballistic Nylon wrap envelops and attaches to the outside of the box, providing additional levels of utility and secure storage. Large zippered and gusseted pockets adorn the front and sides, while a handy mesh pocket spans the back. Up top, a Nylon-covered, comfortable foam pad creates a plush seating surface for waiting out fast-flying game, while a detachable shoulder strap affords comfortable and reliable transport to and from the truck. MSRP $59.99

▲ The fab four waiting patiently. Working three or four dogs at the same time is great, as it teaches them patience. I learned that from Robert Milner's excellent book and video.

For the Dogs

▲ One can work one's dog anywhere. Wellington is sitting alert, waiting for training session to begin. He doesn't just love working, he lives for it.

Orvis

Memory Foam Dog Beds with Bolster—For most of my adult life, I have had at least two dogs living with me, and when I ran a commercial shoot, six. Now that I'm down to my last Labrador and my last spaniel, and as they are best friends, I have bought a couple of the largest Orvis dog beds, one of which I keep in the library and the other in the screened in porch for days when I go out for a few hours and when I know they would be happier outside than in. They enjoy, which means I like, the double-stacked bolsters of these beds, as they can rest their heads on them. The cover is removable and washable, which makes it ideal in case of any accident. One of my dogs vomited once, and after cleaning it up, hosing it down, and then putting it through the washing machine, it was as though the accident never happened. In small to X-large sizes and several color options. MSRP: $219–$349

▲ After a hard day's work, a good dog needs a comfortable place to sleep.

Raised Dog Bowls—One of my dogs twisted his gut and required surgery. Luckily, he made a full recovery, but once he was back on food and off the IV,

▲ Having a raised bowl is better for the dogs digestion.

the vet suggested that I raise his food bowl. I bought the wrought-iron base with stainless steel bowls from Orvis Sandanona, and I could see that he had an easier time feeding. It makes sense for taller dogs. Orvis offers various sizes and both single and double feeders. MSRP: $59–$129

Backseat Hammock

Depending on where I'm going and the weather, my dogs are either in a crate in the back of the pickup or in the backseat. I suppose the world has changed, so if I'm running errands in a shopping mall, for example, I would never leave them in a crate where they could easily be stolen, but if I'm heading off to the woods, the back of the truck is where they are most likely to ride. Still, if it's an exceptionally cold day or I plan to stop somewhere for breakfast or lunch, they may wind up in the backseat of the Ram at some point. Orvis makes a hammock that can nest between the front and the rear headrests. It keeps the back seats clean and dry, no matter how wet or muddy they get. It reduces but does not eliminate the dog's ability to jump into the front, so you may want to combine it with some other guard if Fido is likely to do so. It takes no time at all to install or remove, and it can be cleaned by simply hosing it off allowing it to dry. I've had them for a few years, and my dogs probably ride with me on almost a daily basis, and the hammocks show virtually no signs of wear. It comes in a couple of different sizes. MSRP: $119–$189

▲ Often you won't want to leave your dogs out in a crate in the back of your SUV or pickup, and Orvis's seat covers will keep your vehicle clean and safe. Photo courtesy of Orvis.

Canine First Aid Kit—I was hunting a friend's property in Millbrook 30 years ago with my English setter Buck, when he managed to step on a thorn apple. It was something I could not deal with myself, but luckily I was able to carry him back to my car (I was young and my back wasn't bad then) and drive 10 minutes to a veterinarian. He needed an injection to numb the pain to make removal possible. This is not a DYI project. That said, dogs are often picking up something small, perhaps a bit of debris gets in the eye or they cut themselves. It is therefore imperative that responsible owners have some necessary first aid equipment with them. Orvis has a kit that includes most of what you will need afield. You could put all this together on your own, but I would take a bit of time, might not be as complete, and if you get everything might even cost more money. Items included: scissors, iodine prep pads, cotton tip applicators, parachute cord for leash, tongue depressors/leg splints, antiseptic towelettes, sting relief pads, instant cold pack, tweezers, latex-free rubber gloves, twill tape roll, gauze pads (multiple sizes), elastic bandage, trauma pad, gauze roll, alcohol prep pads, thermal foil emergency blanket, and perhaps most important of all a good but compact first aid guide. MSRP: $35

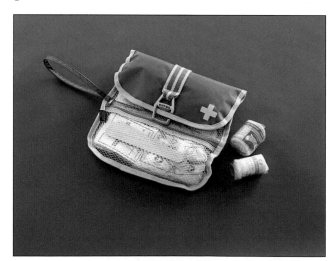
▲ While you can put your own first-aid kit together, these kits are great. Photo courtesy of Orvis.

Super Lightweight Pet Half Ramp—High-density propylene provides a strong yet lightweight non-slip walking surface while the rubber feet on the ground add to its stability. It is supposed to support up to 200 pounds,

which has to be double the weight of any sporting dog I can think of. Weighing a mere seven pounds, this is one of the lightest and strongest pet ramps available, and it gives easy access to minivans and SUVs with lower tailgate heights (full-size pickups will require a longer ramp to offset steepness). MSRP: $89

▲ As our canine companions age, they often need help getting in and out of vehicles. As we age, we are less able to lift them, so a ramp is the ideal solution.

Simple Human

Airtight Stainless Steel Food Bin—This small-footprint stainless bin from Simple Human is a good, hygienic way to store dry dog food. The seal is very tight, which means it is rodent-proof, thereby preventing leptospirosis (Weil's disease in humans and lepto in dogs, for which there is a vaccine.) While it does come with a magnetic scoop attached to the bottom of the top lid, I actually find it easier to use two different mugs, one for my spaniel one for my lab. It also comes with a BPA-free liner, which is excellent

► Mice often make it into country homes. A good container like this keeps your dog's food safe.

as something accidentally spilled in mine once, and I just poured it out and then washed the liner in the shower. It comes in two sizes—32- and 40-pound capacities—so it makes the most sense to buy the size that coincides with your normal dog-food purchase. MSRP: $100–$140

Dog Collars

I have owned hunting dogs for over fifty years. English setters, Labradors, and spaniels have always been an integral part of my life. I even campaigned one dog, Champion Cowboys Footsteps, who won the Canadian Open Shooting Dog Championship, a pretty big-deal stake for pointing breeds.

▲ This is a collar that I've been using, and I find it exceedingly reliable and simple to use. With twenty-one settings, on one of the very lowest settings it does not adversely affect my soft-skinned spaniel. Photos courtesy of SportDOG Brand.

When I started hunting, a small version of a cowbell was all the help we had to track dogs in the woods. While this worked fine on closer-ranging canine companions, the usefulness diminished as the dogs ranged out—and if you are hunting areas where ruffed grouse is the prize and the cover is thick, problems finding your dog and getting to it in time when it is on point is an issue.

Over thirty years ago, the beeper collar was invented. I probably went through a half-dozen of these offered by Orvis and other companies. These were a great improvement over the bell. They normally operated with a constant electronic beeping sound that changed when the dog went on point. They could be heard at much greater distance than the bell. While they did occasionally malfunction, especially if the battery wasn't sufficiently charged, in general they made life a whole lot easier in the field.

Beeper collars were an outgrowth of electronic stimulation training collars, which have earned a number of reputations. Early versions did not have the multitude of settings that the modern collar provides. The early ones were great on hardheaded dogs or for

▲ A lot can be accomplished with the bumper. The tennis ball thrown from a launching arm greatly extends the distance retrieves; mechanical launchers are even better.

snake or deer-proofing any breed. Today, the quality of modern collars is astounding. My spaniel, who is a hunting machine willing to tackle the thickest cover if he thinks a bird is in it, is a gentle soul. If I speak to him in to stern a voice, he will roll on his back and show submission. Considering that he will do his best to retrieve a wounded Canada goose, which comes in at about half his weight, this demonstrates the complexity of psycho-cognitive behavior—and the challenges of judicial e-collar use.

SportDog provides a wonderful training information on using their collars. Delmar Smith taught me how to use them over 30 years ago. You want to start on the lowest setting, and *not* in a field hunting situation, and determine what level of stimulation your dog needs. When he swallows, sighs, or his shoulder shows a twitch, you have achieved the correct level of stimulation that you know gets the dog's attention. These collars are brilliant for reinforcing something the dog has already learned. For example, your dog walks to heel while on the lead, then, with the lead loose, correction applied through the collar and, at least initially coupled with your "heel" command, will quickly have him come to understand that he's to heel whether or not on lead.

I have seen people use collars in an inappropriate manner. Trying to over-control a dog that is ranging out in search of birds, depending on circumstance, can be an example of this. I had a friend for whom I purchased quite a good setter, but he wanted the dog to stay within a 10-yard wide, but 300-yard long sorghum strip while hunting released pheasants at a preserve. (This would've been a job much more suited to a quartering spaniel.) It really wasn't appropriate or fair to the dog to correct every time he got out of walk-up shooting distance, for he was doing what he was previously and professionally trained and his instincts told him to do.

Working my Cowboys Footsteps and my personal dog Buck down in Alabama for quail off horseback, Buck disappeared. We had to circle back and retrace our steps. We found him in the middle of the pine forest holding a covey of quail. Under this circumstance, he was perfectly correct not to come when called. It was *our* mistake for not running him with a beeper collar. And, with today's electronic collars and their built-in GPS, we would have both known where he was *and* that he was on point. That would've saved three of us on horseback about 20 minutes of scouting to find him. Great dog work!

The TEK 2.0 GPS e-collar system (MSRP: $799.95) from SportDOG (www.sportdog.com) allows one to control multiple dogs via e-collar and also to be aware of their location at all times. They are amazingly easy to use and very well designed. While I have not tried it, I know SportDOG also has a model designed specifically for waterfowling, the WetlandHunter (MSRP: $179.95–319.95)—how cool is that? Other models include:

- The FieldTrainer 425X takes the most advanced, industry-leading technology that SportDOG Brand has ever built into its e-collars and

packaged it up in the most compact system ever offered. Ideal for training in the yard, field, or for hunting with close-working dogs. Switch instantly between static stimulation, vibration, and tone to fit the correction or communication to your dog's temperament and learning ability. MSRP $159.95

SportDOG Brand FieldTrainer 425X uses industry leading technology and has packaged it into an ultra-compact system. I use this with my spaniel, as he is a small dog. It has a multitude of settings from soft, which is all Wellington needs, too much stronger simulation required for tougher dogs or to deer proofing a dog. I have used it for yard work and keep it on Wellington to remind him, as he occasionally needs reminding, to hup to flush rather than going straight after the bird. One can switch from static stimulation, to vibrate or tone, as your dog requires and is most compatible with his training regimen.

SportDOG Brand SportHunter 1825X is designed for the wide running dog covering big country as it will work at up to a mile. (Seeing what your dog is doing a mile away and knowing whether he needs reprimanding opens a whole other series of questions. But if you are training an All-Age pointing breed, it is good to know that the dog is not going to range past your ability to control it, or correct it, if necessary.) It has 21 static stimulation levels and the ability to give either a momentary correction or continuous stimulation. It also boasts vibration and tone options to further enhance the customized training program.

CHAPTER 17
Gear–Waterfowl

Clothing and Waders

L.L. Bean—www.llbean.com

▲ Today's waterfowler is spoiled for choice when it comes to camo patterns, so you can pick the pattern that works best with your blind and surroundings. Photo courtesy of L.L. Bean.

This past year was mild for most of the duck hunting season in the Northeast. I have found this jacket to be excellent on its own in the early season or during a mild cold snap, but it also works well in colder weather when layered with thermal underwear, fleece, and sweaters as necessary. The fact that it is perfect in combination with various under layers makes it ideal for anyone who wants one jacket for the entire season. The jacket comes in a wide range of sizes and in a long version for the very tall.

I have also found this coat to be completely waterproof and very well thought out. There are lots of pockets with zippers to keep things organized, separated, and safe. The two large cargo pockets close with magnets, and I find them quite useful for carrying shells. The neoprene closures on the wrist help to seal out water and keep heat in. Even the tab for attaching one's hunting license holder on the back is intelligently

designed. The Mossy Oak Shadow Grass Blades camo works well in most situations.

Should you need to clean it, I would first try brushing or hosing it off, but if it needs more it can be machine washed and dried. MSRP: $239–$249

▲ Besides providing a great camouflage, they are warm and well-made, offering excellent protection from the elements so often encountered in late-season hunts. Photo courtesy of L.L. Bean.

I use these in combination with the above jacket. I like the fact that the waders are fairly lightweight but very roomy, so that I can use them in the early season on their own, then add various insulated undergarments or fleece wader pants to make them sufficiently warm for cold days in duck boats or blinds. The boots are very sturdy and well-made, giving plenty of support.

These waders come with Bean's SuperSeam Technology, which I suppose is a fancy way of saying that the boots and the rest of the waders are less likely to spring a leak. Bean explains the "Stitch-less, cutting-edge adhesive technology gives the waterfowler the edge in these men's stitch-less waders—our lightest, strongest, most comfortable and watertight ever. SuperSeam technology joins fabric with a super-adhesive that increases strength 50 percent while reducing the chance of a leak. This new construction method produces a lighter and more flexible wader, allowing you to move naturally in the water." So far, I have found this to be true. MSRP $299

Decoys and Blinds

Avian-X—www.avian-x.com

AXF Canada Goose Shells

▲ Realistic decoys go a long way to bringing in wary birds. Photo courtesy of Avian-X.

Avian X offers a wide variety of goose decoys from Flocked Honker Shell decoys to floaters and by mixing them you can often get cautious geese to come in for a look. I use these decoys differently than most. I live on a flight line between feeding and roosting areas. When I notice that it is being actively used, especially in the early evening hours, I'll put out some of the shells and put up my portable L.L. Bean blind under a tree and

wait for them.. I don't do this often enough to educate them, but when conditions are right, I am able to bag a few while field-testing goose loads.

The slightly over-sized, Avian-X AXF Flocked Honker Shell Decoys are Canada goose reproductions with deeply-textured bodies composed of Avian-X's advanced rubberized molding material finished with highly-detailed non-chip paint schemes. Sold in six-packs, Avian-X AXF Canada Goose Shells have fully-flocked adjustable heads, which are removable for easy, space-saving stacking during storage and transportation. Each six-Pack contains one Rester, one Alert, two Stretch Neck Feeders and two Short Neck Feeders. MSRP: $159.99

Avian-X Topflight Preener/Sleeper Mallard Floating Decoys

▲ Having quality decoys and placing them correctly will greatly increase the odds of success Photos courtesy of Avian-X.

Again, according to the company, "The out-of-the-way places smart ducks go when pressured are increasingly important locations for the savvy waterfowl hunter. Good scouting is key, and when the strategy is mapped out, it's time to execute. This is no time for the crummy old beater decoys from the shed. This is when you bring a small spread of the most realistic decoys, such as the new Avian-X Topflight Preener/Sleeper Mallards. They perfectly convey the serene behaviors wary ducks expect to see at their hidden honey holes."

These blocks proved very effective this past season as part of my duck blind setup. Molded from carvings by world champion carver Rick Johannsen, they are sold in packs of six that include amazingly lifelike depictions of two hen and two drake mallards preening, plus a pair of sleeper mallards. The floaters feature Avian-X's Weight-Forward Swim Keel, a design that creates natural motion with the slightest breeze or current by simply snapping the line through one of two swim-clip positions. Slightly oversized at 16 inches long, the Avian-X Preener/Sleeper Mallards help "sell-it" to suspicious ducks MSRP: $79.99

LL Bean—www.llbean.com

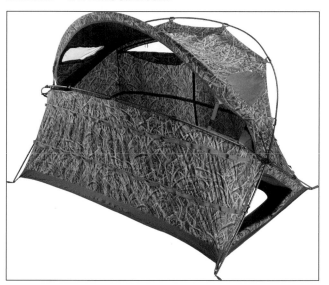

▲ Pop-up deer blinds are very popular, and pop-up duck blinds make sense in many circumstances. Photo courtesy of L.L. Bean.

Duck House Waterfowl Blind—I have a swamp that covers nearly a third of my property and is a magnet for game, especially ducks during the migration. While a permanent blind was built in a good location, it's not always the place to go. I found the L.L. Bean Duck House a brilliant setup, especially early in the season when teal can come in in great numbers.

As L.L. Bean points out on its website, "We designed this innovative pop-up duck blind specifically for duck hunters, with a roof panel that flips or retracts for standing shots and an almost 8-foot-long window for swinging and shooting comfortably." It will hold three hunters plus one dog; I prefer to hunt alone or with a maximum of one pal and two dogs. As it weighs only 12½ pounds and comes in its own sack, it is easy for me to walk the 300 yards from my house to my honey hole carrying it. MSRP: $429

Boats and ATVs

Duck Water Boats—www.duckwaterboats.com

Ocean 21—For those adventurous, rugged outdoorsmen who hunt at sea, the Duck Water Boats' Ocean 21 is a model to consider. It is built from ¼-inch aluminum, and at twenty-one feet long and ninety-six inches wide, it sports enough room for six hunters and their gear. More important, this is a boat designed to go find sea ducks. You still need to know what you're doing before you head out to big waters, as sea swells can always turn ugly and dangerous, but this is a boat to take seriously if this is your sport of choice. MSRP: $22,995

G3 Boats—www.g3boats.com

G3 Boats is a subsidiary of Yamaha, with a number of models that have duck hunters in mind, as well as those that serve a multiplicity of purpose from fishing to drifting rivers in search of moose. Some models are made for shallow running and are specifically designed to be used with Yamaha jet motors. Various lengths are available, as are various camo patterns.

▲ Courtesy of G3 Boats/Yamaha.

Before I go on, let me point out that while these boats were designed for duck hunters, they can certainly do multiple tasks and are very well suited for bass fishing etc. during the warmer months or for a cast and blast excursion.

All of them share many features. In addition to solid colors they can be ordered in Mossy Oak Break-Up or Mossy Oak Shadow Grass, depending on the habitat one hunts. They are also offered in a solid Desert

Brown color. They are also all designed to take trolling motors to be attached to the front. Under the bow you'll find two high intensity LED headlights, and the bows have extended deck plates with build in handholds which can also be used for tiedowns. The bow is especially worth checking out as you will see that it has a double layer icebreaker keel which reinforces the bow of the boat. It also has lockable cases for storing shotguns etc.

Another nifty feature of these boats is that they can be purchased as complete duck hunting packages with the choice of standard or jet outboards from Yamaha.

The DK 15 actually measures 15'5". The DK 16 measures 16'5" and the DK 18 is a good size boat at 18'6". The DK 18 is also available with a built in or rather built on, duck blind. Maximum horsepower's are 40 on the DK 15, 50 on the DK 16, and 70 hp on the DK 18. The first two boats are designed to carry three people maximum whereas the DK 18 is rated for four, and will carry them comfortably.

They all offer various options. But the package even comes with a trailer. My local dealer quoted $13,850 for the DK 15 with a 40 hp Yamaha. For full specs Google www.g3boats.com/duck-hunting-jon-boats which also has links to your local dealer.

▲ Model 1860. Courtesy of G3 Boats.

1860 DK Combo—The 1860 DK Combo from G3 Boats was an exciting new addition to the G3 line for 2016. G3 Boats has teamed with Bust'Em Boat Blinds to create the ultimate in mobile duck blind platforms. The 1860 DK Combo lets you change locations in a matter of minutes, so you're always "where the ducks

want to be," as Steven Matt, wrote to me. It comes in Mossy Oak Break-Up or Mossy Oak Shadow Grass.

▲ G3 boats can be purchased as complete duck hunting packages, with a choice of standard or jet outboards. Courtesy of G3 Boats/Yamaha.

Take the blind off and you can use this boat to get to remote hunting or fishing locations; add a trolling motor and you've got a first-class boat for bass fishing etc.

Gator Trax—www.gatortraxboats.com

Marsh Series—These boats are designed for quick concealment and for running on mud flats. Specifically designed to use with mud motors, this relatively small boat comes in 14- or 16-foot lengths. One to three men can comfortably hunt from this boat. It is perfect for those who hunt shallow lakes or backwaters. MSRP: $4,550–$4,950

▲ A good waterfowling dog is worth its weight in gold . . . and ducks.

CHAPTER 18
Gear—All the Extras

Knives

Buck Knives—www.buckknives.com

I can remember being a young lad, certainly less than ten, lusting after Buck knives. They were the bee's knees: the coolest of the cool. Strangely, while my parents had already given me a .22 (used under their supervision), they felt I was too young to have a serious knife. I guess they were concerned I would chop off my finger while whittling a stick. Maybe they were right. The one thing I know is that one is more easily injured with a dull knife than a sharp one, and one of Buck's beauties is that its knives come sharp and are easily re-honed. When I got older, I bought one for myself, a lovely knife designed to skin a deer, which lived in sheath on my belt.

Today Buck still makes a great knife. Being a country guy, I invariably have one in my pocket. (I always have to check my pockets before going to the airport these days!) Buck Knives have always been and continue to be made in America. I have a number of knives from this company, including the following:

▲ Like many country guys, I feel half naked without a knife, and this is a great one to carry day in day out on one's belt. Photo courtesy of Buck Knives, Inc.

110 Folding Hunter—Al Buck created this knife in in 1963, creating a revolution in knives of sportsmen with the lockblade knife. He took the folding knife to a new level by adding the ability to lock it in place. This gave at the strengths of a fixed blade knife and the compact aspects of a folding knife. It was revolutionary at the time and is still going strong as one of America's best-selling knives. Length 4⅞" closed.; Blade Length: 3¾" (9.5 cm); Weight: 7.2 oz. (205 g);
Handle: Cherrywood. MSRP: $70

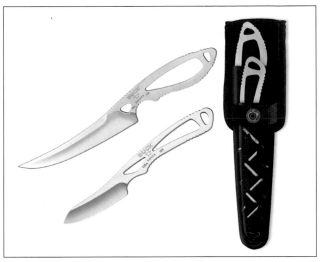

▲ This is a great set of knives that can be carried into the back and beyond when weight is an issue, or for a hunt in your own backyard. Photo courtesy of Buck Knives, Inc.

The PakLite Elite is a two-knife package that includes a lightweight 135 PakLite caper and 136 PakLite boning knife that conveniently share a compact sheath. If you hunt deer with a slug gun, or indeed any rifle or bow, you'll find that it makes the task after the animal is down less onerous. This combination of blades allows efficient, yet precise work to be done as necessary. A bone saw might be a good addition, but on hunts where ounces count, this will get almost all the work done, and done well. MSRP: $120

▲ This is my go-to knife when I head off still hunting for deer. Photo courtesy of Buck Knives, Inc.

Zipper—This is a gut-hook knife with the type of blade that would have horrified a ten-year-old's parents. The combination of edge angle and hook length is why this knife works so well. CJ Buck, the fourth generation involved in the company, helped design the knife which I carry routinely on my belt when I am hunting big game. MSRP: $110–$135

420 HC Steel is Buck knives blade material of choice combining the advantages of high carbon alloys with the corrosion resistance of chromium stainless steel. For those who are technical, they harden it to a Rockwell hardness of RC 58.

Gun-Cleaning Tools

J Dewey Rods—www.deweyrods.com

Larry Weeks, a great guy who has now retired from Brownells after a 36-year career there, turned me on to Dewey products for cleaning rifles decades ago. From coated rods to bore guides, I have found Dewey products to be great. While I got hooked on its products for my rifles, I found them to be great for shotguns, as well.

Dewey provides both nylon-coated and metal rods. Some of the metal rods handle stronger solvents better than the nylon coated rods do, so check out their www.deweyrods.com to see which specific solvent products it recommends *not* using with the non-metal rods.

One-piece nylon coated rods—These rods come in 26- or 34-inch lengths, and except for the shortest barrels, you will need to go to 34 inches, remembering that you do need to pass the brush all the way out the muzzle before beginning the return stroke. They can be purchased individually or as part of a complete kit: MSRP: $45

"Break More Clays" Choke Tube & Chamber Cleaning Kit—Cleans chambers, choke tubes, and choke tube threads. Comes with a fixed handle cleaning rod, spare set screw and hex wrench, 12- and 20-gauge brass core, "no-harm" bronze bristle brushes, 12- and 20-gauge 100 percent cotton mops, long-handled bronze cleaning brush, cotton patches Shooter's Choice MC-702, solvent, and Shooter's Choice G-10CC grease. MSRP: $42.95

PBK-Shotgun Port Cleaning Tool—This tool is just the ticket for those who shoot guns that have been ported to reduce muzzle flip. It comes with three brushes, and additional brushes may be purchased. MSRP: $15.95

Choke Tube Cleaning Tool—Fixed handle with 2-inch black oxide steel shaft with set screw, accepts 5/16 x 27 male threaded brushes and mops. MSRP: $17.95

CHS Shotgun Chamber Cleaning Rod—Brass rod, 9 ½ inches long, 11/32-inch diameter, fixed handle, 5/16 X 27 female threads. MSRP: $11.95

Negrini—www.negrinicases.com

Negrini Luxury Shotgun Wood Cleaning Kit (12- and 20-gauge)—If you're looking for a treat for yourself or a gift for a deserving friend, Negrini makes available a beautiful wooden appearance luxury cleaning kit made by Stil Crin. It has all the necessary parts and accessories for proper cleaning, including a Burmese Teak and recessed brass cleaning rod and the set comes in a Negrini case with LXX Italian leather trim and two combination locks. MSRP: $299.

UPLAND Shotgun Cleaning Kit—Another product of STIL CRIN offered by Negrini, this is a smart choice for those who want an affordable and well-done travel kit. It includes a brass wire brush, hurricane brush, wood cleaning rod, wood chamber brush, grease and lubricant, wool mop, and a nylon brush. In 12-gauge, 20-gauge, and 28-gauge. MSRP: $59

Otis Technology—www.otistec.com

Otis has been offering its cable-based gun cleaning systems for years. The design is particularly handy for revolvers where the barrel cannot be removed, and pistols where it can but it's often easier to clean them with the barrel attached. For any autoloading rifle, like my Volquartsen .17-caliber, it is imperative. This allows one to start cleaning at the chamber and working forward towards the tip of the barrel to avoid damaging the crown. And for slug guns that have pinned barrels, this too is obviously the best way to go most of the time.

Otis Upland Wingshooter Cleaning System—What I really like most about this kit is just how compact it is. All the tools you need fit inside the case that's about the size of one used for a trout reel. This makes it easy to stash in a daypack, so that it is always handy. If the kit has a downside, it's that its instruction manual isn't terribly clear. If you go to Otis's website, you'll find YouTube links that show how to use these products, and I suggest you do so, especially as the patches attach in a unique fashion.

While it is best to give guns a really proper cleaning, critical on rainy days, but also necessary after most outings as even condensation on fouling can cause rust, you can do a decent job quickly with this kit. If you are really pinched for time, the kit's ripcord picks up burnt powder and fouling quite well and both speeds cleaning and increases effectiveness. It is designed for 12-, 20-, and 28-gauge shotguns, with brushes in all three sizes are provided. You also get Otis's rubberized patch savers, 36 inches worth of its Memory-Flex cable, and a T-handle obstruction-removal tool. MSRP: $49.99

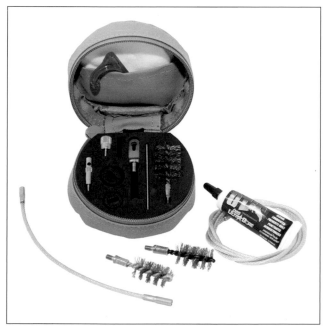

▲ Photo courtesy of Otis Technology.

Ripcord—Though different, Otis's Ripcord offers the same sort of easy cleaning as the Bore Snake. You pass it through your gun from the breach to the muzzle, and, according to Otis, "The rigid, helix-shaped rubber core keeps the cleaning surface pressed against the bore," giving and aggressive clean. As it is part of the Otis system, you can even attach a bore brush at

the breach end to get an even more thorough clean. It is available in both 12- and 20-gauge and works well with rifled barrels, so you can use it on your slug gun, too. MSRP: $14.99

▲ This system is great for a quick clean in the field. Twelve-gauge Otis Ripcord. Photo courtesy of Otis Technology.

Electronics

Red-Dot Optics

Tight patterning chokes and sophisticated loads for both turkey and predator hunting make optics necessary for low light or (relatively) long-range success. Red dots are the choice for both pursuits these days.

There are two basic types of red dots available to the modern hunter. The first was pioneered by Aimpoint, and it has a tube at its core. Some of the newer models look very much like low-powered scopes. The other design is tubeless, sometimes referred to as reflex or holographic sight. Most come with a rheostat for adjusting brightness, and some even do that for you automatically. Normally, they are only a couple of inches long at their widest point, weigh a couple ounces give or take, and offer unlimited eye relief, a real bonus when shooting heavy recoiling guns—and don't fool yourself, 3- and 3½-inch 12-gauge loads on anything less than 8 pounds of gun generate *significant* recoil, sometimes 60 ft.-lbs. or more.

Don't confuse red dots with lasers that project a dot, rather these are optics that you look *through*, and because of unlimited eye relief in most models, and other aspects this allows shooting with both eyes open. You just squeeze when the dot is on the target.

I like these tools, and they're a great bonus for anyone with aging eyes. Here are a few I recommend.

Aimpoint—www.aimpoint.com

9000SC—Predator and turkey hunters should consider the Aimpoint 9000SC, a medium-length optic. The 30mm tube is available with a 2 or 4 MOA dot, with ten illumination settings. Its technology allows tens of thousands of hours of operation from a single battery. It is compatible with many 30mm mounting systems. MSRP: $359

Burris—www.burrisoptics.com

SpeedBead—It is rare that a really innovative design comes along to correct that common problem of so many shotguns: not being drilled and tapped for optic

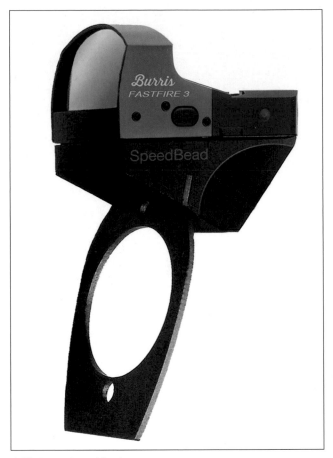

▲ Photo courtesy of Burris.

▲ Photo courtesy of Burris.

mounts. Burris has come up with a "mounting" solution that, as far as I can tell, is unique, innovative, and easy to use. The SpeedBead mounts its tubeless optic between the stock and receiver of many popular shotguns. It mounts low, aligning the red dot just above the bore, thus keeping the center of the optic in line with the rib. You can choose from a wide variety of SpeedBead Systems for the most popular shotgun models—there are various systems for different groups of models of shotguns, but one system or another will work with many Benelli and Berettas, some Franchis, most Remington pumps and autoloaders, and some Winchester and Browning models. The best thing to do is to check the Burris website to determine which system works with the gun you are planning to use. Burris even offers a combination package of the Burris FastFire 3 with SpeedBead Shotgun Mount package.

Burris FastFire III offers 8-MOA red-dot sight for rapid target acquisition. The SpeedBead works with all FastFire models. Its 1x magnification allows for both-eyes-open shooting and is parallax free. Windage and elevation adjustments makes sighting in straightforward and the high-grade optical glass provides excellent brightness and clarity. It is waterproof and fog-proof, and pretty shockproof too, which is a good thing. MSRP: $95–$299

Note: The only other option I know of for guns that are not drilled and tapped are the saddle mounts offered by B-Square (www.b-square.com) and AimTech (www.aimtech-mounts.com). They work with many autoloaders and pumps and do not require a gunsmith to mount.

Bushnell—www.bushnell.org
First Strike—This is an outstanding, precise sight that provides rapid target acquisition, an unlimited field of view, 1x magnification, and superb clarity. Its 5 MOA red dot has a self-regulating brightness. The integrated mount allows you to easily attach it to a most firearms. It is waterproof, fog-proof, and shockproof. The Bushnell First Strike weighs a hair over two ounces, and the mounting length is two inches. MSRP: $120

TRS 1x25 Trophy Red Dot—This tube-bodied 1x25 scope has a 3 MOA red dot and is less expensive than the First Strike. Fast target acquisition is a given. The single CR2032 battery lasts up to 3,000 hours. Available in matte black or in Realtree APGcamo with a built-in mount, the TRS 1x25 is just 3.7 ounces and 2.4 inches long. MSRP: $52.94–$79.78

Leupold—www.leupold.com
DeltaPoint Pro—This reflex sight offers a 7.5 MOA triangular "dot," a lightweight aluminum housing covered in steel for strength, and an aspheric lens that produces a wide field-of-view and excellent image quality. Leupold's patented Motion Sensor Technology recognizes any movement of the sight once it has been turned on and automatically activates the reticle illumination. The 1 MOA elevation and windage adjustments are an improvement over adjustment lock screws on many other makes.

Precision locating pins enable quick removal and remount without a loss of zero. That's a good thing, because changing batteries does require removing the

▲ A top-of-the-line red dot. Photo courtesy of Leupold.

optic. The All Mounts kit features unique plate system that aligns the mount with the gun. It even includes plates for many handguns, allowing for double duty. The cross-slot mount works with Picatinny or Weaver-style rails and bases which is most important for predator hunters using shotgun. MSRP: $519.99

Zeiss—www.zeiss.com
Z-Point—This reflex sight offers a self-regulating dot that automatically adjusts to available light. It needs a battery to activate, but a solar panel powers the dot without draining the battery, greatly extending battery life. Its sealed housing offers dependable protection to optics and electronics. The illuminated dot has a manual as well as an automatic digital control system. Different mounting options are available, including for the popular Weaver and Picatinny rails. LotuTec lens coating means water rolls off guaranteeing clear visibility. MSRP: $489

GPS

Garmin—www.garmin.com
While I am a firm believer in always having a map and a compass when going to the back and beyond, (batteries die, equipment can get lost or broken), a Garmin GPS should make getting lost virtually impossible.

GPSMAP 64st—This handheld is a top-of-the-line product that comes preloaded with topographical maps for the entire U.S., including Alaska. It is a rugged and full-featured device offering GPS, GLONASS, and wireless connectivity via a quad helix antenna and it sports a 2.6-inch sunlight-readable color screen. The preloaded TOPO U.S. 100K maps come with a one-year BirdsEye Satellite Imagery subscription. Map details include national, state and local parks and forests, along with terrain contours, elevation information, trails, rivers, lakes, and more.

The one-year subscription of BirdsEye Satellite Imagery gives you a photo-realistic view. You can add additional maps including Garmin's topographic, marine and road maps. The 8 GB of memory and microSD card slot allows convenient download TOPO 24K maps.

The BaseCamp software enables viewing and organizing of maps, waypoints, routes, and tracks.

Live Tracking allows individuals you to follow your trip in real time. This can add a safety net to the adventure in going into wilderness situations. One can also send an invite via email or social media, and "followers can view live data on Garmin Connect." MSRP: $350

Rangefinders

Halo Optics—www.halooptics.com

Halo XL450 Laser Rangefinder—This is one of the best on the market, especially well-suited for those who are not shooting at extreme distance, as it reads only to 450 yards. For shotgunners, even those using souped-up slug guns, 450 yards is far beyond the ability to kill cleanly, so this is a great model for shotgunners.

What most shotgunners don't realize is that the rangefinder is useful not only for deer or turkey hunting, but for working out the maximum distance you can shoot ducks or geese consistently from your blind using various landmarks, including decoys. Likewise, few sporting clay shooters employ them—and perhaps they should, especially in practice. Most of us are not great at judging distance, and by using the rangefinder, perhaps ranging a tree along a flight path, one can better determine the choke and load to use.

For slug-gun or turkey hunters, few variables play a greater role in success than knowing the actual distance to the target. Halo's new XL450 Laser Rangefinder

▲ Rangefinders are critical for bowhunters and for those taking long-range rifle shots. While not required, they are a great tool for checking patterns at a specific distance and knowing how far away a target really is. Photo courtesy of Halo.

offers high-end performance features at a realistic price. With accuracy to +/- one yard, this unit provides fast ranging out to 450 yards, while its 6x magnification provides bright, clear viewing. An easy-to-read internal LCD displays the reticle, battery status, mode setting, numerical display, and unit of measure in yards or meters as you prefer. MSRP: $99.99

Things That Make Life Easier

Fort Knox—www.ftknox.com

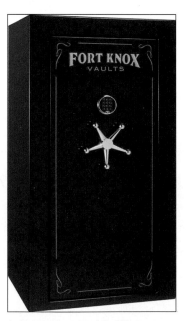

▲ Photos courtesy of Fort Knox.

We all want peace of mind. Responsible gun owner-ship means keeping guns out of the hands of untrained or under-aged family members and the grubby mitts of burglars. A good gun safe is a necessity these days for conscientious gun owners.

When I bought my house, it came with a good-quality gun safe. It is too heavy to move easily, which is why the previous owners offered me a good deal on it. Unfortunately, for my needs it doesn't have enough room for long guns. Also, I find the heated dehumidify-ing rod makes it too warm and I am concerned that it could affect wood and bedding. (I now use this safe for my synthetic-stocked guns, from the Remington 1100 Sporting to my Beretta wildfowl gun, etc.)

If I were starting from scratch, I think I would prob-ably buy a Fort Knox in a large size with plenty of room for my dozens of shotguns and rifles. One of the reasons I would choose Fort Knox is that it offers

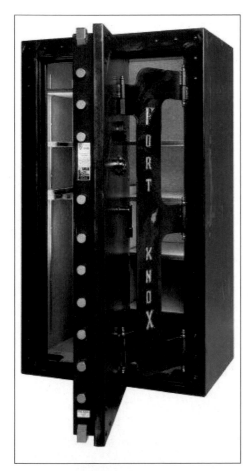

▲ Photo courtesy of Fort Knox.

a variety of interiors to accommodate rifles, shotguns, handguns, and other valuables by using a combina-tion of firearm and modular shelves. The shelves are covered in recycled carpeted.

Fireproofing is essential to any floor safe. Fort Knox's Inferno Shield works, according to the company web-site, like this: "Limiting the thermal conductivity by lining the inside of our vaults with a proprietary blend of a hydrogen bond fireboard and locking it in place using a stud-weld process allows Fort Knox to provide the industry's leading fire protection." This translates into the fact that sometimes houses burned down, but items inside a safe with Infernoshield remain in good shape. For even more protection, Fort Knox's Inferno Shield Level 90 is tested to keep the inside of the vault under 350 degrees while the fire around it can burn up to 1,680 degrees for up to ninety minutes.

Other options with Fort Knox safes include increas-ing the size of the steel doors and walls by adding additional layers of steel so that it stronger and more resistant to attacks. For Knox also allows you to create your vault with a heavier steel body via its Vault Body Upgrade, or increase the level of security with both the vault body and door with the Deluxe Package. MSRP: From $1,500

Loading Your Own

For anyone interested in reloading, the practice of using spent hulls and loading them with a new primer, powder, wad, and shot at home, the No. 1 thing I personally recommend is to read every-thing you can get your hands on written by Tom Roster. He is the true guru in the field of shotgun ballistics and reloading, and he writes a column for *Shooting Sportsman* and a number of other magazines. He also has specialized handbooks on reloading both lead and nontoxic shot. One of his more brilliant articles was in a 2015 issue of *Shooting Sportsman,* in which he went through all the steps he took in creating an optimum HEVI-Shot load for 28-gauge hulls. The meticulous process of trial and testing displays both the depth and breadth of his knowledge, and his attention to detail in the pursuit of (relative) perfection.

While many fellows reload shells to save money, Roster reloads because he can improve on factory offerings. Riflemen, at least serious riflemen and especially benchrest shooters and varmint shooters, have always handloaded because they felt they could improve on factory loaded shells. Until about 1980, factory loads could be easily improved upon both for accuracy and terminal ballistics. (Since then, factory loads have improved dramatically.)

Modern shotgunners can mimic those perfection-seeking riflemen by designing shotshell loads that outperform factory offerings. Whether you fall into this category will depend upon how much you shoot, your own technical inclinations, and whether you want to try and are capable of beating industry norms. For Tom Roster, this is relatively easy. But he is an expert. His manuals and his writings, thankfully, make it more realistic for the rest of us. But before you buy a reloading press that can handle steel shot, for example, you should ask yourself whether the initial outlay for the machine and the time and effort required to set it up properly exceeds the convenience of going to your local gun shop, buying three or four boxes of factory loads, and patterning them in your gun to find a cartridge with which you are happy. Of course, you might be the sort of individual who goes through only a box or two of goose-hunting loads in the season, yet still finds satisfaction in loading your own. Then there are those serious target competitors who shoot many thousands of rounds a year and both want to perfect their loads and save some money over having to buy thousands of factory rounds.

No matter your reason, let's talk about reloading According to a column that appeared in the January/February 2016 issue of *Shooting Sportsman,* Roster believes that the conscientious reloader can produce "a better load—often a much better load—than you can buy." His premise that most factory shotshells are compromises is obviously correct. "By making your own shotshells, you can custom build loads to nearly the exact velocities and pressure levels you're after and use the exact charge weights of the best shot sizes to fit your needs," he writes.

Reloaders are living in a functional Golden Age. Today's shotshell reloading machines and tools are so well made and so well designed that they are almost bombproof (Note: We are not providing any shotshell data here and assume no liability for anyone who does choose to reload their own shells.)

The Reloading Process
While some individuals will start with new, pre-primed shotshells, most begin with previously fired hulls, so let's start there.

The first thing you'll need to do is inspect the hull for signs of stress. It should look as new as possible, with the crimp folds uniformly unfurled and with the hull in one, solid, uniform piece. Discard any that have become severely discolored, have torn crimp fingers, or have splits anywhere along the body, as well as any whose brass head displays a bulge of any kind. With a hull ready to load, you'll need to get rid of its expended primer, a process called, aptly, "depriming." At the same time the shell is deprimed, the metal head (in the old days always brass and commonly called so today even if it is made of a different material), is resized to its original dimensions.

The next step is re-priming, which should be self-explanatory. Any machine from the midrange of the pricing tier on will be set up to feed primers automatically. Next, with a new primer seated in a resized hull, the hull is filled with powder.

This is where some caution is warranted. The worst accidents with handloaded shotshells generally occur as the result of one of two faults during the reloading process: 1). insufficient propellant to get the wad out of the barrel, so that the next load down either bulges the barrel or blows it; or 2). through the use of cheap equipment or lack of concentration during the reloading process that results in a *double* load of powder.

I've had a couple of barrel bulges over the

years from factory loads. Once when shooting in England, using felt-wadded Rio factory shells, I heard a *thwaffff* sound on firing. I knew what the problem was, as I had seen/heard it on clay fields from reloads: a wad stuck in the barrel. As I was shooting double guns, I just used the gun in which the problem had not occurred until the drive was over and I could put a rod down the barrel to push out the offending wad. (I always carry cleaning equipment with me in the field for just this type of occurrence.) As for the double-charge, not only will you definitely know you've shot one, you'll be lucky if you don't cause damage up to and including a catastrophic failure of your shotgun.

Bottom line, you must pay attention to your press during the powder drop phase. Remove the hull from the press and inspect it if you have to and if something doesn't feel right as you operate the press. Weigh the charge if you're unsure. The extra time is surely worth having to replace a barrel. Or worse.

The powder charge is followed by the wad. The size of the wad limits the amount of shot. For the sake of convenience and simplification I will presume that one is using a plastic wad designed with the particular type of shot (lead, bismuth, tungsten, or steel) requirements in mind. There are other permutations of this process (and lots of reloading manuals from the various propellant makers such as Hodgdon, IMR, and others that you should be using as guidance), but for this very basic overview of reloading, I will not go into it in any depth. In a progressive press, both the shot charge and the powder charge are dropped by gravity through separate bushings that control the amounts.

With everything inside the hull that needs to be there, you now need to seal the hull. Your original hull will have either a six- or eight-fold crimp, and you will need a corresponding crimp die tool to replicate that crimp (you really don't want to force a six into an eight or vice-versa) In the next and usually final step, a different die presses down on the cone-shaped top of the crimp left from the last stage, and just like that the shell is complete.

Reloading Presses

Basically there are two types of shotshell presses. The single-stage press means that each time you pull the handle you are just performing one of the steps needed to produce a complete shell. In other words, you'll have to adjust the press, replacing the dies as you go through each step. These are great if you are handloading, say, a small batch of buckshot, goose or turkey loads. Any more than that though and you're going to want a progressive press.

A progressive press is a multi-tasking machine in which every pull of the handle performs all the stages of the reloading process at once. There are even hydraulic units that can be attached to the latter so that it's almost a hands-free operation. All that is necessary is to insert the new hull and a new wad before pulling. If you are shooting tens of thousands of rounds a year on the clay fields, a progressive machine, perhaps with a hydraulic add-on, is justified.

Beyond the two basic types, there are presses designed for loading hard shot such as steel. Some machines will only load a single gauge, while others have die sets that are interchangeable so that you can load a variety of cartridges in a variety of gauges.

From whatever company you buy your press, most likely, Spolar (www.spolargold.com); MEC (www.mecshootingsports.com): or Ponsness-Warren (www.reloaders.com), I highly recommend that you contact Tom Roster at tomroster@charter.net and order his reloading manuals on buffered lead, bismuth, and HEVI-Shot. He also has instructional DVDs and a barrel modification manual that are worth reading. Indeed, if you do start reloading with the idea of outperforming factory loads, they are more than worth reading, they are *required* reading.

Orion Coolers—www.orioncoolers.com

These aren't your father's disposable Styrofoam ice chests. These are rugged, workhorse versions that can be used and almost abused and still keep food cold for days. While this movement was certainly started by Yeti, which probably still has the lion's share of the overall market, Orion coolers are giving that brand a run for the money. And while strangely the Orion coolers are slightly more expensive than the Yeti, they come with more accessories included in the price. For example, there are four bottle openers included, whereas Yeti charges $20 each. Orion coolers also come with a nonslip lid mat, which would set you back another $70 from Yeti. (Believe me, I am not knocking Yeti's product, rather I am reviewing the Orion model I own.) I mention Yeti because it is the one that leaps to mind for most consumers in this product market.

Orion coolers also include a metal gear track for attachments and an internal torch attached to dry rack. Add them altogether and the accessories would cost over $100. I also like the integral rubber nonslip mat, as it does offer a better purchase if you are standing on it. The YakAttack gear track accepts a good range of RAM accessories from rod holders to GoPro mounts, lights, plus Orion's own minibar/cutting board so you can adapt your cooler to your requirements for the particular trip. In other words, it can do double duty for tailgating with family and friends or carrying enough food for a week in the backcountry.

Orion coolers come in 25- to 85-quart sizes and weigh from 21½ to 43 pounds. They also come in a variety of colors. If you are going on an extended

adventure, a model holding over 55 quarts makes sense. I have the 65-quart size, and find it a perfect fit in the back of my Ram truck. You could put a tremendous number of snow geese breasts in these. MSRP: $370–$550.

Streamlight—www.streamlight.com

Streamlight is a leader in lights for sportsman, offering everything from flashlights that pick up blood at night to game-tracking lights for hunting predators. I've used their flashlights for years and have always found them well-made and reliable.

The Streamlight ProTac HL-X

▲ It is rare that I find a single product that is the best of its kind, but the Streamlight flashlight qualifies. Photo courtesy of Streamlight.

This is the single best flashlight I have ever used. It is compact, well-constructed, hard as nails, relatively lightweight, uses either lithium ion batteries or Streamlight's own rechargeable single battery. But what really separates it from the rest of the pack is it sheer power. This is a 1000 lumen tactical flashlight and it gave me great comfort walking from dinner back to my tent in the Save Conservancy in Zimbabwe. We did kill a puff adder in camp during daylight hours, but it is the snake most likely to bite a hunter simply because they are slow-moving and tend not to get out of the way from the vibration of walking the way a cobra would. Unlike the aggressive African mamba or Australian brown snake, they tend not to go after people—but if

▲ Sixty-five-quart Orion cooler. This is a great addition to any extended hunt. Photo courtesy of Orion.

stepped upon or if one simply gets too close to them, they will bite and their venom can be severe, in fact often fatal. This light not only illuminated by path over grass back to the tent but also flooded the dry river-bed below with light which was also comforting as there were a couple of PAC (problem animal control) lioness in the area. I will probably buy another. One will live in my car, or in my day pack if I'm going for an extended hunt with my bird dogs, and another to keep by my bedside should lights fail. (Where I live in upstate New York, that happens 4 to 8 times a year sometimes just for a couple of hours, sometimes for a couple of days or longer.) Simply put, this is the finest flashlight I have ever owned.

Dual Fuel, 1,000 Lumen Tactical Flashlight

New technology for the ProTac HL-X gives users 1,000 lumens of high lumen output, as well as the flexibility of multiple power sources, which helps reduce down time. Features "TEN-TAP" programming, which lets you choose from high/strobe/low; high only; or low/medium/high.

Solid state power regulation provides maximum light output throughout battery life. Uses two CR123A lithium batteries, but also accepts one Streamlight rechargeable 18650 lithium ion battery. The length is 5.43 inches, weight is 5.7 ounces.

Siege AA: Ultra-Compact, Alkaline Hand Lantern

▲ This lantern is a real boon on any camping trip. I leave it in my car, as it is a great source of light if one needs to change a flat after dark.

This is the other new product that I took from Streamlight on Safari. The lanterns normally supplied in the tent really don't give enough light to read comfortably. This does. With 3 power settings, it works well for a number of applications and comes with handy handles so that it can be used standing, hanging, or indeed hanging upside down. The amount of power you use affects the length and life of the batteries but as it uses 3 AAs and, as they are easy to pack, you will find a world of applications for this on every outing after dark. I'm going to leave this in my car when I don't take it traveling with me simply so that if I need to change a tire, etc. in the dark, I will have plenty of light to do so, all hands-free. Again, another product from Streamlight which I cannot recommend too highly–it is just that good!

The light has a polycarbonate glare-reducing cove, which provides soft, even 360-degree light distribution; runtime is seven to thirty-seven hours; length is 5.44 inches, weight is 8.8 ounces.

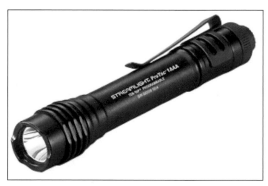

▲ Streamlight ProTac Photo courtesy of Streamlight, Inc.

Streamlight ProTac—This AAA tactical penlight is a great small piece of gear. And when I say little, I mean little! It works on a single AAA or equivalent-size lithium battery. And while it comes in a very compact package, it gives great performance. I really like the fact that it has a little clip on it to attach to the front of a baseball cap, which makes walking in the dark much easier and leaves your hands free. As it weighs so little, it is the perfect light to always have in your shooting vest. Features high/strobe/low (factory default); high only; and low/high.

▲ Where legal and sporting—for example predator control—this lights up the night. Photo courtesy of Streamlight, Inc.

TLR-1 Game Spotter Gun Light—This is designed for long-range nighttime hunting, where legal, and ideal for predator hunting or for culling too many does, again with nuisance permits etc. where legal. The green C4 LED produces a long-range beam with an intense hotspot.

It produces 31,000 candela peak beam intensity; 150 lumens, and has a battery life of nearly 2 hours. It attaches through a Picatinny or Glock-type rail system. And while 350 yards is certainly well past any reasonable shot with a slug, it does mean that you can switch it from your slug gun to a long-range predator rifle and get double duty from one item.

The lens is made of unbreakable polycarbonate with scratch-resistant coating. O-ring sealed. MSRP: $125.99

▲ Streamlight HPL. Photo courtesy of Streamlight, Inc.

Streamlight TLR-1 HPL Gun Light—This is very similar to the model above but with slightly different specifications in terms of beam distance and lumens. Mounts directly to all MIL-STD-1913 (Picatinny) rails and weapons with Glock-style rails. MSRP: Additional accessories are available for both products. See their website www.streamlight.com. (Brownells sells adapters for shotguns without a rail.)

Bugged

I have been bitten by all manner of insects from tsetse flies to blackflies to no-see-ems and ticks. From sleeping sickness, luckily fairly rare, to the all too common Lyme's disease, insect borne illness takes a huge toll on mankind. And while mosquitos kill more humans than any other animal through parasitic and viral infections, including malaria, dengue, West Nile, and others, their bite concerns me less than some others. Moyowoshi in western Tanzania was such a bad tsetse area that as they swarmed, I sometimes found it difficult to concentrate on hunting. I tried 100 percent DEET (Ben's, if memory serves; www.bensmeadows.com), as well as DEET-impregnated jackets and Avon's Skin So Soft (www.avon.com) without discernable improvements. Thankfully, now there are two products on the market that seem to be game-changers.

I saw ElimiTick products on the Orvis website and ordered some and completed my outfit from the Gamehide website (Gamehide manufactures ElimiTick; www.gamehide.com). There is a large swamp on my property, which is home to a multitude of wildlife, including bobcats, bears, coyotes, and deer. It also offers great wild duck shooting. But the transitional areas of woods between the lawn and grass areas and the swamp is as bad a place for picking up deer ticks as anyplace I've been (well, with the exclusion of Hluhluwe in Natal, Republic of South Africa, which has areas with pepper ticks in almost unimaginable numbers). This past fall, in warm weather, I spent hours tracking a deer I'd shot with a crossbow. It rained, washing away the blood trail. Wearing ElimiTick clothes and having spayed Permethrin on my rubber boots, I exited the woods three hours later, and, as best as I could tell, tick free and with my deer.

My bobwhite guide at Gilchrist plantation, Randy Ransom Jr., told me he never hunts turkey without Thermacell (www.thermacell.com). Insects in the South especially in the spring or summer months can drive one bugs—pun intended. This was echoed by a guide Mike Wallace, who guides turkey hunters in upstate New York. Once he turned around and added 45 minutes driving time to his day because he left his Thermacell at home—it is just *that* important to many outdoorsmen.

These products work in different ways, but, importantly, *they both work*. Try them separately or, for maximum protection, together.

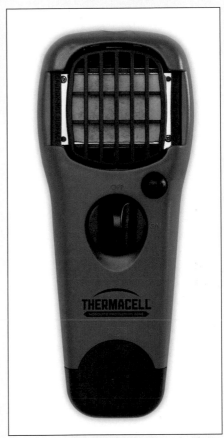

▲ Photo courtesy of Thermacell.

▲ Pierre Villere shooting doves below the Atlas Mountains in Morocco. We met on this trip and have shot together at least once a year since, most often in Britain but occasionally in Spain. According to the CDC, Morocco is malaria-free.

APPENDIX A
The Wingshooter's Essential Library

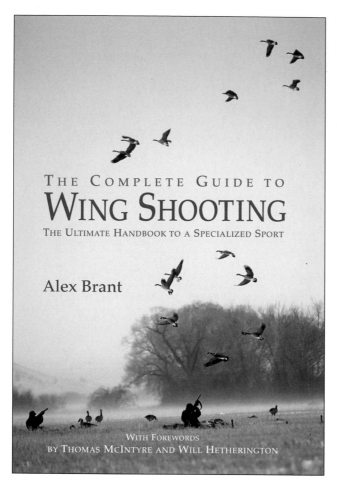

The Complete Guide to Wing Shooting, by Alex Brant.

Rather than reviewing my own book I will take excerpts from some of the reviews others provided. I will say that this book was designed to be an update of Bob Brister's American classic, *Shotgunning: The Art and the Science*.

*Brant has shot a good deal of winged game under many circumstances and has studied shooting and expert shooters of various styles under field conditions. In this important book, he has broken down what he knows about the techniques, attitudes, and equipment that make up excellence in wingshooting. For those who take their shooting seriously—upland, waterfowl, and clays—Brant's book deserves close consideration.—*Gray's Sporting Journal, August 2006

The author offers detailed instruction on how to shoot skeet, trap and sporting clays. The book is less for the beginner than for the already competent who wishes to excel. . . . The text is spiced with stories from Brant's adventures around the world.—The Shooting Sportsman.

Whether you're a novice or experienced shotgunner, you certainly always looking to improve, and if so, this is the book for you. Wingshooting is an art and the science all of its own, and Sports Afield Contributing Editor Alex Brant is one of the most passionate and proficient practitioners. His book provides helpful advice on gun fit, lead, footwork, shooting etiquette, and much more, covering the depth and breadth of the sport from field to shooting stand. It is an all-encompassing guide to the subtleties that make wingshooting so addictive.—Sports Afield

I could not have said it better myself (ha-ha!). But seriously, this book is more for intermediate shots who want to improve than for absolute beginners.

The World's Best Shoots, by Alex Brant.

This book is strongest on European shoots, particularly driven bird shoots in the British Isles and in Spain. Again, I will take excerpts from other reviews, at least to appear less biased, and do note that I have a few copies of first edition, limited numbered signed books that are available for purchase directly.

Brant covers shoots from all over the globe, from the quirky-sounding Crooked Wood to the more exotic Buffalo Springs Ranch and Tswalu Game Reserve, and quarry from goose to grouse to guinea fowl. Most importantly, he has more nous than to judge a shoot on a single day's experience, since circumstances (especially the weather) do not allow for a shoot to go perfectly every day of the season.—The Field, November 2008

When it comes to top-quality shoots, there are few sportsmen who have seen as many as former Shooting Gazette columnist Alex Brant. Although he admits that a better title would have been Alex Brant's Favorite Shoots, his collection of articles, drawn from over 50 years' experience writing for various shooting magazines, is one guaranteed to be read until the pages fall out. Charting shoots in Spain, Great Britain, and Ireland (including Molland, Chargot, and the Duke of Wellington's Stratfield Saye), Scandinavia, Eastern

Europe, North and South America, Africa, and the Caribbean, Brant's writing style is captivating from the first line. The book ends with an appendix on 'protocol for driven pheasant shooting,' great for anyone who has never gone on a driven shoot before. It's a nice little touch, because one thing is for sure, you will be on the phone to a sporting agent in no time.—Shooting Gazette, December 2008

With the help of a handful of friends, the author takes the reader on a world tour that takes in not only Britain and Ireland, but Morocco, Argentina, North America, Spain, Eastern Europe, Africa, and all points between. Light the fire, pull an armchair up, and pour yourself a Scotch, because this one's going to make good winter night reading.—Sporting Gun, Robin Scott, December 2008

If ever there was ammunition for a heated debate during a shoot lunch, Alex Brant has supplied it in the form of The World's Best Shoots. *According to whose criteria and at what price, you might ask. Brant addresses the subjective nature of his book and clearly states that he*

hasn't been to every shoot in the world … but he's seen more than his share, as the subtitle A Sporting Man's Odyssey *suggests. This book reads like the diary dates for a game shot's dream season. From the U.K., premier league names such as Chargot, Molland, Holkham, and Castle Hill are assessed, and while few would argue against their inclusion, the focus is principally on the costly driven bird and the visiting gun. Cartridge ratios, high birds, and hospitality are very much in evidence, with the work required to put on a big day closely analyzed.*—Shooting Times, December 2008

This is a book for dreamers—a tour of the shoots that have achieved a legendary status from Molland to Mexico. So, while you may never command the financial resources to shoot at Holkham or in Argentina, you can at least read about them. And one of the pleasures of Alex Brant's book is that it doesn't simply rhapsodize about endless streams of high birds—oh, there are plenty of them, but Brant also shows that even the best shoots can sometimes fail to reach expectation. Except for one shoot—so bad he would never return—Brant's opinions are based on a number of visits, so they do give a fair assessment, and it is fascinating to compare the great names—and get down to some serious daydreaming.—Shooting & Conservation, November/December 2008

Books may be ordered from the author, autographed and inscribed, a.alexander.brant@gmail.com or abrant1@optonline.net

The Complete Guide to Wingshooting is $30 including postage. Limited edition copies (four hundred) of *The World's Best Shoots,* slipcased, are $200 apiece, including postage, and are already collector's items. This book is becoming highly collectible and I have seen it for hundreds of dollars on some of the book sites, even the Standard Edition if in new condition.

Shotgunning: The Art and the Science, by Bob Brister.

Ernest Hemingway wrote or said that all American literature has its basis in Mark Twain's *Adventures of Huckleberry Finn.* Similarly, there is sort of a before-Bob Brister and an after-Bob Brister in American shotgunning books. Before Bob, who very kindly provided some of his articles for anthology magazines that I put out circa 1980, most of the thinking on shotgun shooting revolved around the British writers. Many of the Brits still cling to old views back when 12-gauge bores measured .728 or .729 and fiber wads were all that were available. Everything has changed since then, and from a mechanical standpoint and metallurgy, everything has improved. If you own only one book on shotgunning in addition to mine, it should be Brister's. Available from Skyhorse Publishing (www. skyhorsepublishing.com).

▲ Photo courtesy of Rizzoli.

Beretta: 500 Years of the World's Finest Sporting Life, by Nicholas Foulkes, photos by Andy Anderson.

Most books focusing on a single gunmaker are dull as mud. While they are certainly of interest to historians, collectors, and, in some cases, technoids, they tend to sit on the shelf. The Beretta book, on the other hand, is a fascinating look at one of the most historic, and certainly the oldest continuously operating, company in the world.

While it does begin with the history of the company, it does so in an entertaining way, and everything is complemented with truly fantastic photography. But unlike most of the other single-gunmaker books, it also looks at the gun from the point of view of those who have owned them, some famous like Ernest Hemingway, Winston Churchill, Norman Schwarzkopf, and Sean Connery, and some less so. It then goes on to "The Sporting Life" and features shoots from around the world.

It is a well-written book, and I presume my friend Peter Horn author of Hunting across the Danube, wrote the short chapter "Memories of a Buffalo Hunter"; it is unattributed, but his style is unmistakable. The writing in a way complements the magnificent photography and beautiful production of this book more than the other way around. As is so often the case, a photo is worth 1,000 words, though, and with the pallet of options available to the photographer, he was able to capture amazing moments and made some ordinary experiences such as climbing into a treestand an experience to be shared. From humans to landscapes, from guns to game, this is a book to be enjoyed, and unlike most shooting books, deserves a place on one's coffee table.

Breaking Clays and The Instinctive Shot, by Chris Batha.

Chris Batha's books are as useful to beginners as more experienced shots. Undoubtedly, this is one of the reasons Chris Batha's book sold much better than mine. (The quality of paper printing and illustrations was a definite step up from my book.)

Chris is one of the soundest guys around, both from the point of view of the gunfitter and an instructor. He is also very knowledgeable when it comes to shotguns. His passion for the sport is infectious. In his two books Breaking Clays and The Instinctive Shot, written in that order, he thanks and mentions every writer under the sun living and dead except for me. Oh well. This is at least slightly confusing in that the first full-page photograph in his second book is a shot of me shooting at West Molland Wood, with Phil Llewellyn loading and the lovely Renata looking on. He also shot duck as our guest at Humewood.

The beginning of the book Breaking Clays is very

much designed for those new to shooting. While I found it personally a little simplistic especially in the early chapters, I must admit that it is all good stuff for beginners. After you get through the first third of the book, there are many things that will appeal to the intermediate and advanced shot. Batha's thoughts on everything from the mental game to improving physical fitness are all valid and useful. This is a very highly recommended book.

I never liked the term "instinctive" applied to shooting. I find it counterproductive. While we do have an instinct that can be honed in terms of hand/eye coordination, we certainly have no innate instinct to shoot, to fish, to play golf, tennis, or ski. These are all learned skills. Much of the second book is the same as the first, including a great overlap in photos and illustrations.

Gun Craft—Fine Guns & Gunmakers in the 21st Century, by Vic Venter.

As the U.K. historic *Shooting Times and Country Magazine* points out, "Thoughtful, intelligent and beautifully written, this is a fascinating and impressive work." While I own a plethora of books on guns and shooting, if I could only have one book on shotguns, this would probably be it. Shotguns from America, Britain, Italy, Spain, and Belgium are covered. Not all makers are included but more importantly those that are done so in depth and with great accuracy. From diagrams showing bolting to excellent photos used to explain many mechanical issues associated with shotguns, to clear explanations on both the mechanical and artistic nature of creating the modern shotgun, everything is accurate, lucid and correct. From jointing to case color hardening, and on to the hand regulation of chokes, this is an in-depth look at the processes that go into making a great gun. Beyond this, the book delves into the artistic aspects and the master artisans who ply their craft. This is the rare tome that combines information, great illustrations and photographs, and is, as a Brit would say, "a jolly good read."

Live Pigeon Trap Shooting, by Cyril Adams.

Just when I thought little new could be written about competitive shotgun shooting, Houston's Cyril Adams has produced a stunning new work. *Live Pigeon Trap Shooting*, the first book published in English on the subject since Captain Albert Money wrote *Pigeon Shooting* in 1896, has given me reason to smile. It is well written and beautifully researched. One of its great strengths, amongst many, is the quality of the illustrations depicting the evolution of the game from live pigeon, both box birds and colombaire, to trap and Helice. I envy Adams's collection of historic illustrations.

While I was certainly aware that live pigeon shooting was closely tied in its early days to the Hurlingham club, of which I am a reciprocal member, I had no idea that the genesis of the Hurlingham club originated in Stephen Grant's gunroom in London. Nor did I know that Annie Oakley, the famous shot often associated with Buffalo Bill's Wild West shows was also a fabulous live pigeon shot having won numerous competitions, and on more than one occasion with a score of 49 out of 50. It is these details that I find so intriguing along with the wonderful section on live pigeon shooting rules, even showing how it had been codified slightly differently at a number of important venues from Hurlingham to the European continent, and back here to America. (Rules for the various clubs/organizations are provided.)

Live pigeon shooting is described in detail along with the lists of winners of major competitions such as the World and European championships. From early in the history of the sport, big prize money, large crowds, and fabulous trophies were associated with it. My great and good friend Jaime Patiño, a Spanish nobleman with more titles than you can shake a stick at and a grandson of Count Teba, one of the greatest shots of all time, has had me stay at the family Palace, Ventosilla, close to Toledo, which is littered with amazing silver trophies.

Live pigeon shooting was also important to the gunmakers. Boss, Holland & Holland, Purdey and Westley Richards and others used the pigeon ring to showcase their shotguns. Monte Carlo, amongst other capitals, such as Madrid, offered live pigeon shooting competitions with serious prize money on the line.

Anyone who is interested in trying this game or Helice would be well advised to buy and read the book. To anyone who is interested in the history of our sport, you'd be foolish not to.

In America it is available directly from Cyril Adams,

4801 Woodway Drive, Suite 300 East, Houston, TX 77056. cyriladams38@gmail.com. $100, including shipping. It is published by The Sporting Library with details at www.thesportinglibrary.co.uk which is associated with FIELDSPORTS magazine, for which I wrote extensively for nearly a decade.

In the Field: A Photographers Journey with Sporting Dogs, by Nancy Whitehead.

Nancy Whitehead has produced the best book of dog portraits that I have ever had the pleasure of viewing. And it is a pleasure! While some photographs show the dogs in action: locked on point, retrieving birds, others provided an intimate glimpse into the heart and soul of our beloved friends. The yellow lab on page 49 sitting in the water drenched obviously enthralled by whatever he's watching or the young English pointer puppy making eye contact with the gamebird on page 72 are absolutely brilliant. There are wonderful photographs of game birds flying, young duck hunters calling, are splendid too but it is the portrait of the dog that takes his book to such a high level.

Nancy is also available for commissions of dogs or hunts which would allow one to capture memories to last a lifetime.

The book is available for $38 directly from her: Nancy Whitehead, P. O. Box 3023, Hailey, ID 83333; phone: 208-481-0034; wnancy42@aol.com; nancywhitehead.com

NRA Firearms Sourcebook

This is one of the most comprehensive reviews of technical gun knowledge, ballistics, safety and firearms history compiled into a single volume. My edition is older and shorter than the current volume, but not really outdated. The newest printing of the NRA Firearms Sourcebook includes updated timelines and sources plus information on gun-safety principles, ballistics data, firearms design and assembly, shooter terminology, and more.

THE BEST OF BRITISH
A Celebration of British Gunmaking, by David Grant & Vic Venters.

Published by Quiller in the U.K. and Stackpole in the USA in 2010. Great photos and well written–can serve as a coffee table book as well as one of the standard references.

Boss & Co., Builders of Best Guns Only, by Donald Dallas.

The definitive history of Boss & Co, fully authorized by the firm. Published by Quiller, 1995.

Purdey, Gun and Rifle Makers: The Definitive History, by Donald Dallas.

This book details the history of James Purdey & Sons, the British gunmaker universally respected and known as makers of the finest quality guns. The second edition, published to coincide with Purdey's bicentennial in 2014, contains additional material plus numerous new photographs. Published by Gardners Books.

Holland & Holland, The Royal Gunmaker, by Donald Dallas.

The complete history of the company, with a foreword by Daryl Greatrex, former managing director of Holland & Holland. Published by Quiller, 2015.

David McKay Brown, Scotland's Gun and Rife Manufacturer, by Donald Dallas.

Fully authorized by David McKay Brown, this is the definitive history of the firm. Published by Quiller 2011.

- **Can be ordered from Donald Dallas:**
- **John Dickson & Son, The Round Action Gunmaker,** leather bound, published 2015.
- **John Dickson & Son, The Round Action Gunmaker,** published 2014.
- **Holland & Holland The Royal Gunmaker, The Complete History,** new edition published 2015.
- **James Purdey and Sons, Two Hundred Years of Excellence,** published 2013.
- **David Mckay Brown, Scotland's Gun And Rifle Manufacturer** published 2011.
- **Boss & Co., Best Gunmakers,** published 1995, 2005.
- **The British Sporting Gun And Rifle, Pursuit Of Perfection 1850–1900,** published 2008.

donalddallas.com balyarrow@aol.com

Best Guns a.k.a. *Fucili D'Autore,* by M. Nobili.

Two classic books on Italian engraving were both authored by Nobili. While they are wonderful reference works and show off some of Italy's greatest gunmakers and engravers, and while they were also translated so that English readers can enjoy them, some of the translation is so bad that it makes you want to laugh out loud. Nobili's later books are much more professionally and accurately translated.

Best Guns was intended to showcase the most important aspects of each make of gun. In addition to discussing many of the finest European gunmakers, the author covers in depth both production and engraving. A gigantic reference item, it is badly translated, which is a shame.

Modern Engraving (*Il Grande Libro Delle Incisioni*), by M. Nobili

A breakthrough book at the time on modern engraving by Italian Masters, it features great pictures of high-grade guns. The current edition of the book will not get updated, as the author is no longer with us. With detailed photography, the book features engravings by Pedretti, Torcoli, Fracassi, Galeazzi, and Creative Art amongst others and showcases guns by Beretta, Fabbri, Piotti, and more. Photographs are in color and black-and-white. Text is in English and Italian; unfortunately, the translation is a bit rough.

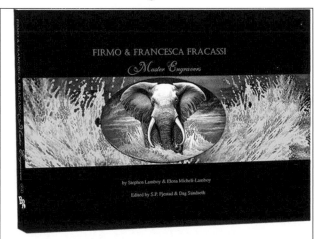

▲ Photo courtesy of Blue Book Publications, Inc.

Master Engravers Standard Edition—Firmo & Francesca Fracassi, by Stephen Lamboy & Elena Micheli-Lamboy, Edited by S. P. Fjestad & Dag Sundseth.

This beautiful, color coffee-table book was the second in a series featuring Italy's master engravers. Firmo Fracassi is, without a doubt, one of the world's finest engravers. There are stunning images of some his finest examples in this landscape-format, 236-page, full-color hardcover book. Firmo's daughter, Francesca, who also has a deservedly great reputation, has her own section. This is the only book ever done featuring Fracassi's finest works.

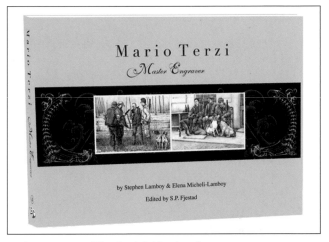

▲ Photo courtesy of Blue Book Publications, Inc.

Mario Terzi—Master Engraver, by Stephen Lamboy & Elena Micheli-Lamboy, edited by S.P. Fjestad

Another master engraver in Blue Book's series, *Mario Terzi–Master Engraver* is still in print. Terzi uses more

▲ Photo courtesy of Blue Book Publications, Inc.

precious metal inlay than most, and his use of enameled figures appeals to many. His subject matter includes fantasy scenes from nudes to creatures. This deluxe hardcover coffee-table book is 288 pages and features Terzi's finest engraving.

Giancarlo and Stefano Pedretti—Master Engravers, by Stephen Lamboy & Elena Micheli-Lamboy, edited by S. P. Fjestad.

Giancarlo and Stefano Pedretti are a father-and-son team of engravers in Gardone, Val Trompia, the epicenter of Italian gunmaking. They specialize in animals, hunting scenes, and gold inlays and are well-known for their engraving of English setters on the run. Their work in Bulino realism has helped transform engraving to fine art. Giancarlo began his engraving career at Beretta as an apprentice at age thirteen. Stefano first considered becoming an artist and attended the Caravaggio School of Art in Brescia, before deciding to follow in his father's footsteps to become a master engraver.

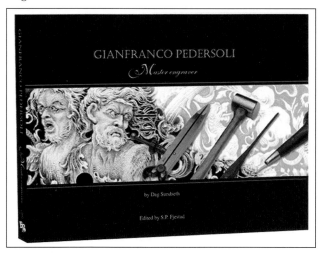

▲ Photo courtesy of Blue Book Publications, Inc.

Gianfranco Pedersoli—Master Engraver, by Dag Sundseth, edited by S.P. Fjestad & Elena Micheli-Lamboy.

The Italian master engraver Gianfranco Pedersoli is one of the giants in the field, and his work has embellished guns for Beretta, Fabbri, Flli. Rizzini, and others. This book was the first in the series. It is out-of-print and seems to command a premium.

ALSO OF INTEREST with brief reviews:

The Gun and Its Development, by WW Greener.
Originally published in 1910, this early seminal work is still of significance. It has been republished many times by many publishing houses (including Skyhorse Publishing).

The Gun Book and The Second Gun Book, by GT Garwood (better known as Gough Thomas).
He was the *Shooting Times* (UK) gun expert for decades and knows his stuff.

Skeet Shooting with D. Lee Braun, by Robert Campbell.
Undoubtedly there are many excellent contemporary books, but I find this little book to be the perfect primer. Braun was the Remington Pro and a many time all-American. Rutledge books 1967.

You and the Target, by Kay Ohye.
Self-published by this renowned trap shooter and coach in 1978, it is an excellent primer for those new to trapshooting or those who want to get better. Very sound.

Game Shooting, by Robert Churchill.
I have an old edition of this book marked 42 shillings. First published by Michael Joseph in 1955, London. Country Sport press in Camden, Maine published a revised edition in 1990, and it has been reprinted more than once.

Shotgun and Shooter, by GL Carlisle and Percy Stanbury.
They also wrote **Shotgun Marksmanship** and **Clay Pigeon Marksmanship**. Stanbury was the chief instructor at West London, whose disciples included Michael and Alan Rose. Stanbury and Churchill differed in their own shooting styles but most of what is commonly, and inaccurately, called instinctive shooting, is based on their methods.

Lock, Stock, & Barrel, by Cyril Adams and Robert Braden.
Another excellent book on British guns and how to

shoot them. Originally published by Safari press in 1996.

Trouble with Bird Dogs and What to Do About Them, by George Bird Evans.

Evans and his Old Hemlock strain of English setters were very well known in the 1950s, 1960s, and 1970s. He wrote frequently for the magazines, and while his type of setter is quite old-fashioned by modern standards, the book is well written and thoughtful. Winchester press, 1975.

The Complete Guide to Bird Dog Training, by John R. Falk.

Johnny Falk was a friend and I gave his son a puppy from my English setter bitch, Rose, when I bred her to my great field trial dog, Champion Cowboys Footsteps, who ran both in open shooting dog and all age competitions. He was the PR man for Winchester when I was beginning my career circa 1980. John Falk was a true gent and a very thoughtful dog trainer. This book and the book on Delmar Smith's method of training are the two books that I go to when I need to check something out. Winchester Press, 1976.

The Best Way to Train Your Gun Dog: the Delmar Smith Method, by Bill Tarrant.

From force breaking a dog to retrieve using a toe pinch, rather than an ear pinch, to understanding a dog psychology and bonding with it, yet maintaining the 'A' position, Delmar was a master. I wrote an article on him for *Gun Dog* magazine decades ago and was lucky to spend time with him in Oklahoma chasing wild quail. He was a true American original. Crown, 1977.

Retriever Training: A Back to Basics Approach, by Robert Milner.

This is my go-to book for working with my labs. David McKay 1977.

Successful Waterfowling, by Zack Taylor.

He was the boating editor for *Sports Afield* in the heyday of the big three outdoor publications. But more than just being interested in boats, he was a master waterfowler. Fairly unique among books on the subject, he showed how to design and build one's own duck boats and blinds. Crown, 1974.

Snipe and Woodcock: Sport & Conservation, by Colin McKelvie.

An interesting book on the intriguing gamebirds.

Gunfitting: Achieving the Ideal Fit for the Game and Clay Shot, by Don Currie.

Don is the Chief Instructor for the NSCA. He is the man who has set up the curriculum for certification up to and including level III instructors.

The is one of the best books on shotgunning to come out in a long time. Although Don does have a lot of information on proper gun fit and the importance of it, this book is about much more than that. It is about shotgun design, the intricacies of gunfitting, and the subtleties often overlooked in many similar, but lesser books, such as the shape of the hand and length of the fingers in relation to the grip so as to get the pad of the finger in the perfect place for shooting—overall length of pull will not be correct unless the finger is comfortably and naturally in the correct spot on the trigger; the effect of canting the gun, not having one's eye in the proper place over the rib, and much more.

I am not sure if the title does the book justice in that it's not merely a book about how to fit a gun as much as it is a book on the importance of proper gun fit and how to work with an expert gunfitter to achieve that fit so that an individual's best performance is most easily realized.

There are many important aspects of shooting covered, from where to focus on the clay to the shotgun's point of impact (POI), which makes tremendous sense because of Currie's expertise as a shooter and coach. This is a sophisticated book for the shooter who wants to achieve his full potential. I highly recommend Stackpole Books, 2021.